KERUX COMMENTARIES

1 & 2 KINGS

KERUX COMMENTARIES

1 & 2 KINGS

A Commentary for Biblical Preaching and Teaching

DAVID B. SCHREINER
LEE COMPSON

KREGEL
MINISTRY

Contents

THE DIVIDED MONARCHY

POLITICAL UPHEAVAL

PROPHETS AND KINGS

POLITICAL UPHEAVAL

JUDAH ALONE

THE GOOD AND THE BAD

THE END

PUBLISHER'S PREFACE TO THE SERIES

Since words were first uttered, people have struggled to understand one another and to know the main meaning in any verbal exchange.

The answer to what God is talking about must be understood in every context and generation; that is why Kerux (KAY-rukes) emphasizes text-based truths and bridges from the context of the original hearers and readers to the twenty-first-century world. Kerux values the message of the text, thus its name taken from the Greek *kērux*, a messenger or herald who announced the proclamations of a ruler or magistrate.

Biblical authors trumpeted all kinds of important messages in very specific situations, but a big biblical idea, grasped in its original setting and place, can transcend time. This specific, big biblical idea taken from the biblical passage embodies a single concept that transcends time and bridges the gap between the author's contemporary context and the reader's world. How do the prophets perceive the writings of Moses? How does the writer of Hebrews make sense of the Old Testament? How does Clement in his second epistle, which may be the earliest sermon known outside the New Testament, adapt verses from Isaiah and also ones from the Gospels? Or what about Luther's bold use of Romans 1:17? How does Jonathan Edwards allude to Genesis 19? Who can forget Martin Luther King Jr.'s "I Have a Dream" speech and his appropriation of Amos 5:24: "No, no, we are not satisfied, and we will not be satisfied until 'justice rolls down like waters, and righteousness like a mighty stream'"? How does a preacher in your local church today apply the words of Hosea in a meaningful and life-transforming way?

WHAT IS PRIME IN GOD'S MIND, AND HOW IS THAT EXPRESSED TO A GIVEN GENERATION IN THE UNITS OF THOUGHT THROUGHOUT THE BIBLE?

Answering those questions is what Kerux authors do. Based on the popular "big idea" preaching model, Kerux commentaries uniquely combine the insights of experienced Bible exegetes (trained in interpretation) and homileticians (trained in preaching). Their collaboration provides for every Bible book:

- A detailed introduction and outline
- A summary of all preaching sections with their primary exegetical, theological, and preaching ideas
- Preaching pointers that join the original context with the contemporary one
- Insights from the Hebrew and Greek text
- A thorough exposition of the text
- Sidebars of pertinent information for further background
- Appropriate charts and photographs
- A theological focus to passages

- A contemporary big idea for every preaching unit
- Present-day meaning, validity, and application of a main idea
- Creative presentations for each primary idea
- Key questions about the text for study groups

Many thanks to Jim Weaver, Kregel's former acquisitions editor, who conceived of this commentary series and further developed it with the team of Jeffrey D. Arthurs, Robert B. Chisholm, David M. Howard Jr., Darrel L. Bock, Roy E. Ciampa, and Michael J. Wilkins. We also recognize with gratitude the significant contributions of Dennis Hillman, Fred Mabie, Paul Hillman, Herbert W. Bateman IV, and Shawn Vander Lugt who have been instrumental in the development of the series. Finally, gratitude is extended to the two authors for each Kerux volume; the outside reviewers, editors, and proofreaders; and Kregel staff who suggested numerous improvements.

—Kregel Publications

PREFACE TO 1 AND 2 KINGS

The book of Kings is a tragedy. There was so much opportunity for God's people in the Iron Age. They were strategically located. They enjoyed the legacy of a charismatic king who was able to build a national foundation and focus a group of argumentative tribes upon unifying goals and a common identity. However, from the opening chapters of Kings, it's clear that things are more complicated than what one would hope. And as the history unfolds, the viability of the nation comes to rest on a knife's edge. Kings, prophets, the average Joe and Jane, and God's designs collide over approximately five centuries to produce a tumultuous period defined by great moments of salvation and great moments of foolishness. Only toward the end of the period, at the beginning of the sixth century BCE, is the trajectory set without hope for reversal. With Manasseh, the son of one of Judah's great reformers, the legacy of David can no longer pacify the Lord's growing anger.

As one would expect, the book of Kings is about Israel and Judah's kings. However, it's more than just a discussion of royal leaders. It's also about those who interacted with them, on personal and national levels, and how choices can have lasting effects, personally and corporately. So, perhaps this is the enduring theological value of this book. In Kings, one observes how choices matter and how choices are not made in a vacuum. Our choices affect not only ourselves, but also those whom the Lord has placed in our sphere of influence. Yet as bad as our choices may get, Kings also shows that God's grace is still present, and his plan of salvation history will unfold. Yes. Kings is tragic. But it's a tragedy nuanced by a cosmic plan of redemption.

EXEGETICAL AUTHOR'S ACKNOWLEDGMENTS

*This book is dedicated not only to my professors
who taught me the importance of wrestling with Israel's history,
but also my family, for their perpetual love and support.*

For whatever reason, ever since I can remember, I've been fascinated by history. During my primary education, I enjoyed learning about early American history, from its Revolutionary and frontier days to the brink of World War I. Consistently then, when it came to the Bible, the stories of David, Elijah, Elisha, Hezekiah, and others were the ones to which I continually returned. If anything, the historical narratives of the Old Testament seemed to be channels to easily enter the world of the Old Testament.

As I started to pursue a vocation in biblical higher education, I began to dive deeper into these familiar narratives. One thing I soon realized in this process was that virtually none of these major characters were flat, nor were the events that they experienced simple. David had a dark side. Solomon was a polarizing figure whose policies were both profitable and extremely problematic. Elijah was at times so myopic that it crippled his perspective and ability to minister. And the Babylonian exile? That was the result of a very complicated convergence of sociopolitical and theological factors. I could go on and on, but I trust you get the point.

I credit my professors at Indiana Wesleyan University and Asbury Theological Seminary for so many things, but in the case of ancient Israel's history, they exposed me to the difficulties of language, the data of archaeology, the confusing extrabiblical sources, the mysteries of the canon and canonization, and other realities in a way that was challenging but not hostile. Both schools were environments that stressed critical thinking for the sake of building a more sustainable faith. All of this helped me wrestle with ancient Israel's history and opened my eyes to the depths and richness of God's revelation to humanity.

If you have not yet learned to struggle well with Israel's history, I hope you'll learn. Ancient Israel's history is complicated, and it's certainly more than the flannelgraphs some of you may have experienced in Sunday school growing up. If you have learned to struggle well, I pray that you help others as well. And perhaps this is really my driving hope for this work. I want to help you discover the theological richness of wrestling with Israel's history.

With all this said, I would be remiss to not mention Herb Bateman IV, Shawn Vander Lugt, and the entire editorial team at Kregel. Herb took a flyer on me when he asked me to come aboard for the series, and for that I am grateful. Shawn has been absolutely excellent as the Managing Editor, as has been the rest of the editorial team. My prayer is that this project brings honor to the kingdom of God.

—David B. Schreiner

PREACHING AUTHOR'S ACKNOWLEDGMENTS

To my wife Stephanie
and sons Tate and EJ—for your
encouragement and love.

Both in my experience as a student and a pastor, I have always been drawn to commentary resources that kept the teacher in mind. So when this opportunity presented itself, I enthusiastically signed up because the goal of this series is to combine the exegetical and the practical.

Philosophically, my approach will be more Christotelic than Christocentric. By that I mean that I will interpret passages with the understanding that they are leading to Christ, but I do so without awkwardly shoehorning Jesus's death and resurrection into every paragraph. I want to honor 1–2 Kings' place in the larger narrative of God's redemptive movement that is leading toward the cross, and ultimately the full establishment of his kingdom in the new heaven and new earth.

In that light, I offer my homiletical contributions not as some hard-and-fast standard. It is not as though one *must* use these outlines, illustrations, and key ideas exactly and exclusively. In fact, as I have preached through these books myself, I have found plenty of places where I needed to alter my own material to better fit my context and audience. My goal is that this will be a catalyst that helps pastors and teachers understand what is going on in the text and figure out how to communicate it effectively.

—Lee Compson

OVERVIEW OF ALL PREACHING PASSAGES

1 Kings 1:1–2:11

EXEGETICAL IDEA
David's physiological deterioration engendered a series of events that saw David sanction Solomon as his successor and present his son with a critical decision about what would define his reign.

THEOLOGICAL FOCUS
The events of life often produce critical junctures, which force us to make choices that determine the ideologies that will define us going forward.

PREACHING IDEA
Despite uncertainties, following God's plan is the best path when at a crossroads in life.

PREACHING POINTERS
The book of 1 Kings begins by describing a time of transition within Israel. Like a sunrise turning into a sunset, David's reign is coming to a close. He is a shell of his former self, his family has splintered, and his kingdom is at risk. Similarly, for the original audience of 1–2 Kings, the people of Israel were facing significant transitions. As they sought to rebuild their lives, questions of leadership, morality, and national identity hung over them. The accounts found in Kings offered them historical examples of how to navigate this uncharted territory. Just as the question for Solomon was how to best navigate these issues and on what foundation he would build his own legacy, the people of the sixth and fifth centuries were compelled to consider what founding principles were going to guide them as they transitioned back into their homeland.

Our lives are also marked by critical periods where we face crucial decisions about how we will move forward. What should we do when we graduate high school? What is the best career path we ought to take? Additionally, how we date and who we marry are decisions that significantly affect the course of our lives. When layoffs unexpectedly hit us or when retirement looms over us, how will we respond? When we are at these crossroads, who will we listen to? What will be our guide? The best path to take is the one where we seek and follow God's plan and not our own.

1 Kings 2:12–2:46a

EXEGETICAL IDEA
The actions of Solomon decisively and finally secured his hold on the throne, although ambiguity surrounding motives, requests, and actions persist throughout the account.

THEOLOGICAL FOCUS

The ambiguity surrounding Solomon's decisions is indicative of life; tackling ambiguity can ultimately produce a level of understanding about God's work in the world not otherwise possible.

PREACHING IDEA

We shouldn't give up—derailing God's plan is difficult to do.

PREACHING POINTERS

First Kings 2:12–46 is filled with questions that are both unanswered and unanswerable. Readers are left to speculate on what might be going on with almost every part of this passage. The original audience of Kings could relate. Uncertainty hung over nearly every aspect of their lives, as they tried to rebuild their cities and society. As documented in the books of Haggai and Zechariah, even in Ezra and Nehemiah, actions and decisions of leadership were hotly debated as the people returned to the land.

As uneasy as we may be with tension, these verses reflect common aspects of our own world. So many circumstances in life are not black and white, and we often find ourselves dealing with the gray area in between. We are compelled to try to interpret situations and actions of others when more than one motive may exist. Should we fear making the wrong conclusions? Will exercising our "free will" hinder what God wants? Thankfully, as this story teaches, God is still at work in the gray areas and we don't have to fear the unknown or worry about ambiguous decisions spoiling his plans.

1 Kings 2:46b–3:15

EXEGETICAL IDEA

With Solomon's kingdom established, he encountered the Lord and ultimately requested wisdom to rule; Solomon's request for wisdom is granted, but not without expectations.

THEOLOGICAL FOCUS

Solomon's interchange with the Lord not only demonstrates how to pray, but also testifies to the character of God and how he relates to humanity.

PREACHING IDEA

God delights in meeting the needs of people who recognize their neediness.

PREACHING POINTERS

By 1 Kings 3, Solomon is now established as king over Israel. He has settled into power after the passing of his father and has tied up loose ends politically. He sits on his throne in security.

So now what? What will his legacy be, and what will he rely on? First and 2 Kings appealed to people who needed to consider the same questions. Jewish exiles returning from captivity were resettling in their homeland and needed to consider Solomon's example as they moved forward with their lives. Rather than security, wealth, or any other self-motivated request, the key to Israel's prosperity would be to humbly discern God's plan as they reestablished themselves as a people in their land.

When we are given new freedom, new power, or new privileges, how do we use them? Many people will default to using any advantage for their own personal gain. We burn through our work bonuses to buy the gadget or toy we've been coveting for a while. Students stop coming to class the moment the teacher mentions an "open-book final exam." Politicians work harder to stay in office than to actually represent the people who elected them. Many people make self-centered decisions in hopes of securing what they think will fulfill them, whether it is happiness, wealth, comfort, or recognition. We could endlessly chase after our own pursuits, or we could recognize what we really need and who can actually provide it for us. God loves to meet the needs of people who recognize their neediness and selflessly seek his plan rather than their own desires.

1 Kings 3:16–28

EXEGETICAL IDEA
Solomon hears the tragic case of an infant's death shrouded by maternal deception, but channeling his divinely apportioned wisdom, the king forces the truth to appear.

THEOLOGICAL FOCUS
The qualities of wisdom exhibited by Solomon prefigures those exhibited by Christ and can still be invoked.

PREACHING IDEA
Some puzzles are only solved supernaturally.

PREACHING POINTERS
In the previous section, Solomon had asked for and received God's wisdom. This passage shows how he put it to use. The original readers of 1 Kings needed to follow the same process. As the returnees from exile were resettling the land, they needed to ask for God's special insight, be ready to receive it, and then put it to good use. The accounts of Ezra and Nehemiah record many of the difficult puzzles and problems those people were facing. After the exile, the spiritual and physical rebuilding of the country was a daunting task. God's people needed to turn to God for his help and wisdom if they were going to succeed.

Individually and corporately, Christians today face complicated puzzles that require God's supernatural insight. We need it when our doctor presents several different options to address our health problem. We need it when our coach is asking us to play a role that we neither like nor feel equipped for. We need it when we are trying to get our new business off the ground in a competitive market. Corporately, we need it as we see our culture change its views on hot-button issues like homosexuality, economic policies, immigration, and war. There may be no quick-and-easy answers, but we need to seek God's supernatural insight to navigate those situations and respond in ways that honor Christ. Will we choose, in faith, what seems best to us even if others don't understand? Are we willing sacrifice for the greater good? Can we live out both biblical truth and biblical love? Solving some of life's puzzles will require supernatural insight.

1 Kings 4:1–34[5:14]

EXEGETICAL IDEA
Solomon's administration translated to a level of opulence that set Solomon above all his peers; however, his method of operation was not above criticism.

THEOLOGICAL FOCUS
Progress at the expense of others does not comport with the character of the Lord or his intentions for the way his people are to live.

PREACHING IDEA
Don't let the light of success blind you to the pitfalls of power.

PREACHING POINTERS
Solomon continues to employ superior wisdom as he sets up his administration and pursues the prosperity of his nation. For us, this chapter might read as a dry record of Solomon's history. To the original audience, this would have been a high point in their nation's history. As the returned Jewish exiles rebuilt the cities that were in disarray and as they reorganized their government and society upon returning to the land, they would read of the glory of Solomon's reign and dream of the day when that grandeur would return. But discriminating readers would take note of the subtle clues within the text that warned of straying from God's directives. Achieving success is a wonderful blessing, but what did it cost in the past and what would it cost in their postexile world?

Success and the desire to attain it are woven into the very DNA of our world, especially in the United States of America. Just in the twentieth century, the United States came out victorious in two World Wars as well as the Cold War. This nation made itself into a nuclear superpower and was the first to put a man on the moon. Winning became assumed and superiority became an expectation. But like King Solomon, are there cracks in the facade of prosperity? Are there people groups neglected? Have morals been sacrificed for the sake of freedom and power? The Larry Nassar-USA Gymnastics scandal provides a revealing example. In pursuit of Olympic glory, an entire organization turned a blind eye to a sexual predator harming kids and abusive coaches fostering a poisonous environment. Gold medals were won, but lives were ruined. Success isn't a bad thing, but we cannot let it blind us.

1 Kings 5:1–18[5:15–32]

EXEGETICAL IDEA
The relationship between Solomon and Hiram channeled the resources necessary to build the temple.

THEOLOGICAL FOCUS
Day-to-day encounters offer evangelistic opportunities.

PREACHING IDEA
Let your light shine—all the time!

PREACHING POINTERS
Solomon's deal with King Hiram of Phoenicia would prove critical for the building of the temple of the Lord. Beyond the transactional aspect of this chapter, there is potentially more to glean from this record of King Solomon's political duties. The people rebuilding Jerusalem and resettling the land could have merely focused on the work, the resources, and the commercial nature of returning from the exile. Yet this chapter offers them a reminder of the covenantal purpose God had for them dwelling in the land in the first place. From the promise to Abraham to the messages of the prophets, God intended them to be a "light to the nations" and to be a redemptive blessing to the Gentile world around them (Gen. 12:2–3; 22:17–18; Isa. 42:6; 49:6). Through informal interactions and official partnerships, they could reach those in spiritual darkness with the light of God. Rebuilding the land was more than just about creating a home; it was about establishing an influence so that all peoples could know Yahweh as the returning Jewish exiles did. God was providing them a new opportunity to be a light as they resettled their homeland.

Today, Christians have a similar calling. In Matthew 5:14–16, Jesus describes us as "the light of the world" whose good deeds will cause people to glorify God. Some people try to shine their lights only at church, while doing whatever they want the rest of the week. God expects us to be lights from Monday through Saturday, not just Sunday. We are called to reflect Jesus to the world whether we are at our jobs, at school, traveling, or relaxing at home. This chapter's business negotiations provide a great practical context for increasing our witness. How we conduct ourselves in meetings, over meals, and even in the day-to-day grind of our jobs can be a shining testimony of our faith in Jesus. We need to let our lights shine—all the time and everywhere we go.

1 Kings 6:1–7:51

EXEGETICAL IDEA
The construction of the temple and the palace is like other accounts found across the ancient Near East; yet in celebrating the glories of Israel's society and the Lord, the biblical account nevertheless tempers any unbridled celebration.

THEOLOGICAL FOCUS
The construction of the temple and the palace anticipates the Babylonian exile, ultimately bearing witness to the potentialities of perpetual disobedience.

PREACHING IDEA
Details determine if our worship flourishes or fails.

PREACHING POINTERS

These chapters are full of details and descriptions recounting the construction of the temple of the Lord. They demonstrate that not only did the completed building facilitate worship, but the preparations themselves also had God's covenant in mind. The building materials and adornments purposefully symbolized God and his covenant with his people. In the end, it was their own failure to remain loyal to God that proved to be their downfall. So the mission for Israel upon returning from exile was clear: rededicate themselves to faithfully following the Lord in every respect. Their ritual sacrifices needed to be accompanied by acts of love and justice, otherwise rebuilding the second temple would be a futile effort (Micah 6:8–10; cf. Ezra 3–6; Neh. 12:27–47).

It might be easy to skim by these passages assuming that they have little bearing on our lives. That would be unwise because as this section shows us, details matter. Just as the details of the temple had greater meaning, so do the little things in our lives. Romans 12:1–2 teaches us that every aspect of our lives is worship. Therefore, all we do matters to the Lord. For example, what we say and how we say it matters. Negatively and positively, our speech reflects our hearts (Prov. 10:11; Eph. 4:22–32; James 3:10–12). Even our interactions with strangers and people "below" us are details that God takes seriously (Matt. 18:1–7; Heb. 13:2–3; James 2:1–10). As in the past, God still expects his people to be committed to obedience in all matters, big and small. Our disobedience won't necessarily lead to national exile as it did for the Israelites given the nature of their covenant relationship with God, but it will negatively affect all of us—in general as citizens of our country, but in particular as believers in Jesus and thus members of the body of Christ—if left unconfessed (1 Cor. 11:28–33; 1 Peter 3:7). How we handle the details in life will determine whether our worship flourishes or fails.

1 Kings 8:1–66

EXEGETICAL IDEA

The temple dedication not only celebrated Jerusalem as the center of the Israelite worldview, but also the intimate relationship between the Lord, his people, the temple, and the Davidic dynasty.

THEOLOGICAL FOCUS

Jerusalem as the cosmic center of Israelite worship testifies to the character of God and prepares his people, as well as all the peoples of the earth, for the "new cosmic" center following Christ's death, resurrection, and ascension.

PREACHING IDEA

Genuine worship is life-changing.

PREACHING POINTERS

The dedication of the temple in 1 Kings 8 is an awe-inspiring event where God and his people come together. The account places strong emphasis on God's glory and his glorious covenant promises. Later readers of this account, especially those of Ezra and Nehemiah's day, would have naturally compared the glory of the original temple with its replacement. Such a comparison led to disappointment for some (Ezra 3:11–13). Eventually the enthusiastic momentum of rebuilding dissipated and the danger of falling back into old habits would return (Neh. 13). This is why there is an emphasis on obeying God's law in connection with God's covenant with David. This worship wasn't dependent on a building achievement nor was it intended to be a one-time event. This was a time of national renewal and commitment to the Lord. The people of Solomon's day, the people of Nehemiah's day, and all the people who would come after were to be mindful of the obedient commitment that is essential to worship.

Jesus is the true fulfillment of the promises that are in view in this passage. He secured our forgiveness, provides our blessings, and is the basis of the hope we have for the future. All of those themes ought to be main ingredients in our worship. Now, there are a multitude of ideas about what makes *good* worship, especially within the American church. There are many different styles, practices, and preferences. This passage offers a pointed evaluation for all of our current forms. Seeking to create the right feelings, the right atmosphere, and a perfect production are all good things in and of themselves. Yet they should be secondary to the themes God highlights in his Word. When we gather to worship, is there an emphasis on presenting and celebrating who God is? Is there a call to obediently respond to what God has done? Genuine worship is an encounter with God that impacts who we are and what we do.

1 Kings 9:1–9

EXEGETICAL IDEA
The Lord endorsed the construction of the temple, but quickly discussed the implications of the dynasty's willingness to live by the covenantal ideal.

THEOLOGICAL FOCUS
The vitality of God's kingdom is renewed with every generation that chooses to learn important lessons and adhere to God's expectations.

PREACHING IDEA
Our accomplishments *for* God won't last without faithfulness *to* God.

PREACHING POINTERS
The original readers of this passage would have heard, seen, and felt the negative consequences that God promises included if his people failed to obey him. Their forefathers neglected faithfulness to the Lord, and now they were picking up the pieces. As they repaired the ruins of the once-great city of Jerusalem, there could be little doubt that God had meant what he said about "turning away" from God's commands and precepts. It was to their national shame that the foreign nations had destroyed their cities and exiled their people. The glory of Solomon's era was long gone because the nation and its leaders had failed to be faithful.

We do not face the same disaster as the nation of ancient Israel did then, but our mission is much the same. Like they were, we are called to faithfully obey God's Word. At the core of our calling as disciples of Jesus is the concept of faithfully passing on the good news of Jesus Christ. Many passages—including Matthew 28:18–20, 2 Timothy 2:1–2, and Titus 2:1–8—underscore this mission. We are called to make disciples by teaching and modeling the way of Jesus to others, especially the next generation. Failure to do so will not bring national disaster because biblically speaking, God's people are no longer defined in terms of a political state. But failure to be faithful to God's calling will bring dishonor to ourselves by weakening the body of Christ. It is not enough to merely attach the label "Christian" to ourselves and think it is enough. Nor is it good enough to build sizable churches and ministries. With all the ministry and service accomplishments we might achieve, it is essential that we pair those with faithfully embodying the mission of God and equipping the next generations to continue God's work. To ensure that our accomplishments leave a lasting legacy, we must be faithful to God in all aspects of our personal and public lives.

1 Kings 9:10–28

EXEGETICAL IDEA
Solomon's policies sought to fulfill geopolitical ambitions, and in turn produced several realities that affected the dynamics of Israel.

THEOLOGICAL FOCUS
Solomon's policies testify to a timeless responsibility of leadership: how to balance traditional values with a responsibility to grow and innovate.

PREACHING IDEA
On the path of success, watch out for the potholes!

PREACHING POINTERS
Solomon pursues progress, growth, and innovation in this passage. These things would have been far-off goals and dreams to the returned Jewish exiles rebuilding their nation. Survival would have been at the top of their minds more than success, with all the work that needed to be accomplished.

That difference between the eras would have actually been advantageous to the wise reader of that day. Many would have been dreaming of "making Israel great again," but astute observers could point to passages like this one and warn of the red flags that come with success. Its practical, detailed accounts of Israel's business are more than just bookkeeping records. It reveals just how tricky leadership can be in times of success. Solomon deals with diplomatic relationships and returning favors with King Hiram. He orders more building projects and makes decisions about enlisting people from his kingdom into labor and military service. One can read of those decisions and see cracks in the facade that will become obvious later. One can also read this in context of God's blessing and the king's faithfulness (v. 25). Both readings can be true. The point is that leading often involves walking a fine line between compromise and courage.

No matter how positively or negatively we want to read it, this passage is a stern warning against blindly pursuing prosperity. Many people aspire to leadership, and every nation/business/ministry pursues success. Are we wise enough to recognize the dangers when we've reached the top? Success will not protect us from mistakes. In fact, more success brings more responsibility. And failing to keep up our responsibilities will undermine our success and undo all the good we accomplish. As we pursue and achieve success in our ventures, we ought to be mindful of the pitfalls and potholes that hinder us along the way.

1 Kings 10:1–29

EXEGETICAL IDEA
The prestige and opulence of Solomon left the Queen of Sheba overwhelmed, yet it alluded to large fractures in Solomon's moral foundation.

THEOLOGICAL FOCUS
The pursuit of excellence may compromise us or our communities if left unchecked.

PREACHING IDEA
Success is a spotlight that magnifies our glory and our shame.

PREACHING POINTERS
The last couple chapters have recorded some of the true high points of Israel's history. The temple's completion was a crowning moment in their spiritual history. In this section, Israel is entering their peak economic period. Yet warning signs have been popping up all along and can no longer be ignored. Solomon is transgressing God's commands and leading the nation toward trouble. The later readers of this and the preceding chapters would feel this tension. As they rebuilt their nation after the exile, they would naturally compare their progress to this previous season of national glory. A wiser, more critical mind would ask a more basic question: Should they seek a return to this kind of power and glory? Deuteronomy 17:14–20 stood as a warning against the extravagance described here. The constant cry of the post-Solomon prophets was for faithfulness and justice on the part of God's people (Isa. 58; Jer. 22; Hos. 4; Mic. 6). First Kings 10 is a record of Israel's glory, wrapped in reminders of God's expectations for his people when they are prospering.

These principles aren't hard to find in the New Testament either. Jesus often gave warnings against loving and pursuing money and wealth (Matt. 6:19–24; Luke 18:18–25). Paul encouraged sacrificial generosity as part of a larger message that we should be selfless in all we do, because of what Jesus has done for us (2 Cor. 5:14–15; 8:1–9:15; Phil. 2:1–11). Success and prosperity are not overtly condemned in the Bible. But what is condemned is the pursuit of success at the expense of God's desires. We are warned that achieving all our wildest dreams may not be all we think it will be. Is the degree I'm pursuing in line with God's true calling on my life or is it just to pad my resume? Are the expectations we set for our kids realistic and in line with God's Word? Have the career decisions I've made been about me or about making an impact for Christ? Success can bring us fame and renown, but it also can reveal our weaknesses and character defects.

1 Kings 11:1–43

EXEGETICAL IDEA
Solomon received a stinging indictment that ultimately rendered him an "evil king," but the expected judgment was pacified by the legacy of David.

THEOLOGICAL FOCUS
The Lord is both just and gracious in his interactions with his people and their leaders.

PREACHING IDEA
God's grace and God's judgment are not mutually exclusive.

PREACHING POINTERS
Solomon's reign began with so much promise, but it ends unceremoniously in shame and strife. Spiritual compromise led to his downfall, and the nation itself would never be the same. While they were several generations removed, the people rebuilding in the postexile and Second Temple periods were living with the consequences of Solomon's failures of leadership. His life would remind them of the importance of spiritual loyalty, especially as they evaluated their own leaders. Their hope was that a son of David would arise who would meet God's ideals and standards.

Jesus is the ultimate fulfillment of what the Davidic kings were supposed to embody. He changed the paradigm as the divine Messiah. For us, national exile is not a potential punishment. Faithfulness is still expected, even though the nature of the consequences is different. God has expectations for us, which he has outlined in his Word to indicate what we should and shouldn't do. If we sin, God still offers us abundant grace and forgiveness. But he does not promise the absence of any consequences. We might face jail time for our crimes and ruin close relationships because of our offenses. At the same time God disciplines us when we get out of line, he also graciously calls us to repentance. God desires to correct us and help us grow. He wants the thief to no longer steal, the cheater to no longer cheat, and the drunk to no longer drown in the bottom of a bottle. And he provides us the power to overcome our weaknesses and failures through the Holy Spirit (1 Cor. 6:9–11; Eph. 5:18–20). God's grace and judgment are not mutually exclusive, and they still have bearing on our daily lives. Our eternal hope is founded on the fact that they were both put on display at Calvary when God revealed himself as perfectly just and perfectly gracious. It is in light of that reality that we can now live into the mission God has given us.

1 Kings 12:1–24

EXEGETICAL IDEA
When Rehoboam rejected the request of the northern tribes to alleviate their terms of service, the kingdom split, and Rehoboam's efforts to reunify the kingdom failed.

THEOLOGICAL FOCUS
The choices of humanity collaborate with divine sovereignty to direct the contours of life within God's providence.

PREACHING IDEA
Don't be surprised when God lets us feed on the fruits of our foolishness.

PREACHING POINTERS
The growing fractures in the kingdom of Israel finally reach their breaking point in 1 Kings 12. The northern tribes split from the southern tribes and reach the brink of civil war. The blame rests squarely on the foolish leadership of Rehoboam, though the author clearly indicates that God was still overseeing these political developments. Interestingly, the original audience was in an almost complete opposite position. They were coming out of the exile and seeking to put their nation back together. The example of King Rehoboam stands as an antitype—an example of what not to do if unification is your goal. They needed to be careful to follow the notion that "the needs of the many outweigh the needs of the few."

How does this matter for us? Our nation has gone through an awful civil war due to a number of factors and causes, including moral failings (i.e., the sin of slavery). But that was more than 150 years ago. Unfortunately, however, our propensity for foolishness did not disappear after the War Between the States. The United States of America has certainly developed into a major superpower on the world stage, but that is not necessarily to be understood as the result of God's blessing because of some kind of extrabiblical covenant between God and America as some Americans believe, nor is it an automatic guarantee of such blessing in perpetuity. Just like the leaders of any other post-Babel nation from antiquity to modern times, if our leaders make foolish decisions, we should expect the consequences. This is perhaps most relevant on the personal level. I can attend a good church, pray often, and serve regularly, which are all good and commendable things. But if I also have a spending problem that I let go unchecked, God won't miraculously erase my credit card balance when it rises to unhealthy levels. We shouldn't be surprised when God allows the logical consequences of our mistakes to become realities in our lives.

1 Kings 12:25–14:20

EXEGETICAL IDEA
Jeroboam's reign is remembered for the king's construction of an illegitimate and heretical religious system that ultimately secured devastating judgment.

THEOLOGICAL FOCUS
The fear and self-preservation at the root of Jeroboam's disobedience is a potentially devastating pair of tendencies in light of humanity's fallen state.

PREACHING IDEA
Depravity leads to disaster, no matter what.

PREACHING POINTERS
Jeroboam's reign comes to a dramatic and ignominious end. Plagued by insecurity over Jerusalem's central place in their nation's religious life, he decides to set up an alternate religious system that was not sanctioned by the Lord. These selfish and fear-driven actions mark

the northern kingdom to such an extent that God announces his imminent judgment. National prosperity and security were certainly highly cherished goals for the returning Jewish exiles and those living in postexilic Israel. Would they, like Jeroboam, choose security over obedience? Would they compromise God's law in the interests of self-preservation?

The people of God have faced these kinds of dilemmas quite often throughout history. Of course, the specifics are often quite different. Today, Christians face these types of choices when considering who to support politically. What do we do if the candidate from "my party" espouses unbiblical views and positions? Beyond individual interests, our communities of faith must wrestle with these issues too. Will our church seek the Spirit's leading or will we split into factions that fight over our preferences? Operating by fear and self-interest is a mark that we are living by the flesh. Living that way for very long will inevitably lead to disaster. We can learn from Jeroboam's poor example and do the opposite when we deal with our own insecurities. Following our own rebellious path will only leave us worse off because depravity leads to disaster, no matter the excuses or circumstances. God calls us to live by faith. While his path may be uncertain, he promises that it will not end in disaster.

1 Kings 14:21–16:20

EXEGETICAL IDEA
Both Judean and Israelite kings generally failed to honor the Lord and his expectations, yet the intensity of judgment was pacified in Judah because of David's legacy and the occasional good king.

THEOLOGICAL FOCUS
Judgment can only be pacified temporarily, for without complete repentance the root of sin will only grow and consume.

PREACHING IDEA
Half-measures of repentance won't cure full measures of rebellion.

PREACHING POINTERS
Both Judah and Israel find themselves in unstable political circumstances in this section. Unlike Israel, Judah does experience brief eras of positivity, because at times their leadership follows the Lord. The original readers of 1 Kings would have been able to clearly recognize the implications for their context. As they rebuilt their nation, they had two paths to choose from. The first was the path of loyalty and faithfulness to God's law. The second was the path of compromise and rebellion. They could imitate the spiritual reforms like Asa and find national success, or they could tolerate pagan worship in their midst and invite God's judgment. Leaders like Nehemiah and Ezra wholeheartedly served so that the former would be true, not the latter.

Today, living under the new covenant, much has changed in God's equation for dealing with sin. Sacrifices are no longer required, and national prosperity is not on the line. The essential acts of confession and repentance have not changed, however. Jesus's sacrificial death provides forgiveness, but it doesn't give us license to live immorally. James 4:7–10 and 1 John

1:7–9 are just two prominent passages among many in the New Testament underscoring the believer's need to address their sin with God and turn from its enticing grip. But we can't just go halfway in dealing with our sinful habits. The Bible uses commands like "cut it off," "flee," and "put to death" when it comes to sin in our lives (Matt. 5:30; 1 Cor. 6:18; Col. 3:5). This means: Take drastic action now! Don't mess around with sin. Counseling or Alcoholics Anonymous meetings may need to be scheduled. Internet or cable access should be canceled. Quitting a bad habit "cold turkey" may be difficult, but it may be the healthiest way forward. We must deal seriously with our sinful habits and tendencies, whatever they may be. Half-hearted repentance won't fix all-out rebellion.

1 Kings 16:21–34

EXEGETICAL IDEA
Omride policies brought an aggressive policy shift that sought to stabilize the region but also brought the entrenchment of Canaanite religion.

THEOLOGICAL FOCUS
The egregiousness of Omride sins exists in their high-handedness, which fundamentally undermines the ethos of God's people.

PREACHING IDEA
Prosperity is a tragedy when it comes at the expense of piety.

PREACHING POINTERS
On a strictly historical level, the Omride dynasty was wildly successful. The northern tribes finally found leaders who gave them stability and security. All was not well, however. King Omri and his son Ahab ushered in an era of religious apostasy that God's people had never experienced. The lesson for the readers of 1 Kings couldn't be any clearer: prosperity shouldn't be pursued apart from piety. Throughout history, God's people would have to hold those two factors in tension. The prophets often chastised Israel for defrauding the impoverished and vulnerable. The postexilic, Second Temple, and New Testament periods were all filled with political struggles for various levels of freedom and independence. Israel always had a spiritual conscience, however, and there were many who sought to spiritually discern how best to pursue those marks of success.

The church in the West has faced this balance between prosperity and piety in historically unique ways. Since the dawn of the twentieth century, American Christians have found themselves citizens of an economically flourishing and politically powerful nation. How have we used our strength and influence? The United States has been a global launching point for the gospel. Many ministries have been created that have sought to use material wealth to help the disadvantaged. However, in some cases, Western culture has been promoted itself rather than our Christ. In some cases, especially within North American evangelicalism, the rights and perspectives of women and ethnic minorities have not been fully acknowledged. In some cases, the church in the West has identified with political movements even when they go against Scripture's admonitions. Those compromises result in a diminished witness, which is a true tragedy.

1 Kings 17:1–2 Kings 1:18

EXEGETICAL IDEA

Elijah embodied the prophetic institution, which was defined not by individual personalities but by its theological and social responsibilities.

THEOLOGICAL FOCUS

The essence of the prophetic institution continues when the Lord brings a specific word to a specific situation by means of Scripture.

PREACHING IDEA

God amplifies prophetic voices when we're having trouble hearing him.

PREACHING POINTERS

At this point in Israel and Judah's history, there is a big enough sample size to declare that the office of the king was failing to properly lead the people of God. King Ahab took over for his father, and like many kings before him he has only worsened the spiritual state of his nation. It is at this time that God raised up key prophets to deliver his message and call the people back to their covenant with the Lord. The message and the ministry of the prophets, especially Elijah, represents God's determination to keep his end of his covenant promises. As Walter Brueggemann (2001) puts it, the main function of the prophets was to "criticize" and "energize" God's people. They challenged the spiritually apathetic while encouraging the disillusioned with the hope of God's plan.

The exiled Israelites and those living in the postexilic world dealt with somewhat different circumstances. Their problem was not the presence of evil leadership—their issue was the lack of any internal leadership at all. That's why God raised up men like Ezra and Nehemiah as the people resettled their ancient homeland. Ezra and Nehemiah provided the godly administrative and spiritual leadership the people needed. As a pair, they encouraged the people in God's law and challenged those who doubted or opposed what God was doing. One can debate whether God still ordains prophets in an official, spiritual gift-type capacity. Yet, if one accepts Brueggemann's premise that prophets primarily served to criticize and energize, this author sees no reason to deny that prophetic voices are applicable and necessary for our day. The writings and ministries of those like A. W. Tozer and Dietrich Bonhoeffer certainly were prophetic in their day. The reality is that every generation has its own pockets of spiritual apathy and blindness. And every generation has pockets of faithful but discouraged believers too. It is for those times and for those people that God amplifies prophetic voices, so that those who need it most can hear God's message.

2 Kings 2:1–13:25

EXEGETICAL IDEA

As a prophet, Elisha served all levels of society to provide social, theological, and political insight, but Jehu's coup inaugurated a period where the basic vitality and effectiveness of

God's people, including the continued existence of the Davidic line, were being compromised by internal and external pressures, which were all linked to shortsighted decisions and covenantal unfaithfulness.

THEOLOGICAL FOCUS
God's grace offers hope in life's precarious situations.

PREACHING IDEA
Desperate times call for divine measures.

PREACHING POINTERS
Turmoil and unrest mark this period of Israel's history. This larger unit is loosely tied together by Elisha's prophetic ministry, as he succeeds Elijah during a tumultuous time for both Israel and Judah. Elisha is described serving in a wide variety of situations, from helping commoners in crisis to advising kings regarding their military campaigns. Besides the prophet, several other leaders are noted for their activities. Some are graded positively, others negatively. What seems clear is that all aspects of life during this time were fraught with instability and anxiety. The Jewish people of the exilic and postexilic periods could relate all too well as they studied this part of their history. Disagreements, conflicts, and uncertainty were the norm as they resettled their homeland. Their one hope would be to follow godly servants and leaders like Elisha and trust the Lord to bring order to their chaos.

We do not lack turmoil in our world today, nor do we have to look very far for reasons to be anxious. Job layoffs, Wall Street fluctuations, and contentious political developments can all directly impact our lives and catch us unprepared. When desperate times arrive, it is natural to wonder what God is up to or even where he is. One helpful response is to take Mr. Rogers's classic advice and "look for the helpers." Has God raised up some individuals or groups that are providing support and service to those in need? Are there leaders who are embodying a response of steadfast faith when others are acting out of fear? Church work teams that help clean up in the aftermath of natural disasters exemplify this, as are Christians who volunteer at homeless shelters or with Big Brothers Big Sisters of America. The common saying is, "Desperate times call for desperate measures." But for people of faith, desperate times call for *divine* measures. We can be the hands and feet of Jesus and make an incredible impact, especially in times of turmoil and unrest.

2 Kings 14:1–16:20

EXEGETICAL IDEA
After the departure of the prophets Elijah and Elisha, this period of the divided monarchy reverted to instability while the presence of the Neo-Assyrian Empire redefined the geopolitical landscape, putting Israel and Judah in potentially compromising situations.

THEOLOGICAL FOCUS
Poor choices that produced a spiritually compromised existence for God's people is a symptom of the fall, yet this situation need not persist.

PREACHING IDEA

Sinful choices lead to serious catastrophe that only God's grace can rescue us from.

PREACHING POINTERS

Political turmoil continued for Judah and Israel, only now those kingdoms were without the divinely empowered prophetic presence of Elijah and Elisha. The focus is primarily on the numerous kings who rise and fall. Almost without exception, these kings stumble into trouble because of the decisions they make as they lead. As the record of 1 and 2 Kings advances closer and closer to the period of exile, the mistakes of their ancestors would become more and more relevant to Israel as they reestablished themselves as a people. Spiritually faithful leaders bring security and stability. Otherwise, this is what happens when rulers rule poorly: political infighting and external pressure from world powers.

As Christians today, we need to be careful about drawing too many political conclusions, as we are no longer identified by ethnic or political traits (Rom. 4; Gal. 3:28; Phil. 3:17–20). We will still struggle with these kinds of sins, however. The temptation to act out of ambition, pride, and selfishness is ever present for us as individuals and groups. Should I push hard for my preferred building proposal rather than wait for a consensus to settle on one of the options? Will my social media presence be driven to enhance my personal brand or for other more worthy causes? Will we do whatever it takes to get our church attendance up, even if it sacrifices some biblical principles? Will we sell out to support a political party or candidate because it will make our lives "easier"? Sinful choices will lead us straight into trouble, whether making decisions about how to lead our church, corporation, research group, family, or just our own lives. God's grace can temper the consequences at times, but catastrophe awaits those who lead by their own sinful desires.

2 Kings 17:1–20:21

EXEGETICAL IDEA

The Assyrian Empire's swift invasion and destruction of Samaria and Israel demonstrated Judah's relative superiority over Israel, yet King Hezekiah's decisions with the Babylonian envoy tempered any unqualified praise and foreshadowed the demise of Judah.

THEOLOGICAL FOCUS

The portrayal of Hezekiah testifies that the success of one's faith journey and legacy for the next generation is contingent upon one's consistent commitment to Christ.

PREACHING IDEA

The difference between victory and defeat is a lived-out faith.

PREACHING POINTERS

This section is a study in contrasts. The Assyrian Empire swiftly conquers the northern tribes of Israel, while the southern kingdom manages to survive that threat. The record of 1–2 Kings has transparently shown all the failings and flaws of both groups as the harsh reality of exile loomed larger and larger over Israel's history. The unwritten question that the author seems to be posing for his readers is, "What is the difference between the two?" or more specifically, "Why did the exile come in stages?" Second Kings 17–21 offers an explanation. More than Israel, Judah maintained at least a semblance of faithfulness to the covenant—and under Hezekiah's leadership, it was more than a semblance. He led significant reforms and remained faithful to the Lord even when his enemies were at his doorstep.

We are not facing an actual military conquest, yet we are engaged in warfare. As Paul describes in Ephesians 6:10–18, Christ-followers must be prepared for spiritual battles by putting on the armor of God. While there is much to say about that passage, what is generally obvious is that the illustration is meant to encourage believers to understand who they are in Christ and "fight" (i.e., live) accordingly. The student who faces antagonistic peers at school can maintain a strong witness by starting each day in the Word and prayer (Eph. 6:17–18). The housewife can parent her young kids with confidence by seeking the Lord's help daily with each parental challenge and difficulty that arises (Eph. 6:16). The aging grandparents can influence the next generation by imparting godly advice, sharing honestly about their own mistakes and successes and how God's grace saw them through it all (Eph. 6:14). Spiritual victory comes when we live out our faith. Defeat follows when we make our own choices and do our own thing no matter what God has said.

2 Kings 21:1–26

EXEGETICAL IDEA
Manasseh undermined the reforms of his father and secured the destruction and judgment of Judah, while Ammon's reign intensified the sociopolitical tensions.

THEOLOGICAL FOCUS
Past faithfulness is no guarantee of future faithfulness, but focused engagement on the Lord's teachings increases the likelihood of future faithfulness.

PREACHING IDEA
Legacies are dismantled much more easily than they are constructed.

PREACHING POINTERS
After the godly reign of King Hezekiah, Judah experiences spiritual whiplash when his son and grandson take over the throne. His son Manasseh seems especially dedicated to reversing the progress and reform Hezekiah had instituted. He leads the nation headlong back into flagrant idolatry. It was at this point that God announced his coming judgment of exile on Judah—the exile that the first readers of 2 Kings would have been all too familiar with. After reestablishing themselves in their homeland, the Jewish people returning from exile now reading this account would have been reminded that all the work they had done could be fumbled away by those who came after them. The only way forward would be to spiritually invest in the next generation, to ensure that their sons and grandsons remained faithful to Yahweh.

Many Christians have lamented the direction of Western culture in the twenty-first century. Few have thought to consider whether Western Christianity is at least in part to blame. For much of the late twentieth century in the United States, conservative Christians sought to carve out cultural influence through political means, by forming the Religious Right voting bloc. Might the results we decry in the 2000s and following decades be a direct consequence of previous generations of Christians pursuing political power at all costs? Subsequent generations seem to be disillusioned by that quest. Many have rejected the faith altogether. The positive legacies of twentieth-century Western Christianity—global missions, scholarship, musical worship, humanitarian aid, civil rights progress—are often disregarded because of the way Christian leaders put the emphasis on the wrong pursuits. Some Christian legacies of recent times need dismantling. But the world around us is increasingly dismissive of the whole, not just the particulars. The Western church needs to move ahead with a greater desire to leave a legacy that is faithful to the gospel. That will entail raising up disciples and leaders who will follow in our faithful footsteps, instead of walking away disappointed by the failings of their spiritual forebears.

2 Kings 22:1–23:30

EXEGETICAL IDEA
King Josiah's extensive spiritual reforms throughout the land of Judah and Jerusalem, while intensely focused on pushing the nation back to the Lord, could not sway the determinations of the Lord.

THEOLOGICAL FOCUS
In certain instances, no amount of repentance will alter the determinations of the Lord.

PREACHING IDEA
God's Word is final.

PREACHING POINTERS
Looking back, Judah's exile was inevitable. Even though King Josiah led extensive spiritual reform, it was not enough to avert God's coming judgment on his people for centuries of sin. As the people returned from this exile and studied this history, they would learn a double-sided lesson. Yes, the Babylonian exile was deserved. The nation's continued faithlessness earned that punishment that God had announced. Yet this period also offers a positive lesson, especially to the original audience of Jews returning from exile to resettle their homeland: Josiah's reign is an example to follow as they rebuild their society. His reforms followed God's Word, thus giving the people one final peaceful era before the end came. God's word of judgment could not be avoided, but it served as the template for a good king leading his people in repentance.

It is in that latter lesson where we find points of relevance for our lives today. Is God's Word our template, our compass that guides our lives? When a classmate stumbles upon essays online that fit the assignments for the class we are taking, will we cheat or will we let God's Word determine what we do? Scripture clearly tells us to "pray continually" in all circumstances and situations. Do we? Or do we try to figure out our own solutions to the issues in front of us? Like a fresh-faced cadet following the orders of his drill sergeant, we need to follow God's Word as our final authority in what we say, think, and do.

2 Kings 23:31–25:30

EXEGETICAL IDEA
The dethronement of King Jehoahaz plunged Judah into a turbulent period defined by new suzerains, rebellion, political gambling, and a tragic end in exile, yet the release of Jehoiachin from prison presented hope.

THEOLOGICAL FOCUS
The hope represented at the end of Kings manifests the grace of God.

PREACHING IDEA
The hope of God still flickers in our darkest days.

PREACHING POINTERS
Even as the tragic end of Judah is vividly depicted, the author of Kings leaves his readers with the faintest glimmer of hope. A king still lives. He is a vassal of a foreign empire, but one who enjoys a modicum of honor and favor. His status is symbolic of the people corporately. While they have been forcefully subjected to a foreign power, they would eventually emerge from their darkest days with their national identity intact. The flicker of hope that Jehoiachin represents would turn into a full-blown flame as God would restore his people to their land.

Since the earliest settlers and the later founding of our nation, Christians have enjoyed a great amount of privilege and freedom in the United States of America. There have not been many prolonged "dark days" for Christians in the West. We can learn a lot from our brothers and sisters in other contexts in this sense. They have much to teach us about holding on to hope, no matter the darkness. We should also be able to relate to this on a personal level. When a health crisis hits and the medical bills pile up, where do we find hope? There are few days as dark as when a marriage falls apart. Christians are also not immune to stressing over political developments. What if churches lost their tax-exempt status? What if our religious freedoms were taken away by the government? Trials have a way of exposing where our hope lies. And if it is set on Christ, we can be confident that we will not be disappointed.

ABBREVIATIONS

GENERAL ABBREVIATIONS

BCE	before the Common Era
CE	Common Era
LXX	Septuagint
NT	New Testament
OT	Old Testament

TECHNICAL ABBREVIATIONS

ca.	circa
cf.	compare (*confer*)
ch(s).	chapter(s)
dat.	dative
e.g.	for example
et al.	and others (*et alii*)
etc.	and so forth, and the rest (*et cetera*)
idem	the same
i.e.	that is (*id est*)
n(n).	note(s)
p(p).	page(s)
repr.	reprinted
rev.	revised
§ (*pl.* §§)	section(s)
s.v.	under the word (*sub verbo*)
temp.	temporal
trans.	translation
txt.	text
var.	variant
v(v).	verse(s)

BIBLICAL

Old Testament

Gen.	Genesis
Exod.	Exodus
Lev.	Leviticus
Num.	Numbers
Deut.	Deuteronomy

Old Testament (continued)

Josh.	Joshua
Judg.	Judges
Ruth	Ruth
1 Sam.	1 Samuel
2 Sam.	2 Samuel

Old Testament (continued)

1 Kgdms.	1 Kingdoms (LXX)
2 Kgdms.	2 Kingdoms (LXX)
1 Kings	1 Kings
2 Kings	2 Kings
3 Kgdms.	3 Kingdoms (LXX)
4 Kgdms.	4 Kingdoms (LXX)
1 Chron.	1 Chronicles
2 Chron.	2 Chronicles
Ezra	Ezra
Neh.	Nehemiah
Esther	Esther
Job	Job
Ps./Pss.	Psalm(s)
Prov.	Proverbs
Eccl.	Ecclesiastes
Song	Song of Songs
Isa.	Isaiah
Jer.	Jeremiah
Lam.	Lamentations
Ezek.	Ezekiel
Dan.	Daniel
Hos.	Hosea
Joel	Joel
Amos	Amos
Obad.	Obadiah
Jonah	Jonah
Mic.	Micah
Nah.	Nahum
Hab.	Habakkuk
Zeph.	Zephaniah
Hag.	Haggai

Old Testament (continued)

Zech.	Zechariah
Mal.	Malachi

New Testament

Matt.	Matthew
Mark	Mark
Luke	Luke
John	John
Acts	Acts
Rom.	Romans
1 Cor.	1 Corinthians
2 Cor.	2 Corinthians
Gal.	Galatians
Eph.	Ephesians
Phil.	Philippians
Col.	Colossians
1 Thess.	1 Thessalonians
2 Thess.	2 Thessalonians
1 Tim.	1 Timothy
2 Tim.	2 Timothy
Titus	Titus
Philem.	Philemon
Heb.	Hebrews
James	James
1 Peter	1 Peter
2 Peter	2 Peter
1 John	1 John
2 John	2 John
3 John	3 John
Jude	Jude
Rev.	Revelation

EXTRABIBLICAL SOURCES

Old Testament Apocrypha

Tob	Tobit
Jdt	Judith
Wis	Wisdom of Solomon
Sir	Wisdom of Jesus the Son of Sirach (Ecclesiasticus)
Bar	Baruch
Ep Jer	Epistle of Jeremiah
Add Esth	Additions to Esther
Add Dan	Additions to Daniel
Bel	Bel and the Dragon

1 Macc	1 Maccabees
2 Macc	2 Maccabees
1 Esd	1 Esdras
Pr Man	Prayer of Manasseh
3 Macc	3 Maccabees
2 Esd	2 Esdras
4 Macc	4 Maccabees

Old Testament Pseudepigrapha

Apoc. Ab.	Apocalypse of Abraham
As. Mos.	Assumption of Moses
2 Bar.	2 Baruch (Syriac Apocalypse)
Ep. Arist.	Epistle of Aristeas
Jos. Asen.	Joseph and Aseneth
Jub.	Jubilees
1 En.	1 Enoch (Ethiopic Apocalypse)
2 En.	2 Enoch
4 Ezra	4 Ezra
Odes Sol.	Odes of Solomon
Pss. Sol.	Psalms of Solomon
Sib. Or.	Sibylline Oracles
T. 12 Patr.	Testaments of the Twelve Patriarchs
T. Benj.	Testament of Benjamin
T. Dan	Testament of Dan
T. Iss.	Testament of Issachar
T. Jos.	Testament of Joseph
T. Levi	Testament of Levi
T. Adam	Testament of Adam
T. Mos.	Testament of Moses
T. Sol.	Testament of Solomon

PERIODICALS

ABSA	Annual of the British School at Athens
AUSS	*Andrews University Seminary Studies*
BA	*Biblical Archaeologist*
BAR	*Biblical Archaeology Review*
BASOR	*Bulletin of the American Schools of Oriental Research*
BBR	*Bulletin for Biblical Research*
Bib	*Biblica*
BJRL	*Bulletin of the John Rylands University Library of Manchester*
BR	*Biblical Research*
BSac	*Bibliotheca Sacra*
CBQ	*Catholic Biblical Quarterly*
CJT	*Canadian Journal of Theology*

CSion	*Cahiers Sioniens*
CTJ	*Calvin Theological Journal*
DRev	*Downside Review*
DSD	*Dead Sea Discoveries*
ETL	*Ephemerides Theologicae Lovanienses*
FM	*Faith and Mission*
HTR	*Harvard Theological Review*
HUCA	*Hebrew Union College Annual*
JAOS	*Journal of the American Oriental Society*
JBL	*Journal of Biblical Literature*
JETS	*Journal of the Evangelical Theological Society*
JJS	*Journal of Jewish Studies*
JNSL	*Journal of Northwest Semitic Languages*
JSJ	*Journal for the Study of Judaism in the Persian, Hellenistic, and Roman Periods*
JSNT	*Journal for the Study of the New Testament*
JSOT	*Journal for the Study of the Old Testament*
JTS	*Journal of Theological Studies*
Mus	*Muséon: Revue d'études orientales*
Neot	*Neotestamentica*
NovT	*Novum Testamentum*
NTS	*New Testament Studies*
PEQ	*Palestine Exploration Quarterly*
RB	*Revue biblique*
ResQ	*Restoration Quarterly*
RevExp	*Review and Expositor*
RevQ	*Revue de Qumran*
RHPR	*Revue de l'histoire et de philosophie*
RTR	*Reformed Theological Review*
ST	*Studia Theologica*
SwJT	*Southwestern Journal of Theology*
TJ	*Trinity Journal*
TynBul	*Tyndale Bulletin*
TZ	*Theologische Zeitschrift*
TZT	*Tübinger Zeitschrift für Theologie*
USQR	*Union Seminary Quarterly Review*
VT	*Vetus Testamentum*
WTJ	*Westminster Theological Journal*
ZAW	*Zeitschrift für die alttestamentliche Wissenschaft*
ZNW	*Zeitschrift für die neutestamentliche Wissenschaft und die Kunde der älteren Kirche*

SERIES

AB	Anchor Bible
AmCNT	American Commentary on the New Testament
ANTC	Abingdon New Testament Commentaries

ANTF	Arbeiten zur neutestamentlichen Textforschung
BECNT	Baker Exegetical Commentary on the New Testament
BZNW	Beihefte zur Zeitschrift für die neutestamentliche Wissenschaft
CBC	Cambridge Bible Commentary
CBSC	Cambridge Bible for Schools and Colleges
ConBNT	Coniectanea Biblica: New Testament Series
DJD	Discoveries in the Judaean Desert
Ebib	Études bibliques
EC	Epworth Commentary
EKKNT	Evangelisch-katholischer Kommentar zum Neuen Testament
FRLANT	Forschungen zur Religion und Literatur des Alten und Neuen Testaments
HNT	Handbuch zum Neuen Testament
HNTE	Handbook for New Testament Exegesis
ICC	International Critical Commentary
JSJSup	Supplements to the Journal for the Study of Judaism
JSNTSup	Journal for the Study of the New Testament Supplement Series
JSOTSup	Journal for the Study of the Old Testament Supplement Series
JSPSup	Journal for the Study of the Pseudepigrapha Supplement Series
KCB	Kregel Charts of the Bible
KEK	Kritisch-exegetischer Kommentar über das Neue Testament (Meyer-Kommentar)
KNT	Kommentar zum Neuen Testament
NAC	New American Commentary
NCBC	New Cambridge Bible Commentary
NIBC	New International Biblical Commentary
NICNT	New International Commentary on the New Testament
NIGTC	New International Greek Testament Commentary
NTD	Das Neue Testament Deutsch
NTL	New Testament Library
NTM	New Testament Message
PCNT	Paideia: Commentaries on the New Testament
PNTC[1]	Pelican New Testament Commentaries
PNTC[2]	Pillar New Testament Commentary
RCRD	Rule of the Community and Related Documents
SBLDS	Society of Biblical Literature Dissertation Series
SBLMS	Society of Biblical Literature Monograph Series
SBLSS	Society of Biblical Literature Supplement Series
SD	Studies and Documents
SP	Sacra Pagina
TBC	Torch Bible Commentaries
THNTC	Two Horizons New Testament Commentary
TNTC	Tyndale New Testament Commentaries
WBC	Word Biblical Commentary
WC	Westminster Commentaries
WUNT	Wissenschaftliche Untersuchungen zum Alten und Neuen Testament

REFERENCE

ABD   Freedman, D. N., ed. 1992. *Anchor Bible Dictionary.* 6 vols. New York: Doubleday.

ANET   Pritchard, James B., ed. 1969. *Ancient Near Eastern Texts Relating to the Old Testament.* 3rd ed. Princeton, NJ: Princeton University Press.

BAGD   Bauer, W., W. F. Arndt, and F. W. Gingrich, and F. W. Danker. 1979. *Greek-English Lexicon of the New Testament and Other Early Christian Literature.* 2nd ed. Chicago: University of Chicago Press.

BDAG   Danker, F. W., W. Bauer, W. F. Arndt, and F. W. Gingrich. 2000. *Greek-English Lexicon of the New Testament and Other Early Christian Literature.* 3rd ed. Chicago: University of Chicago Press.

BDF   Blass, F., A. Debrunner, and R. W. Funk. 1961. *Greek Grammar of the New Testament and Other Early Christian Literature.* Chicago: University of Chicago Press.

COS   Hallo, William W., and K. Lawson Younger Jr., eds. 1997–2016. *The Context of Scripture.* 4 vols. Leiden: Brill.

GKC   Gesenius, Friedrich W. 1910. *Gesenius' Hebrew Grammar.* eds. E. Kautzsch and A. E. Cowley. 2d. ed. Clarendon Press.

IBHS   Waltke, B. and M. O'Connor. 1990. *Introduction to Biblical Hebrew Syntax.* Winona Lake, IN: Eisenbrauns.

ISBE   Bromiley, G. W., ed. 1979–1988. *International Standard Bible Encyclopedia.* 4 vols. Grand Rapids: Eerdmans.

NIB   Keck, L. E., ed. 1994–2004. *New Interpreters Bible.* 12 vols. Nashville: Abingdon.

NIDNTT Brown, C., ed. 1975–1978. *New International Dictionary of New Testament Theology.* 4 vols. Grand Rapids: Zondervan.

NIDOTTE VanGemeren, W. A., ed. 1997. *New International Dictionary of Old Testament Theology.* 5 vols. Grand Rapids: Zondervan.

TDNT   Kittel, G., and G. Friedrich, eds. 1964–1976. *Theological Dictionary of the New Testament.* Trans. G. W. Bromiley. 10 vols. Grand Rapids: Eerdmans.

TDOT   Botterweck, G. J., H. Ringgren, and H.-J. Fabry, eds. 1974–2006. *Theological Dictionary of the Old Testament.* Trans. J. T. Willis, et al. 8 vols. Grand Rapids: Eerdmans.

TLNT   Spicq, C. 1994. *Theological Lexicon of the New Testament.* Trans. and ed. James D. Ernest. 3 vols. Peabody, MA: Hendrickson.

UT   Gordon, C. H. 1965. *Ugaritic Textbook.* Rome: Pontifical Biblical Institute.

Wise, et al. Wise, M., M. Abegg, and E. Cook. 1996. *The Dead Sea Scrolls: A New Translation.* San Francisco: HarperSanFrancisco.

BIBLE TRANSLATIONS

ESV	English Standard Version
NASB	New American Standard Bible
NIV	New International Version
NKJV	New King James Version
NLT	New Living Translation
NRSV	New Revised Standard Version
WEB	World English Bible

INTRODUCTION TO 1 & 2 KINGS

OVERVIEW OF 1 & 2 KINGS

Author: Likely multiple writers; possibly a single writer

Provenance: Multiple contexts associated with the place of the writers; final edition possibly in Mesopotamia but also possibly in Yehud early in the Second Temple period

Date: Earliest portions likely written early in the United Monarchy, and continued until shortly after the fall of Jerusalem

Readers: Israelites, Judeans, and the members of the Second Temple community

Historical Setting: In Israel and Judah, from the United Monarchy through the destruction of Jerusalem

Occasion: To explain the history of Israel and Judah, and ultimately the Babylonian exile

Genre: Ancient historiography

Theological Emphases: Legacies; effects of choices; differences between Judah and Israel; effects of perpetual covenantal disobedience

Kings details the exploits of Judean and Israelite kings, several prophets, foreign kings, as well as the twists and turns of two nations once united. Consequently, one can say that Kings is primarily concerned with people. From Solomon, to Ahab, to Elijah and Elisha, to Hezekiah, and beyond, Kings recounts the exploits of important people across the history of ancient Israel. And this biographical concern only supplements the historiographic intentions of the book. Given the recurring regnal formulas that form the backbone of the book's structural divisions (see below), the book's biographical concerns are presented in the form of a national history. Therefore, Kings argues that individuals

are a part of something larger than themselves. The exploits and experiences, the faith or faithlessness, of individuals can shape the contours of a nation's history.

But is Kings "history?" Should Kings be classified as proper history writing? The complexities of the debate notwithstanding, one should feel comfortable describing Kings as history writing, even "good history writing." Indeed, one should be mindful of the differences between ancient and modern history writing, namely that ancient history writers operated by different canons and conventions. Nevertheless, as long as a modern reader can respect the differences and consider Kings in the vein of *ancient* history writing, the integrity of the account and the theological potency of the text can be appreciated. Kings is a historical account of Israel and Judah that documents their existence within the Promised Land and the rationale for their tragic exile.

AUTHORSHIP OF 1 AND 2 KINGS

Issues of authorship, audience, and date of composition are often intimately connected, and Kings represents a particularly frustrating case. In short, seeking clarity on issues of authorship, audience, and date of composition forces one to consider the literary history behind the final form of Kings, a discussion where ideas are diverse and potentially incompatible.

Jewish tradition holds that Jeremiah the prophet was the author of Kings (*Baba Bathra*, 15a). This is undoubtedly due to the literary connection between 2 Kings 25 and Jeremiah 52, the historical connection between Jeremiah's context of ministry and the fall of Judah, and perhaps the emphasis upon the prophetic institution within Kings. However, Jeremianic authorship is not widely held among modern scholars, although there are exceptions (e.g., Maier 2018, 6–25). Instead, perceptions of authorship and date of composition, which in turn affects audience, is greatly influenced by modern critical theories.[1]

Ideas of authorship for Kings can be categorized in two broad categories.

1. One writer compiled several sources and traditions into a coherent whole. The debate in this category is when to date the work.
2. There were multiple writers, who worked in different social and historical contexts, responsible for the

---

1   Perception of authorship and date of composition, which in turn affects audience, is greatly influenced by modern critical theories. By the late nineteenth century, sources associated with Pentateuchal composition, memorialized by the Graf-Wellhausen Documentary Hypothesis, were being projected on to the Historical Books (Arnold and Schreiner 2017, 252–73). Scholars invoked the so-called J and E sources in their discussions of Joshua, Judges, Samuel, and Kings. The result was a cacophony of voices with no semblance of a consensus. However, in the middle of the twentieth century, Martin Noth presented the idea of the Deuteronomistic History (Noth 1991). This would set a course within critical scholarship for the next seventy-five-plus years.

Noth argued that Deuteronomy, Joshua, Judges, Samuel, and Kings were the result of a singular historian's compilation of different traditions and texts into a coherent history shortly after the sacking of Jerusalem (586 BCE). According to the theory, Deuteronomy articulated the religious ideal that explained the expectations surrounding the nation and the canons for assessing its history that unfolded in Joshua through Kings. Naturally then, Deuteronomy assumed its place at the onset of the history. Noth also argued that the historian organized his work around a series of speeches. Long or short, at critical junctures important people gave important speeches (1 Kings 8 represents one of these speeches). As further substantiation, Noth highlighted similar phraseology, the same theological assumptions, and the cross-referencing of major characters throughout the work.

Scholars quickly embraced Noth's theory, and many today continue to hold to either the theory or the essence of the theory. Consequently, since the middle of the twentieth century a clear majority of scholars associate the composition of Kings with the elusive "Deuteronomistic Historian." In some cases, people refer to an equally elusive "Deuteronomistic School." However, the wide acceptance of Noth's ideas did not mean his theory was without criticism. Most notably, Noth was criticized for not properly explaining the positive elements within the history. For example, the recurrence of David's legacy and covenant looms large, and 2 Kings 25:27–30 can be interpreted as the historian offering a ray of hope. In addition, Noth was criticized because some observed evidence that the historian was working well into the postexilic period.

For a good synopsis of this debate, with a quality bibliography, see Sandra Richter, "Deuteronomistic History," in *Dictionary of the Old Testament Historical Books* (DOTHB; Downers Grove, IL: InterVarsity Press, 2005), 219–30. Also, see Marvin A. Sweeney, *I and II Kings* (OTL; Louisville: Westminster John Knox, 2007), 1–32.

composition of Kings. In this category, there is a host of opinions. Were there two primary historians who each produced an edition respectively? Were there more than two historians, which in turn implies more than two editions? When did the writers produce those editions? Before the exile? During the exile? After the exile? Or, some combination thereof?

DATE OF WRITING

Assuming the two broad categories just mentioned, if one accepts a single author, the issue is determining when the author worked, even though the ending of Kings (2 Kings 25:27–30) suggests the middle of the sixth century as the ending point. For example, Martin Noth argued that a singular historian wrote Kings in the middle of the sixth century (Noth 1991) while Van Seters argued that a singular historian wrote closer to the Hellenistic period (Van Seters 1983).

If one holds to the idea that Kings is the result of a lengthy and complicated history of development, then questions about a "date of writing" will yield multiple answers. For instance, one historian could have worked in the seventh or sixth centuries with a final historian working later in the fifth. Or, there remains a possibility for an initial historian to have worked during the exile with subsequent historian(s) working after the exile. Options and reconstructions are legion.

Second Temple Period

The Second Temple period is defined in several ways. Generally, it designates the time that the second temple existed. Dedicated in 516 BCE, the second temple stood until the Roman general Titus razed it when he sacked Jerusalem in 70 CE. The period was a time of foreign occupation (Persians, Greeks, and Romans) but also a relatively brief period of Jewish independence under the Hasmoneans. As detailed by the Old Testament books traditionally dated to this period (1 and 2 Chronicles, Ezra, Nehemiah, Esther, Daniel, Haggai, Zechariah, and Malachi) and the host of intertestamental literature, the primary concerns of the Jewish community during this period included questions of theology and identity in light of a community that was being spread throughout the ancient Near East and the Mediterranean world. Without an independent kingdom in the Promised Land and a perpetual state of foreign occupation, such questions became critical.

OCCASION FOR WRITING AND AUDIENCE

Predictably then, the question of audience is also complicated. The possibility of a preexilic edition of Kings notwithstanding, the book of Kings in its final form was originally compiled and written for the exilic and Second Temple communities. It was written to give an account of Israelite history and explain the Babylonian exile. It sought to explain who Judah and Israel were and why Israel no longer exists. It also intended to explain what caused the schism between the once-unified countries, and the role of the Mosaic covenant and Davidic promise in the unfolding of these events. Perhaps most importantly, it sought to discuss if there was any hope for Judah and the Davidic line.

As the Second Temple period progressed, so too did the book's importance for the community. Perhaps Ezra's prayer best demonstrates how the book continued to edify the community. Responding to the egregious shortcomings of the Judean leadership, Ezra draws from the lessons found in the book of Kings to declare humiliatingly that his community is on the path to committing the same deeds that precipitated the Babylonian exile (Ezra 9:5–15). Thus, Howard is surely on target when he suggests that the book of Kings functioned in something other than a purely historical capacity. The book of Kings sought to keep the past at the forefront of the mind of the Second Temple community, perpetually reminding them of the consequences of covenantal infidelity and the enduring quality of God's Word (Howard 1993, 196–97).

Yet the Second Temple period ultimately produced social developments and questions that were not directly addressed by the book of Kings nor relevant to the original audience, such as the rising questions about Israel's relationship to an ever-expanding geographic frame of reference. The period produced new questions about the Davidic dynasty's role in an increasingly dominant imperialistic context. But despite these developments, the book of Kings was not abandoned by subsequent generations as an authoritative text. It remained a concise and honest explanation of Israel's darkest moments. But it also became the foundational source for a new historical reflection, 1 and 2 Chronicles. So, while the occasion for writing of Kings is best fixed to the context of the early Second Temple period, its message continued to affect the Judean community well beyond the sixth and fifth centuries.

Deuteronomistic History

The Deuteronomistic History is a scholarly term that refers to a range of books that display theological and thematic uniformity, and there is reason to believe that they may have been composed together. According to the theory classically defined, Joshua, Judges, 1 and 2 Samuel, and 1 and 2 Kings were composed with Deuteronomy in the middle of the sixth century BCE to explain the Babylonian Exile. Deuteronomy, as the lead in the historical account, articulated the theological standard against which Israel and Judah would later be judged. Both countries' inability to live in accord with Deuteronomy's theology secured the destruction of Israel and the exile of Judah.

A RECONSTRUCTION OF THE COMPOSITIONAL HISTORY OF KINGS

Articulating the specifics about who wrote Kings, when they wrote it, and for whom it was written thrusts one into an arena where there is no clear winner. Therefore, the question, "How does one even discuss the question of authorship, date of composition, and audience?" is worth asking.

The way forward is to first frame the boundaries of the debate and allow the conversation to progress within that framework. As such, one must first accept that the canons of history writing and literary composition, including notions about "authorship," were different in antiquity (Rollston, 2010; Schniedewind, 2004; Walton and Sandy, 2013). Thus, we cannot assume that modern ideas of authorship equate to those in antiquity. Second, writing in Israel was a controlled skill that required a certain economic and political infrastructure. Therefore, any statement of dating must account for social and historical contexts that would have been conducive to large-scale literary development. Third, whoever was responsible for the composition utilized source material. Fourth, the ideological imprint of Deuteronomy upon Kings is beyond question. In the words of Richter, Deuteronomy is "the theological foundation of Israel's self-understanding" and represents the "political agreement that dictates the precepts by which Yahweh and Israel had agreed to govern their relationship" (Richter, 2005, 228). Fifth, there is significant literary-critical evidence to suggest that the so-called Deuteronomistic History was published in both preexilic *and* postexilic editions.

Applying this framework to Kings, the book was likely the product of a literary endeavor that transcended the boundaries of Kings. It was likely composed along with traditions that came to constitute elements of other biblical books, namely the books of Deuteronomy and Samuel. The quintessential proof is the Deuteronomic ideology that permeates Kings and the legacy of David that demands a frame of reference offered in the books of Samuel. Also, it is reasonable to think of at least two editions of Kings before the final form. This is based on a few considerations.

First, 2 Kings 18:5 states that Hezekiah "trusted in the Lord the God of Israel; so that there was no one like him among all the kings of Judah after him, or among those who were before him." Similarly, 2 Kings 23:25 proclaims that before Josiah "there was no king like him, who turned to the Lord with all his heart, with all his soul, and with all his might according to the law of Moses; nor did any like him arise after him." These incomparability statements are often understood as climactic statements reminiscent of older editions of Kings.[2] Second, as just alluded, scholarship has produced a variety of literary critical studies that demonstrate 1) that Israelite historians employed ancient Near Eastern literary conventions and 2) that Kings developed analogously to other historical works in antiquity. What started with the work of Cross gave way to Nelson, Halpern, and others. Moreover, Halpern and Vanderhooft have studied the variations within the regnal framework and concluded that there is evidence of subtle shifts in style that are indicative of three editions of Kings: a Hezekian, a Josianic, and a final edition. The cumulative effect of such studies translates into the likelihood that Kings manifests a lengthy and complex history of development punctuated by two editions before the final one.

Nevertheless, to what degree of certainty can one speak of older editions before the final form? And, to what extent do these ideas play into the present task? Admittedly, terms of certainty can only proceed so far. There is no extant manuscript that evidences either a Hezekian or Josianic edition of Kings. Moreover, critical studies are, by nature, tentative and debatable. However, there is a consensus around the idea of a Hezekian and Josianic edition among those who accept the probability of large-scale literary development between 1000–586 BCE. In other words, circumstantial evidence and critical theory establish the warrant to refer to Hezekian and Josianic editions of Kings.[3] However, this does not imply that our exegetical focus will be on a reconstructed early edition of Kings. Rather, the exegetical focus for this project will fall upon the final form of Kings. The literary history of Kings will be considered only when it is deemed to explain or illuminate the final form.

Ultimately, the answer to the question of authorship, audience, and date of composition for Kings is threefold. The first edition of Kings was likely a Hezekian History. This account climaxed with an account of Hezekiah's reign, which included an emphasis upon Jerusalem's salvation. It was likely sanctioned by the Judean royal court in the wake of Sennacherib's third military campaign to answer questions likely circulating about Judah's place moving forward and to emphasize the superiority of Judah versus Israel. Thus, one can speak of a date of composition at the very end of the eighth century or the beginning of the seventh. The Josianic History constitutes the next edition, and it sought to celebrate the exploits

---

2   Yet some do not interpret these incomparability statements as evidence of Kings's literary history. In a famous example, Knoppers interprets them as unifying statements used by an exilic historian (Knoppers 1992). Accordingly, Hezekiah is celebrated as the paradigmatic example of trusting in Yahweh in the middle of political turmoil. Josiah is the quintessential reformer. Admittedly, Knoppers's ideas are possible, but in light of all the other literary critical data in Kings, this possibility becomes less likely. Moreover, the ideas of Knoppers proceed from the questionable assumptions about large-scale literary development within Israel during Iron Age II.

3   This is not to suggest that there was no history writing in Judah and Israel before a Hezekian context. Rather, there is ample evidence to suggest that history writing flourished in ninth and eighth centuries, perhaps reaching back to the era of Solomon and David. Admittedly, such reconstructions rest upon historical critical methods of inquiry, and thus subject to criticism. With respect to the development of the sources utilized by a Hezekian historian, Halpern, Lemaire, and Sweeney have done important work (Halpern and Lemaire 2010; Sweeney 2007, 26–32).

of Josiah and Judah during the waning years of the Neo-Assyrian Empire. The difficulty with the second edition is when to date the composition. Josiah's sudden death occurred shortly before the Battle of Carchemish (605 BCE). Thus, one can make a general statement of composition being at the end of the seventh or at the beginning of the sixth century BCE. The final edition of Kings is the final form, and it, in the vein of Noth, explained Judah's exile to Babylon in 586 BCE. As to a date of composition, the final verses are informative. Because 2 Kings 25:27–30 recounts the house arrest of Jehoiachin, the final edition of Kings was likely not finalized before the middle of the sixth century BCE.

HISTORICAL SETTING

The book of Kings is set in the region of Israel and Judah (often called the Southern Levant) between approximately 1000–586 BCE. This was a period of great social and political fluidity that was largely dictated by the rise and fall of Neo-Assyrian and Neo-Babylonian empires. This period can also be described as the Golden Age of ancient Israelite culture—a time when God's people hit their stride culturally.[4]

While much could be said, there are a few social and historical realities that are particularly important for understanding Kings. First, it's important to realize that for much of their history Israel and Judah were cogs in very large, imperialistic wheels. Initially, Shishak, the Egyptian king (945–924 BCE), made incursions into both Israel and Judah at the end of the tenth century BCE to reassert Egyptian dominance. Then, in the ninth century BCE, Neo-Assyria set its sights on Egypt, which effectively put Judah and Israel in the crosshairs of the Assyrians. Finally, there were the Babylonians, who assumed control of the region when they overran the Assyrians at the end of the seventh century. All of the imperial domination is reflected in the archaeological record (Stern 2001, 14–41; 308–9).

Second, which is related to the first, the book of Kings addresses one of the most fluid social and political contexts of Israelite history. The period of 1000–586 BCE was a time of significant cultural growth and territorial expansion for the Lord's people (Mazar 1990, 368–530). Important early Israelite settlements (in the Central Highlands) were expanded, and new settlements developed in bordering

---

4   Archaeology is responsible for shedding light on the cultural developments of Israel and Judah during the period between 1000–586 BCE. Thus, archaeology constitutes an important element to consult for understanding the full dynamics of Kings. Yet archaeology's role for understanding Kings is complicated. On the one hand, archaeological results are relevant to illuminating the historical setting of Kings. For example, archaeology shows Israel's movement away from traditional kinship-based social structures, which uniquely illuminates the anxiety associated with the growth and power of the monarchical institution and growing social stratification attested to throughout Kings (Faust 2010, 264–66). In some instances, specific finds have illuminated Kings. For example, the Tel Dan Stele verifies the lasting legacy of the Davidic line, as well as the conflict between Israel, Judah, and Aram (Biran and Naveh 1993; 1995). Then there is Shishak's stele, which verifies the biblical testimony of his incursion into the Cis-Jordan (Redford 1992, 121–22).

The results of archaeology have also forced a more sophisticated understanding of Kings. For example, the excavations at Samaria, coupled with the textual data from Neo-Assyrian sources, cooperate to offer a different picture of the Omride dynasty than the one emphasized by the biblical historian. In this case, the interpreter is forced to ponder how the historian balanced the requirement to give an accurate account of the line while emphasizing their profound damage to Israelite society. Similarly, Sennacherib's annals at first glance appear to offer a different account of Jerusalem's siege and Judah's decimation during his third military campaign. In the end, an awareness of the historical setting for Kings must accommodate a wide range of interrelated issues, which have events, cultural change, and hermeneutics as the focal point.

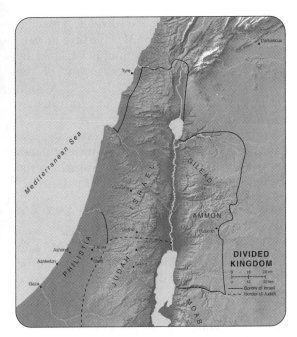

The Divided Kingdom of Israel and Judah
Map by A. D. Riddle

a component of the monarchy's method of operation. Whether King Solomon or the Omrides, marriages to foreigners resulted in an influx of theological influences that eventually brought down both kingdoms. In fact, archaeological data reinforces the historian's concern as it paints a picture of a culture that was extremely diverse in its theological practices (Hess 2007). The inscriptions of Khirbet el-Qom and Kuntillet Ajrud testify to polytheism associated with some views of Yahweh. The so-called Pillar Figurines, other cultic paraphernalia, and iconography found throughout Israel and Judah testify to domestic cultic practices that incorporated elements of Canaanite religion. The high places and standing stones shunned by Kings and the Deuteronomic ideology were ubiquitous throughout Israel and Judah. Consequently, the theological apostasy that characterized the royal courts of Israel and Judah was indicative of a larger social reality.

King Solomon Sacrificing to the Idols
by Sébastien Bourdon. Public domain.

regions (the Shephelah and Negev). Associated with this expanding settlement pattern was also an increase in population density and urbanization whereby several sites displayed important architectural features such as public installations, fortifications, and sophisticated city planning. For example, Beersheba during this period displayed an intricate city design, fortification, and an elaborate waterworks system (Hostetter 2005, 113–16). Most importantly, there are the inscriptions and other evidences of literacy and literary development. In short, the proliferation of epigraphic evidence during 1000–586 BCE is a key marker of cultural development, for literacy and literary development in antiquity required a number of social and political requisites (Rollston 2010; Schniedewind 2004).

But lest one forget, there were also theological implications associated with Israel's cultural development. Throughout its presentation, the book of Kings testifies to them. The clearest example is the negative implications related to politically arranged marriages, which developed as

In sum, 1000–586 BCE was an incredibly strategic era that saw Israelite culture blossom to influence the region. This period also saw the rise and fall the Neo-Assyrian and Neo-Babylonian empires. What is implicit throughout the text of Kings is made abundantly clear through archaeology. Therefore, while the period assumed by Kings was the Golden Age of classical Israelite culture, it also was one that craved guidance by the prophetic voice so that the ebbs and flows of the era could be navigated.

THEOLOGICAL EMPHASES OF KINGS

In what follows is a literary analysis of Kings that emphasizes the literary units of Kings and the relationship between those units. Such an analysis will in turn illuminate the theological themes of the book.

The Major Literary Units of Kings

Kings unfolds in three major units, each of which is set off by a significant development in the regnal framework (see below), most notably in the succession formula. The first unit (1 Kings 1:1–14:20) recounts the final generation of the united monarchy, focusing in large part on the exploits and dramatic rise and fall of King Solomon. The second is the most extensive and details the period of the divided kingdom (1 Kings 14:21–2 Kings 20:21). The final unit recounts the systematic erosion of Judah after the sacking of Samaria and destruction of the northern kingdom (2 Kings 21:1–25:30). Within each major unit, the account can be further divided in accord with distinct segments. The transitions between those segments carry the narrative forward in accord with major themes and structures. The chart below visualizes the breakdown of Kings, and a detailed outline further below offers more information.

Structural Relationships and Themes

First and Second Kings is a complicated and layered account. Therefore, understanding the major themes and structural relationships that are driving the account is paramount. To accomplish this, one must keep a "bird's-eye-view" when identifying key themes and structures. The following themes and structures are the most prominent to the overall flow of Kings.

The Collapse of the United Monarchy					Divided Monarchy			Judah Alone	
1 Kings 1:1–14:20					1 Kings 14:21–2 Kings 20:21			2 Kings 21:1–25:30	
					Political Upheaval	Prophets and Kings	*Political Upheaval*	The Bad and the Good	The End
					14:21–16:34	1 Kings 17:1–2 Kings 13:25	14:1–20:21	21:1–23:30	
Solomon Securing the Throne 1:1–2:46a	Solomon's Wisdom Displayed 2:46b–4:34[5:14]	Solomon's Building Campaigns and Other Endeavors 5:1[15]–9:28	Solomon's Legacy 10:1–29	Dissolution of the United Monarchy 11:1–14:20	Dynastic Stability versus Instability 14:21–16:20 / Omrides Established 16:21–34	Elijah and the Omrides (1 Kings 17:1–2 Kings 1:18) / Elijah and Kings (1 Kings 2:1–2 Kings 13:25)	Internal and External Pressure 14:1–16:20 / Samaria versus Jerusalem 17:1–20:21	Manasseh and Ammon 21:1–26 / Josiah 22:1–23:30	23:31–25:30

1 Kings 1:1–14:20: The Collapse of the United Monarchy

Solomon Securing the Throne 1:1–2:46a	Solomon's Wisdom Displayed 2:46b–4:34[5:14]			Solomon's Building Campaigns and Other Endeavors 5:1[5:15]–9:28						Dissolution of the United Monarchy 11:1–14:20		
Succession of Solomon (1:1–2:11) / Establishing the Throne (2:12–46a)	The Lord's Appearance (2:46b—3:15)	Solomon's Wisdom in Adjudication (3:16–28)	Solomon's Wisdom in the Affairs of the Kingdom (4:1–4:34[5:14])	Preparations (5:1–18[5:15–32])	Building the Royal Precinct (6:1–7:51)	Dedication Speech (8:1–66)	The Lord's Second Appearance (9:1–9)	More Royal Endeavors (9:10–28)	Solomon's Legacy (10:1–29)	The Demise of Solomon (11:1–43)	Schism (12:1–24)	Reign of Jeroboam I (12:25–14:20)

1 Kings 1:1–14:20 as Introduction

First Kings 1:1–14:20 can be understood as an extensive introduction.[5] For starters, and perhaps most importantly, the succession formula, an integral element to the regnal framework, does not begin until 1 Kings 14:21, at which point the flow of the narrative demonstrably shifts to something robotic and more rigid when signaling the onset of a new reign (see below). Such a flow continues until the conclusion of the history.

In addition, the content of 1 Kings 1:1–14:20 is tightly packed over five discernable subunits, which suggests an intentional message.

This unit uses the material associated with Solomon and Jeroboam I to suggest that the monarchy was critical to the Lord's method of operation only with certain unwavering commitments, namely absolute covenantal fidelity. Unfortunately, this unit recounts how both the final king of the united monarchy and the inaugural king of Israel were unable to exhibit absolute covenantal fidelity. Consequently, 1 Kings 1:1–14:20 sets the tone for the remainder of the account and establishes the critical historical question that will inform so much of the book: Why did Judah survive longer but still end up in exile?

---

5   There is no consensus on the structure of the first unit of Kings. Most commentators position the first unit break after chapter 11, and some perceive a very intricate, chiastic structure governing the first unit of Kings (Olley 2003; Walsh 1996). However, placing the transition after chapter 11 disregards the onset of the regnal framework in 1 Kings 14:21. Also, intricate chiasms overwhelm the reader with burdensome cross-referencing (Schreiner 2020).

Throughout this unit, this question is answered in a number of ways, but in one instance it's answered by the symbolic tearing-of-the-garment passages (1 Kings 11:29–39; 14:7–11). The passages are connected by specific words, images, and syntax that simultaneously link Solomon with Jeroboam I and introduce fundamental contrasts between the two. Both kings were remembered for specific covenantal infractions that had lasting effects, but only one saw the continuation of their dynastic line. Indeed, the geographic reach of David's dynasty was undermined, but the dynasty in Jerusalem would endure. And while dynastic stability would define Judah, dynastic instability would define Israel. Thus, the answer to why Judah survived longer is, in part, the legacy of David.

First Kings 1:1–14:20 also introduces the rival worship sites: Jerusalem in the south and Bethel and Dan in the north. Jerusalem is understood as the divinely approved throne of the Lord while Bethel and Dan are two illegitimate worship sites fashioned out of fear and a desire to control the northern populace (1 Kings 12:26–33). Importantly, this contrast is revisited over and over in Kings. Consequently, with the conclusion of 1 Kings 14:20 two major criteria that will be utilized by the historian for the evaluation of the subsequent monarchs is established.

The National Effects of Choices, Prophecy, and Their Climactic Outcome

According to the book of Kings, Israel's history was the product of a nuanced relationship between choice and determinism. On the one hand, the historian explicitly links the historical trajectory of Israel and Judah to the choices of particular kings. For example,

- 1 Kings 11: Verses 9–13 explicitly detail the connections between Solomon's choices and the contours of history. "Then the Lord was angry with Solomon *because* his heart turned away. . . . *Therefore*, the Lord said to Solomon . . . ".
- 1 Kings 14: According to verses 7–16, Jeroboam I failed to exhibit the necessary covenantal obedience like King David (v. 8) and so provoked the Lord to anger with his illegitimate gods (v. 9). *Therefore*, the Lord orchestrated the downfall of his household (vv. 10–11) and the eventual exile of Israel (v. 16).
- 2 Kings 21:10–15: Manasseh's abominable practices secured the judgment of Judah, "*Because* King Manasseh of Judah committed these abominations. . . . *Therefore*, says the Lord . . . I am bringing upon Judah . . . ". Moreover, he earned the characterization of being worse that the Amorite pagans.
- 2 Kings 23:26–27: According to the historian, not even Josiah's incredible reforms could pacify the pending judgment secured by Manasseh. "Still the Lord did not turn from the fierceness of his great wrath . . . *because* of all the provocations with which Manasseh had provoked him . . . 'I will remove Judah also from my sight.'"

On the other hand, Kings also recounts how divine providence shaped the contours of history in a more unilateral way. This is clearly demonstrated in cases where prophecy impacted personal and national histories.

- Josiah fulfills the prophecy spoken against Jeroboam's altars: 1 Kings 13:2 ➔ 2 Kings 23:5–10
- Ahab receives a prophecy that his maneuvers against the Arameans would find success: 1 Kings 20:13 ➔ 20:19–21; 1 Kings 20:28 ➔ 20:29–30

- Dogs will consume the corpse of Jezebel: 1 Kings 21:23 ➜ 2 Kings 9:30–37
- Elisha prophesies about the defeat of the Arameans: 2 Kings 7:1 ➜ 7:16–20
- Elisha prophesies that Israel will reclaim cities under the control of Aram: 2 Kings 13:16–20 ➜ 2 Kings 13:24–25
- Isaiah prophesies that the siege of Jerusalem will fail: 2 Kings 19:32–34 ➜ 19:35–37

Together, all these examples demonstrate a belief that choice and divine sovereignty mutually influence history. It's not solely as an "either/or" proposition, but rather a "both/and" proposition. Israel's history was neither solely the result of the Lord's will nor solely the result of the people's choices.

Assuming this scheme, the text offers a general explanation of the exile. Solomon's lifestyle demonstrated a rejection of Deuteronomic ideals, and so too did Jeroboam I's. Therefore, Solomon's choices secured the schism, and Jeroboam I's set the course of Israel's history. The latter would be defined by apostasy and dynastic instability and ultimately lead to Samaria's destruction in 722 BCE (2 Kings 17). For Judah, its judgment was initially pacified by the legacy of David and Jerusalem, but Manasseh's deliberate apostasy eventually secured its judgment, so much so that even the greatest reform in Judean history could not alter divine determination. Thus, the progression of 1 and 2 Kings is demonstrably negative. While the text remembers positive spells of revival and reform, the account overall manifests a negative trend. Literarily, this renders 2 Kings 25 as a negative climax to the account.

In the Shadow of David and Jeroboam

There is a recurring comparison involving kings David and Jeroboam I. For David, his legacy is invoked in a variety of ways. First, his way of life is the achievable, yet unrealized, standard for Solomon if he wishes to carry forth his dynastic line (1 Kings 3:14; 9:4). But because Solomon, as well as other kings, failed to meet these expectations, David's memory is also periodically used as an indictment, emphasizing the infidelity of particular kings. Prominent examples include Solomon (1 Kings 11), Jeroboam I (1 Kings 14), and Ahaz (2 Kings 16:2). Yet David is also invoked positively, as a comparison to highlight faithful Judean kings (Asa, 2 Kings 15:11; Hezekiah, 2 Kings 18:3; Josiah, 2 Kings 22:2). Most important, however, is how David's covenant helped explain the contours of history. For example, Solomon appeals to the dynastic covenant in his temple dedication prayer (1 Kings 8:15–21; 25–26), and in 1 Kings 11 and 15:4–5, the implications of David's privileged status and covenant are called out as the reasons why Judah remained despite so much disobedience.

Jeroboam's memory is not only more uniform than David's, but it is also more pervasive throughout Kings. In each location, the idolatrous deeds of Jeroboam I inform the regnal evaluations, as if to punctuate the historian's negative assessment of that particular king (1 Kings 15:34; 16:2–3, 7, 19, 26, 31; 21:22; 22:52; 2 Kings 3:3; 9:9; 10:29–31; 13:2–13; 14:23–24; 15:9, 1, 24, 28). This comes to a head in 2 Kings 17:21–23, where Jeroboam's deeds are explicitly linked to the destruction of the northern kingdom.

When he had torn Israel from the house of David, they made Jeroboam son of Nebat king. Jeroboam drove Israel from following the Lord and made them commit great sin. The people of Israel continued in all the sins that Jeroboam committed; they did not depart from them until the Lord removed Israel out of his sight, as he had foretold through all his servants

51

the prophets. So Israel was exiled from their own land to Assyria until this day.

Only in 2 Kings 23:15–16 is Jeroboam I remembered in a relatively positive manner, but it's also indirect. Josiah is the "un-doer of Jeroboam."

Consequently, the historian uses the memory of two different people as baselines for evaluation and explanation. Jeroboam was the architect of so much that was wrong with the northern kingdom. David nullified the faithlessness and disobedience of his descendants at so many turns. In the case of the former, he sowed the seeds of his nation's destruction. With the latter, he was the standard for which all strived, but only few achieved.

Judah versus Israel, and Their Fundamental Differences

Kings understands that fundamental differences existed between the northern and southern kingdoms. Moreover, these differences contributed to the sociopolitical and historical developments within each nation after the schism. First, Judah exhibited dynastic stability, with only one minor interruption during the reign of Athaliah (2 Kings 11). This stability contrasts with the northern kingdom's dynastic instability. In fact, periods of intense political upheaval, which were exacerbated by unstable leadership, bracket the entire history of the northern kingdom (1 Kings 14:21–16:20; 2 Kings 15:1–17:41). Second, Judah enjoyed the temple in Jerusalem, the place where the Lord chose to put his name, but Israel boasted two illegitimate sanctuaries at their northern and southern extremities (Bethel and Dan). To the historian, these sites symbolized all that was wrong with the northern kingdom's religion, and he sought to keep this in the forefront of the reader's mind by making continual reference to them. Third, the miraculous salvation of Jerusalem during Hezekiah's reign stands in stark contrast to the destruction of Samaria and deportation of the northern kingdom (2 Kings 17–19), perhaps even functioning as the quintessential proof that Judah was superior to Israel.

The Framework

First and Second Kings is framed by a recurring framework. While not identical, each occurrence displays a remarkable amount of continuity, and Wiseman articulates a useful, threefold breakdown of this framework (Wiseman 2008, 49–55).

- First, there is an introductory component, which includes the king's name, relationship to his predecessor, date of ascension, length of reign, and place of reign. For Judean kings, the age and mother are also disclosed. Most importantly, within the introductory comments a pithy evaluation declares whether the king did "right" or "evil" in the eyes of the Lord.

- The second component offers the historical account of each king, and it is here where significant variation occurs. Some kings are discussed extensively, but others are not. The reason for such disparity can be linked to a number of possibilities, including authorial preference or a lack of sources.

- The final component includes any citation of other, nonextant literary sources, additional notes and/or postscripts, succession information, and a notation of death and burial.

The following table exemplifies this and has been composed considering Wiseman's scheme and ideas from Mark Leuchter and David Lamb (Leuchter and Lamb 2016, loc. 5046).

Components	Israelite Formula (2 Kings 13:1–9)	Judean Formula (2 Kings 14:1–21)
Introductory Components: Name; Relationship to Predecessor; Date of Ascension, Length of Reign, Place of Reign; Mother's Name; Age; Evaluation	In the twenty-third year of King Joash son of Ahaziah of Judah, Jehoahaz son of Jehu begin to reign over Israel in Samaria; he reigned seventeen years. He did what was evil in the sight of the Lord, and followed the sins of Jeroboam son of Nebat, which he caused Israel to sin; he did not depart from them.	In the second year of King Joash son of Joahaz of Israel, King Amaziah son of Joash of Judah began to reign. He was twenty-five years old when he began to reign, and he reigned twenty-nine years in Jerusalem. His mother's name was Jehoaddin of Jerusalem. He did what was right in the sight of the Lord, yet not like his ancestor David; in all things he did as his father Joash had done. But the high places were not removed; the people still sacrificed and made offerings on the high places.
Second Component: Historical Account	The anger of the Lord was kindled against Israel, so that he gave them repeatedly into the hand of King Hazael of Aram. . . .	As soon as the royal power was firmly in his hand he killed his servants who had murdered his father the king. . . .
Concluding Components: Other Citation; Other Sources; Notes and Postscripts; Death and Burial Notice	Now the rest of the acts of Jehoahaz and all that he did, including his might, are they not written in the Book of the Annals of the Kings of Israel? So Jehoahaz slept with his ancestors, and they buried him in Samaria; then his son Joash succeeded him.	Now the rest of the deeds of Amaziah, are they not written in the Book of the Annals of the King of Judah? They made a conspiracy against him in Jerusalem, and he fled to Lachish, and killed him there. They brought him on horses; he was buried in Jerusalem with his ancestors in the city of David. All the people of Judah took Azariah, who was sixteen years old, and made him king to succeed his father Amaziah.

Since the rise of critical scholarship, the framework of Kings has been the subject of numerous studies, often with the intention of discovering how it aides the reconstruction the literary history of Kings. Recently, Shoshana Bin-Nun, Baruch Halpern, and David Vanderhooft have offered significant analyses (Bin-Nun 1968; Halpern and Vanderhooft 1991). For the purposes of understanding the final form of Kings, however, the framework is important because it drives the work as a whole. As stated above, the onset of the introductory component moves the account into its second major unit, and the cessation of the synchronization formula moves the account into the third. Within the second unit, the framework organizes the account, interchanging between Israelite and Judean kings so that relationships and explanations can be effectively communicated.

More generally, the framework shows that the account mixed efficiency with creativity. Certain elements needed to be included in a national history, such as who succeeded whom, when the transfer occurred and under what conditions, and if the king was generally good or bad. The historian understood such requirements, and the framework ensured conformity to such expectations. Yet it also offered the opportunity to expand, emphasize, and explain points where necessary. Such dynamics display the conventions and beauty of ancient history writing.

Atmosphere and Tone of Kings

Any historian seeks to examine and explain more than entertain. Such a purpose, therefore, dictates a certain tone or atmosphere. Generally speaking, histories appeal to the mind and reason more than humanity's emotional spectrum. Yet this is not to say that history is not emotional. Rather, it suggests that the emotional impact of history writing is largely determined by the "closeness" of the reader to the subject matter. Thus, an Israelite audience would be more emotionally invested in Kings than, say, a Mesopotamian audience.

For Kings, the tone and atmosphere are measured. The positive memories are not permitted to overwhelm the reader, and the negative memories are flavored by the notion that they were in accord with what was to be expected. For example, nestled amid celebrating Josiah's reforms, the text interjects the sobering comment that those celebrations did not dissuade the Lord from judgment that was secured under Manasseh (2 Kings 23:26–27). Solomon's temple dedication, which constitutes the high point of his reign alludes to disobedience and eventual exile (1 Kings 8:22–53). Hezekiah's successful reign is rounded out with an act of shortsightedness that opens the door for the Babylonian exile (2 Kings 20:12–19).

In addition, there is the progression of the narrative that builds until it reaches its fulfillment in 2 Kings 25 (see The National Effects of Choices and Prophecy and Their Climactic Outcome above). Cumulatively, Kings does not celebrate Israel's history. Rather, it mourns it through a sobering and critical evaluation. The Babylonian exile was the logical result of Israel's and Judah's course of action. Corporately and individually, the nation exhibited a propensity to abandon the Deuteronomic ideals that were necessary for a long and vibrant life in the Promised Land. If there are any surprises inherent to the account, it is the pacifying impact of David's legacy and covenantal promise.

OTHER IMPORTANT INFORMATION

The Prophetic Institution

Prophets are just as much a part of Kings as the kings. In fact, within the second major literary unit of Kings the text shifts the exploits of the royalty to the side so that the exploits of Elijah, Elisha, and others can move into focus.

Therefore, it is important to consider the nature of the prophetic institution and its function within Israelite society.[6]

The prophetic institution was common across the ancient Near East. Fundamentally, prophets served two identifiable but

---

6   Prophecy was ubiquitous across the ancient Near East, and thanks to archaeology, this institution has been illuminated in profound ways over the past century. The Mari and Nineveh archives have proven to be particularly influential (Gordon 1995; Hayes 2014, 235–38). Speaking to a number of social topics, including political crises and day-to-day life, these texts demonstrate alongside the Bible's testimony that prophets simultaneously satisfied sociological and theological roles, both of which are mutually influential and cannot be neatly separated. Prophets were either intuitive or professional, and they brought a specific message from the divine to a specific audience. Prophetic messages would either be fundamentally encouraging or chastising, and they also would come in a variety of circumstances. However, during times of transition and social crisis, they were particularly prevalent, not to mention welcome.

As to how the messages were gleaned, one can describe two categories (Hayes 2014, 236). First, prophets employed inductive methods. This means that prophets observed tangible, concrete phenomena and then evaluated against accepted canons of interpretation. Second, there were noninductive methods, which are described as people carrying "a message" to an audience at the bidding of the divine. In this scenario, one can see why prophets were often described as "mouthpieces," or spokespeople, for the divine being that they represented. In the case of the Bible, noninductive methods appear to have been the method of preference. (This is not to suggest that inductive methods were not used. For example, the Urim and Thumum are examples of inductive prophecy, although attached to cult. Nevertheless, Deuteronomy's legislation against particular inductive forms of prophecy in preference for the spoken word is informative. See Deut. 18:9–22.)

The comparative data also illuminates other aspects about the institution. First, prophets were associated with certain spheres of society. As such, they can be described as either central or peripheral (Malamat 1995, 53). Central prophets were associated with the central power structures, such as the royal court or the temple. For example, Isaiah has unfettered access to the royal court, and Nathan comes and goes, and even influences policy, without hindrance. However, other prophets operated on the fringes of society away from those central power structures. For example, Elijah and Elisha existed on the margins of Israelite society and often confronted the exploits of the monarchy. However, this is not to suggest that central prophets never criticized the structures with which they were associated. The Old Testament recounts a number of examples where central prophets openly criticized the central power structures. For instance, Isaiah chastises Hezekiah for opening up the treasure houses of Judah to the Babylonian envoy (2 Kings 20:12–19).

Finally, it is clear that the prophetic institution cannot be boiled down to one term. Mari and Neo-Assyrian texts refer to prophets by a number of terms, which may be related to particular realities of their prophetic action (Stökl 2012, 19). Similarly, the Old Testament eclectically employs נָבִיא, חֹזֶה, רֹאֶה and other more generic terms (e.g. "man of God").

Yet what gives Israelite prophecy its distinctive quality? Why do prophets occupy so much space within this historical presentation? In short, the distinctiveness and historical prominence is linked to the pervasiveness of the covenant between God and his people and how it dictated the contours of Israelite society and history. According to Deuteronomy, the prophet was one of the community's critical social institutions (Deut. 16:18–18:22), and, as it appears last in that section, one could argue that perhaps it was viewed as the most important. Nevertheless, Deuteronomy envisions the prophets as the descendants of Moses (Deut. 18:9–22). Thus, they were the mouthpiece of the Lord and demanded the respect of the community at large. Most importantly, the prophets, like Moses, were to be the guardians of the covenant, the definitive ideology that defined Israelite society. This, more than any other quality, explains the boldness of Elijah, Elisha, Micaiah ben Imlah, and others. The prophets understood that they fulfilled the legacy of Moses and that they carried the burden of guiding the community in times of transition and crisis in a way that the community's ideological foundation would not be forgotten or ignored.

mutually related functions. On the one hand, they performed a sociological function. On the other hand, they performed a theological function. As the deity's or deities' intermediary, prophets brought the divine word to the community. As for how this word or message was brought, there were inductive and noninductive means. Noninductive prophecy refers to an authoritative message impressed upon the prophet's mind. For example, the prophet may state that a "word" had come upon him or her. On the other hand, prophetic acts were a type of inductive prophecy, which refers to the assessment of observations against an accepted standard. For example, a prophet may examine the entrails of a sacrifice and prophesy based upon what physiological features are observed. Prophets were both professional and intuitive. Professional prophets and prophetic guilds trained as prophets, but intuitive prophets were called into the office for a variety of reasons for a finite amount of time. Prophets also gravitated toward times of crisis and were fixed to the central and peripheral spheres of society. For example, Elijah and Elisha were both professional, peripheral prophets (Schreiner 2019, 30–34).

Consequently, it is not difficult to understand why the prophetic voice is so critical to Kings. As discussed above (see Historical Setting above), 1000–586 BCE was one of the most fluid eras within Israel's history. Israelite culture was developing at the same time that numerous pressures were being externally applied. Thus, the ideological fabric that had defined the community for so long was at risk. In this context came the Lord's ambassadors, charged with boldly applying the expectations of the covenant to new situations.

Chronology

Perhaps the single most difficult historical issue associated with 1 and 2 Kings is establishing a chronology of Israel and Judah. Who reigned when, and for how long? When did they assume the throne? How do the events recounted in Kings correlate to other events across the Mediterranean basin and Mesopotamia? Unfortunately, there is no consensus, and several issues, including the textual traditions, the chronographic method of the Israelite historian, and general chronographic conventions, complicate any reconstruction (Maier, 45–92; Howard 2013, 207–12).[7]

Ultimately, chronological reconstruction is possible only to a certain point. It should be held loosely and valued more for its general information than minute details.[8] See a chart below that contextualizes the reigns of Israelite and Judean Kings against the most important reigns of the ancient Near East. It is based off Rainey and Notley's *The Sacred Bridge* (2006).

---

7   Important textual traditions of Kings display significant variations between their respective chronologies, including the length and coordination of reigns (Sweeney 2007, 32–40). Thus, the relationship between the Masoretic Text and the Septuagintal or Lucianic textual traditions is an important consideration. For example, is the Masoretic Text a deliberate alteration of some "parent tradition," or are the difference between traditions the result of an attempt by the Septuagintal and Lucianic traditions to rectify an otherwise "impossible chronology?" (Sweeney 2007, 40). Further complicating any chronological reconstruction is the issue of which calendar to assume. Did the year start in the fall or the spring? Both were widely attested throughout the ancient Near East, including Israel (Kitchen 2005, 184). Finally, how the historian calculated the length of a reign is also problematic. There is evidence that Kings amalgamates an accession and non-accession system (Kitchen 2005, 184–85).

On the discipline of textual criticism in general, see Emanuel Tov 2001; Ernst Wurthwein 1995.

8   See Kitchen, "Chronology," 186.

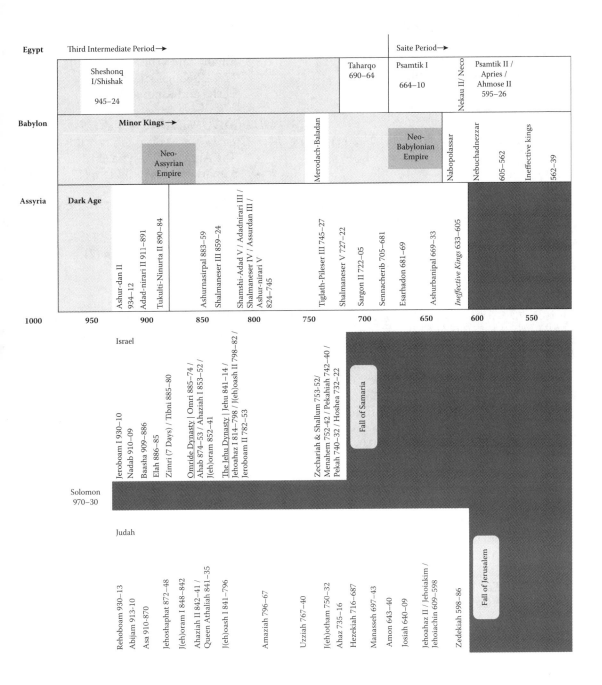

Egypt	Third Intermediate Period→							Saite Period→				
	Sheshonq I/Shishak 945–24						Taharqo 690–64	Psamtik I 664–10	Nekau II / Neco	Psamtik II / Apries / Ahmose II 595–26		
Babylon	Minor Kings →					Merodach-Baladan		Neo-Babylonian Empire	Nabopolassar	Nebuchadnezzar 605–562	Ineffective kings 562–39	
		Neo-Assyrian Empire										
Assyria	Dark Age	Ashur-dan II 934–12 / Adad-nirari II 911–891 / Tukulti-Ninurta II 890–84	Ashurnasirpal 883–59 / Shalmaneser III 859–24	Shamshi-Adad V / Adadnirari III Shalmaneser IV / Assurdan III / Ashur-nirari V 824–745		Tiglath-Pileser III 745–27	Shalmaneser V 727–22 / Sargon II 722–05	Sennacherib 705–681 / Esarhadon 681–69 / Ashurbanipal 669–33	Ineffective Kings 633–605			

1000	950	900	850	800	750	700	650	600	550

Israel

Jeroboam I 930–10
Nadab 910–09
Baasha 909–886
Elah 886–85
Zimri (7 Days) / Tibni 885–80
Omride Dynasty | Omri 885–74 /
Ahab 874–53 / Ahaziah I 853–52 /
J(eh)oram 852–41
The Jehu Dynasty | Jehu 841–14 /
Jehoahaz I 814–798 / J(eh)oash II 798–82 /
Jeroboam II 782–53

Zechariah & Shallum 753–52/
Menahem 752–42 / Pekahiah 742–40 /
Pekah 740–32 / Hoshea 732–22

Fall of Samaria

Solomon 970–30

Judah

Rehoboam 930–13
Abijam 913–10
Asa 910–870
Jehoshaphat 872–48
J(eh)oram I 848–842
Ahaziah II 842–41 /
Queen Athaliah 841–35
J(eh)oash I 841–796

Amaziah 796–67

Uzziah 767–40

J(eh)otham 750–32
Ahaz 735–16
Hezekiah 716–687
Manasseh 697–43
Amon 643–40
Josiah 640–09
Jehoahaz II / Jehoiakim /
Jehoiachin 609–598
Zedekiah 598–86

Fall of Jerusalem

OUTLINE

THE COLLAPSE OF THE UNITED MONARCHY
(1 KINGS 1:1–14:20)

The first major literary unit in Kings is 1 Kings 1:1–14:20, which describes the collapse of the united monarchy. This major unit may be divided into four sections: first, Solomon securing the throne (1:1–2:46a); second, Solomon's wisdom displayed (2:46b–4:34[5:14]); third, Solomon's building campaigns and other endeavors, ending with his legacy (5:1[5:15]–10:29); the fourth section recounts the dissolution of the united monarchy (11:1–14:20).

Across these sections, there are numerous preaching units: 1:1–2:11; 2:12–46a; 2:46b–3:15; 3:16–28; 4:1–34[5:14]; 5:1–18[5:15–32]; 6:1–7:51; 8:1–66; 9:1–9; 9:10–28; 10:1–29; 11:1–43; 12:1–24; 12:25–14:20. Moreover, the types of texts across these sections are diverse, thereby creating eclectic homiletical opportunities.

SOLOMON SECURING THE THRONE
(1 KINGS 1:1–2:46A)

The first section of the first major literary unit in Kings is 1 Kings 1:1–2:46a, which describes Solomon securing the throne. This first section may be divided into two preaching units: first, the succession of Solomon as the sanctioned Davidic king in the wake of David's deterioration (1:1–2:11); second, how through a series of actions Solomon establishes the throne (2:12–46a). Together, the passages in this section the kingdom and power to rule are handed over from David to Solomon, although not without opposition or challenges to the throne.

1 Kings 1:1–2:11

EXEGETICAL IDEA

David's physiological deterioration engendered a series of events that saw David sanction Solomon as his successor and present his son with a critical decision about what would define his reign.

THEOLOGICAL FOCUS

The events of life often produce critical junctures, which force us to make choices that determine the ideologies that will define us going forward.

PREACHING IDEA

Despite uncertainties, following God's plan is the best path when at a crossroads in life.

PREACHING POINTERS

The book of 1 Kings begins by describing a time of transition within Israel. Like a sunrise turning into a sunset, David's reign is coming to a close. He is a shell of his former self, his family has splintered, and his kingdom is at risk. Similarly, for the original audience of 1–2 Kings, the people of Israel were facing significant transitions. As they sought to rebuild their lives, questions of leadership, morality, and national identity hung over them. The accounts found in Kings offered them historical examples of how to navigate this uncharted territory. Just as the question for Solomon was how to best navigate these issues and on what foundation he would build his own legacy, the people of the sixth and fifth centuries were compelled to consider what founding principles were going to guide them as they transitioned back into their homeland.

Our lives are also marked by critical periods where we face crucial decisions about how we will move forward. What should we do when we graduate high school? What is the best career path we ought to take? Additionally, how we date and who we marry are decisions that significantly affect the course of our lives. When layoffs unexpectedly hit us or when retirement looms over us, how will we respond? When we are at these crossroads, who will we listen to? What will be our guide? The best path to take is the one where we seek and follow God's plan and not our own.

SUCCESSION OF SOLOMON (1:1–2:11)

LITERARY STRUCTURE AND THEMES (1:1–2:11)

King Solomon is the central character in 1 Kings 1–11, and chapters 1 and 2 detail how he came to the throne and solidified his administration. In chapter 1, the scene is typical of times of transition for ancient Near Eastern monarchies. As one reign closed, questions of succession became critical.[1] Here, one reads about ambition, political posturing, and subterfuge, which incidentally establishes a sense of irony for the opening chapters of Kings. The section can be subdivided threefold: David's impotence, a competition for the throne, and David's last testament.

- *David's Impotence (1:1–4)*
- *A Competition for the Throne (1:5–53)*
- *David's Last Testament (2:1–11)*

EXPOSITION (1:1–2:11)

David's physiological deterioration (1:1–4) triggered a series of events that sought to clarify who the next king would be. However, it was an extremely messy process, defined by political ambition, potential manipulation, and bloodshed (1:5–53). Eventually, David identifies Solomon as the next king and personally addresses him (2:1–9) prior to his death (2:10–11). Solomon is presented with potential scenarios that will define his tenure moving forward.

David's Impotence (1:1–4)

1:1–4. David's physiological deterioration

Old Testament Scene (Solomon and King David) by Francúzsky Maliar. Public domain.

caused a series of actions and questions about his ability to perform his duties as a king.

Translation Analysis: וְלֹא יִחַם לוֹ
The ESV, NASB, NIV, NKJV, NLT, and NRSV all render this clause as "he could not get warm," which is the result of reading an impersonal verbal construction (*DCH*, 3:256). However, it is also possible to understand לוֹ as a reflexive phrase, thereby rendering "he could not warm himself."

The most perplexing element in the succession account is David's relationship with Abishag. David was "old and advanced in years" and had trouble keeping warm. The phrase "old and advanced in years" is relatively straightforward, but there has been significant debate over the meaning of the phrase "he could not

---

1   Of course, this historical principle was not absolute. For example, the Vassal Treaties of Esarhaddon intended to secure the transition from Esarhaddon to his son Ashurbanipal (Barré 1992, 6:656).

get warm" (Hess 2009, 427–38; Meek 2014, 1–14). The Hebrew can communicate that David "could not warm himself." When this is considered alongside other sexual connotations of verses 1–4, namely, verse 4 and its statement that David did not have sexual relations with the beautiful virgin (וְהַמֶּלֶךְ לֹא יְדָעָהּ), as well as the ancient Near Eastern conceptions about virility, this phrase is likely a euphemism. David was impotent.

But why is this physiological development so significant? Why did David's impotence warrant a national search for a beautiful young virgin (נַעֲרָה בְתוּלָה)? As Sweeney (2007, 53) has shown, kings in the ancient Near East relied on their virility for diplomatic reasons. Marriages were used to seal alliances and gain political favor. Thus, David's impotence signified his inability to satisfy this diplomatic responsibility, which was also a hallmark of his rise to power (Levenson and Halpern 1990, 507–18). In addition, there existed a perception in ancient Near Eastern thought that a virgin could potentially rejuvenate an impotent man, which is supported by the Sumerian folktale "The Old Man and the Young Woman" (Alster 1975, 90–99; Meek 2014, 1–14). Possibly sharing this perception, the royal attendants may have sought a young woman to either rejuvenate David's virility or confirm that he was impotent. When the latter scenario proved to be true, the royal attendants could only wonder about the viability of David's reign (Schreiner 2018).

A Competition for the Throne (1:5–53)

Through the aid of others, Solomon becomes David's sanctioned successor in front of his older brother Adonijah.

1:5–10. Verse 5 begins with a disjunctive clause in the Hebrew (וַאֲדֹנִיָּה), "Now Adonijah son of Haggith exalted himself," and thus ushers in a new scene and new characters amid a larger narrative (*IBHS*, §39.2.3c). Naturally, "What is the logical relationship between verses 1–4

King David Presenting the Sceptre to Solomon
by Cornelis de Vos. Public domain.

and verse 5 and following?" One explanation is implicit causation. David's impotence is the impetus for Adonijah's movement toward the throne. Perhaps more important than the logic of Adonijah's actions is how the narrative produces ironic questions about the effectiveness of the dynastic covenant. David's impotence initiates a chain of events that plunged Israel into a period of sociopolitical uncertainty—something that the idea of a dynastic covenant sought to prevent.

There is, however, very little ambiguity in the actions of Adonijah. According to verse 5, he "exalted himself" and boldly proclaimed, "I will be king." Yet he does not make his move without consultation (v. 7), although the writer suggests a certain level of impropriety. First, his debonair looks and chariot parade recalls images of Absalom and echoes his older brother's coup respectively (2 Sam. 15). Second, that there were some who were not invited to his coronation ceremony suggests that his action was at least suspicious. Moreover, it is telling that a priest, a prophet, and elements of David's personal guard (i.e., "David's own warriors") avoided association (לֹא הָיוּ עִם־אֲדֹנִיָּהוּ).

1:11–27. Ultimately, the text does not explicitly say why Solomon, Nathan, or Benaniah were not invited. Based on verse 12, however, Adonijah may have felt threatened. Nevertheless, Nathan masterfully orchestrates a delicate plan of political posturing that would come to have a tremendous impact on the nation's future. First, Nathan exploits fears of succession that inflict any royal house during times of transition. He understands that efforts to secure a throne could easily include the death of any perceived rival. So, the prophet offers Bathsheba life-saving advice (v. 12). In the process, Nathan also seeks to force David's hand by constructing a coordinated plan of persuasion that ultimately conveys Solomon as the ethical choice. According to the plan, Bathsheba ushers in the first front, appealing to a specific oath otherwise not explicitly documented (vv. 15–21).[2] Nathan piggybacks her appeal, entering "while she was still speaking" (v. 22). Nathan in turn echoes Bathsheba's complaint by recounting Adonijah's celebratory sacrifices (v. 9) and his selective support (vv. 19, 26).

Interestingly, Nathan's appeal is subtly different from Bathsheba's. While Bathsheba invokes a specific oath ostensibly offered to Solomon (v. 17), Nathan wonders aloud how any bequest to Adonijah could have been offered (vv. 24–27). Thus, Nathan effectively shifts the onus back onto the king, suggesting that an approval of Adonijah as king is an injustice.

1:28–48. David's response is decisive. First summoning Bathsheba, David swears an oath that Solomon shall be his rightful successor (vv. 29–30). David then summons Zadok the priest, Nathan the prophet, and Benaiah the soldier, instructing them to coordinate and officiate an official coronation ceremony (vv. 32–37). Solomon is to ride David's mule to the Gihon Spring, where Nathan and Zadok would anoint him. All of this, including the trumpet-laced public proclamation, functions to emphatically counter Adonijah's move. In fact, this is so emphatic that David accepts Solomon's immediate role as king, saying that "he will rule in my place" (v. 35). Therefore, what is implied early in the text is now verified. Adonijah's move toward the throne was illegitimate, which forces the king to conjure up his failing strength to ensure that his succession proceeds as desired.

Translation Analysis: In verse 35, the clauses וְאֹתוֹ צִוִּיתִי לִהְיוֹת נָגִיד עַל־יִשְׂרָאֵל וְעַל־יְהוּדָה and וְהוּא יִמְלֹךְ תַּחְתָּי are disjunctive clauses that can be understood as the cause of the actions discussed (cf. *IBHS*, §39.2.3b). They are to anoint Solomon *because* he shall be king and a *nagid* over Israel and Judah. The term *nagid* (נָגִיד) connects Solomon with David and Saul, but it is used in this context generically, merely as "ruler."

According to verse 38, Zadok, Nathan, and Benaiah faithfully carry out David's orders. In the process, they are joined by the Cherethites and the Pelethites, both of whom, according to 2 Samuel 8:18 and 20:23, were (foreign) military units under the command of Benaiah (Wiseman, 2008, 79). Adonijah's fifty-plus men processional is dwarfed by Solomon's military processional. Again, Adonijah's move is emphatically countered. Moreover, Solomon's celebration was so loud that the writer says that "the earth quaked." It is therefore no surprise that when the sound of the celebration reached the ears of Adonijah and his audience, fear descended upon the crowd. With the arrival of Jonathan's news, Abiathar the priest's son, their fears were confirmed. Adonijah and his party are left with one option—dispersion.

---

2   According to 1 Kings 1:30, David appears to acknowledge that an oath was made on behalf of Solomon's succession. However, it is unclear if David has been duped, which is entirely possible if David's physiological deterioration included a cognitive deterioration.

1:49–53. Per verse 49, the banquet broke and everyone "went their own ways." However, Adonijah found it necessary to grasp the horns of the altar, which signaled a fearful capitulation to the events that countered his own. Adonijah knew that his efforts toward securing the throne had failed, but he was still apparently uncertain if his life would be spared by his rival. Therefore, understanding the sanctity of the altar, Adonijah sought refuge there until he would be assured safety (v. 51). Solomon obliges (v. 52), saying that if Adonijah accepts his new role and lives within the parameters established, he would be safe. If he should transgress those boundaries, then the consequences would be dire. This conditionality will prove crucial (see below).

Behind 1 Kings 1–2

In a recent article, Joyce Willis, Andrew Pleffer, and Stephen Llewelyn analyzed conversation scenes within 1 Kings 1–2 to understand their subtleties (Willis, Pleffer, and Llewelyn, 2011). Convinced that conversations within a narrative offer a unique set of considerations for characterization and other literary concerns, they focus on the ambiguities and gaps in the narrative as well as the differences between important statements. For the authors, the subtleties are striking enough to reconstruct an anti-Davidide tradition that accused Solomon of a coup. Therefore, 1 Kings 1–2 was fashioned by the historian, at least on one level, for apologetic purposes.

Did Solomon wrestle the throne away from a more rightful heir? Were Nathan, Bathsheba, and others deceptively involved? Such questions carry far-reaching implications that ultimately inform how one understands the nature of Scripture. Such questions force the reader to consider how sociopolitical realities influenced the composition of the Old Testament. For some, such questions are unwelcome, for a variety of reasons. Nevertheless, one must realize that several factors influenced the composition of the Old Testament. The writers were real people in real space and time, and their experiences influenced their theology. Ultimately, studies that look "behind" the text, often labeled historical critical studies, have their place. The critical issue is properly appropriating those studies.

It is likely that there were anti-Davidide factions within Israelite society that sought to accuse and slander Solomon, and it is not problematic to conclude that Scripture itself contains the evidence of their contrary traditions. However, one cannot stop there, for the final form is what matters. Nevertheless, such behind-the-text studies shed light on the historian's ability to appropriate diverse tradition for a singular purpose.

Verses 52–53 are also significant because these are the first words attributed to Solomon. Until this point in the narrative, Solomon is a completely passive character. He neither speaks nor acts. Everything is done for him by other people. He merely exists. Moreover, prior to 1 Kings 2:13, these verses are the only place where Solomon speaks. The result is something subtle and calculated. The historian, on one level, is creating an apologetic for the new king. As if to counter any accusation against Solomon's ascent to the throne that may have been circulating in the minds of his audience, the historian is suggesting that Solomon rose to power by the efforts of others who demanded that David hold true to his word in the twilight of his life.

David's Last Testament (2:1–11)

David's last testament forces Solomon to consider the ideology that will define his reign.

2:1–9. Within verses 1–9, there are two distinctive components. First, David exhorts Solomon to be fiercely faithful to the covenant. In typical Deuteronomistic fashion, in ways that echo the central message of

Deuteronomy, he is to walk in the ways of the Lord and keep his statutes, commandments, ordinances, and testimonies—just as it is written in the "law of Moses" (v. 3). *If he can do this*, David foresees success that will also solidify the dynastic promise offered to him. In other words, David is encouraging his son to forsake any selfish perspective for one that instead looks beyond himself. He wants his son to understand how his faithfulness can have lasting implications.

On the other hand, David urges his son to revisit the past, namely, the actions of Joab, Barzillai, and Shimei. In the case of Barzallai and Shimei, David's exhortations are clear. The call to show favor to the sons of Barzallai is rooted in their father's willingness to support David during Absalom's revolt. Conversely, Shimei publicly opposed David during the same event, and for this he needed to be dealt with (2 Sam. 16:5–13). In the case of Joab, the circumstances around his actions are more ambiguous. Technically speaking, Joab's killing of Abner and Amasa were justifiable (2 Sam. 2–3). Yet David is ostensibly convinced that he had incurred a bloodguilt. So, David is declaring that the responsibility falls upon Solomon, and he is to use his wisdom in order to ensure that Joab will not die in peace. One cannot help but wonder if verse 6a is a leading statement, particularly since the succeeding clause issues a call that Joab's gray hair should not go down to Sheol in peace.

In the end, David's last testament adds to the irony and intrigue of the opening chapters. David preaches fidelity to the covenant at the same time he encourages questionable actions aimed at silencing some of his enemies—feats that he was either incapable of and/or unwilling to do. Surely then Sweeney is at least on track when he describes a complex character that exhibits a "warped understanding of Torah observance." Yet it's not clear whether the dynasty was "corrupt at its very foundation" (Sweeney 2007, 60–61). Nevertheless, for Solomon everything has been leading to this choice: What will define his rule?

2:10–11. This segment closes with David's death notice. In terms that will become very familiar, there is a notation of where David was buried and how long he reigned.

There has been debate on whether verse 12 or part of verse 12 constitutes the end of this segment. For example, Sweeney places verse 12 with the next segment, while Wiseman understands verse 12 to be the conclusion of David's death notice (Sweeney 2007, 62; Wiseman 2008, 84–85). From a grammatical point of view, verse 12 cannot be separated, as some commentators do.[3] As we shall see, verse 46a echoes verse 12 and therefore creates a bracket for the next section of text.

THEOLOGICAL FOCUS

The exegetical idea (David's physiological deterioration engendered a series of events that saw David sanction Solomon as his successor and present his son with a critical decision about what would define his reign) leads to this theological focus: The events of life often produce critical junctures, which force us to make choices that determine the ideologies that will define us going forward.

The various choices made and the ideologies those choices thus determined apply both for the person involved and those associated with that person. For Solomon, David's physiological deterioration kick-started a series of events that eventually brought him to a critical juncture. At this moment, Solomon was faced with a choice. What would define his rule? Covenantal fidelity or kinship

---

3   The antecedent on "his kingdom" is Solomon, which suggests that verse 12a not be separated from verse 12b. Walsh, however, separates verse 12a from verse 12b (Walsh 1996, 151).

obligations? What's more, amid this juxtaposition is a fatherly call to be wise (v. 6). Thus, the text creates a layered question about wisdom and its role in one's choices. What is "wisdom?" What defines "wisdom?" Is it something defined by popular sentiment? Or, is it defined by something more specific, say God's revealed truth? Applied to Solomon, will Solomon's wisdom be defined by the "law of Moses" or by the personal feelings of his father and kinship obligations?

What is described here is not anomalous. Plenty of other passages in Scripture describe critical junctures where so much falls upon whether the parties involved will live in accord with the Lord's ideals. Nevertheless, two examples rise above the rest. The exhortation to Solomon to "be strong" echoes Joshua 1, where the Lord exhorts Joshua to "be strong and courageous." Moreover, just as Solomon's choice will affect the nation, so too will Joshua's willingness to fiercely adhere to the Lord's expectations directly impact the nation. Success is a very real possibility, but it is contingent upon an ability to faithfully live in accord with the covenant.

Second, Ezra is likewise encouraged to "be strong" and do what is necessary (Ezra 10:1–4). However, in contrast to Joshua and Solomon where the future is conditionally bright, Ezra's future appears dark. Ezra is faced with a tough situation, and he realizes what must be done. The community is committing the same covenantal infractions as they did in the past. Consequently, they are in dire straits, on the verge of repeating what sent them into exile. Strict adherence to Torah is the only remedy, but to do that would require a stark course of action.

Consequently, the canon of Scripture speaks a unified message. Critical junctures come in all shapes and sizes, and the choices that characterize them force one to decide whether or not they will yield to the Lord's ideals.

PREACHING AND TEACHING STRATEGIES

Exegetical and Theological Synthesis

Solomon is essentially a passive actor in this part of the story. Actions of others and developments beyond his control force him to face a critical juncture in his life—his elevation to kingship. His own father provides direct advice about how to lead as the ruler of God's people. That advice is somewhat mixed in its message, however. On the one hand, David exhorts Solomon to remain faithful to the Lord. On the other, David encourages him to deal with personal offenses that were left unaddressed. This is potentially wise political advice, but the text leaves the reader with some tension between these orders and the call to be loyal to God's covenant.

It is clear that Solomon's greatest concern as he begins his reign is how he will approach his newly acquired power and position. The natural approach is to use one's power and position for selfish ends. God's desire is that we use our privilege to invest in what he values. He honors those who follow his ways rather than the path of self-centeredness. Most of us will not achieve the level of power that Solomon did. Yet God is still interested in how we use the resources, privileges, and power he does give us. Whether it's our financial status, our job title, our educational opportunities or our natural talents, God expects us to use what he's given us for his honor. If we let his Word and his Spirit guide us, we will find genuine success in whatever circumstances bring us to a crossroad in life.

Preaching Idea

Despite uncertainties, following God's plan is the best path when at a crossroads in life.

Contemporary Connections

What does it mean?

What does it mean that despite uncertainties, following God's plan is the best path when at a crossroads in life? This passage offers a clear example of the importance of the choices and decisions we make. Scripture repeatedly affirms God's control over our world, but it also affirms the freedom we have to make our own choices. It also highlights the impact our decisions have on ourselves and others around us. Therefore, we must remember the Lord's values, principles, and commands when find ourselves in critical situations whether similar to or different from what Solomon faced in 1 Kings 1:1–2:11.

When we are weighing our college options, for instance, we should assess the financial, academic, and social components of the schools. But we also need to consider how each school might help us grow in our faith. Christian and secular universities offer different benefits and challenges that deserve to be evaluated with respect to how they will affect our individual spiritual walks. Similarly, career decisions should be judged for how well they align with our spiritual priorities, not just for the salary package. A higher-paying job may allow us to give more, but will it also eliminate our ability to serve locally with our church or participate in cross-cultural missions? These decisions will not always be easy. That is why it is important to rely on God's wisdom through Scripture, through godly counsel, and through the Spirit's inner prompting. In doing so, we will be faithful to God's plan, and we can approach these defining crossroads with confidence.

Is it true?

Is it true that despite uncertainties, following God's plan is the best path when at a crossroads in life? Both through examples and plain teaching, Scripture strongly affirms that following God's plan is the best path to take when at a crossroad in life. The entire book of Proverbs is devoted to the idea that God blesses those who abide by his commands. Historical figures like Joseph underscore this truth as well. Even when doing the right thing got him into trouble, he remained faithful, and he ultimately found himself in an important position with the ability to help save many lives, including those of his own estranged family. Elijah, Daniel, and Ruth offer additional godly examples as well.

A more recent example of the truth of this principle is the life of Fred Rogers, more popularly known as TV's "Mister Rogers." While studying to be a Presbyterian minister, Rogers felt called to get involved in the television industry. He completed his theological education, even balancing his studies while developing his children's shows. Upon his ordination, he was encouraged to continue his work in media and not pursue a formal pastoral position.[4] Here was a man who came to a crossroads in life, and for him, being true to God's plan for his life meant television, not a pulpit. His positive influence on generations of people was beyond what he could have imagined. That's the kind of impact we can have when we remain true what God wants of us.

Now what?

If it's true that despite uncertainties, following God's plan is the best path, how can we follow God's plan when at the crossroads in life? If we are going to follow God's plan at life's crossroads, we first need to *understand what God's plan is.* Just as David called on Solomon to be faithful to God's law, our lives ought to be founded on God's Word. We live in a world where Bibles and Bible study materials are prevalent and easily accessed. There is no excuse for ignorance as to what God's wisdom is or what God's Word says. Children can be led by their parents to read and even memorize short passages of Scripture, "hiding God's

---

4   "Fred Rogers," Wikipedia, https://en.wikipedia.org/wiki/Fred_Rogers (accessed February 23, 2022); and "Won't You Be My Neighbor?" Independent Lens, https://www.pbs.org/independentlens/documentaries/wont-you-be-my-neighbor (accessed February 23, 2022).

Word in their heart." Teenagers should be encouraged to explore God's Word for themselves, aided by devotionals that relevantly get them asking questions and digging into the meaning of the passages. Adults need to be challenged in this as well. Reading plans that guide the reader through the entire Bible are prevalent and can be a helpful supplement to popular-but-basic devotionals.

From there, it is crucial to *remember that God's best is really worth sacrificing for*. Missionaries give up many creature comforts to further God's kingdom. Regular everyday Christians give up time, money, and other worldly priorities in order to invest themselves in eternal things. It is a sacrificial investment to follow God's plan, and we may not always see the fruit right away. However, God is faithful and over time we will be able to look back and recognize that his path is the one that will bring us the greatest payoff, the greatest reward, and the greatest fulfillment. Desmond Doss, whose story was immortalized in the movie *Hacksaw Ridge* (directed by Mel Gibson, 2016) serves as a real-life example of this. Despite the hostility he endured for being a pacifist while serving in the army during World War II, he remained committed to his spiritual convictions. In the end, he was instrumental in saving about seventy-five lives at Hacksaw Ridge and became the first and only conscientious objector to receive the Medal of Honor during World War II. Though he shunned the title of conscientious objector and was known to describe himself as a "conscientious cooperator" because he wanted to serve his country and help his fellow man, his refusal to bear arms against another invited mocking and derision from his fellow soldiers. But in the end, God's plan for him had a greater payoff. It was worth sacrificing for.[5]

Creativity in Presentation

The GPS or Global Positioning System is one of the most common navigational systems in the world today. From our phones to our computers to our cars, we can find the best way to get to any destination at the push of a button. It has taken over our lives in a very real way. A GPS offers a natural way to illustrate following God's will. Of course it would depend on one's particular context, but a range of possibilities could be used—from referencing a recent personal trip to pulling up a destination live onscreen. By utilizing current brands like Google Maps, one could cite how we are given alternative routes. This provides a natural connection to the spiritual lessons of this passage as we compare it to the alternative choices to God's wisdom that exist.

Beyond the symbolic illustrations, though, presenting personal testimonies would be an excellent option. Whether on recorded video or live from the stage, personal stories are powerful. For instance, find a businessman or businesswoman who made a difficult career choice for the right reasons. Or maybe their choice was fueled by the wrong reasons. Either way, to hear the experience of a fellow member and their crossroads moment will have a lasting effect. For older members, hearing from a Christian investment agent could be utilized. It would be very beneficial for many to hear tips from a Christian professional on how to invest and what to consider when stewarding one's retirement.

The key idea to communicate is that despite life's uncertainties, following God's plan is the best path when at a crossroads.

The passage for this preaching unit can be outlined as follows:

- We can trust God with what we can't control (1:1–53).

---

5   "Private First Class Desmond Thomas Doss, US Army: Medal of Honor Series," The National WWII Museum | New Orleans, accessed June 30, 2018, https://www.nationalww2museum.org/war/articles/private-first-class-desmond-thomas-doss-medal-of-honor.

- ○ Trust him with his timing (1:1–4).
- ○ Trust him to work on our behalf (1:5–27).
- ○ Trust him to enable the fulfillment of his promises (1:28–53).
- We can entrust to God what's under our control (2:1–11):
  - ○ By obeying his will with unwavering commitment (2:1–4)
  - ○ By seeking his will in uncertain decisions (2:5–11)

DISCUSSION QUESTIONS

1. What is the significance of the fact that David "could not warm himself"?

2. While Solomon is the central figure of these chapters, what are the crossroads that David and Bathsheba each face in this passage? How do they proceed? What could we learn from them?

3. How are Bathsheba's and Nathan's approaches with David similar, and how are they different?

4. What is David's primary concern for Solomon (vv. 1–3)?

5. How might you defend David's instructions in 1 Kings 2:5–9 as fitting with God's law? How might you criticize them as not fitting with God's law?

6. How do David's instructions to settle these old scores fit with Christ's commands in passages like Matthew 5:38–48?

1 Kings 2:12–46a

EXEGETICAL IDEA

The actions of Solomon decisively and finally secured his hold on the throne, although ambiguity surrounding motives, requests, and actions persist throughout the account.

THEOLOGICAL FOCUS

The ambiguity surrounding Solomon's decisions is indicative of life; tackling ambiguity can ultimately produce a level of understanding about God's work in the world not otherwise possible.

PREACHING IDEA

We shouldn't give up—derailing God's plan is difficult to do.

PREACHING POINTERS

First Kings 2:12–46 is filled with questions that are both unanswered and unanswerable. Readers are left to speculate on what might be going on with almost every part of this passage. The original audience of Kings could relate. Uncertainty hung over nearly every aspect of their lives, as they tried to rebuild their cities and society. As documented in the books of Haggai and Zechariah, even in Ezra and Nehemiah, actions and decisions of leadership were hotly debated as the people returned to the land.

As uneasy as we may be with tension, these verses reflect common aspects of our own world. So many circumstances in life are not black and white, and we often find ourselves dealing with the gray area in between. We are compelled to try to interpret situations and actions of others when more than one motive may exist. Should we fear making the wrong conclusions? Will exercising our "free will" hinder what God wants? Thankfully, as this story teaches, God is still at work in the gray areas and we don't have to fear the unknown or worry about ambiguous decisions spoiling his plans.

ESTABLISHING THE THRONE (2:12–46a)

LITERARY STRUCTURE AND THEMES (2:12–46a)

It's unclear how much time has elapsed between Solomon's deal with Adonijah (1:51–53), David's final words (2:1–9), and the events of 2:12–46. The NRSV's translation of verse 13 emphasizes the sequence of events when it reads, "Then Adonijah," which can be understood with a sense of temporal proximity. However, the NIV and NASB better testify to the ambiguity inherent to the Hebrew with the translation, "Now Adonijah." What is unambiguous is Solomon's decisive response to Adonijah's request. The passive character in chapter 1 gives way to an assertive one; Solomon is remarkably different in 2:12–46a. This section consists of two scenes: verses 12–18 and verses 18–46a. In the latter, Solomon's authority is fully displayed and fully experienced by Adonijah, Abiathar, Joab, and Shimei.

- *Adonijah's Request (2:12–18)*
- *Solomon's Decisive Responses (2:19–46a)*

EXPOSITION (2:12–46a)

Solomon transitions from a passive character to an active one when he violently asserts his dominance in the wake of Adonijah's request for Abishag. By the end of the chapter, Solomon's reign is introduced by a trail of violence and death. However, there is a striking amount of ambiguity in the passage, suggesting that Solomon is a very complex character.

Translation Analysis: Verse 13 begins with a wayyiqtol (or, waw-consecutive) form, וַיָּבֹא. Possibilities for articulating the logical relationship between this verb and the section that immediately preceded it include sequential, consequential, narratival, exegetical, and dependent. See Arnold and Choi 2018, §3.5.1.

Adonijah's Request (2:12–18)

Despite the ambiguity around Adonijah's request and Bathsheba's motives, Bathsheba approaches Solomon on behalf of Adonijah.

Translation Analysis: The clause in 2:15, כִּי מֵיהוָה הָיְתָה לּוֹ, should be understood causatively, demonstrating that the Lord was understood to be the author of the events of chapter 1. IBHS, §38.4a.

2:12–15. Adonijah's request in verse 15 reveals Adonijah's capitulation that Solomon's rule was "from the LORD." Thus, when Adonijah reappears on the scene the reader is tempted for just a moment to think that Solomon's older brother has accepted his subordinate status. However, the circumstances are such that the reader cannot help but wonder if this was another attempt by Adonijah to secure the throne. Even Bathsheba, when she asks, "Do you come peacefully?," appears to wonder about his motives. There is a palpable sense of ambiguity here, and throughout this section.

2:16–18. The conversation between Adonijah and Bathsheba is ostensibly private, and it is intriguing that Adonijah presses the queen to commit to his request without first hearing it (v. 16–17). Such a method may suggest a less than admirable motive, but it may also suggest that Adonijah wants to ensure that his request will not be dismissed out of hand. As for the request, it is critical to note that control of the harem signaled control of the kingdom (2 Samuel 3:6–7; 12:8; 16:21–22). Yet David's lack of sexual contact with Abishag raises questions about her place and function within the court. Thus, it is unclear if Adonijah's request for her carry the same connotations as if she were a normal concubine. It is also unclear if Adonijah understood his request as a subtle movement to the throne or something more innocuous. Again, ambiguity.

But why did Bathsheba willingly go to Solomon with the request? Merely making the request could have given the impression that she was an accomplice or supporter of Adonijah. Or, did she know what she was doing? Given that she already demonstrated a certain level of political acumen by taking part in Nathan's scheme (1 Kings 1), it's likely Bathsheba knew exactly what she was doing. As long as Adonijah breathed, she likely understood him as a threat. By going to her son and relaying Adonijah's request to Solomon, she started a process that would secure Adonijah's fate as well as the fate of others.

Solomon's Decisive Responses (2:19–46a)
Solomon responds to Adonijah's request definitively, although questions about those actions remain.

2:19–25. True to her word, Bathsheba obtains an audience with the king "on behalf of Adonijah" (v. 19). Upon her arrival, the queen mother is shown great respect. Solomon rises to meet her (וַיָּקָם הַמֶּלֶךְ לִקְרָאתָהּ) and bows before her (וַיִּשְׁתַּחוּ לָהּ). She is then given a throne at the right of her son, a clear sign of honor. These actions are provocative and certainly indicative of Bathsheba's influence. Moreover, her description of her request as "one small request" (שְׁאֵלָה אַחַת קְטַנָּה) and preemptive plea not to be refused only heighten the intrigue. When Solomon obliges her request of non-refusal, Bathsheba bluntly relays Adonijah's desires in the form of a personal request.

Solomon blows his top. He first publicly chastises his mother. "And why do you ask Abishag the Shunammite for Adonijah? Ask for him the kingdom as well! For he is my elder brother, ask not only for him but also for the priest Abiathar and for Joab son of Zeruiah" (2:22 NRSV). But apparently chastisement was not enough. The king follows his invective with an oath that secures the death of his older brother under the rubric of failing to keep the terms of his oath (vv. 23–24). In fact, Solomon's actions quickly move into their second phase—the removal of four individuals from the political scene.

Sweeney (2007, 68–70) notes numerous tensions informing the atmosphere of this section. They include the peculiar posturing of Solomon before his mother, the irony of her "small request," the repeated declaration that Solomon will not refuse his mother, the recognition that Adonijah is older, and the king's dealing with Adonijah's supporters, namely Joab and Abiathar. However, perhaps the greatest element contributing to the tense atmosphere of this section is the methodical movement within the text. Through a string of wayyiqtol forms, the narrative creates the impression that Bathsheba's request fostered a singular obsession within Solomon that would not be satisfied until all potential problems were removed. Moreover, the events of 2:25–46 apparently answer the question posed by David's last testament (2:1–9). Solomon's administration will not be defined by a fierce allegiance to the law of Moses. Rather, things will be complicated. Solomon indeed displays an inclination to give the benefit of the doubt, but if certain elements are introduced, he also displays the capacity and willingness to act swiftly and brutally.

Translation Analysis: Solomon is the subject of a string of wayyiqtol forms that create a fast-paced narrative: וַיִּשָּׁבַע (v. 23)…וַיִּשְׁלַח (v. 25)…וַיְגָרֶשׁ (v. 27)… וַיִּשְׁלַח (v. 29)…וַיֹּאמֶר (v. 31)…וַיִּתֶּן (v. 35)… וַיִּשְׁלַח (v. 36).

2:26–46a. During Solomon's bloody purge, it is noteworthy that he exercises some restraint. This only deepens the complexity of his character. He only banishes Abiathar to the village of Anatoth, approximately three miles from Jerusalem. The reason for his leniency? Abiathar "carried the ark of the Lord GOD" and "shared in all the hardships" of David (v. 26). Thus, exile takes the place of deserved execution.[1] Restraint is also exhibited, at least initially, in the case of Shimei. According to verses 36–38, Solomon and Shimei agree to a "fair sentence" (טוֹב הַדָּבָר) for his actions against his father. He is granted house arrest in the immediate vicinity of Jerusalem. However, three years later, while acting within his rights as a slaveholder to pursue two slaves who apparently went AWOL, Shimei violated that agreement—a reality that Solomon emphatically reiterates just before the pronouncement of his death (vv. 42–43).

Yet there is more ambiguity, which has been detailed by Sweeney (2007, 71). It is possible to understand Shimei's trek to Philistine territory as an attempt to usurp David's line on behalf of his lineage under the guise of social prerogative. If true, Solomon's actions are reasonable. However, it is equally possible to understand Shimei's actions more innocently, which is evidenced chiefly by the reality that Shimei does not stay in Philistine territory but rather comes back to Jerusalem.

In the end, it is impossible to determine precisely the motive behind Shimei's action. More importantly, the reader should embrace the ambiguity, for it has come to characterize this section of text. This literary phenomenon likely reflects a historical reality—the complexity of the person Solomon.

Translation Analysis: Much has been said about the function of 2:46. Does it conclude chapter 2 or introduce chapter 3? Sweeney (2007, 72–78) and Nitsche (2015, 36 and *passim*) read 2:46b with chapter 3, but DeVries (2003, 41) and Wiseman (2008, 87) read the clause with chapter 2. Ultimately, verse 46b is best understood as a clause that introduces 1 Kings 3:1, so rendered, "Now when the kingdom was established in the hand of Solomon, Solomon became a son-in-law to Pharaoh."

THEOLOGICAL FOCUS

The exegetical idea (The actions of Solomon decisively and finally secured his hold on the throne, although ambiguity surrounding motives, requests, and actions persist throughout the account) leads to this theological focus: The ambiguity surrounding Solomon's decisions is indicative of life; tackling ambiguity can ultimately produce a level of understanding about God's work in the world not otherwise possible.

"Ambiguity" is the word for this section. The section opens ambiguously, and ambiguity colors the requests of Adonijah and the actions of Shimei. Ambiguity also colors Solomon. If the king's interpretation of Adonijah's request and Shimei's actions was correct, then Solomon's decisive actions are commendable. Yet the reader cannot help but wonder if Solomon interpreted things correctly, particularly the actions of Shimei. Was Solomon acting presumptuously? Perhaps duplicitously? In the end, this suggests that one must fight the urge to simplistically interpret life as "black and white."

Ultimately, the passage is engaging precisely *because* of the ambiguity, which is by no means unique in Scripture.[2] Ambiguity describes so much of life, and so in this sense 1 Kings 2

---

1   This exile fulfilled the oracle of judgment against the priesthood of Eli for its corruption, immorality, and ineffectiveness (1 Sam. 2:27–36).

2   Consider the final words of Job (Schreiner 2016, 22–23), or the multivalent symbolism inherent to apocalyptic texts like Daniel and Revelation. Are Haggai's final words (Hg 2:20–23) a call for insurrection of a call to stand firm and wait upon the Lord's perfect timing (Schreiner 2015, 191–204)?

reflects a universal reality. Moreover, embracing and wrestling with life's ambiguity produces a level of theological insight that would have been difficult to achieve otherwise. And practically speaking, this suggests a very important lesson about the dynamics of divine providence vis-à-vis humanity. As God was able to navigate humanity's complex pursuits of power, security, and validation in 1 Kings 2 to accomplish his goals, God continues to perform similar feats to this day.

PREACHING AND TEACHING STRATEGIES

Exegetical and Theological Synthesis

From characters' questionable actions to their unstated motives, this passage invites many questions while providing few clear answers. By and large, 1 Kings 2 records the political machinations of an administration still getting settled. Adonijah makes a potentially dangerous inquiry and the king's mother goes along with it. Solomon then begins to exercise his kingly authority with both that particular inquiry and with other situations his father had advised him about earlier. All of this dramatic political uncertainty is not beyond the reach of God's hand, however. To the astute reader, the Lord can still be seen within this ambiguous text, establishing the son of David in his place on the throne of Israel.

This passage offers great comfort to us when we find ourselves dealing with uncertain motives of coworkers or unclear decisions where none of our choices sit well with us. No matter the unanswered questions about motives and tactics, God's plan moved forward in these early days of Solomon's reign. God's plan will still move forward with us, even when we make mistakes or others make flawed decisions that affect us. Our plans for our lives are of course easily altered. But if we are faithful in following God's big picture, macro-plan, the micro-plan he has for us will fall into place.

Preaching Idea

We shouldn't give up—derailing God's plan is difficult to do.

Contemporary Connections

What does it mean?

What does it mean that we shouldn't give up because derailing God's plan is difficult to do? Some stories have principles clearly embedded in them for our instruction. First Kings 2:13–46a is not one of those passages. Each and every character is described taking curious, if not questionable, action. As we struggle to interpret the specific parts of this story, it is helpful to assess the results of these actions. A wise reader can see that through all of this political maneuvering, God is fulfilling his covenant with David (2 Samuel 7:12–16). Solomon is sitting on the throne of Israel, having taken care of a number of potentially threatening situations.

Is it true?

Is it true that we shouldn't give up, since derailing God's plan is difficult to do? The developments recorded in this passage offer support to the consistent biblical theme that God's plan and his grand purposes cannot and will not be thwarted by humanity's scheming. He has a macro-plan where he is directing all of human history toward an ultimate end. That big-picture plan involves the individual micro-plans for our lives. Personally, we can certainly cooperate with God's plan or we can try to resist it, but we can't alter God's overarching control of our world and our reality (Ps. 115:3; Prov. 16:9; James 4:13–15).

It is a fact of life that at one time or another, everyone will resist God's plan, whether on a macro-level or a more personal micro-level. And when that happens, regret is a common emotion that follows. Even with past decisions that aren't explicitly sinful, shame and disappointment can haunt us whenever we dwell on those things. A teacher can look back on their long career and think, "I wish I would have done it better." An advertising executive finishes a project dogged by the nagging thought, "if only I'd had more time." An athlete falls short of their goals and is haunted by the mishit, missed shot, or missed play that could have made the difference. Thankfully this story encourages us that nothing we've done will derail God's plan. No matter our age or status, the very fact that we are still breathing should tell us the final chapter of our lives has not been written. God has grace for all people. Our churches all too often marginalize those who have made past mistakes. But God doesn't. Our ideal plan for ourselves may fall apart, but God still has a redemptive use for us. This is true for divorcees, those who've had abortions, and those who have battled addiction. God has a long history of furthering his plan through people with checkered pasts.

Now what?

If it's true that we shouldn't give up because derailing God's plan is difficult to do, what then should we do? For starters, it is important that we *accept God's forgiveness for our past sin*. We are clothed in the righteousness of Christ, and God no longer sees us as sinful or shameful (Isa. 61:10; Rom. 13:14; Gal. 3:27; 1 John 1:9). Accepting God's forgiveness is not only a one-time heart decision. It may require consistent discipline of our minds when memories come flooding back, triggering feelings of sorrow and shame all over again. Those are flaming arrows of our enemy who wants us to doubt our status and God's grace.

For those past regrets that continually bother us but can't be pegged as "sinful," we must *trust God and remember that he is in control*. We don't need to obsessively dwell on such matters. God's plan is not easily derailed; in fact, it's downright impossible. We can trust that he was and is still at work, even in our missteps and even in our uncertainty. This also applies to those situations that are beyond our control. So when we completely botch a witnessing opportunity, God can still work. When we lose our jobs because of someone else's incompetence, we can still trust God to provide. When a family member cuts themselves off from us, creating turmoil for us and those we love, we can cling to God as our anchor and our peace. Sometimes all our options are less than ideal. Sometimes people's motives are murky. Sometimes God just wants us to make our decisions and trust him. We cannot sabotage God's will. We can trust him, knowing his plan will move forward.

Creativity in Presentation

In 1993, former college basketball coach Jim Valvano gave a speech at an awards show for ESPN. As his own body was succumbing to cancer, he attended the event and announced the formation of a foundation in his name that would be 100 percent dedicated to funding research to cure the disease that was going to take his life. Even though he'd won hundreds of basketball games and an NCAA championship, he created an enduring legacy that night with his ten-minute speech. He implored those watching to stand with him to give of their resources to fund the fight against cancer. His words inspired millions and started a surge in cancer-fundraising that has saved countless lives and supported many research advancements. The crux of his speech that started it all was the simple message, "Don't give up, don't ever give up." That message offers a fitting application for this passage. For those who think their past has disqualified them or ruined their chance to be used by God: we shouldn't give up—derailing God's plan is difficult to do. For those affected by decisions beyond their control: we shouldn't give up—derailing God's plan is difficult to do.

Another way to illustrate this story might be to include personal anecdotes about pursuing romantic relationships. Almost everyone at some point has done something ill-advised in hopes of making a love connection. Maybe it was making sure you crossed paths with someone to see if you could catch their attention. Maybe it was volunteering for something in hopes of getting to know the individual better. Maybe it was concocting a grand gesture to let the other person know how you felt about them. Maybe it was just starting up an innocent conversation in hopes of developing a relationship. Stories of that kind that helped start a relationship will be funny, or embarrassing, but also support the idea that despite ulterior motives or cringeworthy actions, God can still work.

The key idea to communicate is that we shouldn't give up—derailing God's plan is difficult to do. From the perspective of Solomon, this passage as a preaching unit can teach us this:

- God's plan isn't derailed by shady motives (2:13–25).
- God's plan isn't derailed by dubious tactics (2:26–46).

DISCUSSION QUESTIONS

1. In view of 2 Samuel 16:20–22, why does Solomon get so upset at Adonijah's request?

2. Bathsheba has shown significant political savvy already in this book (1 Kings 1:11–21). How might her actions be interpreted similarly in 1 Kings 2:19–25?

3. Does Solomon violate Exodus 21:12–14 when he has Joab killed? Why or why not?

4. How could Shimei's actions be understood innocently? Why might Solomon see them as suspicious?

5. How could Solomon's actions be justified? Why could they be criticized?

6. How should we handle situations where motives, answers, and even the choices themselves are morally unclear?

SOLOMON'S WISDOM DISPLAYED
(2:46b–4:34[5:14])

The second section of the first major literary unit in Kings is 1 Kings 2:46b–4:34[5:14], in which Solomon's wisdom is displayed. This second section may be divided into three preaching units: first, the Lord's appearance to Solomon (2:46b–3:15); second, Solomon's wisdom in adjudication (3:16–28); third, Solomon's wisdom in the affairs of the kingdom (4:1–34[5:14]). Together, the passages in this section offer a comprehensive description of Solomon's divinely appropriated wisdom.

1 Kings 2:46b–3:15

EXEGETICAL IDEA

With Solomon's kingdom established, he encountered the Lord and ultimately requested wisdom to rule; Solomon's request for wisdom is granted, but not without expectations.

THEOLOGICAL FOCUS

Solomon's interchange with the Lord not only demonstrates how to pray, but also testifies to the character of God and how he relates to humanity.

PREACHING IDEA

God delights in meeting the needs of people who recognize their neediness.

PREACHING POINTERS

By 1 Kings 3, Solomon is now established as king over Israel. He has settled into power after the passing of his father and has tied up loose ends politically. He sits on his throne in security.

So now what? What will his legacy be, and what will he rely on? First and 2 Kings appealed to people who needed to consider the same questions. Jewish exiles returning from captivity were resettling in their homeland and needed to consider Solomon's example as they moved forward with their lives. Rather than security, wealth, or any other self-motivated request, the key to Israel's prosperity would be to humbly discern God's plan as they reestablished themselves as a people in their land.

When we are given new freedom, new power, or new privileges, how do we use them? Many people will default to using any advantage for their own personal gain. We burn through our work bonuses to buy the gadget or toy we've been coveting for a while. Students stop coming to class the moment the teacher mentions an "open-book final exam." Politicians work harder to stay in office than to actually represent the people who elected them. Many people make self-centered decisions in hopes of securing what they think will fulfill them, whether it is happiness, wealth, comfort, or recognition. We could endlessly chase after our own pursuits, or we could recognize what we really need and who can actually provide it for us. God loves to meet the needs of people who recognize their neediness and selflessly seek his plan rather than their own desires.

THE LORD'S APPEARANCE (2:46b–3:15)

LITERARY STRUCTURE AND THEMES (2:46b–3:15)

This segment can be divided twofold. First is the seemingly abrupt comment about Solomon's marriage to an Egyptian princess and the notation of national worship in the absence of the temple (2:46b–3:2). Second is Solomon's first supernatural encounter with Yahweh (3:3–15). Together, these verses transition 1 Kings 1:1–11:46 out of the succession accounts and closer to its point of focus—the construction of the temple.

- **Solomon's Marriage and Popular Sacrifice (2:46b–3:2)**
- **Solomon Encounters the Lord at Gibeah (3:3–15)**

EXPOSITION (2:46b–3:15)

The text transitions from a concern of who will follow David to an explanation of what that successor did and accomplished. However, the transition is introduced by a quick statement of Solomon's marriage to the Egyptian princess. Therefore, such an introduction subtly encourages the reader to consider Solomon's great wisdom and acts through the reality that he married a foreign princess.

Solomon's Marriage and Popular Sacrifice (2:46b–3:2)

The notation of Solomon's marriage to Pharaoh's daughter introduces the accounts that follow and subtly alludes to his eventual demise.

2:46b–3:2. As stated above, 2:46b should be understood as an introductory clause for 3:1–2. Yet the placement of verses 1–2 is difficult. The verses appear abrupt, perhaps intrusive, and some scholars are inclined to see the verses as a later insertion (e.g., Sweeney 2007, 78–79).[1] Moreover, the issues in these verses are not obviously related: marriage and worship. Nevertheless, the function of 2:46b–3:2 is introductory.

Recall that there was a concern among David's servants over the king's impotence, linking it to an inability to fulfill his diplomatic duty (1 Kings 1:1–4). Therefore, when Solomon "became a son-in-law with Pharaoh, king of Egypt" (וַיִּתְחַתֵּן שְׁלֹמֹה אֶת־פַּרְעֹה מֶלֶךְ מִצְרָיִם) (1 Kings 3:1), the historian signals that Solomon satisfied the issues that started the succession fiasco. Yet the reader may also detect another level of significance in these verses. This short statement foreshadows the problems that will eventually secure Solomon's downfall. His marriages, and the theological implications of those marriages, will begin moving front and center and eventually come to a head in chapter 11.

Consequently, one can appreciate the placement and association of verses 1–2. Alliances, building campaigns, the temple, and worship will highlight the administration of Solomon, and yet some of these foci will also have disastrous implications. The historian is using these

---

1   Scholars observe an intrusiveness about verse 2, and they cite the initial רַק as support, claiming that it lacks an antecedent. However, this restrictive particle does not require an explicit antecedent, and an emphatic function is possible. IBHS, §39.3.5c.

statements to set the reader up for what will follow.[2]

Solomon Encounters the Lord at Gibeah (3:3–15)

Appearing at Gibeah, a historic location, Solomon encounters the Lord and requests wisdom based on his understanding of the Lord's actions. He secures wisdom that will be beyond comparison, but it's not without certain expectations.

3:3–4. Verse 3 states, "Solomon loved the LORD by walking in the statutes of David his father" (וַיֶּאֱהַב שְׁלֹמֹה אֶת־יְהוָה לָלֶכֶת בְּחֻקּוֹת דָּוִד אָבִיו). This harkens back to David's final words to Solomon (2:1–9), and initially creates the impression that Solomon heeded his father's final exhortation. However, the restrictive clause at the end of the verse tempers any overwhelming positivity. Incidentally, it also produces a question: How can the historian say that Solomon *loved* the Lord while also admitting that he sacrificed and burnt incense at the high places? These contradictory descriptions are there to highlight the gravity of Solomon's supernatural encounter at Gibeon.

Gibeon, modern-day Tel El-Jib, is an important site within the biblical tradition (Arnold, 2:1010–12). It was associated with Joshua's conquest of the Promised Land (Josh. 9–10) and the earliest stages of the United Monarchy (2 Sam. 2:12–32; 20:8–13; 21:1–9). According to Kings, "the great high place" (הַבָּמָה הַגְּדוֹלָה) was located there, and Solomon preferred this place for his sacrifices (1 Kings 3:4b). While Kings is not clear on what attracted Solomon to this location, the Chronicler reveals that Gibeon was the resting place of the tabernacle (1 Chron. 16:39; 21:29; 2 Chron. 1:3, 13). The appearance of the Lord to Solomon in a dream, therefore, is another point in a history of divine presence associated with Gibeon.

3:5–9. The rhetoric of Solomon's words in verses 5–9 is enlightening. Solomon appeals first to the Lord's relationship with the late king David: "You have shown great and steadfast love to your servant my father David, because he walked before you in faithfulness, in righteousness, and in uprightness of heart toward you; and you have kept for him this great and steadfast love, and have given him a son to sit on his throne today" (1 Kings 3:6). "Steadfast love" (חֶסֶד), is a covenantal term, and here it simultaneously recalls the memory of the dynastic covenant (2 Sam. 7) and functions as the chief warrant for Solomon's appeal. Yet also important is the particle כַּאֲשֶׁר in verse 6. The NRSV translates this "because," but it's more precise to understand a temporal relationship (*IBHS*, §38.7a; "when"), which suggests a reciprocal connection between the Lord's lovingkindness and David's lifestyle. Thus, Solomon begins his supplication by describing a circular relationship, implying that the Lord's actions and humanity's actions mutually influence each other.

But for Solomon, verse 6 is merely a preparation for the main point of his supplication, signaled by the particle וְעַתָּה in verse 7 (*IBHS*, §39.3.4; "And now . . . ," NRSV). The passage quickly moves into verses 8–9, and taken together the verses show Solomon's understanding that relationships and piety can move beyond an immediate context and impact others. More importantly, Solomon seeks to exploit this reality. David's relationship with the Lord was fueled by his way of life, and Solomon's opportunity as the nation's king is one that he dares not squander. So, when offered essentially a blank check, knowing that the Lord committed himself to granting that request (v. 5), Solomon exhibited wisdom beyond his age. He requests "an understanding mind" for the expressed purposes of governing the people (לִשְׁפֹּט אֶת־עַמְּךָ) and discerning between good and evil (לְהָבִין בֵּין־טוֹב לְרָע). The Hebrew

---

2 Similarly, Wiseman describes the verses as the "forward" to his reign. Wiseman, *1 and 2 Kings*, 89.

can be literally translated as "a heart of listening" (לֵב שֹׁמֵעַ), and all the terms converge to illustrate clearly that Solomon's foremost concern was administrative insight.

3:10–15. Merely to say that Solomon's request registered positively with the Lord would be an understatement. Not only does verse 10 mention that "it pleased the Lord" (וַיִּיטַב הַדָּבָר בְּעֵינֵי אֲדֹנָי), but in verses 11–14 the Lord reveals an extravagant blessing that is rooted in Solomon's humble request. Because (יַעַן אֲשֶׁר) Solomon put others and the duties of his throne over any selfish ambition, the Lord graciously offers the king what he could have requested. Honor and riches will accompany unprecedented wisdom (v. 13). In fact, "no other king shall compare" (v. 13).

Yet it is worth mentioning that all this is restricted. Verse 14 concludes with a conditional clause. If Solomon performs in the same manner as his father—faithful to the covenant's expectations—then he will also be granted long life. In the context of 1 Kings 1–11, like verses 1–2 of chapter 3, this condition anticipates what will follow.

THEOLOGICAL FOCUS

The exegetical idea (With Solomon's kingdom established, he encountered the Lord and ultimately requested wisdom to rule; Solomon's request for wisdom is granted, but not without expectations) leads to this theological focus: Solomon's interchange with the Lord not only demonstrates how to pray, but also testifies to the character of God and how he relates to humanity.

The logic of Solomon's interchange with the Lord is important. It appeals to the effects of personal piety and how one's relationship with the Lord—just like any relationship—is not unilateral. Most importantly, this conviction informed Solomon's method of prayer as he (1) appealed to the Lord's past faithfulness and (2) prayed with humility and an awareness

of his context and community all for the advancement of the kingdom.

Such general logic is not unique in the Old Testament. Moses appeals to the exodus when trying to intercede on behalf of Israel (Num. 14:13–19). Later, Solomon will assume the Lord's faithfulness when he anticipates how the temple will be the focal point of repentant prayer (1 Kings 8). Consequently, Solomon's prayer in chapter 3 invites a critical assessment of our own method of prayer. Do we approach the Lord with an awareness and appreciation of what he has done in the past? Do we allow those past provisions to combat any anxiety and fear that we may have over a current situation? Do we pray for selfish reasons, even at the expense of the kingdom's pursuits?

This interchange also speaks to the character of God. It shows that the Lord is not latent. Rather, he desires the see relational possibilities reach their full potential. He wants excellence and extravagance to be realized. Yet full potential requires maximum effort from all parties involved. In this case, the question of maximum effort never rests with the Lord, but with the human side of the equation, hence the qualifications of verse 14.

PREACHING AND TEACHING STRATEGIES

Exegetical and Theological Synthesis

This episode in Solomon's life is a pivotal one. Solomon exhibits a keen sense of the reciprocal nature of God's relationship with his people. He understood from his father's life that God's covenantal love and blessing brought with it expectations of faithfulness. Thus, Solomon asked for God's wisdom to fulfill his duties in a way that would please the Lord. God was delighted with this and decided to abundantly bless this new king, recognizing that Solomon was looking beyond himself as he began his reign. God continues to operate in the same way with his people today. While he has blessed us beyond measure in Jesus, that blessing is not detached from the clear ethical standards marked out in His Word. God expects his people to live lives that please Him because of all he's done for us. Doing so begins with humbly recognizing our neediness and realizing that God is the only one who can help us.

Preaching Idea

God delights in meeting the needs of people who recognize their neediness.

Contemporary Connections

What does it mean?

What does it mean that God delights in meeting the needs people who recognize their neediness? As Solomon's throne is established, it becomes apparent that he sought out God because he knew he needed to follow in his father's faithful footsteps. God responds by essentially offering Solomon a "blank check." Solomon understood that his greatest need—wisdom to govern—was more important anything he selfishly may have wanted.

The importance of faithfulness to God and humility before God stand out in this passage. It shows us that instead of selfishness, we please God if we would consider the unselfish path instead. God's response to Solomon is significant too. It shows us that when we seek God to meet our needs, we can be confident he will provide for us just as he delighted to provide for Solomon.

Is it true?

Is it true that God delights in meeting the needs of people who recognize their own needs? Over and over again, Scripture describes God as a provider who has always loved to meet the needs of his people. He demonstrates this in individual cases like Elijah and the widow of Zarepath in 1 Kings 17. He also promises to provide on a larger scale, as we see in 2 Chronicles 7:14. The teachings of Jesus, Paul, and James also underscore the truth that God delights to provide for those in need (Luke 11:9–13; Phil. 4:19, James 1:5–8).

The challenge for us is that the world around us tries to convince us we can provide for ourselves, and we don't need anyone else's help. The American dream idolizes the self-made man or woman who "pulls themselves up by their own bootstraps." This self-sufficient mentality tries to convince us that we can figure a way out of our financial problems. It tells us we should keep our mental health struggles to ourselves because we are strong enough to work them out on our own. This self-centered mentality can also twist our view of God, turning him into a cosmic Santa Claus who will just give us whatever we want. The Bible pictures God as delighting in answering our prayers, but only when we approach him in humble faith (James 1:5–8; 4:1–10). We need to be open about our weaknesses and needs with ourselves, others, and especially God. He is the one who can ultimately provide anything we need. All we need to do is ask Him. He delights in providing for those who recognize their neediness.

Now what?

If it's true that God delights in meeting the needs of people who recognize their neediness, how should we respond and what should we do? A natural way to apply this passage is to *pray for wisdom*. When we, like Solomon, are faced with a task or decision that seems beyond our abilities, asking God for wisdom and direction should be our first response. Maybe it involves choosing a major in school, getting a promotion at work, or signing up to coach a youth sports team. Many opportunities in life will stretch us and test our expertise. In those moments we can turn to God for his supernatural insight and power to successfully tackle the task in front of us.

This story doesn't just teach us *what* to pray for; it also teaches us *how* to pray. Solomon responded to God's offer with a selfless answer and a submissive attitude. We too need to *pray with humility* whenever we are given new responsibilities, new powers, or new privileges. In his book *Quiet Strength*, Super Bowl–winning coach Tony Dungy recalls his journey through the NFL. After losing his first five games as a head coach, his Tampa Bay team broke through in a big way on their sixth try. In the postgame celebration, the team gathered for their traditional postgame prayer. It was a significant moment, Dungy says, because "We had already prayed together following our five losses. I wanted them to know that a great win would not change our core values. We would thank God both as gracious losers and as grateful winners" (Dungy and Whitaker 2007, 121). That is the kind of humble approach to prayer that pleases God. In our successes and in our struggles, we should recognize our neediness before God.

Creativity in Presentation

The offer God makes to Solomon is the kind of thing people dream about. Scenarios involving winning the lottery or being handed a blank check excite our imaginations as we brainstorm about all we might do.

A pastor could capitalize on this in many interesting ways. The pastor could hold up a hundred dollar bill and ask the congregation to write down three to five things they would do with that money. Then a random audience member could be chosen and given the money. The stipulation could even be made that if they accept the money, their list would be read from the pulpit. This is logically an introductory exercise to get people interacting with the passage's scenario before delving into the positive lessons we should embrace. To shift to the central preaching idea, try highlighting the items from the winning list that are needs and point out how this gift can help meet those needs. Alternative versions of this could also be employed. If using actual money is not realistic, having people make this kind

of list and share it would still be relevant. To pivot to the central idea, have personal examples ready of God providing what was needed. Or if your preaching environment allows, invite people to share how God met their needs in unique ways.

The key idea to communicate is that God delights in meeting the needs people who recognize their neediness. To show how God meets our needs, the passage for this preaching unit can be outlined as follows:

- When we fail, God meets our needs (2:46b-3:2).
- When we earnestly seek him, God meets our needs (3:3–9).
- When God meets our needs, we should respond with gratitude (3:10–15).

DISCUSSION QUESTIONS

1. What are the potential red flags in Solomon's life that are introduced in 3:1–2?

2. How does Solomon demonstrate that he was listening to his father's final instructions (2:1–9, 3:3–4)?

3. How does Solomon describe God's relationship with David? What significance does it have for him (3:5–7)?

4. Why is Solomon's request met with such appreciation from God (3:10–13)? What might this teach us about our prayer life?

5. What is the condition or expectation that God puts on his blessing of Solomon (3:14)? Does God have similar expectations for us?

1 Kings 3:16–28

EXEGETICAL IDEA
Solomon hears the tragic case of an infant's death shrouded by maternal deception, but channeling his divinely apportioned wisdom, the king forces the truth to appear.

THEOLOGICAL FOCUS
The qualities of wisdom exhibited by Solomon prefigures those exhibited by Christ and can still be invoked.

PREACHING IDEA
Some puzzles are only solved supernaturally.

PREACHING POINTERS
In the previous section, Solomon had asked for and received God's wisdom. This passage shows how he put it to use. The original readers of 1 Kings needed to follow the same process. As the returnees from exile were resettling the land, they needed to ask for God's special insight, be ready to receive it, and then put it to good use. The accounts of Ezra and Nehemiah record many of the difficult puzzles and problems those people were facing. After the exile, the spiritual and physical rebuilding of the country was a daunting task. God's people needed to turn to God for his help and wisdom if they were going to succeed.

Individually and corporately, Christians today face complicated puzzles that require God's supernatural insight. We need it when our doctor presents several different options to address our health problem. We need it when our coach is asking us to play a role that we neither like nor feel equipped for. We need it when we are trying to get our new business off the ground in a competitive market. Corporately, we need it as we see our culture change its views on hot-button issues like homosexuality, economic policies, immigration, and war. There may be no quick-and-easy answers, but we need to seek God's supernatural insight to navigate those situations and respond in ways that honor Christ. Will we choose, in faith, what seems best to us even if others don't understand? Are we willing sacrifice for the greater good? Can we live out both biblical truth and biblical love? Solving some of life's puzzles will require supernatural insight.

SOLOMON'S WISDOM IN ADJUDICATION (3:16–28)

LITERARY STRUCTURE AND THEMES (3:16–28)

In the following verses, one sees an example of Solomon's wisdom. Perceptive and bold in his adjudication, the king was able to force the best course of action to appear in a situation that seemed to elude justice. This translated into an unprecedented level of fame for Solomon.

- *The Case of the Two Women (3:16–22)*
- *Solomon's Verdict (3:23–28)*

EXPOSITION (3:16–28)

In one of the most famous episodes of Solomon's reign, he brilliantly forces the truth to appear in a dispute that seems destined for gridlock. This episode becomes foundational evidence of Solomon's wisdom and ability to adjudicate, ensuring his presence among the wisest kings of the ancient world.

The Case of the Two Women (3:16–22)

3:16–22. Two prostitutes come to Solomon seeking adjudication for a situation that stemmed from the tragic death of one of their babies.

This scene is one of the legendary scenes in the Old Testament. It opens as a classic case of "she-said–she-said," which often defy any satisfying solution. Conventional wisdom, therefore, would suggest that at least one party would leave devastated. However, as this scene will demonstrate, Solomon does not wield conventional wisdom.

Two prostitutes who share living accommodations come before Solomon with a tragic story. According to the accuser, her housemate smothered her child in the middle of the night (v. 19) and deceitfully swapped her dead child for the living one (v. 20). When the accuser awoke, she quickly noticed that the dead child was not hers (v. 21). Of course, the accused vehemently denied the charges and their testimony ends with the two arguing before the king.

The scene is simple but effective. Not only does it tug the reader's emotions, but it also creates the impression of a hopeless situation. How will the king be able to resolve this issue? Indeed, one may wonder about some details, like why the two were living in the same house? Or, why did one sleep so heavily so as not to notice the swapping of the infants? Yet this ambiguity adds to the gravity and desperation of the scene.

Solomon's Verdict (3:23–28)

3:22–28. Solomon's bold action forces the truth to appear.

Solomon finally responds in verse 23. He first summarizes the case and then, in stride, calls for a sword. The reason for his request is not immediately divulged, and so the suspense builds. Eventually, it's revealed that the king aims to cut the living child in half and give one section to each party. Indeed, such a ruling is appalling to modern sensibilities. Yet this is the point. In the face of a situation that presents no solution, Solomon, channeling his divinely appropriated wisdom, forces the solution to reveal itself. Aware of the primal and unique bond between a mother and her child, he counts on it to produce a particular response.

His hopes are realized. When the true mother realizes the king's plan, her deep-seated desire to see her child live takes over. She pleads with the king to give the child to the accused. This is all that Solomon needs to identify the true mother. Solomon renders his verdict and declares that the living child be returned to the rightful mother.

Of course, this entire scene is a means to an end. It's building to verse 28, which states that "all Israel" heard and were amazed. With this statement, Kings states that Solomon achieved a desire common to virtually all ancient Near Eastern monarchs—legendary wisdom.

The Wisdom of Solomon
by James Tissot. Public domain.

THEOLOGICAL FOCUS

The exegetical idea (Solomon hears the tragic case of an infant's death shrouded by maternal deception, but channeling his divinely apportioned wisdom, the king forces the truth to appear) leads to this theological focus: The qualities of wisdom exhibited by Solomon prefigures those exhibited by Christ and can still be invoked.

"Wisdom" as a concept in the Old Testament is hard to pin down. Not only are there many Hebrew words that can be glossed with a general sense of "wisdom," the semantic range of חָכְמָה, the term most often glossed as "wisdom," exhibits a diverse semantic range. Nevertheless, in this context the concept of wisdom is qualified. Here, it's an ability to perceive right and wrong, to adjudicate effectively. But Solomon's wisdom also shows an ability to be creative and a willingness to pursue the truth of a situation with a certain level of boldness and vigor. It also implies a certain level of confidence in one's abilities.

But the immediate context of this scene further clarifies how wisdom can be understood. Effective wisdom—wisdom that allows one to navigate what appear to be hopeless situations—is a gift from God. First Kings 3:5–9 informs us that Solomon asked such a gift, and the populace realized that the king's abilities stemmed from wisdom that originated with God (3:28; חָכְמַת אֱלֹהִים). But perhaps most importantly, such wisdom is not a gift locked to a particular historical context.

Centuries after Solomon, the incarnation of divine wisdom would walk among Israel and exhibit a similar vigor, boldness, and creativity. Yet whereas Solomon's case was a judicial one, Jesus's case would be a soteriological one. Nevertheless, just as Solomon needed to consider his situation from a different angle so that a way forward could be revealed, Jesus too would come at his situation from an unanticipated angle so that a solution would be revealed. And if the general exhortation of James is to be heeded, then such qualities of wisdom are still available to the believer (James 1:5–8). All they must do is ask.

PREACHING AND TEACHING STRATEGIES

Exegetical and Theological Synthesis

Solomon has received God's blessing of divine wisdom and now it is put on display for all to see. He is confronted with a seemingly unresolvable "she-said–she-said" situation involving the tragic death of an infant and possible sinister deception by one of mothers. Employing divine wisdom, he settles on a solution that draws out the truth. The infant's life is spared and the rightful mother takes custody of her child.

Later on in his life, Solomon will encourage God's people to seek the same supernatural insight that guided him. Beginning with the posture of "fearing the Lord," he points the way to truly effectual wisdom in the book of Proverbs. Ultimately, Jesus was the embodiment of God's wisdom, pointing the way to a truly fulfilling life (John 1:1–4; Col. 1:15–20; cf. Jer. 10:12). Now it is our privilege to obtain the same divine insight, by simply asking in humble faith like Solomon (James 1:5–8; 3:13–18).

Preaching Idea

Some puzzles are only solved supernaturally.

Contemporary Connections

What does it mean?

What does it mean that some puzzles are only solved supernaturally? Life has a way of presenting challenges that are often beyond our level of expertise. Health problems arise that require choosing between options that are all difficult. Job market uncertainties can threaten our families' financial stability. We will face crises of various kinds at various times. Neat and tidy answers don't always exist.

Some well-meaning Christians believe "God won't give you more than you can handle" and insist that is a biblical promise. Yet if that were true, when would we need faith? God calls his people to dependence which by very definition is a call to face things that are beyond our control and beyond what our strength can tackle. The bigger, more complex the puzzle God gives us in life, the more directly we must turn to the Lord for clarity, wisdom, and solutions because some puzzles are only solved supernaturally.

Is it true?

Is it true that sometimes life gives us a puzzle that requires supernatural insight to solve? Yes, God has put even his most faithful servants in such predicaments. He called Abraham to sacrifice his son Isaac. Gideon was tasked with leading a short-handed army to liberate his nation. Mary became pregnant with Jesus before marrying Joseph.

There are plenty of examples of this for us too. Talking heads on TV endlessly debate immigration and how to fix it. Christians wrestle with who to vote for when no major candidate fits their standards. These puzzles often go beyond the societal level and meet us in a personal way. A single parent begins to suspect their troubled teenager is stealing from them. A newly hired employee discovers their boss is "fudging the numbers" to please the corporate higher-ups. Life will present us with dilemmas that common sense can't solve easily. It is in these circumstances and with these issues that we need to lean on God's direction.

Now what?

If it's true that sometimes life gives us a puzzle that requires supernatural insight to solve, how can we obtain the wisdom we need to know what to do? While a debate on TV may not demand our immediate response, what are we supposed to do when we encounter complicated issues that do require our action? How do we solve seemingly impossible problems?

From Solomon's example, we can learn *to assess the situation carefully*. Solomon listened to the testimony of both women, hearing in painful detail both versions of events. Any wise detective or impartial jury will consider all the evidence before moving forward. Likewise, we ought to listen to both sides if mediating a dispute. We will need to examine all possible courses of action and how they might lead to resolving the situation. We should ask trusted friends for their input and seek counsel from pastors or other godly people if possible. Assessing God's Word and being sensitive to the Spirit's leading as we pray are important at this point as well. A wise decision cannot be made unless all of the information is presented, thus we need to take time to evaluate the full picture.

Once we have assessed the situation carefully, we can then *boldly act in faith*. Like Solomon's solution, it may seem extreme. We shouldn't actually suggest cutting children in two when a divorced couple approaches with a family dispute. But a young man struggling with pornography should consider eliminating his internet connection. A young woman with body image issues can throw away her fashion magazines. Dave Ramsey's programs offer wise steps for those people struggling with financial problems. These aren't guaranteed cure-alls of course. Additional bold steps may be needed. However, boldly acting in faith will lead us to freedom and hope in difficult situations.

Creativity in Presentation

Comparing this story to a puzzle offers some good, creative options to illustrate or introduce the passage. In the long history of the game show *Wheel of Fortune*, there have been some amazing guesses that solved the puzzle with only a letter or two on the board. Playing a YouTube clip of one of those would be a great way to grab the audience's attention. There are numerous compilation videos that could be used to get the viewer wondering, *How did they come up with that?*

Another option would be to get a jigsaw puzzle and try to put it together without having the picture in front of you. A volunteer could be used and the scenario could be set up where all of the pieces are upside down and cannot be turned over. Various levels of puzzles could be used depending on how complicated it needed to be or how much time was available. Having two people try to put together identical puzzles, one with the picture and one without, might be a fun way to do it as well. Handicapping the task in any of these ways would effectively drive home the point that it takes extra help to complete the task and solve the puzzle.

The key idea that the sermon needs to convey is that some puzzles can only be solved supernaturally. We must look to God to give us his divine wisdom when conventional common sense falls short. The passage for this preaching unit can be outlined in the following points:

- Assess the puzzle carefully (3:16–22).
- Boldly act in faith (3:23–28).

DISCUSSION QUESTIONS

1. What are the elements of this situation that make it seemingly impossible to know the truth (3:16–22)?

2. How could this situation turn out bad for those involved?

3. Why is Solomon's seemingly rash proposal actually really wise (3:23–27)?

4. What is the result of this episode, and how does it relate back to the beginning of the chapter (3:28)?

1 Kings 4:1–34[5:14]

EXEGETICAL IDEA

Solomon's administration translated to a level of opulence that set Solomon above all his peers; however, his method of operation was not above criticism.

THEOLOGICAL FOCUS

Progress at the expense of others does not comport with the character of the Lord or his intentions for the way his people are to live.

PREACHING IDEA

Don't let the light of success blind you to the pitfalls of power.

PREACHING POINTERS

Solomon continues to employ superior wisdom as he sets up his administration and pursues the prosperity of his nation. For us, this chapter might read as a dry record of Solomon's history. To the original audience, this would have been a high point in their nation's history. As the returned Jewish exiles rebuilt the cities that were in disarray and as they reorganized their government and society upon returning to the land, they would read of the glory of Solomon's reign and dream of the day when that grandeur would return. But discriminating readers would take note of the subtle clues within the text that warned of straying from God's directives. Achieving success is a wonderful blessing, but what did it cost in the past and what would it cost in their postexile world?

Success and the desire to attain it are woven into the very DNA of our world, especially in the United States of America. Just in the twentieth century, the United States came out victorious in two World Wars as well as the Cold War. This nation made itself into a nuclear superpower and was the first to put a man on the moon. Winning became assumed and superiority became an expectation. But like King Solomon, are there cracks in the facade of prosperity? Are there people groups neglected? Have morals been sacrificed for the sake of freedom and power? The Larry Nassar-USA Gymnastics scandal provides a revealing example. In pursuit of Olympic glory, an entire organization turned a blind eye to a sexual predator harming kids and abusive coaches fostering a poisonous environment. Gold medals were won, but lives were ruined. Success isn't a bad thing, but we cannot let it blind us.

SOLOMON'S WISDOM IN THE AFFAIRS OF THE KINGDOM (4:1–34[5:14])

LITERARY STRUCTURE AND THEMES (4:1–34[5:14])

The text now turns to another example of Solomon's wisdom—his ability to effectively organize and rule a kingdom. This segment recounts the individuals to whom Solomon delegated authority, the administrative districts of the kingdom, and the opulence of the kingdom.

- *Solomon's Administrators (4:1–19)*
- *Solomon's Opulence (4:20–34[5:1–14])*

EXPOSITION (4:1–34[5:14])

This section demonstrates Solomon's wisdom in organizational effectiveness. He organizes his kingdom to maximum effect, which translates into unprecedented opulence and opportunity. Together with 3:16–28, these passages establish the broad-reaching wisdom of Solomon, which in turn prepare the reader for the king's most memorable action—the construction of the temple.

Solomon's Administrators (4:1–20)

The lists of Solomon's administrators and districts reveal a layered governmental system that operated in a particular way.

4:1–6. It is reasonable to suggest that the details in these verses reflect actual royal documents. The text acknowledges secretaries within the royal court (v. 3; סֹפְרִים), and

administrative lists were common across the ancient Near East. However, any further conclusion regarding their origin may be too speculative.[1] Nevertheless, the presence of Abiathar among the list of "high officials" (הַשָּׂרִים) is interesting (v. 4). It suggests that this list predated the banishment of the priest (cf. 2:26–27) and reinforces the reality that the historian's organization of 1 Kings 1–11 was driven by concerns other than those of chronology.

Lexical Analysis: The noun שַׂר is widely attested across the ancient Near East and refers to several different administrative positions. In this context, it broadly categorizes numerous specific functions and important positions, hence the rendering "high officials" (*HALOT*, 1:1350–53).

Adoniram's role as overseer of forced labor (הַמַּס) is also interesting, as it explicitly acknowledges Solomon's imperial ambitions (*HALOT*, 1:603–04). Moreover, certain positions within the court were apparently hereditary. For example, Zadok was a priest (v. 4), and so too was his son Azariah (v. 2). Most importantly, this list attests that Solomon's administration was not a simplistic one. There were layers of authority and responsibility. Azariah son of Zadok functioned as the high priest (lit., "the priest"; הַכֹּהֵן), Azariah son of Nathan "was over the

---

1 For example, was there a relationship between these lists and the referenced Book of the Acts of Solomon (cf. 1 Kings 11:41)? If so, what was the nature of that relationship? These are legitimate questions, but they cannot be answered with any level of certainty.

officials," who are detailed beginning in verse 7 (עַל־הַנִּצָּבִים), and, if Sweeney (2007, 83) is correct in his suspicions, then Azariah son of Zadok, Elihoreph, Ahijah, and Jehoshaphat constitute an upper echelon that enjoys a closer proximity to the king.[2]

Name	Lineage	Title	Function
Azariah	son of Zadok	"the priest," הַכֹּהֵן	the high priest
Elihoreph	son of Shisah	"scribe," סֹפֵר	responsible for several administrative duties requiring written records (Fox, 2000, 96–99; 101–10)
Ahijah	son of Shisah	"scribe," סֹפֵר	responsible for several administrative duties requiring written records
Jehoshaphat	son of Ahilud	"the secretary," הַמַּזְכִּיר; served under King David (2 Sam. 8:17)	possibly a royal emissary (cf. 2 Kings 18:18; Isa. 36:3)
Benaiah	son of Jehoiada	commander of the army; lit., "over the army," עַל־הַצָּבָא; served under David as leader of a specific military unit (2 Sam. 8:18)	leader of Solomon's standing army
Zadok and Abiathar	no lineage given	both were "priests," כֹּהֲנִים; both served David as priests	responsible for leading cultic duties
Azariah	son of Nathan	leader of the district officials; lit., "over the officials," עַל־הַנִּצָּבִים	apparently managed the district officials detailed in verses 7–19
Zabud	son of Nathan	priest and advisor; lit., "friend of the king," כֹּהֵן רֵעֶה הַמֶּלֶךְ	led cultic functions and likely served as a personal advisor
Ahishar	no lineage given	palace administrator; lit., "over the house," עַל־הַבָּיִת	managed day-to-day operations of the palace and royal property
Adoniram	son of Abda	supervisor of forced labor; lit., "over the forced labor," עַל־הַמַּס	responsible for the management of the king's conscripted labor force

---

2   Sweeney (2007) bases this suspicion in the lack of a waw-conjunctive prefixed to these names.

4:7–20. When it comes to the twelve administrative districts, it's first notable that each district was responsible for supplying the court and royal properties for one month of the year (v. 7), suggesting that taxation was the reason behind developing the districts. Second, the districts were northern districts, and, in light of Judah's appearance as the thirteenth district (v. 19)—which is also the third point—Judah may have enjoyed a different status among the others. Fourth, the descriptions of the districts fall into one of two categories. On the one hand, some districts are described in terms of traditional tribal affiliations. On the other hand, some districts are described in terms of their settlements and cities. Why? It is difficult to say definitively, but Rainey is on track when he says that the different descriptions are indicative of the diverse demographics within the kingdom, perhaps even the differences between traditional Israelite territories and Canaanite areas that had been consumed by Israel's growth (Rainey and Notley, 2006, 177; also Wiseman 2008, 98). Sweeney (2007, 89–95), interestingly, proposes the idea that the different descriptions evince the intentional weakening of the powerful northern tribes.

Tiphsah

Tiphsah is called out as one of Solomon's boundary cities (1 Kings 4:24). If this reference refers to the site of Thapsakos (modern Dibseh), then Kings appears to be establishing Israel's northernmost boundary in northern Syria, hundreds of miles from Jerusalem. Logistically, such a reality would present serious logistical hurdles. However, Tiphsah is also mentioned in 2 Kings 15:16, a site on the receiving end of Menahem's brutal military advances. There Tiphsah is contextualized in the vicinity of Tirzah, an early capital of the northern kingdom.

There, some Greek manuscripts transpose Tiphsah for Tappuah, which may bear witness to an alternative name for the site.

Anson Rainey has suggested that the boundary descriptions of 1 Kings 4:24–25[5:4–5] refer to two realities: a sphere of influence and a geographic boundary. Solomon's sphere of influence reached from Egypt to northern Syria, but his country was geographically limited to what was Dan to Beersheba (Rainey and Notley 2006, 164). Such a distinction is useful because it accommodates the tendencies of royal rhetoric.

Solomon's Opulence (4:21–34[5:1–14])
Solomon's opulence is reminiscent of common ancient Near Eastern descriptions of celebrated monarchs. But there are also hints of criticism.

4:21–28[5:1–8]. These verses are best understood against royal motifs common across the ancient Near East. The consumption and reputation of one's kingdom were normally points of emphasis in royal literature. Ironic here is that the descriptions exist in tension with the law of the king in Deuteronomy 17:14–20. There, a commitment to the תּוֹרָה is to define an Israelite king, not the amassment of riches, military might, and worldly prestige. Thus, it's possible to understand a subtle criticism of Solomon's opulence, reputation, and military might. A similar atmosphere is echoed in chapter 10.

Regarding the extent of Solomon's kingdom, virtually all English translations refer to the river Euphrates as one of the nation's northern boundaries (4:21[5:1]; 4:24[5:4]). However, there is debate over the actual extent of Solomon's kingdom.[3] But regardless, these verses

---

3   The term "Euphrates" does not appear in the Hebrew. The Hebrew can be translated as follows:
    "Now Solomon was ruling over the entire kingdom, from the river to the land of the Philistines to the border of Egypt" (4:21[5:1]).

celebrate the extent and relative security Israel enjoyed under Solomon. "Judah and Israel were as numerous as the sand upon the sea," and they ate, drank, and were merry (4:20). Moreover, Judah and Israel, "from Dan to Beersheba, lived in safety" (לָבֶטַח...וַיֵּשֶׁב; 4:25[5:6]). Images of peaceful solitude under trees and in vineyards are invoked, and when used alongside the catalog of Solomon's formidable and well-fed cavalry, as well as the enormous daily provisions of his court (4:26–28[5:7–9]), a powerful image of peace and abundance is created.

Nevertheless, such a catalog glosses over the realities of imperialism, namely, taxation. Without the significant burden imposed upon the other twelve districts of Israel (cf. 4:7–19), all this would not be possible.

4:29–34[5:9–14]. This section closes with a description. Solomon's wisdom is contextualized by a series of superlatives. Being "as vast as the sand on the seashore," the limits of his wisdom could not be reached, nor even quantified. Moreover, it surpassed the wisdom associated with Egypt and the East, both of which enjoyed prestigious reputations on the topic of wisdom, as well as Ethan, Heman, Calcol, and Darda, all of whom were likely well-known to the audience and may have been famous cultic personnel (Pss. 88; 89; 1 Chron. 2:6; Sweeney 2007, 101). To support these claims, the historian references Solomon's copious literary works as well as the global audience that he attracted. All of this is an emphatic generalization to a section devoted to teasing out the wisdom of Solomon (2:46b–4:34[5:14]).

THEOLOGICAL FOCUS

The exegetical idea (Solomon's administration translated to a level of opulence that set Solomon above all his peers; however, his method of operation was not above criticism) leads to this theological focus: Progress at the expense of others does not comport with the character of God or his intentions for the way his people are to live.

Solomon's wisdom produced a level of achievement that is difficult to overstate. However, a dark side to Solomon's achievements is difficult to ignore. Solomon's administrative system required a significant level of taxation. Consequently, what was viewed as a ground for praise by some would undoubtedly have been viewed as cumbersome and quasi-oppressive by others.

All of this ultimately raises certain ethical questions. But most pointedly, at what point does one set aside the well-being of a few for the well-being of the whole? Even more fundamental, does such a scenario even align with the character of the Lord and his covenantal ideal? Some of the prophets didn't think so.

In chapter 3 of his prophecy, Micah laments the lack of justice for the larger populace, so much so that he describes the situation in grotesque, cannibalistic terms (Mic. 3:1–3). The oracle builds to a climatic pronouncement of Jerusalem impending desolation, and a chief reason is the abolition of justice, the perversion of equity, and the building of Zion "with blood" and "with wrong" (3:10). Zephaniah decries Jerusalem's predatory leadership (Zeph. 3:3), but perhaps Isaiah's criticisms are most telling.

"Indeed, he was exercising dominion over all the region west of the river, from Tiphsah to Gaza, over all the kingdom west of the river" (4:24[5:4]).

Many commentators state, based on the testimony of passages like Genesis 15:18, Deuteronomy 1:7, 11:24, and Joshua 1:4, that "Euphrates" is implied. However, Baruch Halpern has pondered the rhetoric involved, asking if the "river" (הַנָּהָר) is the Jordan (Halpern, 2001, 128; 248–49). Therefore, "How big was Solomon's kingdom?" —an intriguing theory, as difficulty surrounds the mentioning of Tiphsah in verse 24[5:4]. If Tiphsah is also a city near Tirzah (cf. 2 Kings 15:16), then Halpern's more modest reconstruction may be in order, which would align well with Notley and Rainey's ideas of geographic boundaries and spheres of influence.

Nestled in his oracle against Jerusalem (Isa. 22) stands a quick but specific criticism: "You counted the houses of Jerusalem, and you broke down the houses to fortify a wall" (22:10). Later, Isaiah specifically criticizes Shebna for what appears to be the unlawful annexation of land for his personal tomb (22:15–16).

In all these cases, unbridled progress and innovation seem to conflict with the covenantal ideal that was supposed to define Israel's community, particularly since it put certain elements in society under extreme pressure. Indeed, the prophetic critique of Micah, Zephaniah, and Isaiah appear later in the history of Israel and Judah and so represent the outcome of a lengthy process, along which there were countless chances to make the necessary adjustments. However, the historian is suggesting that the seeds of such poisonous pursuits were planted in the policies of Solomon.

PREACHING AND TEACHING STRATEGIES

Exegetical and Theological Synthesis
Solomon's divine wisdom is not just limited to individual situations like the previous chapter. The construction of his government results in great national prosperity (vv. 22–28) in addition to his personal renown (vv. 29–34). On the surface, this passage paints an ideal picture of the kingdom of Israel blossoming under Solomon. There is little doubt that God's covenantal promises to David are being fulfilled (2 Sam. 7:9–14). Yet under closer examination, there are some questionable details about the possible undermining of northern Israel, the heavy load of taxation, and how the kingdom's grandeur fits with God's Law.

Success is not inherently bad. This chapter is clearly advocating that God is blessing the nation through Solomon. God is fulfilling his promises that he originally made to David. God's blessings don't ensure perfection though. When we find ourselves in a position of blessing, do

we get so busy enjoying life that we ignore everything else? We would do well to consider the cost of our success. God's blessings are not divorced from his ethical and moral standards. Ends do not justify means in God's kingdom, and there are pitfalls we need to watch out for when we achieve success.

Preaching Idea
Don't let the light of success blind you to the pitfalls of power.

Contemporary Connections

What does it mean?
What does it mean to not let the light of success blind you to the pitfalls of power? What does it look like to be blinded by success? The drive to achieve success can be unhealthy for people of all ages and in all kinds of circumstances. It drives the student who is striving for perfect grades in order to secure recognition, scholarships, and an esteemed future career. It drives the employee to work longer and longer hours in hopes of earning a prestigious promotion or bonus. It drives the coach to hang on one more year in hopes of breaking that historic wins record.

Those goals are not bad per se, yet so often pursuing those goals comes at the expense of family, friendships, personal health, or moral integrity. And if the pursuit does not cause compromise, the actual success and accomplishment might. We should not celebrate our achievements so much that we lose sight of what is good and right. What we do with our power, position, or influence is very telling. Christ would have us help and serve others rather than use our power, position, or influence to build ourselves up (Matt. 20:25–28; Luke 6:27–36; Eph. 4:28; Phil. 2:1–4; Heb. 13:16).

Is it true?
Is it true that the light of success can blind you to the pitfalls of power? Success certainly brings pitfalls and traps that can result in trouble and

disaster. Solomon's life will ultimately teach this as well as many of his predecessors who later ruled Israel and Judah. Of course, almost every major scandal in our society speaks to this also. From the USA gymnastics downfall to the housing market crash of the mid-2000s to the Harvey Weinstein revelations, the glimmer of glory distracted so many from the horrific realities of what was really going on. Modern Christianity is not immune to this either. Prosperity gospel preachers make negative headlines with alarming regularity because of financial mismanagement. Bill Hybels's ignoble departure from Willow Creek Church exemplified that even those close to a leader can fail to see the warning signs of immorality in ministry. The light of success will often blind people to the pitfalls that surround them. Another recent example is the late Ravi Zacharias, whom multiple sources have accused of serious sexual misconduct, which has resulted in incalculable damage to his family, his world-renowned reputation, his ministry, and all the victims of his abuse—while deceiving himself and everyone around him for who knows how long.

Now what?

If it's true that the light of success can blind you to the pitfalls of power, what can we do about it? What can we do to avoid being blindsided by success or having a downfall due to power? Just because there are pitfalls doesn't mean we should fear success. God's blessings are not something to be dismissed or denied. But we ought to be careful with how we pursue success and how we handle it once we get it.

One way to ensure that we handle success well is to *give out of our abundance*. Adopting this approach to our time, money, and material resources will take discipline. But helping those who have less than us will help to keep our perspective in the right place. Sponsoring a child through World Vision or Compassion International is way simple way to do this. For less than fifty dollars a month, the practical needs of an underprivileged child can be met, and a relationship can be formed that encourages both the sponsor and the child. Americans have so much in comparison to the rest of the world, so giving out of our abundance is one way to serve and bless others.

Another way to ensure that we handle success well is to *surround ourselves with trustworthy people*. The list of Solomon's staff and advisors is not the most exciting text in Scripture, but it reminds us of the importance of who we choose to surround ourselves with. A coach needs team captains who will listen well and follow instructions. A CEO needs a board of reliable people who set the course of their business. A pastor needs elders and deacons of high integrity to help lead the church. Whatever our position, it's important that we surround ourselves with good friends and influencers. Entering into an accountability relationship is a wise practical step to take. Men and women of all walks of life can benefit from regularly meeting with trusted confidants who will ask hard questions and check in to encourage them.

Creativity in Presentation

One of the newer technologies in the auto industry is blind spot detection. This safety feature offers a good illustration for this passage. Travelers can be driving along, thinking they are safe and aware of their surroundings, only to start changing lanes and then get warning lights and sounds alerting to them to traffic in their blind spots. Playing video examples of this or simply describing your experience with it may suffice to connect to the central idea of this story. My wife and I (Lee) went on vacation with some friends who drove their car, which had one of these sensor systems. It made the trip a whole different travel experience, and it became obvious that it is a necessary safeguard when riding with a driver who sometimes easily got distracted from the road. Even when we believe that things are good, safe, and secure, we need to pay attention to warning signs that are alerting us to potential pitfalls.

The United States has enjoyed a prominent status as a world superpower for several generations. The real-life examples mentioned above can easily be used to further illustrate how dramatically compromised our society has become. The Penn State abuse scandal, the Larry Nassar story of abuse, the #MeToo movement, and revelations of the Catholic and evangelical churches of the past decade are all evidence that we have succumbed to the pitfall of sexual immorality. But our success has blinded us to more than just sexual sin. The Flint water crisis in Michigan, the housing market crash of the 2000s, and the increasing racial tension in our nation are just a few examples that point to other issues needing our attention.

Preaching on this passage will not be easy, given that the first half is comprised of lists of strange names and places. Even the second half is complicated because it seems like the kingdom of Israel had turned into some heaven-on-earth utopia. But there are clues within the whole chapter that teach us to avoid letting the light of success blind us to the pitfalls of power. The passage for this preaching unit can be outlined in the following points:

- Surround yourself with straight shooters (4:1–20).
- Seek the good of everyone (4:21–34).

DISCUSSION QUESTIONS

1. Why is Abiathar mentioned in 4:4 after his banishment of 2:26–27?

2. What do the descriptions of the twelve districts tell us, and how might they foreshadow future conflict (4:7–19, 27)?

3. How does Solomon's success fit positively with 2 Samuel 7:9–14?

4. How does Solomon's success fit negatively with Deuteronomy 17:14–20?

5. Beyond 1 Kings, what are some other biblical examples of Solomon's greatness and wisdom?

SOLOMON'S BUILDING CAMPAIGNS AND OTHER ENDEAVORS (5:1[5:15]–9:28)

The third section of the first major literary unit in Kings is 1 Kings 5:1[5:15]–9:28, which describes Solomon's building campaigns and other endeavors. This third section may be divided into six preaching units. First, there is a discussion of the preparations for Solomon's building projects (5:1–18[15–32]). Second, this is followed by the construction of the royal precinct, featuring the temple (6:1–7:51). Third, Solomon's dedication speech constitutes a distinct subsection itself (8:1–66). Fourth, the Lord then appears for a second time to Solomon (9:1–9). Fifth, more royal endeavors of Solomon are described (9:10–28). Sixth, Solomon's legacy is considered (10:1–29). This third of the four sections is the largest within 1 Kings 1–11. All the passages in this section are connected by an appeal to the temple's construction (cf. 9:1, 10) and constitute the point of focus for 1 Kings 1–11.

1 Kings 5:1–18[5:15–32]

EXEGETICAL IDEA
The relationship between Solomon and Hiram channeled the resources necessary to build the temple.

THEOLOGICAL FOCUS
Day-to-day encounters offer evangelistic opportunities.

PREACHING IDEA
Let your light shine—all the time!

PREACHING POINTERS
Solomon's deal with King Hiram of Phoenicia would prove critical for the building of the temple of the Lord. Beyond the transactional aspect of this chapter, there is potentially more to glean from this record of King Solomon's political duties. The people rebuilding Jerusalem and resettling the land could have merely focused on the work, the resources, and the commercial nature of returning from the exile. Yet this chapter offers them a reminder of the covenantal purpose God had for them dwelling in the land in the first place. From the promise to Abraham to the messages of the prophets, God intended them to be a "light to the nations" and to be a redemptive blessing to the Gentile world around them (Gen. 12:2–3; 22:17–18; Isa. 42:6; 49:6). Through informal interactions and official partnerships, they could reach those in spiritual darkness with the light of God. Rebuilding the land was more than just about creating a home; it was about establishing an influence so that all peoples could know Yahweh as the returning Jewish exiles did. God was providing them a new opportunity to be a light as they resettled their homeland.

Today, Christians have a similar calling. In Matthew 5:14–16, Jesus describes us as "the light of the world" whose good deeds will cause people to glorify God. Some people try to shine their lights only at church, while doing whatever they want the rest of the week. God expects us to be lights from Monday through Saturday, not just Sunday. We are called to reflect Jesus to the world whether we are at our jobs, at school, traveling, or relaxing at home. This chapter's business negotiations provide a great practical context for increasing our witness. How we conduct ourselves in meetings, over meals, and even in the day-to-day grind of our jobs can be a shining testimony of our faith in Jesus. We need to let our lights shine—all the time and everywhere we go.

PREPARATIONS (5:1–18[5:15–32])

LITERARY STRUCTURE AND THEMES (5:1–18[5:15–32])

Verses 1–12 recount the relationship between Solomon and the Phoenician king Hiram. Verses 13–18 offer greater detail concerning how that relationship was nurtured. Together, these verses detail the preparatory logistics of the temple's construction.

- **Treaty Between Solomon and Hiram (5:1–12[5:15–26])**
- **The Workforce and Preparatory Labor (5:13–18[5:27–32])**

EXPOSITION (5:1–18[5:15–32])

Solomon and the neighboring king Hiram of Tyre enjoyed a mutually successful relationship. Through the exchange of resources, Solomon was able to procure the materials necessary for the construction of the temple.

Treaty Between Solomon and Hiram (5:1–12[5:15–26])

Upon hearing of Solomon's coronation, King Hiram of Phoenicia sends a delegation to determine if positive relations will continue between Israel and Phoenicia. The two kings ratify a parity treaty.

5:1[5:15]. When he hears about Solomon's coronation, the Phoenician king Hiram dispatched an envoy (כִּי שָׁמַע כִּי אֹתוֹ מָשְׁחוּ לְמֶלֶךְ תַּחַת אָבִיהוּ). On one level, this envoy was congratulatory. Yet it also aimed to determine whether relations between the two regional powers would continue to be amicable (2 Sam. 5:11–12; 10:4). Solomon's response was positive, but it was also certainly calculated as he used the meeting to solicit building materials for the construction

of a national temple (v. 4[18]). Hiram would send lumber, and, as one would expect in a parity treaty (v. 12[26]), Solomon would in turn provide daily provisions for the Phoenician court (5:8–11[5:22–25]). The workforce, tellingly, was to be shared, and ultimately, this transaction signaled the continuation of positive relations.

> *Translation Analysis:* Virtually all English translations read "his feet" in 5:3[17] (רַגְלוֹ). However, the Masoretes suggest reading "my feet" (רַגְלָי). If the Masoretic suggestion is preferred, Solomon's self-comparison over his father is intensified.

5:2–6[5:16–20]. The logic of Solomon's response to the Phoenician envoy is intriguing. He first appeals to a kernel of mutual knowledge to set up a contrast between him and his father. Hiram apparently knew that David aspired to build a temple (cf. 2 Sam. 7). Appealing to that historical reality, therefore, Solomon positions himself as greater than his father. He boldly asserts that he will accomplish what his father could not. Such an assertion undoubtedly sought to silence any anxiety that may have existed in Hiram's mind over Solomon's abilities or ambitions. Furthermore, Solomon appeals to the word of the Lord (v. 5[19]) as well as the "peace" and "security" of his reign, something that his father, who was occupied by conflict (מִפְּנֵי הַמִּלְחָמָה) (v. 3[v. 17]), was unable to obtain. Thus, when Solomon exhorts Hiram to cut cedars and combine labor (v. 6[20]), he is also effectively encouraging the Phoenician king not to worry.

5:7–12[5:21–26]. Upon hearing Solomon's proposal, the Phoenician king "rejoiced greatly"

(וַיִּשְׂמַח מְאֹד), even going so far to bless the Lord (בָּרוּךְ יְהוָה). Such a response is distinctive of what Wiseman describes as a "typical diplomatic correspondence" (Wiseman 2008, 107). In turn, Hiram offered another correspondence that verified the agreement and further articulated the details. Hiram committed to satisfying all of Solomon's needs "in the matter of cedar and cypress timber" (v. 8[22]) as well as a specific method of delivery (v. 9[23]). The price, which was initially left open-ended by Solomon, was food and provision for the royal court. Solomon agreed and thus the treaty was ratified, installing a partnership between peers and becoming another manifestation of Solomon's wisdom. This is substantiated by a subtle syntactical connection set off by a disjunctive clause in the original Hebrew: "So the LORD gave Solomon wisdom, as he promised him. There was peace between Hiram and Solomon; and the two of them made a treaty" (5:12[26]).

Who Was Hiram?

King Hiram of Tyre was a contemporary of David and Solomon, and their dealings centered on the provision of building materials for David and Solomon's building campaigns. According to 1 Kings 9:10–14 and 9:26–28, Hiram reluctantly accepted a payment of twenty cities in Galilee for the lumber, and he was involved in the construction of a maritime fleet for Solomon based in Ezion-geber.

Hiram is a shortened form of Ahiram, which means "my brother is exalted." He was the son of Abibaal and was responsible for improving the infrastructure of the Byblos.

Yet information about Hiram largely comes from the Old Testament, Flavius Josephus (*Ant*

8.50–60), and a small number of Byblian inscriptions. Hiram's sarcophagus was discovered in 1923 and is housed in Beirut.[1]

The Workforce and Preparatory Labor (5:13–18[5:27–32])

To accommodate Solomon and Hiram's treaty and ambitions, a conscripted workforce was marshalled.

5:13–18[5:27–32]. Conscripted labor was a ubiquitous phenomenon across the ancient Near East. Virtually every imperial power documented the forced labor under their control. If the consensus numbers of 2 Samuel 24:9 are taken literally, then the 30,000 men referenced in 1 Kings 5:13[27] represent approximately 5 percent of the total population.[2] Regardless, this labor should be considered another form of taxation, which eventually agitated the northern tribes enough to become a point of concern leveled at Rehoboam (cf. 1 Kings 12:4).

THEOLOGICAL FOCUS

The exegetical idea (The relationship between Solomon and Hiram channeled the resources necessary to build the temple) leads to this theological focus: Day-to-day encounters offer evangelistic opportunities.

As mentioned, the quick comment of 5:12[26] suggests that the partnership between Solomon and Hiram can be understood as another manifestation of Solomon's wisdom. However, for those who know how the Solomonic account ends, this is ironic. Political alliances were sealed by marriages. So, when 1 Kings 11 says that Solomon loved foreign women and had an astronomical number of wives and concubines, one also

---

1   Koowon Kim, "Hiram, King of Tyre," *LBD*, Logos Bible Software 9.0; Keith Whitelam, "Hiram (Person)," *ABD*, 3:203–04.

2   Scholars disagree on how to interpret the figures of 2 Samuel 24:9. Not only does 1.3 million capable men create a population level that was not sustainable for the ecological and demographic framework of Iron Age II, but there are also noticeable divergences in the Chronicler's tallies (1 Chron. 21:15).

senses a criticism of his administrative policies. Yet in this context, there is no hint of a spiritual compromise. Furthermore, the objective of this partnership—the construction of the temple—is foundational to the historian's understanding of history. So, it raises the question: What is one to make of the historian in one context openly discussing the tendencies that he will later intensely disparage? According to the flow of the narrative, the Phoenician-Israelite connection is a benefit to the Lord as it positively affected the construction of the temple. Thus, the historian paints a fine but discernable line. It's not necessarily counterproductive to praise the diplomacies of Solomon here and then criticize those same tendencies just a few chapters later.

Yet let's move beyond the plain sense of the text to consider another angle. Perhaps we can say that relationships and partnerships that ultimately benefit all parties should be praised. As for those relationships and partnerships that expose people outside of the faith community to the workings of the community, perhaps they should be praised even more. The agreement between Solomon and Hiram would have placed Israelites working next to Phoenicians in the context of the temple's construction. Given the dynamics of interpersonal contact, it's reasonable to assume that ideas, experiences, even theology would have been shared.

In fact, the notion of interpersonal contact in close quarters inviting evangelism can be observed elsewhere in Scripture. According to Acts 16:25, fellow prisoners were exposed to the gospel merely by sharing a prison facility with Paul and Silas. In Philippians 1:13–14, Paul acknowledges that the imperial guard had been made aware of the circumstances surrounding his imprisonment, which implies a certain awareness of his message as well. Finally, Acts closes with a statement that Paul continued to minister fervently while under house arrest in Rome. Consequently, these examples suggest an awareness on the part of the believer that his

or her day-to-day dealings are critical contexts for evangelism.

PREACHING AND TEACHING STRATEGIES

Exegetical and Theological Synthesis

King Solomon and King Hiram establish a good relationship between their nations, continuing the history of positive interactions between Israel and Phoenicia. An advantageous way to demonstrate this goodwill was to coordinate and secure resources for the building of the temple in Jerusalem. Solomon has embraced his father's dream of building a place of worship to honor the Lord and he wisely uses this established ally to help achieve that end. Utilizing these political connections also allows Solomon and Israel to redemptively impact the nations just as God desired them to do.

Many times in their history, God warns Israel to remain distinct and set apart from the pagan peoples around them because compromise will undermine their identity as God's people (Exod. 20:1–17; Deut. 12:30–31; 14:1–2; Josh. 23:6–16; 24:14–28). Yet this collaboration is different. Working on this project does not involve any real risk of spiritually compromise. Instead, it provides the people chances to work with the Phoenicians on a project that could enhance their own religious life, and the temple itself would stand as a glorious tribute to Yahweh. Consequently, both in the personal interactions and the project itself, Israel is given prime opportunities to spread the truth of who God is and what He has done for them.

Preaching Idea

Let your light shine—all the time!

Contemporary Connections

What does it mean?

What does it mean to let your light shine all the time? Does it mean we have to be sharing the gospel with everyone, everywhere we go? No, not necessarily. But we should realize that wherever we go, whatever we do, and with whomever we meet, we represent Jesus. Paul calls us "Christ's ambassadors" whom God uses to help reconcile lost people to himself (2 Cor. 5:19–21). That means we ought to be ready to help a stranger fix a flat tire. It means we should be Christlike to our overbearing boss, treating him or her with honesty, grace, and respect. It means we should not swear like a sailor around our buddies, even when their off-color jokes and four-letter words are conversational norms. It is probably not the most effective witness to preach on a downtown street corner or cover our car in Christian bumper stickers. But we should see our entire lives as being a light in a dark world, no matter who we are with or where we are at.

Is it true?

Is it true that we should let our light shine all the time? Absolutely. God's Word repeatedly uses light as a metaphor for our life's witness. Most directly, Christ commands it in the Sermon on the Mount, in Matthew 5:14–16 (NIV):

> You are the light of the world. A town built on a hill cannot be hidden. Neither do people light a lamp and put it under a bowl. Instead they put it on its stand, and it gives light to everyone in the house. In the same way, let your light shine before others, that they may see your good deeds and glorify your Father in heaven.

One does not need to parse all of those Greek verb tenses to understand that Jesus desires his followers to consistently live in a way that appeals to others and honors God. The rest of the Sermon on the Mount certainly reinforces the idea that every facet of our life should be God-honoring. At all times—at work, at play, at home, in the classroom—we should live to glorify our Savior.

Now what?

How are we to shine our light all the time? Try asking the waiter or waitress at your favorite restaurant if there is any way you can pray for them. Is there a way you might encourage that friend from college you've reconnected with on social media? You could try starting spiritual conversations with your coworker whom you know is dealing with some hard life circumstances. Not all are called to be pastors or missionaries, but everyone is called to make disciples and point others to Jesus (Matt. 5:14–16; 28:18–20). We shouldn't view other people as "evangelism projects" but should be sensitive to how God may want to use us to lead them to Jesus. There are good programs out there that teach good methods on how to share your faith. However, just being a kind, listening friend will often be the most effective way to be a light to people struggling in darkness.

Creativity in Presentation

"Let your light shine" is a metaphor that naturally offers creative ways to drive home this passage's central point. One creative illustration would be to shut off all the lights in the sanctuary and let people really "feel" the darkness. After a few moments, pull out a flashlight from the pulpit and have them turn on their cell phone lights. After some time adjusting to that environment, have the lights turned back on and begin to make the connection to the idea of shining our lights and being people of the light.

Additional ideas could include utilizing testimonies from members who see their careers as platforms for ministry. Hearing from local businessmen and businesswomen about how they live out their faith in the marketplace would illustrate this passage very effectively. Also, for a secondary illustration, you might feature the children's song "This Little Light of Mine." It would not need to be part of a worship set; simply humming it from the pulpit would connect to audience members of certain generations and introduce the song to younger generations.

This is a classic narrative passage that doesn't necessarily fit neat outline forms. But bridging this political treaty agreement to letting your light shine is not too much of a stretch. We can break the passage down into the "when", "who", and "what" of opportunities that God gives us. The "when" would cover some of the contextual history of chapters 1–4. The "who" would feature the Israelite-Phoenician interactions. The "what" would revolve around this temple building project but also apply to any job or task God gives us.

The key idea to communicate is to let your light shine—all the time! To show how we can let our light shine, the passage of preaching unit can be outlined as follows:

- *Whenever* God provides the opportunity (5:1–4)
- With *whomever* God sends your way (5:1–4, 7–12, 13–16)
- In *whatever* God calls you to do (5:5–6, 13–18)

DISCUSSION QUESTIONS

1. How does Solomon respond to King Hiram's envoy (5:2–6)?

2. What is the result of this correspondence, and how does it reflect Solomon's great wisdom (5:12)?

3. Later on, Solomon is criticized for his political policies. How is this different?

4. Read Matthew 5:14–16, 1 Corinthians 10:31, and Philippians 1:13–14. How do these New Testament passages reflect this passage's main theme?

1 Kings 6:1–7:51

EXEGETICAL IDEA
The construction of the temple and the palace is like other accounts found across the ancient Near East; yet in celebrating the glories of Israel's society and the Lord, the biblical account nevertheless tempers any unbridled celebration.

THEOLOGICAL FOCUS
The construction of the temple and the palace anticipates the Babylonian exile, ultimately bearing witness to the potentialities of perpetual disobedience.

PREACHING IDEA
Details determine if our worship flourishes or fails.

PREACHING POINTERS
These chapters are full of details and descriptions recounting the construction of the temple of the Lord. They demonstrate that not only did the completed building facilitate worship, but the preparations themselves also had God's covenant in mind. The building materials and adornments purposefully symbolized God and his covenant with his people. In the end, it was their own failure to remain loyal to God that proved to be their downfall. So the mission for Israel upon returning from exile was clear: rededicate themselves to faithfully following the Lord in every respect. Their ritual sacrifices needed to be accompanied by acts of love and justice, otherwise rebuilding the second temple would be a futile effort (Micah 6:8–10; cf. Ezra 3–6; Neh. 12:27–47).

It might be easy to skim by these passages assuming that they have little bearing on our lives. That would be unwise because as this section shows us, details matter. Just as the details of the temple had greater meaning, so do the little things in our lives. Romans 12:1–2 teaches us that every aspect of our lives is worship. Therefore, all we do matters to the Lord. For example, what we say and how we say it matters. Negatively and positively, our speech reflects our hearts (Prov. 10:11; Eph. 4:22–32; James 3:10–12). Even our interactions with strangers and people "below" us are details that God takes seriously (Matt. 18:1–7; Heb. 13:2–3; James 2:1–10). As in the past, God still expects his people to be committed to obedience in all matters, big and small. Our disobedience won't necessarily lead to national exile as it did for the Israelites given the nature of their covenant relationship with God, but it will negatively affect all of us—in general as citizens of our country, but in particular as believers in Jesus and thus members of the body of Christ—if left unconfessed (1 Cor. 11:28–33; 1 Peter 3:7). How we handle the details in life will determine whether our worship flourishes or fails.

BUILDING THE ROYAL PRECINCT (6:1–7:51)

LITERARY STRUCTURE AND THEMES (6:1–7:51)

Having secured the materials, Solomon sets out to build a national temple. Chapters 6 and 7 recount, in glorious terms and elaborate detail, the construction of the temple. Such a literary endeavor was a common concern in ancient Near Eastern royal literature. As Christopher Hays states, "Along with military exploits, building campaigns were the primary achievements for which ancient Near Eastern kings took credit in their own inscriptions" (Hays, 207). Hays further suggests that many ancient Near Eastern building accounts assume a common form, which can also be observed within the biblical account. The following chart adapts Hays's ideas (Hays, 206–7):

Element	Biblical Parallel
Circumstances and Decision to Build	1 Kings 5:1–5
Preparations for Construction	1 Kings 5:6–18
Description of Building	1 Kings 6:1–7:51
Dedication of Rites	1 Kings 8:1–11; 54–66
Prayer of the King	1 Kings 8:12–30
Blessings and Curses	1 Kings 9:3–9

Another useful analogy has been made by Richard Hess, who compares the Masoretic Hebrew account[1] with a Luwian text of King Katuwas. Hess argues that the sequence of the temple's construction within the Masoretic tradition is similar to a Luwian text (Hess 2012, 171–82; 2016, 277). Ultimately, the comparisons of Hays and Hess firmly root this section of text in an ancient literary environment, which provides valuable insight for interpretation.

This block of text can be subdivided in accordance with Hess's ideas (Hess 2016, 277). First, there is a focus upon the building of the temple (6:1–38). Next, there is a focus upon the construction of the palaces (7:1–12). Finally, the historian returns to the temple's furnishings (7:13–51).

- *The Temple Building (6:1–38)*
- *Constructing the Palace (7:1–12)*
- *The Temple Furnishings (7:13–51)*

EXPOSITION (6:1–7:51)

Chapters 6 and 7 document the construction of the temple, in all its glory. As presented in Kings, the construction of the temple represents the pinnacle of Solomon's reign. And by introducing its description by a reference to the exodus from Egypt and making allusions to the creation traditions, the historian puts the temple's historical, theological, and cultural importance beyond question.

The Temple Building (6:1–38)

Introducing the construction account by mentioning Israel's greatest national memory,

---

1 On the differences between the Masoretic Text's account and the Septuagint's account of this account and the immediate context, see Percy Van Keulen (2005).

the historian documents the details of the temple.

6:1. Chapter 6 opens with a chronological marker: "In the four hundred eightieth year after the Israelites came out of the land of Egypt, in the fourth year of Solomon's reign over Israel, in the month of Ziv, which is the second month, he began to build the house of the LORD." To many, this is integral to establishing the date of the exodus, despite the well-known difficulties of such a ceremonial number.[2] However, Wiseman acknowledges a particular modus operandi among ancient writing; often construction texts begin with a reference to a national memory (Wiseman 2008, 111–13). If preferred, then the appeal to the exodus would invoke the memory of Sinai and the tabernacle rather than any specific date of the exodus event. Regardless, this marker ultimately secures a connection between Israel's religious past and present, which will be dramatically reinforced in 8:11–13.

> *Syntactical Analysis:* The protasis of the conditional clause begins in verse 12 and consists of three verbal clauses: תֵּלֵךְ בְּחֻקֹּתַי, תַּעֲשֶׂה אֶת־מִשְׁפָּטַי, and שָׁמַרְתָּ אֶת־כָּל־מִצְוֹתַי לָלֶכֶת בָּהֶם. The apodosis is represented by two syntactically equal clauses. First, הֲקִמֹתִי אֶת־דְּבָרִי אִתָּךְ, which is modified by the relative clause אֲשֶׁר דִּבַּרְתִּי אֶל־דָּוִד אָבִיךָ. Second, שָׁכַנְתִּי בְּתוֹךְ בְּנֵי יִשְׂרָאֵל. Thus, the syntax shows that Solomon's fidelity will have a twofold effect.

6:2–10. Verses 2–10 offer a general description of the temple. As a long-axis temple, it would be similar to other temples across the region. With three distinct delineations of sacred space, the worshipper first encountered the (אוּלָם), commonly translated as porch (*HALOT*, 1:41). The (הֵיכָל) was the main

sanctuary (*HALOT*, 1:245), which separated the exterior from the inner sanctuary, the (דְּבִיר; *HALOT*, 1:208). The דְּבִיר was also known as the Holy of Holies, the Lord's throne room, and the place where the ark of the covenant rested (6:19). The dimensions of the temple were approximately ninety feet in length, thirty feet in width, and forty-five feet high (v. 2). According to verses 5–6, the exterior of the building was bordered by a three-story chamber complex (Hurowitcz 1994, 24–36).

6:11–13. Verses 11–13 are intrusive. Moving against the grain of the building account, the historian interjects to emphasize the conditionality of things and Solomon's covenantal fidelity. *If* Solomon adheres to the covenantal expectations of walking, obeying, and keeping the commandments, then the Lord will dwell among his people and not forsake them. Consequently, these verses stress the reality that obedience will ensure presence. And nestled in the statement is also an assurance of dynastic stability. Thus, the text intimately connects the vitality of the dynasty with the perpetual presence of the Lord. What's more, such a point of emphasis so early in the building account prevents the reader from being caught up in the splendor of the account. Covenantal fidelity matters, and the temple is an important cog in a complex theological system that encompassed a god, a dynasty, a temple, and a city.

6:14–36. Verses 14–36 offer specific details of the temple's decorations. While there is great difficulty here, as many of the terms in the Hebrew are notoriously enigmatic, the most important details are discernable. The temple was constructed of stone hewn off-site (v. 7), but no stone was exposed in the interior

---

2   If the fourth year of Solomon's reign fell between 966 and 956 BCE, merely adding 480 years results in a mid-fifteenth-century date. For the chronological details of Solomon's rule vis-à-vis King Hiram of Phoenicia, see Wiseman (113, n. 55). On the problems of the early date, see the comprehensive discussions of Ralph Hawkins (2013, 49–90) and John Walton (2003, 258–72).

(v. 18). Cypress wood covered the floors, and cedar the walls. The cedar walls were also decorated with flora carvings and overlaid with gold. In fact, gold, a sign of perfection, decorated everything (v. 22). The floral carvings were diverse and recalled Eden, thereby creating a cosmic connection. The Creator of the cosmos now resides in a "new garden," in the midst of Jerusalem (Hurowitz 1994, 24–36; Keel 1997, 163–70; Richter 2008, 125–26).

The cherubim are the focus of verses 23–36. The inner sanctuary was dominated by these impressive creatures. Furthermore, the walls and door carvings throughout the complex intermingle gold, flora, and cherubim.[3]

6:37–38. Verses 37 and 38 conclude the account of the temple's construction; it was finished "in all its parts, and according to all its specifications" (כָּלָה הַבַּיִת לְכָל־דְּבָרָיו וּלְכָל־מִשְׁפָּטוֹ). It took seven-and-one-half years to complete—just under half the amount of time it took Solomon to build his palace (7:1).

Constructing the Palace (7:1–12)

A discussion of the temple's construction is interrupted by a discussion of the construction of Solomon's palace.

7:1. This section begins with a disjunctive clause in Hebrew. By establishing a contrast with the previous section and signaling a "shift in the scene" (IBHS, §39.2.3c), the text digresses from the temple. The Septuagintal tradition transposes verses 1–12 after verse 51, but as Hess has shown, the order in the Masoretic tradition has comparative support. Furthermore, Olley has argued that this digression is intentional, functioning as a subtle criticism of Solomon (Olley 2003, 357–59; 68–69).

7:2–12. What did Solomon's palace look like? Contrary to the preceding chapter, the text is not overly descriptive. According to verses 2–5, Solomon's palace was accented by a building termed "The House of the Forest of Lebanon" (בֵּית יַעַר הַלְּבָנוֹן). This ambiguous building was one hundred cubits long, fifty wide, and thirty tall. Its name was apparently derived from its prominent cedar decorations as well as its central pillars, beams, and rafters. As for the palace building, scholars have debated if it was a *bīt ḫilāni* style or something else. Regardless of the debate, the point is that Solomon's building campaigns tapped into the innovations and architectural trends of his

---

3   Cherubim enjoy a recurring role throughout the Old Testament. Composite creatures, they are associated specifically with the ark of the covenant (Exod. 25:18–22; 1 Sam. 4:4; 6:12), generally with the decorations of the cultic complexes (Exod. 26; 36; Ezek. 41:18–25; 1 Chron. 28:18; 2 Chron. 3:13, and here), and are recognized as heavenly beings (Gen. 3:24; 2 Sam. 22:11 and Ps. 18:11; Ezek. 9–11; 28:11–19). And because the Old Testament bears witness to a variety of understandings, there is no singular understanding of these creatures, what they looked like, or what they did. But in the end, the cherubim are best described as supernatural quadrupedal composite creatures that guarded sacred space. Over time they became agents of praise populating the divine realm (Wood 2008, 205).

Cherubim enjoy wide attestation across the ancient Near East, which in some ways adds to the difficulty in understanding these creatures. Each culture across the ancient Near East apparently had a unique understanding of this celestial beast. For example, the sphinx in Egypt and the winged bulls and lions that guarded the Neo-Assyrian throne rooms are best understood as cultural manifestations of a common concept. Consequently, an understanding of their function must be determined from the context of the passages in which they appear, which brings us to the other half of the difficulty. There is no statement of function in 1 Kings 6, only details about construction. Perhaps this was due to the nature of the historian's sources, or perhaps their function was so widely known that the historian thought it superfluous to mention it (Wood 2008, 41–42). What is beyond question is that all who entered the temple would know that they had entered the Lord's throne and the cherubim were there to guard its sanctity.

day and spared no expense. His palace was no exception.[4]

The Temple Furnishings (7:13–51)

While ambiguous in function, the temple furnishings are described.

7:13–14. This section returns to focus upon the temple and begins by introducing the chief craftsman, Hiram from Tyre (חִירָם מִצֹּר). There is a debate whether this Hiram is the same as King Hiram referenced earlier, but it is unlikely. A royal figure being introduced merely as a skilled craftsman is unorthodox.[5] Therefore, Kings appears to reference two men with the same name.

Throughout this section, Hiram is pitted alongside Solomon. In numerous locations, Hiram is documented as the builder (e.g. 7:14–18; 21–23; 27; 37–40; 45). However, in verse 48 Solomon is said to have "made all the vessels" (וַיַּעַשׂ שְׁלֹמֹה אֵת כָּל־הַכֵּלִים), and according to verse 51 Solomon "did" (עָשָׂה) all the work. The historian, though, is not confused. Rather, he is subtly recognizing the worker-benefactor relationship. Hiram was the craftsman and builder, but the king supplied the goods. Solomon's money and Hiram's prowess were both utilized, and so both are associated with the temple's construction.

7:15–51. The introduction of Hiram gives way to an account of the work (vv. 15–50). The construction of the two entrance pillars (vv. 15–22), the Molten Sea (vv. 23–26), the ten stands (vv. 27–37), and the smaller instruments (vv. 38–40a), such as the basins, shovels, and pots, are recounted before a summary Hiram's work (vv. 40b–47). Solomon's provision rounds out the section (vv. 48–50). Verse 51 constitutes a conclusion to the section, but also mentions how the temple functions essentially as a national bank.

Without a doubt, the critical interpretive issue is the ambiguity surrounding the identification and function of these furnishings. As Wiseman notes, the "technical terms are not precisely known and hamper interpretation" (Wiseman 2008, 122). The function of the pots, shovels, basins, and stands is easy enough to deduce—to facilitate the handling, offering, and cleaning of the sacrifices—but deducing the function of the two massive pillars and the Molten Sea, is more difficult.[6] There is no explicit statement. This suggests that a level of familiarity between the historian and the audience, which unfortunately is difficult for the modern reader. Nevertheless, what is on more firm ground is the symbolism of these furnishings. As pondered by Sweeney (2007, 121–24), the floral symbols on the two pillars represent fertility and perhaps even fecundity. The Sea likely had something to do with purification, but it could have also represented the primordial sea out of which creation came. The twelve bulls likely represented the twelve tribes and

---

4   Baruch Halpern has stated that the *bīt ḥilāni* architecture "formed the heart of Solomon's palace in Jerusalem" (Halpern 1988, 47). He emphasizes the "Hall of Pillars" (אוּלָם הָעַמּוּדִים; v. 6), the "Hall of the Throne" (אוּלָם הַכִּסֵּא; v. 7), and the "Hall of Justice" (אֻלָם הַמִּשְׁפָּט; v. 7), and that the king's living quarters were behind (v. 8) these halls as supporting evidence. David Ussishkin echoes many of the same conclusions (Ussishkin 1973, 78–105). However, Gunnar Lehmann and Anne Killibrew suggest that Solomon's palace was not a *bīt ḥilāni*, but rather a "Central Hall Tetrapartite Residence." Such a building was multipurpose and likely received its conceptual impetus from the four-room pillared house, a standard model among Israelite domestic architecture (Lehmann and Killibrew, 2010, 28).

5   (וַיִּמָּלֵא אֶת־הַחָכְמָה וְאֶת־הַתְּבוּנָה וְאֶת־הַדַּעַת לַעֲשׂוֹת כָּל־מְלָאכָה בַּנְּחֹשֶׁת) Hiram has a parallel within the biblical tradition. Bezalel and Oholiab are described with similar terms (Exod. 31:1–11).

6   According to 2 Chronicles 4:6, the Sea was used for priestly washing. However, a height of five cubits and a diameter of ten means that the Molten Sea was a small pool. Nevertheless, the tabernacle utilized a large basin reserved for ceremonial washing (Exod. 30:17). The pillars are clearly symbolic, but whether they represent strength and stability of the Lord's relationship with his people, or something similar, is a matter of debate (House 1995, 133).

may have also represented religious iconography indigenous to the region. Lions, bovines, and cherubim are also common Iron Age icons, and the lampstands along with the incense certainly symbolized divine presence.

THEOLOGICAL FOCUS

The exegetical idea (The construction of the temple and the palace is like other accounts found across the ancient Near East; yet in celebrating the glories of Israel's society and the Lord, the biblical account nevertheless tempers any unbridled celebration) leads to this theological focus: The construction of the temple and the palace is recounted in way that anticipates the Babylonian exile, ultimately bearing witness to the potentialities of perpetual disobedience.

The temple's construction account is given in accord with a widely attested literary convention across the ancient Near East (Horowitz 1992). Such accounts could be a part of a larger literary endeavor, but, as emphasized by Hays, they always served distinctly propagandistic purposes (Christopher Hays 2014, 209).[7] The opulence of the construction testified to the greatness of the society, the king, and ultimately the deity. However, the Israelite account, particularly in the context of Kings, has a more nuanced function. It is more sobering than merely offering braggadocious claims.

As argued in the introduction, 1 Kings 1:1–14:20 juxtaposes rival religious centers. Jerusalem, with its temple, is set against Bethel and Dan, each with its own respective worship center. Yet as the larger account unfolds, Jerusalem, Bethel, and Dan are revisited in ways that not only nudge the lengthy history along but also set the reader up for a painful climax. When the text reaches 2 Kings 25, the historian recounts the utter destruction and pillaging of the temple in images that remember its construction. The bronze pillars and the Molten Sea were broken into pieces and carried off to Babylon (2 Kings 25:13). The pots, shovels, basins, vessels, and all other furnishings were also carried off (2 Kings 25:14–15). In other words, the construction recounted in 1 Kings 6–7 is eventually "deconstructed" in 2 Kings 25.

Yet the tragedy of Kings is more than just the destruction of a revered building. It is the destruction of *the Lord's house*—the Lord's place of dwelling among his people. So, when readers encounter the opulence and minute details of the temple in 1 Kings 6–7, they must move beyond architectural descriptions and technical terms to think about what all the details signified. The historian is celebrating the society, the king, and the presence of the Lord among his people in great detail, knowing full well where the nation would ultimately end up. So, the details point to a historical tragedy that bears witness to the results of perpetual sin and a lack of sustained repentance.

PREACHING AND TEACHING STRATEGIES

Exegetical and Theological Synthesis

Building a temple for the Lord was a daunting task that required careful planning and skilled craftsmanship. Attention was given to every part of the process because this building would not only be where God met with his people, but it would be a constant reminder of God's covenant promises and covenant expectations. The same care and attention given to the construction also need to be applied to the worship that will be conducted in and around the temple moving forward. There are two digressions within the flow of these chapters that only underscore the importance of continuing loyalty to God. The message Solomon receives from the Lord in 6:11–13, plus the additional description of Solomon's palace construction in 7:1–12,

---

7   For example, Hays draws attention to the annals of Tiglath-Pileser I. He suggests that one could argue that Tiglath-Pileser's annals build from his military accounts and climax in his construction account.

seem intended to give the reader pause. God is emphasizing undivided loyalty in the former, while the king seems preoccupied with building his own house in the latter passage. Clearly God wants to bless his people and even dwell among them in the temple, yet seeds have been planted for the future failure of Solomon and the people.

God desires all of our devotion, not just most of it. Careers, relationships, sports, and family life are all good things that can compete for our loyalty to God. We should strive to honor God in those pursuits rather than let them detract from our faithfully following the Lord. Being committed to the Lord in the little decisions is just as important as obeying him with the big decisions. He has always desired full devotion from his people and if we are faithful in the details, our lives will flourish, and we will become all he wants us to be.

Preaching Idea

Details determine if our worship flourishes or fails.

Contemporary Connections

What does it mean?

What does it meant that details determine if our worship flourishes or fails? Coach John Wooden won more championships than any other college basketball coach in history. Even as he grew more and more successful, he always drilled his players on doing the little things correctly. No detail was insignificant. He even instructed them on to how to properly put their socks and shoes on before hitting the court. He understood that the small details mattered. That principle is reflected in this passage and clearly relevant to more than just basketball or temple-building. Details affect and even determine whether our worship flourishes or fails. And when we see our entire lives as worship, we will understand the significance of our words, thoughts, attitudes,

and deeds. Even if no one notices, getting the details of our lives aligned with what God values and wants is important. We should confess our sin, own up to our mistakes, and seek honest accountability from others in case there are blind spots in our lives.

Is it true?

Is it true that details determine if our worship flourishes or fails? Over and over again, Scripture demonstrates how Israel's faithfulness to God's law affected the quality of their worship and the prosperity of their nation. It comes as no surprise then that this was a major emphasis when it came to the construction of the temple. Even the details within the preparation reveal spiritually significant truths about God and what he expects of his people. In those ancient times, religious worship mostly revolved around a central location. When Jesus arrived, all of that changed for true worshippers of God. New Testament authors John, Paul, and Peter all assert that God's people are now God's true temple—he dwells in us (John 2:13–22; 1 Cor. 3:16–17; 6:19; 1 Peter 2:4–10).[8] While the location of God's presence has changed, it is still essential that we pay close attention to the details. God still desires our loyalty, dedication, and commitment in all facets of our lives. After identifying us as "a spiritual house" and "a royal priesthood," 1 Peter 2:11–12 (NIV) exhorts us:

> Dear friends, I urge you, as foreigners and exiles, to abstain from sinful desires, which wage war against your soul. Live such good lives among the pagans that, though they accuse you of doing wrong, they may see your good deeds and glorify God on the day he visits us.

God desires his people to be Christlike in all they say and do. In Joshua 7, Achan's sin led

---

8   Konkel offers good insights into John 2 and Hebrews's implications on this subject (Konkel 1997, 147).

to the whole nation feeling the consequences. In Acts 5, Ananias and Sapphira gave to God's work but lost their lives because they blatantly lied about it. First John 1:8–2:2 underscores our need to take care of any and all sin in our lives. Our worship, even our lives, will flourish if we address sin issues that come to light. And conversely, our worship, even our lives, will falter and fail if we treat these issues as no big deal.

Now what?

If it is true that details determine if our worship flourishes or fails, how should we envision worship? What should we do to ensure that our worship and our lives flourish? I once served with a pastor friend who would occasionally remark, "They pay me to do the administrative stuff, but I'd do the evangelism, outreach, and discipleship for free." He was expressing his biblical and personal calling to share the gospel and reflecting what his giftedness was. I totally understand the sentiment because there are things I *love* to do in ministry, and others that seem more like a chore. On the other hand, that implies that some tasks are honorable while others are merely requirements that come with the job. God's Word reminds us that we should serve God in all aspects of our lives and that all tasks are viewed as acts of worship. First Corinthians 10:31 (NIV) reminds us that in "*whatever* you do, do it *all* for the glory of God." Some parts of serving God may not be exciting or fun, but they do have eternal value.

Therefore, *we should see all things as worship* and *we should do little things to worship*. Small gestures can go a long way. Sending a card to someone in the hospital is an easy act of service. Smiling at your cashier can be a little detail that brightens their day. Even personal steps like fasting from social media for a week can benefit your own emotional health. They may not be big dramatic gestures that many notice, but God can use them to bless others and bless you.

Creativity in Presentation

Cooking is a part of life that offers a plethora of possibilities to illustrate how details affect and even determine whether something flourishes or fails. Obviously, making lobster bisque or baking a pie from scratch will require careful attention to following the recipe. But even in the simplest of dishes, things can go wrong if details are ignored.

My wife and I (Lee) share cooking responsibilities in our home. A few years ago, I grabbed a can of soup out of the cupboard to prepare for dinner as my wife was coming home from work. I believe it was tomato soup, and without even checking I added a cup of water to the pan and heated it up on the stove. Turns out, this particular brand didn't require any water added. So as we were eating the finished product, we both noticed that something was off. She asked if I had added water and if the directions had called for it. To my everlasting embarrassment, I checked the can to discover my mistake. While I take pride in being able to cook a decent amount of things, I had messed up canned soup because I hadn't paid attention to the details. A story similar like mine can be used to readily exemplify the idea that details matter, and that they affect and even determine whether our worship flourishes or fails.

It will probably be preferable to accentuate the positive when preaching through this passage. Outlining it as we do below will underscore the goal of experiencing flourishing worship. The passage's main points don't flow out of the exact order of the paragraphs, so some jumping around may be necessary. Leaving the clues about Solomon's divided loyalty (1 Kings 7:1–12) until the end is advisable to bring the central point back into focus as the conclusion is made.

The key idea to communicate is that details determine if our worship flourishes or fails. The passage for this preaching unit can be outlined as follows to show what flourishing worship requires:

- Flourishing worship demands proper preparation—even in the details (6:1–10, 14–36; 7:15–51).
- Flourishing worship demands living out our loyalty—even in the details (6:11–13, 7:13–14; 7:1–12).

DISCUSSION QUESTIONS

1. What historical event does 6:1 call back to? What is the spiritual relevance to this project?

2. What is God's message to King Solomon as the construction gets underway?

3. Read 1 Kings 6:23–30, along with Genesis 3:24, Psalm 18:9–11, and Exodus 25:18–22. Who were the cherubim and what are they associated with?

4. What is the subject of 1 Kings 7:1–12 and why could it be negative commentary on King Solomon?

5. What is the probable symbolism behind the creatures made for the temple furnishings (7:25, 36)?

1 Kings 8:1–66

EXEGETICAL IDEA
The temple dedication not only celebrated Jerusalem as the center of the Israelite worldview, but also the intimate relationship between the Lord, his people, the temple, and the Davidic dynasty.

THEOLOGICAL FOCUS
Jerusalem as the cosmic center of Israelite worship testifies to the character of God and prepares his people, as well as all the peoples of the earth, for the "new cosmic" center following Christ's death, resurrection, and ascension.

PREACHING IDEA
Genuine worship is life-changing.

PREACHING POINTERS
The dedication of the temple in 1 Kings 8 is an awe-inspiring event where God and his people come together. The account places strong emphasis on God's glory and his glorious covenant promises. Later readers of this account, especially those of Ezra and Nehemiah's day, would have naturally compared the glory of the original temple with its replacement. Such a comparison led to disappointment for some (Ezra 3:11–13). Eventually the enthusiastic momentum of rebuilding dissipated and the danger of falling back into old habits would return (Neh. 13). This is why there is an emphasis on obeying God's law in connection with God's covenant with David. This worship wasn't dependent on a building achievement nor was it intended to be a one-time event. This was a time of national renewal and commitment to the Lord. The people of Solomon's day, the people of Nehemiah's day, and all the people who would come after were to be mindful of the obedient commitment that is essential to worship.

Jesus is the true fulfillment of the promises that are in view in this passage. He secured our forgiveness, provides our blessings, and is the basis of the hope we have for the future. All of those themes ought to be main ingredients in our worship. Now, there are a multitude of ideas about what makes *good* worship, especially within the American church. There are many different styles, practices, and preferences. This passage offers a pointed evaluation for all of our current forms. Seeking to create the right feelings, the right atmosphere, and a perfect production are all good things in and of themselves. Yet they should be secondary to the themes God highlights in his Word. When we gather to worship, is there an emphasis on presenting and celebrating who God is? Is there a call to obediently respond to what God has done? Genuine worship is an encounter with God that impacts who we are and what we do.

DEDICATION SPEECH (8:1–66)

LITERARY STRUCTURE AND THEMES (8:1–66)

The temple dedication can be broken down into the following scenes: (1) the processional (vv. 1–11), (2) Solomon's speeches (vv. 12–61), (3) Solomon's sacrifices (vv. 62–66). Solomon's speeches can be further divided—an address (vv. 12–21) and a prayer (vv. 22–61). Important themes include Deuteronomistic ideology and the Davidic covenant, and various ideals ubiquitous in the ancient Near East inform the message of the section.

- **The Processional (8:1–11)**
- **Solomon's Speeches (8:12–61)**
- **Solomon's Sacrifices (8:62–66)**

EXPOSITION (8:1–66)

This chapter recounts the grandeur of the temple's dedication. Beginning with a processional that was typical of the ancient Near East, the chapter proceeds to recount Solomon's famous words and the sacrifices that accompanied them. Thus, Solomon's legacy is intimately connected to this event, an event that finally realized a lengthy process of the Lord establishing a permanent house among his people. However, by knowing the ending of the story, when one reads this account, there is an inevitable connection to the final chapters of Kings.

The Processional (8:1–11)

Solomon celebrates the processional of the ark of the covenant into the temple, which establishes Jerusalem as the center of Israel's cultic life and the epicenter of its perception of the universe.

8:1–4. Here, Solomon assembles the leaders of the nation to himself, in Jerusalem. This group includes the elders, the heads of the tribes, and the leaders of the households of Israel. Also taking part in the ceremony were the religious leaders, namely the priests and the Levites. There, the ark of the covenant of the Lord (אֲרוֹן בְּרִית־יְהוָה) passes by the assembly, moving from "the city of David," or Zion, to the temple. In addition, all the sacred vessels were also transposed from the tabernacle to the temple.

Syntactical Analysis: The phrase מֵעִיר דָּוִד הִיא צִיּוֹן shows that "Zion" is equated with the "City of David," demonstrating that "Zion" need not refer to the city as a whole. In fact, according to Groves, the tendency of Kings is to use "Zion" to refer a section within the city (Groves 2005, 1020).

This entire processional, from the people involved to the vessels used, is reminiscent of other ancient Near Eastern processional ceremonies. In such ceremonies, a nation's deities were transported back into their respective worship site in a ceremonial fashion as a sign of renewed commitment. This processional, therefore, powerfully celebrates Israel's renewed commitment to Yahweh.

8:5–11. The text also recounts how copious sacrifices were offered—both cattle and sheep, too numerous to count (צֹאן וּבָקָר אֲשֶׁר לֹא־יִסָּפְרוּ). Such a qualification signifies another overlap with the larger ancient Near Eastern milieu. Yet the climax of this processional appears as the priests vacate the Holy of Holies. "And when the priests came out of the holy place, a cloud filled the house of the LORD" (1 Kings 8:10). To be more precise, the cloud was so

119

intense that the priests could not perform their duties (v. 11).

Such an image recalls Sinai, when the glory of the Lord descended upon the mountain and the tabernacle. However, the description here points to something deeper than merely contact with the past. Jerusalem has replaced Sinai as Israel's cosmic mountain, becoming the central location of Israel's perception of the world (Sweeney 2007, 132; Levenson 1985). Interestingly, such a perception would be reinforced when Jerusalem was miraculously saved from Sennacherib's forces during Hezekiah's reign (2 Kings 18–19) but erroneously foster futile sentiments of invincibility in Jeremiah's day.

The Cosmic Mountain

In antiquity, humanity's fascination with how the divine interacted with the physical realm often led to ideas of a cosmic mountain. Such a concept held that a mountain functions as the meeting place of the gods, the source of water and fertility, the battleground of conflicting natural forces, the locale where heaven and earth meet, and the locale where effective decrees are issued (Clifford 1972, 3). In other words, it was where the physical and spiritual realities gathered and where cosmic order was maintained. For Israel, "The cosmic mountain presents itself most dramatically in the beliefs surrounding Mount Zion. A hill between the Tyropoen and Kidron valleys in Jerusalem, it is overshadowed in the east by the Mount of Olives and in the west by another mountain . . . . This low and undistinguished mound is nonetheless called in the Bible the tallest mountain in the world, the place which God has chosen for his dwelling place, the place protected in a special way from enemies who can only stand at its base and rage, the place of battle where God's enemies will be defeated, the place where God dwells, where fertilizing streams come forth" (Clifford 1972, 3).

Solomon's Speech (8:12–61)

Solomon's address celebrates the intimate relationship that God's people enjoy with the Lord.

8:12–13. The particle אָז sets off verse 12, marking it as the next segment within the section. Put on the lips of Solomon (אָמַר שְׁלֹמֹה), the historian recounts the Lord's desire to settle "in the deep darkness" (בָּעֲרָפֶל)—a description that again recalls Sinai (Exod. 20:21) and reinforces the perception that the temple is the new cosmic center of the world. The Lord's house is also described as a "lofty" house (בֵּית זְבֻל), a place for his eternal residence (מָכוֹן לְשִׁבְתְּךָ עוֹלָמִים). However, the more important issue for verses 12–13 is the syntax. The Lord spoke (אָמַר) and Solomon acted (בָּנֹה בָנִיתִי). Consequently, Solomon is displayed as a paradigm of piety, and with this established at the onset of his speech, the text provides a lens for the following verses.

8:14–21. Verse 14 begins the meat of Solomon's speech. Turning to the crowd, the king addresses his audience and frames everything as a blessing to the Lord. Yet the nuances of the speech go deeper. On the one hand, Solomon subtly fixes the spotlight upon him. David may have desired to build a temple, but he was rebuffed (vv. 17–19). Instead, Solomon was established, currently sits on the throne, and has built the temple. All of this is a point of emphasis communicated by the string of first-person verbal forms (וָאָקֻם...וָאֵשֵׁב...וָאֶבְנֶה). In other words, the Lord has been faithful to Solomon and has established his promise through Solomon, not David.

On the other hand, Solomon also fuses in his prayer Davidic ideals with the traditions of the exodus. In verses 16 and 21, the exodus is referenced in a way that highlights the criticality of this moment. Since the time when the Lord brought Israel out of Egypt, he did not choose a place for his name, although he did choose the Davidic dynasty. Instead, Solomon's temple has resulted in that place of rest. In other words, the temple's dedication is presented as the culmination of a historical process, a process that began with the exodus and sees Solomon prominently standing at the end.

8:22–53. At this point, Solomon subsequently turns to face the altar of the Lord. He stretches out his hands heavenward (וַיִּפְרֹשׂ כַּפָּיו הַשָּׁמָיִם) only to quickly double down on the implications of the Davidic covenant. In verse 23, he proclaims the superiority of the Lord—declaring that there is none like him whether on the earth or in the heavens. He then quickly shifts the focus by means of two independent relative clauses back to the relational dynamics between the Lord and David. Thus, the syntax creates an impression that the superiority of the Lord is evidenced not merely in his character or general interaction with history. Rather, the Lord's superiority is also manifested in his unique benevolence to David's family.

However, such declarations are not just for the sake of declaration. They are for the sake of calling the Lord to action. The syntax of verses 23–26 is tight. Verses 23–24 establish the basis for the call to action in verses 25–26 (וְעַתָּה). Solomon is essentially saying, "There is none like you . . . and you have made these great promises . . . *so now* . . ." Solomon, the paradigm of piety, is seeking a reciprocation. So, the prayer takes a turn in verse 27. Many English translations render a contrastive particle to emphasize the verse's negative rhetorical question and highlight the irony of the whole endeavor. Nevertheless, Solomon persists and exhorts the Lord to turn his face and listen to his prayers (vv. 28–30).

As the prayer progresses, Solomon repeatedly offers scenarios that allude to specific curses found in Deuteronomy 28. Therefore, verses 31–53 assume a conviction, which incidentally exists at the heart of the Israelite worldview. Despite the Lord's awesomeness and transcendence, he will listen to his people, even at their lowest points. The only caveat is confession. Consequently, it seems that Solomon is anticipating the future, calling upon the Lord to commit to undoing the curses *so long as* the people take the proper steps.

8:54–61. Before closing his prayer, Solomon again turns and blesses the entire assembly. Verses 54–61, with verses 14–21, form a nice inclusio around verses 22–53. Blessings aimed at the gathered assembly bracket a call to action rooted in the Lord's relationship with the Davidic line. Yet where the first blessing praises the Lord for the Davidic covenant, the second rendition is more general and universal. In verses 54–61, the Lord is praised for the rest given that was executed perfectly in accord with what was spoken through Moses (v. 56). Moreover, Solomon exhorts the Lord to be consistent and to perpetuate the relationship inaugurated with Israel's forefathers. He calls him to not leave or forsake them so that their hearts and actions may be in tune with covenantal expectations (vv. 58, 61).[1] Solomon also implores that his words would be allowed to "draw near" to the Lord, for the sake of daily obedience and universal acknowledgment of the Lord's uniqueness (v. 60). All of this is theologically significant, for it creates the impression that there is a connection between covenantal fidelity, the Lord, and his people. In short, the fidelity of the Lord will affect the fidelity of the people.

Solomon's Sacrifices (8:62–66)

8:62–66. The celebration concludes, and the historian intimately connects the fates of the Davidic dynasty and the temple.

When Solomon is finished, he and "all Israel with him" offered sacrifices to the Lord (v. 62).

---

1   This nuance of purpose is created by a series of infinitives (לְהַטּוֹת...לָלֶכֶת...וְלִשְׁמֹר...לָלֶכֶת...וְלִשְׁמֹר). On the function of the infinitive, see John A. Cook and Robert D. Holmstedt (2013, 74–75).

The reader will quickly note the king's priest-like role in this context, a phenomenon that was common in the ancient Near East but troublesome within the Israelite system.[2] However, it is noteworthy that Solomon *and* all Israel offered the sacrifices. Could it be then that Solomon is given credit for the nation's participation? Yet verse 62 constitutes a circumstantial clause for verse 63. So, together they can read, "Now while the king and all Israel with him were sacrificing sacrifices before the Lord, Solomon sacrificed the sacrifice of well-being."

In the end, it seems then that Solomon did indeed carry out priestlike actions, which only contributes to the elusive characterization of Solomon observed throughout 1 Kings 1–11. What is beyond question is the emphatic celebration and abundance of the scene. The text informs us that a myriad of animals were sacrificed, and multiple types of sacrifices were offered, including the sacrifices of well-being, burnt offerings, and grain offerings. Thus, Sweeney (2007, 136) is on target when he alludes to the broad function of this celebration. A multifaceted celebration was necessary to consecrate the complex relationship between a holy God and his people.

> *Syntactical Analysis:* Verse 62 reads
> וְהַמֶּלֶךְ וְכָל־יִשְׂרָאֵל עִמּוֹ זֹבְחִים זֶבַח לִפְנֵי יְהוָה. This clause is subordinate to the main clause which begins in verse 63 with וַיִּזְבַּח שְׁלֹמֹה אֵת זֶבַח הַשְּׁלָמִים. According to Arnold and Choi, predication by a participle in circumstantial clauses often highlights a concurrent relationship (2018, 182–83).

Verse 65 draws the temple dedication scene to a close, and as it ends, the subtleties of verse 66 are important. Here the historian declares that the people departed "joyful and in good spirits because of all the goodness that the LORD had shown to his servant David and to his people Israel." This brings the emphasis upon the Davidic line and the Davidic covenant, which has permeated the entire dedication ceremony, back into focus. The historian makes it clear that the Davidic dynasty and the temple are essentially two halves of the same coin. They are inextricably linked, and their futures intertwined.

THEOLOGICAL FOCUS

The exegetical idea (The temple dedication not only celebrated Jerusalem as the center of the Israelite worldview, but also the intimate relationship between the Lord, his people, the temple, and the Davidic dynasty) leads to this theological focus: Jerusalem as the cosmic center of Israelite worship testifies to the character of God and prepares his people as well as all the peoples of the earth for the "new cosmic" center following Christ's death, resurrection, and ascension.

At the heart of 1 Kings 8 is a relatively simple equation: the heavenly realm is intersecting with the earthly realm, and Solomon is celebrating this with a lavish festivity typical of his day. Yet it's the details that give the passage its potency.

In this scene we see that Jerusalem supplants Mount Sinai as the cosmic mountain, and thus becomes the focal point of the Israelite worldview. Moreover, it symbolizes a central reality of the Israelite religious consciousness: the holy, creator God descends from his heavenly abode to nurture a relationship with his people, a relationship that has been conceptualized by the concept of a covenant. By implication, at the heart of this relationship are mutual expectations between the Lord and his people. What's important in this context is that Solomon seizes them in verses 22–53. The cumulative effect, therefore, is that one cannot read this passage and say that God is keeping his people at arm's length, hindered by a rigid system of rituals

---

2   For example, no priestly function is articulated in Deuteronomy's law of the king and Uzziah is famously punished because of his stubborn insistence in offering a sacrifice (2 Chron. 26:16–21).

and legal expectations. It's the opposite. It's a celebration of the mechanisms that allowed the Lord's people to get close to their suzerain. In other words, this entire scene powerfully testifies to the character of the Lord. The holy Creator seeks to break into the human experience to nourish the relationship he has with his people and, by extension, the world.

But let's not forget how this plays out canonically. According to the Lucan writer, at a critical juncture in his ministry Jesus "set his face" to Jerusalem (Luke 9:51). Why? Because there, at Israel's cosmic center, the incarnate God would be crucified and raised from the dead. But shortly thereafter, the writer begins to reveal how Jerusalem will fade to the background, as the gospel's movement will take it away from Jerusalem and into Judea, Samaria, and the ends of the earth (Acts 1:8). Thus, the Lucan writer is making a bold claim. No longer will a geophysical location be perceived as the "cosmic center" for the kingdom of God. Rather, the center will be a divine person by means of his Spirit dwelling in every believer, regardless of his or her nationality.

PREACHING AND TEACHING STRATEGIES

Exegetical and Theological Synthesis

The completion and dedication of the temple is one of the great highlights in Israel's history. God's presence had led them out of Egypt, into the Promised Land, and had guided them as they established their society. Now the people could properly offer their worship to the Lord according to his design in his Law. All the pieces were set in place for God's people to commune with him in his city, at his temple. As was fully appropriate, Solomon leads the people in paying extravagant homage to the Lord. Through ritual sacrifices, speeches of dedication, and prayer, God's people celebrate their intimate communion with the Creator of the universe.

Preaching Idea

Genuine worship is life-changing.

Contemporary Connections

What does it mean?

What does it mean that genuine worship is life-changing? It is not too difficult to imagine what this means for our present-day context. Most churches heavily invest their efforts into creating impressive weekend worship services. Music, messages, and the overall atmosphere are carefully constructed to help the congregation worship the Lord.

But what if there's more to consider than just our Sunday morning services? What if our worship involved a greater commitment than one hour a week on one day of the week? What if our worship looked more like . . . football fans?

For every Sunday during each fall, you can spot what team an individual cheers for. They proudly display their team's flag or bumper sticker. Many shell out significant portions of their hard-earned money to purchase the jersey of their favorite player. Then there are the committed fans that paint their faces and wear funny hats on game days. They even set their entire calendars to revolve around the team's schedule. They are willing to make sacrifices to make sure they can attend the games in person or at least catch it on TV. They take great pleasure in their team's success and deeply despair when the losses pile up.

Those fans "worship" their teams in ways that encompass their entire lives. Our worship of God ought to look the same in that respect. All of our lives—from our finances to our calendar to our attitudes—can reflect our commitment to the Lord. We should not shy away from the whole-life calling that Christ makes to all of his followers.

Is it true?

Is it true that genuine worship is life-changing? If we understand genuine worship to be more of a complete commitment as described above, then it is inherently life-changing. In Romans 12, Paul calls for a worship commitment that involves presenting our "bodies as a living sacrifice" and being "transformed by the renewing our mind." That is a standard that involves our whole lives, not just part.

I met a friend in college who had only recently given his life to Christ after living rebelliously for much of his life. He told me that one of the first things he did after coming to Christ was to trash all his secular music. He literally burned all of his CDs, as I recall. That story shows a) how long ago the early 2000s were, and b) how serious my friend was about guarding the influences over his life. That may not be a step every new Christian should make. It is a good example, though, about how when we decide to worship Christ, it will affect and change our lives.

Now what?

If it is true that genuine worship is life-changing, how should this change our lives? How should genuine worship affect who we are and what we do? This passage records a religious ceremony to end all religious ceremonies. All the preparations have been made and a great celebration is unleashed as Solomon, the priests, and the people dedicate this temple to the Lord. Every aspect of this event is meant to honor God for who he is and what he's done. They are remembering God's provisions and his promises and are committing themselves to obeying him.

Arranging a beautiful worship celebration is certainly a way to apply this story to our day. But as we mentioned above, there's a commitment aspect to this passage that should impact our entire lives. Genuine worship will change us.

Inwardly, we can be transformed when we *meditate on what God has done*. The temple dedication was filled with references directing the people's attention to God's past actions. Almost three thousand years later, with God's Word in hand, we should also worship by reflecting on what God has done. We have a complete picture of God's redemptive plan for mankind that centers on the divine son of David whose name is Jesus. Romans 12:1–2 encourages us to "be transformed by the renewing of our mind" as part of our worship. Practically speaking, we might try journaling and using personal devotions that incorporate more of the Scripture. Taking some time off for a spiritual retreat can help remove distractions and meditate on the wonderful grace and love God has shown us in Christ.

Worship ought to change us on the outside as well. We can *be a mirror of God*, reflecting the glory of God to others. Scripture tells us that the world around us will see who God is when we show love for others and follow the Spirit's leading (John 13:34–35; 2 Cor. 13). Those principles have countless possibilities for living out. A few would include volunteering at a soup kitchen, helping a motorist who is stranded on the side of the road, or striking up a conversation with your coworker who has seemed down for a while. Those kinds of everyday opportunities are worship encounters where we can reflect the goodness of God to others in need.

Creativity in Presentation

During my (Lee's) most recent trip to the dentist, I couldn't help but notice a poster hanging up promoting some sort of teeth-whitening treatment they were offering. The poster prominently displayed the before and after pictures of some anonymous patient's mouth accentuating the difference the whitening had on their smile. Diet and health companies often use similar marketing to promote their systems. I know people whose lives have improved because of their experience with various programs.

Worship can have that same kind of effect to an even greater extent. As we encounter God's presence, consider his promises, and are empowered by his Spirit, we can live changed lives that honor him.

Using visual examples like the ones I saw in my dentist's office will provide a nice lead-in to the idea that genuine worship changes us. Many people like to share and hear about life-changing experiences in other ways too, whether it be trips around the world, starting a family, meeting a hero, having a career-defining conversation, and the like. The fact that things as trivial as a meal can be hyperbolically referred to as "life-changing" demonstrates that this is fertile ground for using something transformational on one level to build a bridge to the greater transformation available when we worship our Lord.

Genuine worship will change us. When we encounter the presence of God, we can't help but be humbled. As we meditate on God's promises as found in His Word, it infuses us with hope. If we depend on the Spirit, we will be empowered to live lives that honor and glorify Jesus. As indicated below, the preacher can find natural extensions of these lessons from 1 Kings 8 in New Testament passages. Our context is different now that God's presence dwells in us, but the general truths remain the same.

The key idea to communicate is that genuine worship is life-changing. The passage for this preaching unit can be outlined as follows:

Our lives will change when:

- We respond to the presence of God (8:1–21, 62–66; John 4:23–24);
- We reflect on the promises of God (8:14–21, 54–61; John 14:1–6; 15:9–16; Heb. 4:14–16); and
- We rely on the Spirit of God (8:22–53).

DISCUSSION QUESTIONS

1. What are some of the ways this ceremony is celebrating the nation's commitment to the Lord?

2. What was the effect of God's presence filling the temple (8:6–11)?

3. What are some of the theological truths that Solomon emphasizes in his prayer to God (8:22–30)?

4. What is the purpose of Solomon's description of future scenarios in which the people might find themselves in 8:31–53?

5. How might this celebration inform our worship?

1 Kings 9:1–9

EXEGETICAL IDEA

The Lord endorsed the construction of the temple, but quickly discussed the implications of the dynasty's willingness to live by the covenantal ideal.

THEOLOGICAL FOCUS

The vitality of God's kingdom is renewed with every generation that chooses to learn important lessons and adhere to God's expectations.

PREACHING IDEA

Our accomplishments *for* God won't last without faithfulness *to* God.

PREACHING POINTERS

The original readers of this passage would have heard, seen, and felt the negative consequences that God promises included if his people failed to obey him. Their forefathers neglected faithfulness to the Lord, and now they were picking up the pieces. As they repaired the ruins of the once-great city of Jerusalem, there could be little doubt that God had meant what he said about "turning away" from God's commands and precepts. It was to their national shame that the foreign nations had destroyed their cities and exiled their people. The glory of Solomon's era was long gone because the nation and its leaders had failed to be faithful.

We do not face the same disaster as the nation of ancient Israel did then, but our mission is much the same. Like they were, we are called to faithfully obey God's Word. At the core of our calling as disciples of Jesus is the concept of faithfully passing on the good news of Jesus Christ. Many passages—including Matthew 28:18–20, 2 Timothy 2:1–2, and Titus 2:1–8—underscore this mission. We are called to make disciples by teaching and modeling the way of Jesus to others, especially the next generation. Failure to do so will not bring national disaster because biblically speaking, God's people are no longer defined in terms of a political state. But failure to be faithful to God's calling will bring dishonor to ourselves by weakening the body of Christ. It is not enough to merely attach the label "Christian" to ourselves and think it is enough. Nor is it good enough to build sizable churches and ministries. With all the ministry and service accomplishments we might achieve, it is essential that we pair those with faithfully embodying the mission of God and equipping the next generations to continue God's work. To ensure that our accomplishments leave a lasting legacy, we must be faithful to God in all aspects of our personal and public lives.

THE LORD'S SECOND APPEARANCE (9:1–9)

LITERARY STRUCTURE AND THEMES (9:1–9)

The Lord's second appearance to Solomon happened after the completion of his building campaigns. Exactly when and where, the text is not clear. What's clear, however, is the comparison set up by the clause "just as [the Lord] appeared to him at Gibeon" (כַּאֲשֶׁר נִרְאָה אֵלָיו בְּגִבְעוֹן; v. 2). The second encounter explicitly recalls the first, and with this, the different tone between the two visitations becomes clear. This scene pivots at verse 6, when the singular subject gives way to a plural subject.

- *Addressing Solomon (9:1–5)*
- *Addressing the Royal Line (9:6–9)*

EXPOSITION (9:1–9)

After the dedication of the temple, and in response to his prayer, the Lord revisits Solomon again. However, the tone is very different from the initial visitation. Here, the focus is upon the dynasty faithfulness to the covenant. And by explicitly linking any dynastic covenantal infidelity to punishment, the two institutions are inextricably linked.

Addressing Solomon (9:1–5)

9:1–5. The Lord verifies that he will honor Solomon's requests of chapter 8, only to quickly move to covenantal fidelity.

Verse 1 states that Solomon's second divine encounter happened after the king successfully built the temple, his palace, and everything else. We are not told when this second encounter happened, and verse 3 answers any question that remains about whether the Lord would honor Solomon's requests of chapter 8: "The LORD said to him, 'I have heard your prayer and your plea, which you made before me; I have consecrated this house that you have built, and put my name there forever; my eyes and my heart will be there for all time.'"

Verse 4 is set off syntactically by the disjunctive marker וְאַתָּה. Moreover, verse 4 begins to get to the real issue: covenantal fidelity. This is accomplished by two lengthy conditional clauses (vv. 4–9). The first conditional clause (vv. 4–5) discusses a positive scenario: if Solomon will mirror his father and exhibit a life that is fully committed to the Lord's expectations, then the Lord will ensure dynastic stability. The words used in this clause are both comprehensive and vivid. Thus, there is no ambiguity here. If there is to be a Davidic line upon the throne in Israel, then fidelity to the Lord's covenant will be critical.

Addressing the Royal Line (9:6–9)

Speaking to both Solomon and his sons, the Lord clearly lays out the cursed state of affairs that awaits the dynasty if they choose infidelity to the covenant.

9:6–7. The second conditional clause begins in verse 6, alongside an observable shift in the grammar. The subject of the verbal forms is now plural, addressing both Solomon and his sons (וּבְנֵיכֶם). Moreover, these verses address the negative scenario (versus the positive scenario in verses 4–5): if David's line turns from the Lord by not keeping the covenant or by chasing after foreign gods, then the Lord will cut his people from the land, cut down their temple that he just consecrated, and render his people cursed in the eyes of humanity. It's a very clear statement about what expectations Solomon and his sons should have if the covenant is abandoned.

9:8–9. Verses 8 through 9 linger upon this negative scenario, dwelling upon the potential shame of Israel. Here there may be a wordplay that recalls 2 Samuel 7. In the Samuel text, the writer played off the semantic range of "house," בֵּית. Essentially, David asked to build the Lord a house (i.e., temple), to which the Lord essentially responded, "I don't need a house [i.e., temple], but I'll build you a house [i.e., dynasty]." One may sense some of the same semantic blurring in 1 Kings 9:8–9. The house that lay in ruins (i.e., the temple) symbolizes the house (i.e., the dynasty) that has been disposed.

Clear is how the ruins of Jerusalem will bear witness to the dynasty's choices. Jerusalem's ruins will testify how the dynasty and the nation forsook the one who brought then out of Egypt for other gods. Their broken allegiance will be the reason why the Lord "caused all this calamity to come upon them" (v. 9).

example, the psalmist of Psalm 78 declares that the deeds of the Lord will not be withheld from the next generation (78:4). The first eight chapters of Proverbs read as a lecture aimed at enlightening an unnamed "child." And the entirety of Deuteronomy, being Moses's final exhortation, intends to teach a new generation about the covenantal ideal. In the New Testament, Paul exhorts his Corinthian congregation to heed the lessons of ancient Israel's wilderness wanderings and choose to live a life of spiritual purity so that their future can be secure (1 Cor. 10).

Consequently, these examples suggest that there is a conviction across the canon that perpetuating memories and lessons across generations is critical for the vitality of the faith. Thus, the future of God's kingdom is renewed with each generation taking up the mantle of obedience. It's not secured by the presence of a building, which is a lesson that God's people failed to realize.

THEOLOGICAL FOCUS

The exegetical idea (The Lord endorsed the construction of the temple, but quickly discussed the implications of the dynasty's willingness to live by the covenantal ideal) leads to this theological focus: The vitality of God's kingdom is renewed with every generation that chooses to learn important lessons and adhere to God's expectations.

The atmosphere surrounding the Lord's second appearance to Solomon is very different from the first. The first was very celebratory. Conversely, the second is terse. It quickly gets down to business, which addresses not only Solomon's fidelity to the covenant but also the fidelity of those that come after him. Thus, intergenerational dynamics are a hallmark of this second encounter.

The importance of intergenerational influence is not unique to this passage. At various points throughout Scripture, the importance of the next generation is recognized. For

PREACHING AND TEACHING STRATEGIES

Exegetical and Theological Synthesis

Unlike the previous chapter, the specific physical context of 9:1–9 is not important to the author of 1 Kings. The exact setting fades into the background so as to put proper emphasis on what God said to Solomon. This hyperfocus on the message is fitting because the Lord stresses just how important it is that Solomon and his descendants remain faithful to his covenant. If the king and the people obey his laws and worship him exclusively, then they will prosper. If they stray by going after other gods and neglecting the law, their glorious temple will be destroyed and shame will cover the people.

Preaching Idea

Our accomplishments *for* God won't last without faithfulness *to* God.

Contemporary Connections

What does it mean?

What does it mean that our accomplishments *for* God won't last without faithfulness *to* God? When Billy Graham's career as a preacher and evangelist began to take off, he and his wife Ruth sought the counsel of someone who might give them good advice about what to expect when ministry and fame mixed. That person was Nell Sunday, whose husband Billy had been one of the America's most famous revivalists a generation before. Nell urged them to make sure Ruth made it a priority to parent their children. Nell herself had not done so while their three sons were growing up, instead plunging completely into organizing and assisting Billy's ministry. By the time they were adults, all three of their sons had become embroiled in some of the very scandals Billy was famous for preaching against. Their oldest even committed suicide. Nell strongly advised the Grahams to make sure Ruth cared for their children away from the spotlight because it was the Sundays' greatest regret that their children had struggled so much. The Grahams heeded that advice, as they navigated their own family journey down the path of world-wide ministry.

That example is what it looks like when we set out to do great things for God but neglect faithfulness to him in significant ways. Billy Sunday's ministry was far-reaching and many decisions for Christ were made along the "saw-dust trail." But his success is not without blemish. Graham, on the other hand, has not only left his own mark on American Christianity but his legacy lives on through many of his children and grandchildren and the Christian service they participate in.

Is it true?

Is it true that our accomplishments *for* God won't last without faithfulness *to* God? If we achieve great things for God, but don't remain loyal to him and his Word, will all of our achievements disappear? God gave Israel and her kings plenty of chances over several centuries after Solomon, but eventually he did mete out his promised punishment when they remained committed to their faithlessness. For us on a personal level, there's no absolute answer. Only time will tell how God's sovereign plan will work itself out. God in his grace may allow some of our accomplishments to last beyond us in spite of our inconsistency. But it is more likely than not that our legacy will be irreparably tarnished when our hypocrisy reveals itself.

Jim Bakker and Jimmy Swaggart built thriving ministries and found fame proclaiming the gospel on television. Ted Haggard did the same and was at one time the president of the National Association of Evangelicals. All now are known not for their faith but for their moral failures. First Corinthians 3:10–15 (NIV) offers a complementary New Testament passage to 1 Kings 9 when it reminds us:

> By the grace God has given me, I laid a foundation as a wise builder, and someone else is building on it. But each one should build with care. For no one can lay any foundation other than the one already laid, which is Jesus Christ. If anyone builds on this foundation using gold, silver, costly stones, wood, hay or straw, their work will be shown for what it is, because the Day will bring it to light. It will be revealed with fire, and the fire will test the quality of each person's work. If what has been built survives, the builder will receive a reward. If it is burned up, the builder will suffer loss but yet will be saved—even though only as one escaping through the flames.

Our accomplishments for God won't truly last through eternity unless we are faithful to Him as loyal servants.

Now what?

If it's true that our accomplishments *for* God won't last without faithfulness *to* God, what should we do to cultivate faithfulness on the one hand and avoid faithlessness on the other hand? This passage records a hopeful warning from God, if there is such a thing. There is the promise of hope and an affirmation of his previous promises to David's line. There is also the warning of the judgment that will come should they not keep up their end of the covenant.

From this hopeful warning, we can learn a couple lessons. First, *be careful to be faithful, especially when you are successful.* Solomon had just completed one of his life goals with the completion of the temple. Now God was urging him to remain faithful and encourage his descendants to remain faithful as they moved forward. As we find success in life, we also need to be very intentional about obeying God. We cannot let success blind us to what God wants of us. Across many different sports, the term "trap game" is often used to describe how danger often accompanies victory. Within their season, a particular team will often get on a winning streak and then face a lesser opponent. That particular contest is often labeled a "trap game" because all the expectations are for victory, and the players themselves may not quite prepare as hard or put in the extra work they did before. The strong temptation is to underestimate the lesser opponent and neglect the efforts that brought success in the first place. To avoid failing in our "trap games," we need to be faithful, especially when we are successful.

The second lesson we can take away from this is to *be careful to be faithful by equipping others to carry on God's work.* God's warning is not just for Solomon. It's an ongoing command that would apply to all his descendants. The implied expectation of this passage is that each generation will instruct the next on what it means to be loyally devoted to God and his law. This implied expectation is explicitly stated in other places in the Old Testament and continues in the New Testament (Deut. 6; Judg. 2; Matt. 28:10–20; Eph. 4:11–16; 2 Tim. 2:2; Titus 2:1–5). We are called to leave a legacy after we are gone. It is not a legacy of great accomplishments necessarily, but one where we have guided people in walking in the truth and being devoted followers of Jesus. If we serve God in a practical way, we should be bringing someone along with us to learn the ropes and be ready to take over when our time is done.

The popular family-friendly musical drama film *The Greatest Showman* (directed by Michael Gracey, 2017) offers a great illustration of this in its third act. This fictionalized account of P. T. Barnum's life concludes with Barnum (played by Hugh Jackman) turning over the reins of the circus to Phillip Carlyle (played by Zac Efron). Whether it's a circus or a church—or a church that's run like a circus—we would be wise to equip others who can carry on God's work after us.

Creativity in Presentation

The illustrations and examples above offer plenty of good and creative ways to better communicate the principles in this passage. Another unique out-of-the-box idea would be to introduce the message by displaying a series of pictures of closed churches.

Whether closed, abandoned, or even re-purposed, pictures of those shuttered buildings or facilities offer a strong visual showing the temporal nature of ministry. If background stories for several of the photos are able to be ascertained, that would add to the power of the illustration as a cautionary tale: "After a season of successful kingdom work, this is what happened to this church—and now look at it." An effective preacher will bring it to bear on his own context and audience, casting the rhetorical but challenging questions, "What will our church look like in twenty-five years?

Where will we be, and how can we avoid the fate of these churches?" Those are ideas many church members probably don't think through very much. But they are important ideas that remind us of the key idea to communicate that our accomplishments *for* God will not last without our faithfulness *to* God.

The passage for this preaching unit can be outlined in the following points:

- God blesses our faithfulness in our success (9:1–5).
- God opposes our faithlessness in our success (9:6–9).

DISCUSSION QUESTIONS

1. What are the similarities and differences between this second visit from the Lord in 1 Kings 9 and Solomon's interaction with him in 1 Kings 3?

2. What is God's favor dependent on, according to 9:4–7?

3. How does 1 Kings 9 preview what would happen later on in 2 Kings 24:1–4, 19?

4. Who are some personal positive examples of faithful people who've left good legacies for Christ? Who are some negative personal examples?

1 Kings 9:10–28

EXEGETICAL IDEA
Solomon's policies sought to fulfill geopolitical ambitions, and in turn produced several realities that affected the dynamics of Israel.

THEOLOGICAL FOCUS
Solomon's policies testify to a timeless responsibility of leadership: how to balance traditional values with a responsibility to grow and innovate.

PREACHING IDEA
On the path of success, watch out for the potholes!

PREACHING POINTERS
Solomon pursues progress, growth, and innovation in this passage. These things would have been far-off goals and dreams to the returned Jewish exiles rebuilding their nation. Survival would have been at the top of their minds more than success, with all the work that needed to be accomplished.

That difference between the eras would have actually been advantageous to the wise reader of that day. Many would have been dreaming of "making Israel great again," but astute observers could point to passages like this one and warn of the red flags that come with success. Its practical, detailed accounts of Israel's business are more than just bookkeeping records. It reveals just how tricky leadership can be in times of success. Solomon deals with diplomatic relationships and returning favors with King Hiram. He orders more building projects and makes decisions about enlisting people from his kingdom into labor and military service. One can read of those decisions and see cracks in the facade that will become obvious later. One can also read this in context of God's blessing and the king's faithfulness (v. 25). Both readings can be true. The point is that leading often involves walking a fine line between compromise and courage.

No matter how positively or negatively we want to read it, this passage is a stern warning against blindly pursuing prosperity. Many people aspire to leadership, and every nation/business/ministry pursues success. Are we wise enough to recognize the dangers when we've reached the top? Success will not protect us from mistakes. In fact, more success brings more responsibility. And failing to keep up our responsibilities will undermine our success and undo all the good we accomplish. As we pursue and achieve success in our ventures, we ought to be mindful of the pitfalls and potholes that hinder us along the way.

MORE ROYAL ENDEAVORS (9:10–28)

LITERARY STRUCTURE AND THEMES (9:10–28)

First Kings 9:10–28 can be broken into three sections, whereby the first (9:10–14) and the third (9:26–28) bracket a middle section that's concerned with "the account of labor" (דְּבַר־הַמַּס; 9:15–25). Hiram, king of Phoenicia, appears again in the first and third sections, but here his parity relationship with Solomon is concerned with ventures more diverse than just building the temple.

- ***The Sale of Territory to Hiram (9:10–14)***
- ***The Account of Labor (9:15–25)***
- ***Hiram and Solomon's Maritime Venture (9:26–28)***

EXPOSITION (9:10–28)

In these verses, the geopolitical ambitions of Solomon are put on display. However, they are presented in a way that continues to reveal the social and theological problems associated with such ambition.

The Sale of Territory to Hiram (9:10–14)

Solomon sells northern land to Hiram in conjunction with a new business venture, based on the success of previous ventures.

Syntactical Analysis: The Hebrew particle אָז is important. It recalls the phrase מִקְצֵה עֶשְׂרִים שָׁנָה and marks the start of the main clause. Thus, relative clauses of verses 10–11, one of which is unmarked, signify that allocation of the Galilean cities occurs at the end of a twenty-year period defined by Solomon's building campaigns.

9:10–11. These verses in the NRSV reads as follows. "At the end of twenty years, in which Solomon had built the two houses, the house of the Lord and the king's house, King Hiram of Tyre having supplied Solomon with cedar and cypress timber and gold, as much as he desired, King Solomon gave to Hiram twenty cities in the land of Galilee." Important here are the phrases "At the end of twenty years . . . as much as he desired." Together, they constitute a lengthy preparatory statement for the main idea, Solomon's liquidation of northern tribal allotments. It does not appear that the transaction was indicative of any complex repayment system or a need for capital, as some have suggested.[1] Rather, it seems that previous ventures are invoked to remember a lengthy and prosperous relationship as a way of legitimizing new business ventures.

9:12–14. Hiram paid 120 talents of gold for the land (v. 14), but more importantly, why was Hiram disappointed in the allotment (vv. 12–13)? The Plain of Acco and the Galilean regions are certainly not pristine real estate, but there were worse territories.[2] Unfortunately,

---

1 Fensham alludes to this when he says, "[Solomon] needed gold for his treasury, and for both wood and gold he ceded the cities to Hiram" (Fensham 1960, 59). Fensham draws parallels between the biblical text and the Alalakh tablets and argues that this account is a standard covenantal transaction. DeVries assumes Fensham but suggests that Solomon's transaction with Hiram may have been over a border dispute that did not compromise the territory of Asher (DeVries, *1 Kings*, 132).

2 The Plain of Acco and the Galilean regions: The Hebrew literally reads "in the land of Galilee." This ambiguity allows three possible regions: the Plain of Acco, upper Galilee, and lower Galilee. Both lower and upper Galilee are

very little is clear. What is clear is that Hiram felt slighted, an emotion clearly revealed in verse 12, reinforced by the sarcastic question of verse 13 and, possibly, by the term "Cabul"—if the suggestion of wordplay is in order.[3] Nevertheless, verses 26–28 suggest that the relationship between the Phoenician and Israelite kings was not too adversely affected.

The Account of Labor (9:15–25)

This portion of text testifies to various dynamics associated with Solomon's building campaigns.

9:15–21. The account of Solomon's labor force (דְבַר־הַמַּס) begins in verse 15 via a disjunctive clause, marking a shift in focus. The witness of the various textual traditions suggests a complicated history, but its location here suggests a subtle criticism of Solomon's policies.

Verses 15–25 can be understood as a unit that digresses on key terms. The account of Solomon's labor force was necessary to complete the king's building campaigns. These campaigns featured prominent cities such as Gezer (v. 15), which was presented by Pharaoh after his conquest as a gift to his daughter (שִׁלֻחִים לְבִתּוֹ), and other important cities (vv. 17b–19). Naturally, then, labor was a critical commodity as the success of the campaigns depended on it. Satisfaction came from indigenous Canaanites, the remnants of those that were not *ḥērem*-ed: Amorites, Hittites, Perizites, Hivites, and Jebusites.[4]

9:22–23. Verse 22 is set off by another disjunctive clause, and according to this verse the conscription of the indigenous Canaanites differed from how the "sons of Israel" were used. The sons of Israel were not made into slaves (לֹא־נָתַן שְׁלֹמֹה עָבֶד), but "men of the army" (כִּי־הֵם אַנְשֵׁי הַמִּלְחָמָה). The last half of verse 22 shows a list of nouns, and it's possible to understand the listing as a specification of the "men of the army." Thus, the sons of Israel became the king's infantrymen, charioteers, and leaders of military divisions. Verse 23 also divulges that the sons of Israel were appointed to other administrative positions, as leaders of the supervisors (שָׂרֵי הַנִּצָּבִים) who oversaw the royal projects (עַל־הַמְּלָאכָה לִשְׁלֹמֹה), 550 projects to be more specific. Therefore, it's likely that the sons of Israel served in a more honorable sphere of society, either in civil or military service. Yet it's still difficult to rectify these statements with the previous declaration that the king conscripted labor from "all Israel" (5:13[27]). It's possible to see the previous statement as a general one and this statement as a more specific catalog.

9:24–25. These verses are very difficult. The restrictive adverb אַךְ opens verse 24, but it's not clear what verse 24 is clarifying: the immediately preceding verses, which catalog Solomon's administrators, or verses 16–17? If so, then verse 24 is very intrusive. If verses 24–25 are read immediately after verse 16, then does this imply that Pharaoh's daughter left Jerusalem (מֵעִיר דָּוִד) for Gezer, which was

---

characterized by hills and valleys of varying heights and widths. Sufficient rain, however, run down the hill and into the valleys, establishing adequate farmland there. The Plain of Acco sits immediately west of Galilee but is characterized by swampy terrain due to the lack of efficient drainage from the Galilean hills in the Mediterranean Sea. With its rough natural coastline, if the Plain of Acco is the reference, it is understandable why Hiram would have been disappointed (Rasmussen 2010, 37–38).

3   The Hebrew כָּבוּל may be the product of an elaborate play on words: the כְּ preposition fixed to the negation בַּל may have been crossed with גְּבוּל, a common word for "territory." Thus, something akin to "like nothing territory."

4   On the concept of *ḥērem* (חֵרֶם), see Versluis 2016.

given to her (v. 16)?[5] Her palace that Solomon constructed was referenced in 1 Kings 7:8, but there is no specific location mentioned. What is the relationship between verses 24 and 25? Where did Solomon go thrice per year to offer a variety of sacrifices? Many scholars understand this to be an allusion to the three major pilgrimage festivals in the Israelite religious calendar (e.g., Sweeney 2007, 146; Wiseman 2008, 137–38), but if so, why not mention the "house of the Lord"? Most importantly, why do these verses appear where they do?

Definitive answers to these questions are not possible. It seems prudent, therefore, to understand these verses as a return to specific details about Solomon's building campaigns after a short digression that detailed Solomon's labor force.

Ezion-geber

Named in six distinct contexts (Num. 33:35–36; Deut. 2:8; 1 Kings 9:26; 22:48; 2 Chron. 8:17; 20:36), Ezion-geber defies identification. Nelson Glueck identified it with modern-day Tell el-Kheleifeh situated on the Gulf of Elath. However, this identification has been severely criticized. Other proposed sites include Jezirat Faraun, a small coastal island near Elath (Lubetski 1992, 2:723–25). The location of Ophir is even more cryptic. Suggestions have ranged from the African coast, around the Arabian Peninsula, and to India, but none are conclusive (Baker 1992, 26–27; Wiseman 1996, 849–50).

Hiram and Solomon's Maritime Venture (9:26–28)

9:26–28. Hiram was a critical partner to Solomon's geopolitical ambitions.

According to verses 26–28, Hiram embarked on a maritime venture with Solomon along the coast of the Sea of Reeds (יָם סוּף), at Ezion-geber. Ezion-geber was "in the land of Edom" (בְּאֶרֶץ אֱדוֹם), and the site of Ophir (אוֹפִירָה) may be a staging site or the origin of the gold. Either way, this notation suggests Israelite influence in the region, a mark of geopolitical ambitions.

Verse 27 implies that Hiram's people were critical to the success of the venture, but Sweeney (2007, 146) understands this as Hiram exerting his dominance over Solomon in response to the less-than-desirable land transaction. But this need not be the case. Ultimately, 1 Kings 9:10–28 is a segment of text bracketed by Solomon's relationship with Hiram.

THEOLOGICAL FOCUS

The exegetical idea (Solomon's policies sought to fulfill geopolitical ambitions and in turn produced several realities that affected the dynamics of Israel) leads to this theological focus: Solomon's policies testify to a timeless responsibility of leadership: how to balance traditional values with a responsibility to grow and innovate.

Sweeney (2007, 146) argues that this section of text has been molded by its overall arrangement and strategic mention of Egypt to critique Solomon. "The result is a portrayal of Solomon as king who has transformed Israel into a nation like Egypt of the exodus tradition, who allows Canaanites to remain in the land, who turned Israelite cities over to a Phoenician/Canaanite king, and who sends his people back across the Red Sea to amass wealth from Egypt contrary to [Deuteronomic] law" (Sweeney 2007, 146–47). While the emphasis upon the passage's rhetoric and criticism of Solomon is laudable, the notion of a kingdom "like Egypt" seems overextended. Rather, the criticism is more general.

---

5   There is a very complicated textual-critical problem associated with verses 15–25. A variety of textual witnesses have certain elements of these versions linked to other portions of 1 Kings 1–11. For a brief statement, see Sweeney (2007, 141–43). Again, this reality testifies to specific intentions shaping the message of 1 Kings 1:1–14:20.

Apparently in pursuit of new business ventures, Solomon sold off land to finance a maritime start-up. Moreover, his political relationship with Egypt opened possibilities to expand and fortify his infrastructure. Yet in pursuing these endeavors, the dynamics within Israelite society changed. Thus, the text speaks to a delicate balance of leadership: preserving traditional values and the advancement of the institution that they lead. Where is the line where the integrity of the institution is compromised by a responsibility to develop and innovate?

According to the larger narrative, Solomon was unable to hold this delicate balance. As will be shown in later chapters (ch. 12), his policies produced a burden from under which the northern tribes sought to escape. And this leads to a question: How can leaders avoid emulating such mistakes? It's interesting that the text declares that Solomon went to worship the Lord three times per year. If this is the text's way of indicating that one's connection to the Lord is the critical ingredient, it's also an indication that the act of worship does not guarantee wise decision-making. Solomon failed, and so there must be something more.

PREACHING AND TEACHING STRATEGIES

Exegetical and Theological Synthesis

At face value, there doesn't seem to be much theology to analyze in 1 Kings 9:10–28. These paragraphs describe business ventures, construction projects, and policy details. Through these details, one gets a sense of how King Solomon was leading Israel in a time of fresh prosperity. Clearly, these pursuits were benefiting his power and his nation's wealth. The question lingers, however, of whether there are any disadvantages to all this growth and development. As time will tell, the table is being set for later developments that reveal the negative consequences of how his leadership affected his people.

Preaching Idea

On the path of success, watch out for the potholes!

Contemporary Connections

What does it mean?

What does it mean to watch out for the potholes when on the path of success? Whether we are seeking personal or professional success, we should be mindful of the drawbacks that come along with that pursuit. Even when we are achieving our goals, we need to be realistic about the potholes that are found along the road of prosperity.

For instance, when we are considering a promotion or major career move, it is natural to be enticed by a bigger paycheck or greater notoriety. But what will it cost in terms of stress, health, and personal relationships? Sometimes more is not better. The same applies to ministry as well. The newest method may be embraced by all the other churches around us, but does that mean it is the true solution to exponential growth? The latest fad may indeed help numerical or financial growth. But does it fit with the core of what Jesus has called us to do? Those questions are critical as we evaluate the choices we make on the path of success. Otherwise, we are likely to run right into one of the potholes that will sneak up on us and cause us problems we had not foreseen.

Is it true?

Is it true that there are potholes to avoid when on the path of success? Being on top is never as glamorous as it may seem. This has always been true. Alexander the Great legendarily wept when he realized he had no other lands to conquer. World-famous actors have the private details of their lives splashed across the headlines of supermarkets all over the country. Urban Meyer became a college football coaching icon when he won championships with the Florida Gators and Ohio State. He had to retire from both schools not because of failures on the field, but because in his pursuit of winning his health deteriorated, and many of the organizational decisions he made with players and coaches were widely criticized. Even when he tried coaching in the NFL, his personal and professional decision-making undermined his tenure, which lasted less than a year.[6] From politics to entertainment to business to our personal lives, success is always accompanied by pitfalls that can damage what we have worked so hard to attain.

Now what?

If it is true that the path of success includes potholes, what can we do to avoid them? Being able to spot coming potholes in the road is the key to avoiding them when driving. The same is true for us personally too. If we are aware of the dangers, we can navigate around them and avoid any harm or damage we would otherwise encounter.

But how can we spot these figurative potholes? One good practice is to *get advice from wise advisors*. We need to surround ourselves with people of integrity who can speak from experience to issues we are facing. This can take the form of having a mentor who has the freedom to be blunt and honest with us. Friends and contacts we make while networking in our field can also help us evaluate our decisions. Another practice to embrace is to *learn how to self-evaluate*. A good self-evaluator will be someone who listens to wise counsel, as mentioned above. But they will also be the kinds of people who proactively make changes without having to be told. They will set goals and honestly assess where they need to improve when they fall short. To properly self-evaluate, keep victories and failures in proper perspective—not focusing too much on either. Good self-evaluators will reveal themselves by the choices they make. They might decline certain opportunities for the sake of their family. They may take a step back from their position or move down the chain of command when they determine their personal wellness is being adversely affected. Abraham Lincoln with his "team of rivals" offers a positive example of a leader open to counsel from differing perspectives. He had enough self-awareness to invite criticisms and viewpoints that could help him make the best decisions in tumultuous times.[7]

Creativity in Presentation

In the summer of 2018, Domino's Pizza announced a new initiative aimed at "saving pizza" from bad roads. They began filling potholes in roads across the country in an effort to help their customers and their drivers make it home with their pizzas without incident. "Have you ever hit a pothole and instantly cringed?" Russell Weiner, president of Domino's USA explains, stated in a press release: "We know that feeling is heightened when you're bringing home a carryout order from your local Domino's store. We don't want to lose any great-tasting pizza to a pothole, ruining a wonderful meal."[8] Domino's knew rough roads were an impediment to their business and creatively marketed their idea. Who doesn't veer around a rut, or recoil every time they hit a hole they just can't avoid?

---

6   John Breech, "Urban Meyer Fired by Jacksonville Jaguars as Controversies Rock His First Season as Head Coach," CBS News, December 16, 2021, https://www.cbsnews.com/news/urban-meyer-jacksonville-jaguars-fired-controversies-first-season-head-coach.

7   Lincoln admirably involved a number of his fiercest political rivals in his administration and on his cabinet. Doris Kearns-Goodwin, *Team of Rivals: The Political Genius of Abraham Lincoln* (New York: Simon & Schuster, 2005).

8   Aarthi Swaminathan, "Domino's Pizza Unveils U.S. Infrastructure Project Filling Potholes," Yahoo! Finance, June 11, 2018, https://finance.yahoo.com/news/dominos-pizza-unveils-u-s-infrastructure-project-filling-potholes-130802630.html.

As jarring and damaging as those fissures can be when we are traveling down the road, there are potholes of a different kind that can be just as harmful as we are traveling down the road of success in life. We may think we are taking a ride down "easy street" but there are plenty of challenges that accompany prosperity. Decisions become more impactful, promises more meaningful, and results are more consequential. The more successful we become, the more we need to recognize the weight of our choices, words, and actions. Achieving our goals can be a wonderful thing, but we can't be blinded by our ambitions and neglect doing what God wants us to do.

The key idea to communicate is the warning to watch out for potholes when on the road of success. The passage for this preaching unit can be outlined as follows:

- Pothole #1: The Cost of Doing Business as a Success (9:1–14, 26–28)
  - Love of Wealth (Deut. 17:17)
  - Relational Missteps
- Pothole #2: The Unintended Consequences of Success (9:15–25)
  - Foreign Influence
  - The Need for Further Security
  - Societal Shifts

DISCUSSION QUESTIONS

1. How does this account of Solomon's new business ventures mesh with the previous section's emphasis on remaining faithful to the Lord?

2. How did the foreign King Hiram help Solomon with his projects? How does Solomon repay him (vv. 10–14)?

3. What does the introduction of Pharaoh's daughter, along with the mention of non-Israelites in the land, foreshadow the potential of in Solomon's life?

4. What compromises might we face when we find ourselves enjoying prosperity?

5. What positive note is given about Solomon in verses 25–26?

6. What are some pitfalls or potholes that we encounter as we are pursuing success?

1 Kings 10:1–29

EXEGETICAL IDEA
The prestige and opulence of Solomon left the Queen of Sheba overwhelmed, yet it alluded to large fractures in Solomon's moral foundation.

THEOLOGICAL FOCUS
The pursuit of excellence may compromise us or our communities if left unchecked.

PREACHING IDEA
Success is a spotlight that magnifies our glory and our shame.

PREACHING POINTERS
The last couple chapters have recorded some of the true high points of Israel's history. The temple's completion was a crowning moment in their spiritual history. In this section, Israel is entering their peak economic period. Yet warning signs have been popping up all along and can no longer be ignored. Solomon is transgressing God's commands and leading the nation toward trouble. The later readers of this and the preceding chapters would feel this tension. As they rebuilt their nation after the exile, they would naturally compare their progress to this previous season of national glory. A wiser, more critical mind would ask a more basic question: Should they seek a return to this kind of power and glory? Deuteronomy 17:14–20 stood as a warning against the extravagance described here. The constant cry of the post-Solomon prophets was for faithfulness and justice on the part of God's people (Isa. 58; Jer. 22; Hos. 4; Mic. 6). First Kings 10 is a record of Israel's glory, wrapped in reminders of God's expectations for his people when they are prospering.

These principles aren't hard to find in the New Testament either. Jesus often gave warnings against loving and pursuing money and wealth (Matt. 6:19–24; Luke 18:18–25). Paul encouraged sacrificial generosity as part of a larger message that we should be selfless in all we do, because of what Jesus has done for us (2 Cor. 5:14–15; 8:1–9:15; Phil. 2:1–11). Success and prosperity are not overtly condemned in the Bible. But what is condemned is the pursuit of success at the expense of God's desires. We are warned that achieving all our wildest dreams may not be all we think it will be. Is the degree I'm pursuing in line with God's true calling on my life or is it just to pad my resume? Are the expectations we set for our kids realistic and in line with God's Word? Have the career decisions I've made been about me or about making an impact for Christ? Success can bring us fame and renown, but it also can reveal our weaknesses and character defects.

SOLOMON'S LEGACY (10:1–29)

LITERARY STRUCTURE AND THEMES (10:1–29)

This chapter focuses on the international prestige of Solomon, but it's divided into two distinct sections. The first, which is demarcated by a notation that the queen of Sheba came to Solomon (v. 1) and went home (v. 13), discusses the visitation of the anonymous queen of Sheba (vv. 1–13). The next section is more generalized and describes the level of opulence associated with Solomon's reign. Together, these verses create a picture of Solomon that alludes to the complexity of his character.

- **The Queen of Sheba Visits (10:1–13)**
- **Solomon's Opulence (10:14–28)**

EXPOSITION (10:1–29)

Solomon's fame reaches a global level, and so he kindly obliges to accept an audience from the queen of Sheba. She is overwhelmed with her experience. However, the presentation of Solomon's wealth and fame alludes to the so-called "Law of the King" in Deuteronomy 17

(17:14–20). Therefore, there is more than what meets the eye.

The Queen of Sheba Visits (10:1–13)

The queen of Sheba comes to inquire many things of Solomon, and she left overwhelmed but fully satisfied.

10:1–5. It's not clear where the kingdom of Sheba was located. Some connect its location with Ethiopia (Ullendorff 1968), but others connect it with the ancient kingdom of Saba, near modern-day Yemen (Kitchen 1995; Sweeney 2007, 149; Wiseman 2008, 139). The latter option is the more likely, particularly since it enjoys the support of archaeological and Assyrian evidence.

What is clear is the occasion for the queen's visit. The "fame of Solomon" (10:1; שֵׁמַע שְׁלֹמֹה) was the impetus for the visit.[1] And she arrives with the expressed purpose of testing (נסה) Solomon with (חִידוֹת)—the NRSV and many other versions render this term "hard questions," which is a bit too generic. According to Wilson, the word חִידָה has two discernible senses: a

---

1   The Fame of Solomon. A peculiar textual phenomenon surrounds verse 1. The NRSV translates the Hebrew, "When the queen of Sheba heard of the fame of Solomon (the fame due to the name of the LORD)." The parenthetical phrase attempts to make sense of the awkward לְשֵׁם יְהוָה, which the editors of the BHS suggest be deleted under the apparent conviction that this phrase was likely a marginal gloss that inadvertently made its way from the margin into the body of the text. Second Chronicles 9:1 and the Targum tradition are cited as evidence. Nevertheless, the phrase לְשֵׁם יְהוָה as it stands is not impossible to explain grammatically. Wiseman articulates one possible example when he reads a nuance of specification (*IBHS*, §11.2.10d), "with reference to the name of the Lord" (Wiseman 2008, 139). The implication of such a decision is significant because it informs the overall tone of this passage. One the one hand, the impressiveness of Solomon is on full display. However, the Lord intriguingly recedes to the background. He is barely mentioned (vv. 5, 9, 24), and when he is mentioned, Solomon quickly resumes functioning as the object of emphasis (see below). If the phrase in verse 1 is not original, the foregrounding of Solomon is that much more potent and לְשֵׁם יְהוָה is likely a scribal attempt to insert the Lord into the equation. Interestingly, Wiseman interprets the phrase שֵׁם יְהוָה as a reference to the temple, meaning that Solomon's reputation is linked to his status of the temple-builder (Wiseman 2008, 139).

riddle and "difficult speech requiring information" (Wilson 1997, 2:107). Given the entourage and cargo described in chapter 10, the queen is about more than just entertainment. Instead, the sense of the passage appears to be making inquiries designed to determine the king's capabilities. Wiseman suggests that this is no "wisdom contest," but a test to determine Solomon's abilities in trade (Wiseman 2008, 139). Sweeney (2007, 150) sees the interchange as typical of royal interchange in the ancient Near East. Regardless, the text is clear that Solomon performed beyond expectations. Nothing was left unanswered (v. 3), and after the interchange "there was no more spirit" left in the queen (v. 5). The queen came with the intention to exhaust Solomon mentally, but she was the one who ended up exhausted.

10:6–12. Throughout the chapter, the narrator's voice dominates, except in verses 6–9 where the words of the queen are recounted. She cannot help but declare that Israel is blessed to have Solomon as their king, and she's convinced that the tales of Solomon do not do justice to reality. In a testament to the pervasive effect of Solomon upon all levels of society, happiness is declared across the board.

The historian concludes by highlighting that 120 talents of gold, precious stones, and an unprecedented amount of spices were offered to Solomon. Yet as if it was not enough, verses 11–12 detour to remember the joint venture with Hiram and the unprecedented amount of imported wood used in Solomon's building campaigns. Such

The Visit of the Queen of Sheba to King Solomon by Sir Edward John Poynter. Public domain.

descriptions lead the reader into the next portion of the chapter.

Solomon's Opulence (10:14–29)

The opulence of Solomon's wealth recounts elements of Deuteronomy 17:14–20, suggesting that a subtle criticism may in view.

10:14–29. Back in verse 11, the historian began to detail the economic success of the king. Indeed, the historian has discussed the success of Solomon previously, but the details in this passage are overwhelming. Gifts from Solomon, gifts to Solomon, commercial success, international relations, precious metals, and other valuable raw materials are all documented in awesome quantities on the heels of each other. The result is an image of a monarch with inexhaustible resources and influence. Moreover, the cultural sophistication of Israelite society is celebrated by the details of the ornate decor throughout the palace complex. And as if the picture did not do justice, the historian offers an explicit statement of summarization in verses 23–25. Solomon was second to none, and everyone knew it. In braggadocious fashion, "the whole earth" (כָּל־הָאָרֶץ) came to secure an audience, bringing even more valuables in the process.

Nevertheless, there's more than meets the eye, particularly if Deuteronomy 17:14–20 is considered. First, chapter 10 ends with a notification that Solomon amassed a formidable chariot corps (vv. 26–29), and that those horses were from Egypt and Kush. Second, Solomon was apparently so successful in his commercial ventures that silver, precious stones, and valuable lumber were so ubiquitous that they became the norm. Indeed, an impressive picture. Yet in Deuteronomy 17:14–20, three specific prohibitions are articulated. The king shall not (1) "acquire many horses for himself, or return the people to Egypt in order to acquire more horses" (v. 16); (2) "not acquire many wives for himself" (v. 17a); nor (3) amass silver and

gold "in great quantity" (v. 17b). Consequently, it's difficult not to make a connection. In this chapter, one reads about Solomon's violation of at least two of the three prohibitions. And if Sweeney (2007, 152) is correct in suggesting that this episode leads into 1 Kings 11, then the third violation is imminent. Thus, the placement of verses 26–29 solidifies a subtle criticism that has been building throughout this section of text.

THEOLOGICAL FOCUS

The exegetical idea (The prestige and opulence of Solomon left the Queen of Sheba overwhelmed, yet it alluded to large fractures in Solomon's moral foundation) leads to this theological focus: The pursuit of excellence may compromise us or our communities if left unchecked.

Oddly, the Lord is largely absent from this section of text. The nouns יְהוָה and אֱלֹהִים appear only in four (or five) passages.

- In verses 5 and 12, יְהוָה is referenced in passing—as an absolute noun in a construct chain with בֵּית.
- Verse 24 subordinates its reference to the feats of Solomon. Indeed, the grammar stresses that the king's wisdom originated with God, but this admission appears deep within a passage devoted to describing Solomon's prestige.
- Verse 9 gives more attention to the Lord, but even here the grammar ensures that Solomon remains firmly in the picture: "Blessed be the LORD your God, who has delighted in *you* (Solomon) and set *you* (Solomon) on the throne of Israel! Because the LORD loved Israel forever, he has made *you* (Solomon) king to execute justice and righteousness" (emphasis mine).

Adding to this, the narrator talks about Solomon but attributes no quotations to the king; Solomon says nothing. Yet this chapter revolves tightly around him and his exploits. And the centrality of Solomon is furthered by noting that he is the object of so much action. The queen came *to test him* (vv. 1–2), to discuss *with him* "all that was on her mind" (v. 2). She gave *him* gold and other valuables (v. 10). Moreover, amazing quantities of gold *came to* Solomon (v. 14) by merchants, dignitaries, and his own business ventures (vv. 15, 20).

Together, these features display an interesting truth: the pursuit of excellence, success, and garnering the respect of others is innocuous. However, given that this passage relegates the Lord to the background in passing references and that the shadow of Deuteronomy 17:14–20 looms ever larger, there's a need for a larger perspective. Consequently, while Solomon's pursuits appear innocent and celebratory on the surface, moving beyond the immediate thrill by reading the account in the context of Scripture as a whole allows problems to become visible. It's worth considering if our pursuits eventually open us up to forces that will ultimately undo us or the community in which we live.

PREACHING AND TEACHING STRATEGIES

Exegetical and Theological Synthesis

Solomon's fame is growing and Israel is flourishing. His personal success is described in the account of his interaction with the queen of Sheba (vv. 1–13). His professional success and the prosperity of his kingdom are outlined in verses 14–29. All of this success is described in lavish terms. But where does God fit in all of this? How does this fit with the warnings in God's law that too much success will be a bad thing? When one reads this in light of Deuteronomy 17:14–20, some problems in this season of success become quite evident.

Some people naively assume that because they are successful, God must be pleased. That may be true, or it may be false. It may even be partially true, where God is pleased with parts of our lives, but not with everything we are doing. The one thing many do not realize about success is that it brings as much scrutiny as it does glory. Your wisdom, skills, and abilities may be lauded by many, but your flaws will get exposed just as much. If we are hot-tempered, we need to understand that we are likely to be triggered more often as the stakes get higher. If we are prone to cut corners, we should prepare to be tempted to cheat more and more as the pressure rises. Our penchant for greed will not be satisfied by the next big commission. Our flaws will not be hidden by success; they will only be amplified.

Preaching Idea

Success is a spotlight that magnifies our glory and our shame.

Contemporary Connections

What does it mean?

What does it mean that success is a spotlight that magnifies our glory and our shame? The greater the level of success one reaches, the greater the glory and the greater the scrutiny. In October of 2018, Amazon announced it was raising its minimum wage for all U.S. employees to $15 per hour, in response to public criticism about its wage disparity.[2] The online retailer knew it could silence a lot of detractors and do a lot of good for their workers by giving more of their profits to their employees. Their example stands in contrast to Walmart. The retail giant has long been criticized for treating their workers poorly while padding the pockets of the Walton family.[3] To their credit, they did also raise the starting raise for all employees—but it

---

2 Sara Salinas, "Amazon Raises Minimum Wage to $15 an Hour for All US Employees," CNBC, October 2, 2018, https://www.cnbc.com/2018/10/02/amazon-raises-minimum-wage-to-15-for-all-us-employees.html.

3 "How Rich Are the Waltons?", accessed July 7, 2020, http://changewalmart.org/how-rich-are-the-waltons.

was only up to $11 an hour, and coincided with an announcement that they were closing more than sixty stores.[4] Both Amazon and Walmart are terrific American business success stories. But only one was willing to make the changes so that their workers could earn a living wage, whereas the other has seemed much more concerned about profits.

No company will be a perfect model of this biblical principle in a positive sense. The business world does offer a plethora of examples for the negative side of this lesson. From the business world to politics to even our home life, everyone is after success in one form or another. It can be a wonderful thing when it is achieved. Yet we must not ignore the fact that success shines a bright light on who we are, revealing the good and the bad.

Is it true?

Is it true that success is a spotlight that magnifies our glory and our shame? Power, prestige, and success certainly reveal the character of those who obtain them. Writing in the early 1880s about Abraham Lincoln, author Robert G. Ingersoll stated, "Most people can bear adversity; but if you wish to know what a man really is give him power. This is the supreme test."[5]

As Solomon's kingdom prospers in greater and greater ways, the regime's shortcomings grow in significance as well. Success will inherently bring applause and approval. But what many don't expect is how it also magnifies flaws.

Now what?

If it is true that success is a spotlight that magnifies our glory and our shame, how can we best prepare ourselves for this revealing evaluation of our character (who we are) and conduct (what we have done)? How will we respond to success? When we move from middle management to the executive board, we ought to treat those under us as we had hoped to be treated before our promotion. When we reach retirement later on in life, what we do with our 401(k) funds says a lot about us. Are we buying all the creature comforts and toys we've always coveted? Or are we generous, wise, and looking to invest in things that matter for eternity?

One surefire way to keep this in check is to *be faithful in small things*. If we develop good habits before we attain all our goals and earn all the success we are dreaming about, we will do well. If we are faithful, generous, and selfless behind the scenes, when the spotlight does come, it will reveal moral strength and not moral weakness. Jesus's words from Luke 16:10–11 (NIV) certainly apply: "Whoever can be trusted with very little can also be trusted with much. . . . So if you have not been trustworthy in handling worldly wealth, who will trust you with true riches?" We may not ever enjoy the glorious material prosperity that Solomon did, but if not, we also will not likely experience the sharp downfall Solomon and Israel did later on either. Be faithful in the small things—and then when the big opportunities come, we will have the habits established to honor God at those times as well.

Creativity in Presentation

If available, the use of a spotlight would be an obvious way to creatively illustrate the lesson of preaching idea. Shine it on an individual member of the congregation and threaten to leave it on them the entire service. One could use cameras and the projection screen to similar effect. Most people might enjoy the little ploy for a bit but will undoubtedly grow uncomfortable

---

4   Abha Bhatt`arai and Todd C. Frankel, "Walmart Said It's Giving Its Employees a Raise. And Then It Closed 63 Stores," *Washington Post*, January 18, 2018, https://www.washingtonpost.com/news/business/wp/2018/01/11/walmart-to-raise-starting-hourly-wage-to-11-offer-paid-parental-leave/?utm_term=.19ae6c5f33f6.

5   "Nearly All Men Can Stand Adversity, But If You Want To Test a Man's Character, Give Him Power," Quote Investigator, accessed July 7, 2020, https://quoteinvestigator.com/2016/04/14/adversity.

and self-conscious the longer the act goes. Speakers may even want to point this out. Why do we get self-conscious the longer the spotlight is on us? The reality is, it that the light will focus on every move we make and reveal every flaw or idiosyncrasy we have. If a spotlight or camera close-up is not realistic, use the auditorium lighting to make the same sort of point. The lights allow the people to see the speaker clearly and also allow them to see when they unknowingly have their shoe untied, hair sticking up, shirt untucked, or a stain on their pants.

One could naturally use pop-culture stories of bands, athletes, or actors who found stardom and then broke down because they couldn't handle success. The stories of musicians like Keith Moon (English drummer for the rock band The Who), Kurt Cobain (American front man of the rock band Nirvana), and R. Kelly (American R&B singer) would exemplify how tragedy, controversy, and trouble will often plague those who reach the pinnacle of success.

The story of 1 Kings 10 is not all negative, of course. But the lesson below the surface is the one to take to heart. Not only does success draw attention to our accomplishments, but it also will put our flaws in full view.

The key idea to communicate is that success is a spotlight that magnifies our glory and our shame. The passage for this preaching unit can be outlined as follows:

- God-given success can enhance our personal reputation (10:1–13).
- God-given success can enhance our professional standing (10:14–29).
- God-given success can lead us into compromise.
  ◦ The accumulation of wealth (vv. 10–13, 14–16)
  ◦ The focus on Solomon's power (vv. 1–5, 18–20)
  ◦ The building up of the nation's commercial and military resources (vv. 21–29)

◦ The clear standard of God's will (Deut. 17:14–20)

DISCUSSION QUESTIONS

1. How would you characterize the interaction between King Solomon and the queen of Sheba? What was the result of the visit?

2. What point might the author be making by circling back to the subject of Solomon's deals with King Hiram in 10:11–12?

3. What kind of impact does Solomon's leadership have on his nation (vv. 14–29)?

4. How many of the prohibitions of Deuteronomy 17:14–20 does Solomon violate just in this chapter?

5. What kind of warning does Solomon's violations serve about pursuing such glorious success?

6. What are some ways we are tempted to compromise when we are successful?

7. What are some ways we might resist that temptation to compromise?

DISSOLUTION OF THE UNITED MONARCHY
(1 KINGS 11:1–14:20)

The fourth and final section of this major literary unit in Kings is 1 Kings 11:1–14:20, which describes the dissolution of the united monarchy. This fourth section may be divided into three preaching units: first, Solomon's demise (11:1–43); second, schism between Israel and Judah, including the reasons for the schism (12:12–24); third, the reign of Jeroboam I, which involves the shortcomings of Israel's first dynasty and more. Most importantly, this section sets the stage for the comparative history that follows.

1 Kings 11:1–43

EXEGETICAL IDEA

Solomon received a stinging indictment that ultimately rendered him an "evil king," but the expected judgment was pacified by the legacy of David.

THEOLOGICAL FOCUS

The Lord is both just and gracious in his interactions with his people and their leaders.

PREACHING IDEA

God's grace and God's judgment are not mutually exclusive.

PREACHING POINTERS

Solomon's reign began with so much promise, but it ends unceremoniously in shame and strife. Spiritual compromise led to his downfall, and the nation itself would never be the same. While they were several generations removed, the people rebuilding in the postexile and Second Temple periods were living with the consequences of Solomon's failures of leadership. His life would remind them of the importance of spiritual loyalty, especially as they evaluated their own leaders. Their hope was that a son of David would arise who would meet God's ideals and standards.

Jesus is the ultimate fulfillment of what the Davidic kings were supposed to embody. He changed the paradigm as the divine Messiah. For us, national exile is not a potential punishment. Faithfulness is still expected, even though the nature of the consequences is different. God has expectations for us, which he has outlined in his Word to indicate what we should and shouldn't do. If we sin, God still offers us abundant grace and forgiveness. But he does not promise the absence of any consequences. We might face jail time for our crimes and ruin close relationships because of our offenses. At the same time God disciplines us when we get out of line, he also graciously calls us to repentance. God desires to correct us and help us grow. He wants the thief to no longer steal, the cheater to no longer cheat, and the drunk to no longer drown in the bottom of a bottle. And he provides us the power to overcome our weaknesses and failures through the Holy Spirit (1 Cor. 6:9–11; Eph. 5:18–20). God's grace and judgment are not mutually exclusive, and they still have bearing on our daily lives. Our eternal hope is founded on the fact that they were both put on display at Calvary when God revealed himself as perfectly just and perfectly gracious. It is in light of that reality that we can now live into the mission God has given us.

SOLOMON'S DEMISE (11:1–43)

LITERARY STRUCTURE AND THEMES (11:1–43)

First Kings 11:1–43 is one of the most important chapters in all the Old Testament. It recounts the specific indictments leveled against Solomon and the consequences that followed. Ultimately, this chapter argues that Solomon began a process that would eventually bring about the split between the northern and southern kingdom. However, the legacy of David casts a long shadow across the geopolitical landscape. First Kings 11:1–43 can be subdivided into three sections: Solomon's indictment (vv. 1–13), Solomon's adversaries (vv. 14–40), and Solomon's death notice (vv. 41–43).

- *Solomon's Indictment (11:1–13)*
- *Solomon's Adversaries (11:14–40)*
- *Solomon's Death (11:41–43)*

EXPOSITION (11:1–43)

As one of the most critical chapters in the book of Kings, not to mention the Old Testament as a whole, 1 Kings 11 recounts the tragic downfall of Solomon. His covenantal infidelity is linked to his numerous marriages, and his adversaries are discussed. Most importantly, we are introduced to the man who would take away most of the kingdom from David's family. However, cutting across this tragedy is the legacy of David, which ensures that a small portion of the kingdom will remain for the Davidic dynasty.

Solomon's Indictment (11:1–13)

Solomon receives a stinging indictment that is graciously pacified by the legacy of David.

11:1–10. The indictment of Solomon follows a general logic. The king loved foreign women who turned his heart away from the Lord. This angered the Lord to the extent where judgment had to come (foreign women ➔ apostasy ➔ anger of the Lord ➔ judgment). More specifically, Solomon brazenly "loved many foreign women" with whom Israel was commanded not to intermarry (vv. 2–3). "Clinging" to these women, there were also three hundred concubines in the mix, and together they collaborated to compromise the king's allegiance to Yahweh, his resources, and his energy. According to verses 7–8, Solomon built high places (בָּמוֹת) for the pagan gods and goddesses in the region, all of which secured the indignation of the Lord. This is particularly shocking given Solomon's previous encounters with the Lord (v. 9). Most importantly, and most tragically, Solomon's actions secured the evaluation that "Solomon did . . . evil in the eyes of the LORD," as he did not follow the commands as his father David (v. 6). This is a remarkable statement given all the accomplishments of the king in the previous chapters. However, as we have seen, it has not been without warning.

Syntactical Analysis: Verse 11 exhibits an emphatic predicate construction: קָרֹעַ אֶקְרַע. The direct object is "the kingdom" (הַמַּמְלָכָה), and the prepositional phrase מֵעָלֶיךָ finishes the clause. The next clause is syntactically linked by expressing the purpose of tearing (וּנְתַתִּיהָ לְעַבְדֶּךָ), "so that I may give it to your servant." This specific syntax connects this passage with others in the Old Testament: 1 Samuel 15:28; 28:17; 1 Kings 11:31; 14:8; 2 Kings 17:21.

It's tempting to see Solomon's indictment here as a product of an inability to harness one's sexual urges. However, the collaboration of the verbs "to love" (אהב) and "to cling" (דבק) points to a deeper indictment. In certain contexts, these verbs appear together to speak to fierce allegiance to Yahweh and his ideals (e.g., Deut. 11:22; 30:20; Josh. 22:5). Thus, Solomon's infractions are spiritual. By loving foreign women and clinging to them (versus Yahweh), the writer is revealing that Solomon's international policies, which were built upon treaties and alliances, put the community at risk by introducing deities that would ultimately compete for allegiance earmarked for the Lord. In other words, Solomon's method of rule and leadership was problematic. It violated divine decree, and, by implication, subjected the people to poisonous influences. Consequently, the full force of judgment upon this royal house is the only logical outcome.

11:11–13. However, in an act of "unfathomable grace," the narrator reveals that the full force of judgment will neither be experienced by Solomon nor be taken to its logical extreme (Maier 2018, 886–87). The text shows clear causation (v. 11). Covenantal infidelity produced judgment—the tearing away of the kingdom to give it to another. Yet "for the sake of David" and "for the sake of Jerusalem," the kingdom will be torn from the hand of Solomon's son, not from Solomon himself. This too is a remarkable statement that is set off by the Hebrew syntax (אַךְ־בְּיָמֶיךָ לֹא אֶעֱשֶׂנָּה). The legacy of Solomon's father, long after his death, is still protecting the nation that he worked so hard to forge. In fact, this pacifying dynamic will be revisited periodically throughout the account.

Solomon's Adversaries (11:14–40)

Solomon's adversaries are some of the mechanisms used by the Lord to bring judgment in the wake of the king's covenantal infidelity. However, the fullness of judgment is offset by the legacy of David.

11:14–25. Verse 14 begins with וַיָּקֶם, which is sometimes translated causatively with verses

1–13. So, the NRSV and NIV read, "Then the LORD raised up." Such translations make explicit what is otherwise implicit. There is no explicit causative relationship between verses 1–13 and verses 14–40, but the juxtaposition, particularly with the stinging indictment of verses 1–13, implores such a relationship. The adversaries—Hadad, Rezon, and Jeroboam—are external mechanisms by which the united monarchy comes undone.

Both Hadad and Rezon are called adversaries (שָׂטָן), which should be understood in a terrestrial sense (Hamilton 1996, 986). They were geopolitical foes who actively worked throughout Solomon's tenure to undermine Israelite ambitions (v. 25). Yet, the association of both Hadad and Rezon with Israel began with an action performed by David's administration. Hadad, who was of the "royal house of Edom," fled to Egypt when Joab established a military presence in Edom. Hadad, with others, found refuge in Egypt, even finding "great favor" in Pharaoh's eyes (וַיִּמְצָא הֲדַד חֵן בְּעֵינֵי פַרְעֹה מְאֹד) and marrying into the family. This signified a diplomatic relationship between Egypt and Edom. Moreover, it's possible that this political alliance helped sway the Pharaoh into letting Hadad return (v. 22) upon the event of David's death (v. 21).

Rezon was an outcast, and, like David, the leader of a group of men defined by a particular social stigma (שַׂר־גְּדוּד). According to verse 24, and similar to Hadad, Rezon's adversarial role transpired in the wake of David's "killing." The text is unclear whom David killed, but the nearest antecedent for "them" is the "men" gathered to Rezon. It seems, then, that Rezon, fugitive from King Hadadezer of Damascus (v. 23), assumed the leadership role of a raiding party after David took down some of their members.

11:26–40. The final adversary is Jeroboam. While his description lacks the term שָׂטָן, it's clear that his role was similar to that of Hadad and Rezon. Jeroboam's efforts to disrupt Israel, however, were far more successful. Verse 26 tells us that he rebelled against Solomon (lit., "he raised his hand against the king"; וַיָּרֶם יָד בַּמֶּלֶךְ). What's more, Jeroboam's adversarial role enjoyed prophetic sanction.

Jeroboam is described as a "servant of Solomon" (עֶבֶד לִשְׁלֹמֹה) and a "man of valor" (גִּבּוֹר חָיִל). However, he was also a self-made member of the royal administration. His lineage was that of Ephraim, but the text reveals that Solomon "observed the young man" and was apparently impressed with his work ethic (v. 28). The king then promoted him to oversee the forced labor over the northern tribes.

> *Syntactical Analysis:* Verse 31 includes the phrase הִנְנִי קֹרֵעַ אֶת־הַמַּמְלָכָה. The Hebrew conveys a sense of immediacy and suggests that the "tearing of the kingdom"—that is, Israel's rebellion—is either already underway or on the immediate horizon.

Jeroboam's future was revealed to him outside of Jerusalem when he encountered the Shilohite prophet, Ahijah. The prophet was wearing a new garment, which was promptly torn into twelve pieces (vv. 29–30). Ten pieces were given to Jeroboam as a sign of his imminent kingship over Israel. Moreover, the prophetic oracle reveals that Jeroboam was offered a dynastic promise akin to David's in 2 Samuel 7 (vv. 37–38). Interestingly, throughout the entire encounter not one word is attributed to Jeroboam. In a way, then, Jeroboam recalls Solomon of 1 Kings 1. Jeroboam is a passive character who merely receives what has been given to him.

The rationale for dividing up the kingdom in two is offered in detail in 1 Kings 11:31–38. But these verses represent one of the most grammatically convoluted passages in Kings.

Without a doubt, the history of development behind the book of Kings (see Introduction) and textual history are largely responsible. Nevertheless, the final form preserves several reasons for the preservation of Judah vis-à-vis the establishment of Israel, suggesting a community that has refined its historical awareness through time. According to the oracle, one tribe shall remain for Judah—because of Jerusalem, the city that the Lord chose; David, the Lord's servant who was also chosen by the Lord; and the territorial dominion promised to David.[1] This is a shocking revelation, as the covenantal logic should dictate that the kingdom be forfeit. Solomon failed to live properly like his father David, forsaking the Lord to worship the pagan deities of Canaan. Yet because of the legacy of David, which is closely associated with Jerusalem, judgment is pacified.

Of course, when Solomon discovered this turn of events, he "sought to kill Jeroboam." However, Jeroboam fled to Egypt, like Hadad, gaining refuge with Shishak until the death of Solomon.

Solomon's Death (11:41–43)
11:41–43. Solomon enjoys an honorable death, despite being an "evil king."

These verses will be common throughout the rest of Kings. They constitute a formal death notice, an integral component to the regnal formula (see Introduction). They reveal that while Solomon is ultimately judged to be an "evil king" (v. 6), he enjoyed a peacefully and honorable death.

THEOLOGICAL FOCUS
The exegetical idea (Solomon received a stinging indictment that ultimately rendered him an "evil king," but the expected judgment

---

1   The notion of territorial dominion arises most pointed in verse 36 and the Hebrew term נִיר. This term is often, but incorrectly, translated as "lamp" (see Schreiner, 2014; 2017). For example, the NRSV reads for 11:36, "Yet to his son I will give one tribe, so that my servant David may always have a lamp before me in Jerusalem, the city where I have chosen to put my name."

was pacified by the legacy of David) leads to this theological focus: The Lord is both just and gracious in his interactions with his people and their leaders.

First Kings 11 is arguably one of the most important chapters in the Old Testament. As a watershed moment, 1 Kings 11 shows how the nation could never go back to the way things were largely because of one leader's proclivity to sin. In fact, the implications of the participial construction in verse 29 implies that at the time of Ahijah's proclamation, the schism was already unfolding. Yet 1 Kings 11 is also about a critical question that not only drove the historical account but also forces the reader to wrestle with the character of the Lord. Why was Judah preserved in the face of such egregious covenantal infidelity?

To answer this question, one should consider the intersection of justice and grace. On the one hand, justice demanded that the Davidic dynasty be punished. Solomon failed to be faithful to the covenant, which meant that Davidic succession should have been severed (1 Kings 9:1–9). On the other hand, the legacy of David loomed large. Thus, in the face of all judicial logic, the Lord graciously allowed the fidelity of one man to trump the infidelity of his kin.

Consequently, the picture that emerges is that of a God who defies any simplistic characterization, as if judicial logic or intimate relationships are all that matter. Rather, it's a God who dynamically interacts with his people through a mysterious rubric that is fundamentally just and gracious. Yet there is another reality that appears in this scene. Actions matter, even late in life. Moreover, actions can potentially undo the good of previous actions. The fact Solomon's history ends with such a negative picture, emphasized by the statement that Solomon's wives turned his heart away in his old age (v. 4), suggests this.

PREACHING AND TEACHING STRATEGIES

Exegetical and Theological Synthesis

First Kings 11 begins by expounding on the extent of Solomon's sin. It ends by describing the resulting judgment of God. Solomon is condemned for serious and blatant rebellion against the Lord. The cracks in the facade that have been previously noted have now become deep fissures (1 Kings 4:26–28; 10:14–29; cf. Deut. 17:14–20). He has amassed great fortune, military power, and now a multitude of foreign wives. These relationships in particular lead him to spiritual compromise. His sins were not merely sexual in nature; rather, they are heart-level failings that mark a divided allegiance to the Lord.

The text also makes it plain that God directly brings his punishment on Solomon and the people by raising up enemies from the north, the south, and even from inside the kingdom. Solomon is given the honor of dying before Israel fractures and splits, but the wheels were set in motion during the end of his reign.

It might seem okay to compartmentalize our lives in similar ways. We may think that our compromises won't really hurt anyone. But this is just self-deception. God desires us to take up our cross and follow him and that is impossible to do when our loyalties are divided. We need to ask ourselves, is our speech around our coworkers the same as it is at church? Do our families see a different person when we are in public versus when we are in private? Are there aspects of my life that I am holding on to selfishly and not giving over to the Lord? Sooner or later, God will get his way. He will use his grace and discipline to make us into the people he wants us to be—and that can be good news or bad news or both all in one.

Preaching Idea

God's grace and God's judgment are not mutually exclusive.

Contemporary Connections

What does it mean?

What does it mean that God's grace and God's judgment are not mutually exclusive? Or in other words, what does it mean that God's grace and God's judgment are often both in play as he works in our lives? It means that when he acts, he's not vindictive, but he's also not a pushover. It means that while he will not mete out eternal judgment to his people for their failings, there will be consequences. Even when forgiveness is sought and given, it will take work to repair relationships. A repentant felon will still have to pay court costs, live under the terms of probation, and live with the consequences of a criminal record. God's grace does not eliminate any and all penalties of past infractions.

But on the flip side, God's grace isn't nullified by our sins either. The church should celebrate troubled teens who gives their lives to Christ. A couple who gets pregnant out of wedlock shouldn't be shunned for their mistake but encouraged by our attitude of non-condemnation like Christ in John 8. God's grace extends to all of our sin, and our grace should extend as far as God's does.

Is it true?

Is it true that God's grace and God's judgment are not mutually exclusive? Is it true that both are often in play as he works in our lives? God's grace and judgment may seem like opposites, like theological oil and water, yet this passage points us to a greater truth. God's grace can exist within his judgment. Solomon is judged by God for his evil ways, yet he is spared from living through the full extent of the consequences. The New Testament certainly supports this as well. Passages like Hebrews 12:4–11 tell us that God disciplines us out of his love for us as his children. Hardships aren't necessarily punishment, but we should view them as discipline.

The flip side of this coin is true too as well. God's grace is not a hall pass to do whatever we want, consequence-free. Paul powerfully demonstrates this in his classic treatise in Romans 6. He demonstrates how it is totally inappropriate for the child of God to use God's grace as an excuse to live sinfully. First Peter 2:13–25 calls us to be willing to suffer for what is right and adds that suffering for any other reason is just getting what we deserve.

The author of Hebrews uses the illustration of parenting to flesh out this principle in Hebrews 12:7–11. That illustration still resonates for us today. Godly parenting will not be domineering nor will it be carefree. It will mix discipline and kindness. Its discipline will be done in love and its love will involve discipline. Within our own family life, God has provided a way for us to understand this truth.

Now what?

If it is true that God's grace and God's judgment are not mutually exclusive, that often both are in play as he works in our lives, how should we reconcile these two very different aspects of who God is and what he does? This passage depicts the beautifully profound way that God weaves two aspects of his nature that we often understand as polar opposites. Lawyers and judges are trained to do their jobs based on black-and-white laws and codes. Counselors, caretakers, and pastors are examples of people who are expected to shepherd, nurture, and listen to others in their struggles. It is a rare thing to see a judge who moonlights as a pastor or a counselor who finds fulfillment as a lawyer.

But this passage speaks to us on a level that transcends our careers. How do we live and act in our jobs, at home, and at church? Two related suggestions rise to the surface. The first suggestion is *don't be fearful*. Avoiding God's punishment is a poor motivation to obey God. We should obey because of God's goodness to us. Ask any high school or college coach and they will quickly be able to tell you which of their athletes is training in the off-season to reach greatness and who is training just to satisfy the minimum requirements set by their coaches. Likewise, we need to walk by grace not by fear.

The second suggestion is *don't be careless.* Grace isn't a hall pass or a get-out-of-jail-free card. God disciplines us and sends his corrective consequences to help us get back on the right path when we stray. Modern history is littered with examples of innovative companies who rested on their laurels and got passed by because of their complacency and carelessness. The same thing can happen with God's people, especially when they are prospering. Flourishing churches get undercut by their own pride. Well-meaning parents avoid setting wise boundaries with their children in an effort to be "loving" or "trusting," only to see their kids make avoidable mistakes. We ought to walk by grace but not carelessly, as we live out our lives as church members, parents, and even as employees.

Creativity in Presentation

During the golden age of Disney animated movies, *The Fox and the Hound* (directed by Ted Berman, Richard Rich, and Art Stevens, 1981) was one movie that always melted my heart when I (Lee) watched it as a child. It tells a poignant story of two animals who became lifelong friends even though they were supposed to be enemies. These two opposites getting along can be a creative way to illustrate how God's grace and judgment are intertwined in this chapter.

If that movie is too dated, the beauty of this idea is that the animal kingdom offers real-life examples of this kind of story. One such example is the chimpanzee Anjana and two white tiger cubs named Mitra and Shiva. The tiger cubs were born during Hurricane Hannah and had to be separated from their mother. Under the watch of caretaker China York, Anjana acted as surrogate mother to the cubs, bonding, nurturing, and even feeding them.[2]

As mentioned above, the lives of parents who are trying to wisely raise their kids offer fertile ground for illustrations too. A loving parent will be firm and unyielding in some ways so as to protect their children from harm. That sternness should be balanced by grace of course as well.

We have tried to make the case that there is a subtle but significant difference between the punishment Israel faced in 1 Kings 11 and the discipline we are subject to as God's children adopted by his grace under the new covenant. It might be helpful for pastors preaching this passage to clearly delineate this point for their audience, especially when addressing verses 11–13. To whatever extent preachers see the need to do so, they should not shy away from the complex central truth we see rising from this chapter, which is the key idea to communicate in the sermon, namely, that God's grace and God's judgment are not mutually exclusive.

The passage for this preaching unit can be outlined as follows:

- God's grace doesn't shield us from God's judgment (11:1–10, 14–40).
  - Failing to be faithful leads to serious consequences (vv. 1–10).
  - Failing to be faithful leads us straight into serious conflict (vv. 14–40).
- God's judgment won't exclude us from God's grace (11:11–13, 41–43).
  - We don't always get what we truly deserve (vv. 11–13).
  - We sometimes get what we don't deserve (vv. 41–43).

---

2 "Pictured: Two White Tiger Cubs Find an Unusual Surrogate Mum . . . Anjana the chimpanzee," *Daily Mail*, October 11, 2008, https://www.dailymail.co.uk/news/article-1076572/Pictured-Two-white-tiger-cubs-surrogate-mum--Anjana-chimpanzee.html. See this link for further examples: https://www.boredpanda.com/unusual-animal-friendships-interspecies/?utm_source=google&utm_medium=organic&utm_campaign=organic.

DISCUSSION QUESTIONS

1. Why did Solomon marry so many women (11:1–10)?

2. How specifically did they lead to his downfall (11:7–8)?

3. How could this apply to our lives and the relationships we have?

4. What is surprising about God's pronouncement of judgment (11:11–13)?

5. Who are the enemies that God raises up, and what are their specific backgrounds with relation to Israel (11:24–40)?

6. How have you seen God's grace and judgment interconnected in your life?

1 Kings 12:1–24

EXEGETICAL IDEA
When Rehoboam rejected the request of the northern tribes to alleviate their terms of service, the kingdom split, and Rehoboam's efforts to reunify the kingdom failed.

THEOLOGICAL FOCUS
The choices of humanity collaborate with divine sovereignty to direct the contours of life within God's providence.

PREACHING IDEA
Don't be surprised when God lets us feed on the fruits of our foolishness.

PREACHING POINTERS
The growing fractures in the kingdom of Israel finally reach their breaking point in 1 Kings 12. The northern tribes split from the southern tribes and reach the brink of civil war. The blame rests squarely on the foolish leadership of Rehoboam, though the author clearly indicates that God was still overseeing these political developments. Interestingly, the original audience was in an almost complete opposite position. They were coming out of the exile and seeking to put their nation back together. The example of King Rehoboam stands as an antitype—an example of what not to do if unification is your goal. They needed to be careful to follow the notion that "the needs of the many outweigh the needs of the few."

How does this matter for us? Our nation has gone through an awful civil war due to a number of factors and causes, including moral failings (i.e., the sin of slavery). But that was more than 150 years ago. Unfortunately, however, our propensity for foolishness did not disappear after the War Between the States. The United States of America has certainly developed into a major superpower on the world stage, but that is not necessarily to be understood as the result of God's blessing because of some kind of extrabiblical covenant between God and America as some Americans believe, nor is it an automatic guarantee of such blessing in perpetuity. Just like the leaders of any other post-Babel nation from antiquity to modern times, if our leaders make foolish decisions, we should expect the consequences. This is perhaps most relevant on the personal level. I can attend a good church, pray often, and serve regularly, which are all good and commendable things. But if I also have a spending problem that I let go unchecked, God won't miraculously erase my credit card balance when it rises to unhealthy levels. We shouldn't be surprised when God allows the logical consequences of our mistakes to become realities in our lives.

SCHISM (12:1–24)

LITERARY STRUCTURE AND THEMES (12:1–24)

First Kings 12:1–24 recounts a watershed moment in Israel's history, when Solomon's indictment is brought to fruition and Ahijah's prophecy is fulfilled. Moreover, from this point on, the united nation of Israel was split into the northern kingdom of Israel and the southern kingdom of Judah. The section can be subdivided twofold: the first recounts the schism (vv. 1–17), and the second recounts the immediate aftermath and Rehoboam's futile attempts to reunite the nation (vv. 18–24).

- **The Schism at Shechem (12:1–17)**
- **Failed Reunification (12:18–24)**

EXPOSITION (12:1–24)

The separation of the northern and southern tribes is recounted when the new king Rehoboam attempts to secure the allegiance of the northern tribes at Shechem. It's hard to imagine how things could have gone worse. Instead of a posture of service, Rehoboam relies on bad advice and adopts a posture of dominance. The north separates, and the Lord sanctions the development in the process.

The Schism at Shechem (12:1–17)

Rehoboam rejects the request by the northern tribes and the advice of council, which results in the split of united Israel.

Shechem

Ancient Shechem sits about forty miles north of Jerusalem in a fertile valley between Mount Gerizim and Mount Ebal in the heart of the Central Highlands. During the Bronze Age, Egyptian and Canaanite textual evidence shows that it was a regionally important site. For the patriarchs, it was a critical juncture along their seasonal migrations, and it was the place of Joshua's farewell and covenantal renewal ceremony. After the exile, its stature grew in conjunction with the rise of the Samaritan community. Archaeological excavations have revealed a history marked by violent destruction and subsequent rebuilding. During the Iron Age, Shechem was a main administrative center for the northern kingdom and thus its occupational history reflects the historical ebbs and flows of the northern kingdom (Negev 1990).

12:1–5. Chapter 12 opens with Rehoboam's assembly at Shechem, a strategic choice. This signaled an awareness of the north's political capabilities and a certain level of appeasement in the wake of Solomon's administrative policies. According to 1 Kings 4:7–19, Solomon leveled a significant amount of taxation upon the northern territories, and verse 4 of 1 Kings 12 makes it clear that Solomonic policies were oppressive. The northern elders therefore requested that their "yoke" (עֹל) be lightened.

This assembly also has implications for the return of Jeroboam. The text-critical problems between the LXX and the MT notwithstanding, verses 2–3 suggest to the reader that Jeroboam returned from Egypt at the request of the northern delegation to attend the assembly. Regardless of whether Jeroboam returned before the assembly (per the LXX tradition) or not, it is highly provocative that the individual to whom Ahijah declared to be the first king of the soon-to-be northern kingdom was in attendance. Perhaps Jeroboam's presence at the coronation scene emboldened the northern tribes to take a hard line against Rehoboam.

12:6–11. In response to the request to lighten the north's burden of taxation, Rehoboam sends the delegation away for three days to take things under advisement. Rehoboam considers two options. First, the advisors of Solomon (lit., "the elders who stood before the face of Solomon his father") suggested that Rehoboam essentially capitulate. They suggest that Rehoboam be "a servant to this people," serving them and speaking good words to them. In return, the advisors are confident that they would reciprocate faithful service. Second, Rehoboam considered the advice of those with whom he grew up. The terms "elders" and "kids" are contrasted (זְקֵנִים vs. יְלָדִים), as is the advice. Whereas the elders advised appeasement and service, the youth advised Rehoboam to make an emphatically unyielding and insulting statement. Essentially, the advice was that Rehoboam needed to make clear that he would advance things where Solomon left off. Things would be noticeably worse under Rehoboam.

12:12–17. When the ceremony reconvened on the third day, the text suggests that Rehoboam wasted no time in communicating his decision. Moreover, it was done "harshly" (v. 13). Rehoboam "forsook" the advice of the elders and regurgitated the advice of the inexperienced youths. Whereas Solomon made their yokes heavy, Rehoboam would increase that yoke's weight. Whereas Solomon chastised them with whips, Rehoboam's chastisement will be laced with venom. Consequently, the response of the northern delegation is predictable, although the logical sequence is worth noting. The northern secession was declared only after Rehoboam laid out his decision. Thus, blame is effectively laid of the feet of Rehoboam. Israel's rejection of Davidic kingship, their return to traditional social order (v. 16), was due to an unwillingness to appease, instead preferring authoritarian policies.

Nestled in the midst of this sequence is the short parenthetical statement of verse 15:

Rehoboam's Insolence by Hans Holbein the Younger. Public domain.

"So the king did not listen to the people, because it was a turn of affairs brought about by the LORD that he might fulfill his word, which the LORD had spoken by Ahijah the Shilonite to Jeroboam son of Nebat." Thus, there is the revelation of a tension. On the one hand, Rehoboam had a choice. On the other hand, this entire sequence was ordained by God and his prophetic word. This tension—between the choices of people and the fulfillment of God's prophetic word—marks so much of the historian's historiographic methods.

Failed Reunification (12:18–24)

12:18–24. Rehoboam's attempts to coerce reunification fails, undermined by divine sovereignty.

Rehoboam's counterresponse could not have gone any worse. His first move apparently happened at Shechem, and it was extremely provocative. He dispatched the leader of his forced labor program, Adoniram, for some undisclosed reason, perhaps to negotiate a settlement. Violently, he was met with a volley of stones. The delegation killed him. In the face of all this, Rehoboam quickly harnessed his chariot and fled to Jerusalem.

Israel's response was conclusive. They installed Jeroboam as their king (v. 20), which explains, to a certain degree, Rehoboam's efforts to coerce reunification. According to verse 21, Rehoboam marshalled 180,000 "chosen troops" for making war and forcing the northern tribes to return to Rehoboam. Yet cutting across all this was divine providence. Verse 22 reveals that "a word of God" came to Shemaiah, a word that left no ambiguity. Addressing Rehoboam and everyone else, the prophet explicitly denounced any effort to force reunification through war. The reason? Because this matter was from the Lord (v. 24). So, cutting across all the emotion and passion displayed up to this point, the war party obliged and disbanded.

THEOLOGICAL FOCUS

The exegetical idea (When Rehoboam rejected the request of the northern tribes to alleviate their terms of service, the kingdom split, and Rehoboam's efforts to reunify the kingdom failed) leads to this theological focus: The choices of humanity collaborate with divine sovereignty to direct the contours of life within God's providence.

Rehoboam's coronation scene at Shechem was wild. But it was typical of things in Iron Age Syria-Palestine. One must remember that times of political transition have always been, and continue to be in many parts of the world, extremely tense. Will all parties go along with the status quo? Or, will one party assert itself, effectively threating the equilibrium? Such was the case at Shechem. Yet what makes this scene so intense is the weight of Rehoboam's decision. The fact that the northern tribes were emboldened enough to request respite suggests that Rehoboam did not enjoy the political clout of his father and grandfather. Therefore, the vitality and nature of his kingdom hung in the balance. Foolishly, Rehoboam chose to heed the advice of the inexperienced youths, who appealed to the young king's ego and pivoted on the conviction that unestablished leadership should be concerned above all else with credibility for itself, even at the expense of others. Such selfish ideology secured the schism within the kingdom.

However, cutting across the notion that Rehoboam had a choice in the matter is the realization that God sanctioned all of this. Verses 15 and 24 recount the words of the narrator and Shemaiah the prophet and so provide an authoritative commentary on the scene. This transpired because it was willed by the Lord. Naturally then, one can only wonder about how much blame one should actually lay on Rehoboam's shoulders. He made a terrible decision, but it all transpired in cooperation with divine providence. Consequently, this scene sheds light on the perplexing but important interaction between human agency and divine sovereignty. The contours of life are the result of a mysterious collaboration between the choices of humanity and the intentions of God. In fact, this collaboration bubbles below the surface for the entire record. The historian is convinced that the contours of history are determined both by the choices of people and the determinations of the Lord.

PREACHING AND TEACHING STRATEGIES

Exegetical and Theological Synthesis

As glorious as the dedication of the temple was in 1 Kings 8, the account of Israel's division in 1 Kings 12 is equally overwhelming. Rehoboam makes the grave mistake of not listening to wise counsel, and when he tries to repair the damage, it's too late. God is a God of grace, but that grace cannot be assumed. The Lord sovereignly raises up opposition to the grandson of David so that Israel is split in two. God's will and human responsibility are closely intertwined here as God's chosen people enter a new phase in their relationship with him.

Preaching Idea

Don't be surprised when God lets us feed on the fruits of our foolishness.

Contemporary Connections

What does it mean?

What does it mean that we shouldn't be surprised when God lets us feed on the fruits of our foolishness? What does it look like when God allows this to happen? It looks like the simple principle of cause and effect. If we habitually ignore speed limits and traffic laws, we are highly likely to receive more tickets and get into accidents.

This cause-and-effect principle can work itself out in a myriad of situations, and it would be ridiculous to expect good results to come from bad decisions. For example, in early 2014 a British woman named Jane Mulcahy tried to sue her divorce lawyers for, of all things, securing a divorce from her spouse. Her lawsuit argued that her divorce lawyers should have made it clear that her divorce would end her marriage. She wanted only a separation, apparently for religious reasons. In the end her suit was dismissed because when you hire lawyers to help you get divorced, you shouldn't be upset when they deliver.[1] Likewise when we make reckless choices, we shouldn't be upset with God when those choices birth negative consequences.

Is it true?

Is it true that we shouldn't be surprised when God lets us feed on the fruits of our foolishness? Common sense would tell us "yes, of course," all actions have consequences. Yet Christians in particular can fall into the trap of presuming upon God's grace. We emphasize God's forgiveness so much that we ignore admonitions like the ones in Romans 6:1–2 and Galatians 6:7–9 which warn us about fooling ourselves into thinking that God's grace will automatically shield us from negative outcomes that naturally come from our poor choices. So the next time you get pulled over for speeding, don't complain if a ticket gets handed to you. God may be letting you feed on the fruits of our foolishness.

Now what?

If it is true that we shouldn't be surprised when God lets us feed on the fruits of our foolishness, what should we do to avoid the consequences of foolish decisions and instead make wise and

---

1   Tomas Jivanda, "Woman Claims Lawyers Should Have Told Her Divorce Would End Her Marriage," *Independent*, January 10, 2014, https://www.independent.co.uk/news/uk/home-news/woman-claims-lawyers-should-have-told-her-divorce-would-end-her-marriage-9051550.html.

better choices in all areas of life? Admittedly, this is a "downer" of a passage because it records the extensive negative consequences of faithlessness that began with Solomon and peaked with Rehoboam. The principle of cause and effect, or the so-called law of the harvest, reaping what we sow, is evident. Clearly, what we do with this story and how we apply it needs to rely heavily on avoiding the actions and steps of the prime actors.

To start with, we need to *listen to and live by wisdom*. Rehoboam got in trouble by not listening to his elders, who offered him wise counsel. As we guide our churches, our businesses, even our families, we ought to seek the advice of those who have been there before. It might not appeal to our desires or satisfy our ego, but we should trust the guidance of those who are experienced. I (Lee) remember hearing mentors of mine teach about intentionally "dating" your spouse when you start having kids. I am pretty sure I taught it myself at one point or another. But it wasn't until my wife and I had our first child that I realized just how hard and important that principle is. Raising a family takes emotional and physical effort. Our calendars and schedules dramatically change when our duet becomes an ensemble. The husband-wife dynamic will naturally change, but it should not be deprioritized. Because that piece of wisdom has always stuck with me, I have tried to discipline myself to intentionally do things that help our love grow, progress, and deepen. We try to weekly have a pizza-and-movie night like we did before we were parents. I have tried to get little gifts like flowers more often to show I appreciate her. And I have had to adjust my planning mindset to think ahead about special date nights where we can secure child care. All of the above ideas have been life adjustments we have had to make in order to follow that sage advice.

Creativity in Presentation

Since the early 1990s, the Darwin Awards have highlighted the ill-advised decisions certain individuals have made that led directly to their deaths: "We commemorate those who improve our gene pool—by removing themselves from it in the most spectacular way possible."[2]

While some of these verified reports can be morbid, many offer illustrations that leave the reader wondering "what were they thinking?" The skilled expositor can bring this directly to bear on his audience by asking them to consider how often they have texted while driving, drank to excess, or ignored a doctor's instruction because of convenience. Those and other more "acceptable" forms of foolishness can effectively challenge the audience to consider our passage's central truth.

The key idea to communicate in the sermon is, don't be surprised when God lets us feed on the fruits of our foolishness. The passage for this preaching unit can be outlined in the following points:

- Fools don't listen to wise advice (12:1–8).
- Fools choose short-term selfish wants over long-term selfless needs (12:9–17).
- Fools don't realize how harmful they can be (12:18–24).
- Fools can't upset God's plans (12:15, 21–24).

---

2   "Darwin Awards," accessed May 25, 2019, https://darwinawards.com.

DISCUSSION QUESTIONS

1. How might have things turned out differently if Rehoboam had listened to the wise counsel (12:6–7)?

2. Why would Rehoboam choose to adopt the harsher policies advocated by his younger advisors (12:8–11)?

3. How do the northern tribes respond to Rehoboam's announcement (12:18–20)?

4. How does the theological tension between God's sovereignty and human responsibility play out in this story?

5. How might a passage like Romans 6:1–4 relate to the lessons of this story? What other biblical passages or stories might relate to this chapter?

1 Kings 12:25–14:20

EXEGETICAL IDEA
Jeroboam's reign is remembered for the king's construction of an illegitimate and heretical religious system that ultimately secured devastating judgment.

THEOLOGICAL FOCUS
The fear and self-preservation at the root of Jeroboam's disobedience is a potentially devastating pair of tendencies in light of humanity's fallen state.

PREACHING IDEA
Depravity leads to disaster, no matter what.

PREACHING POINTERS
Jeroboam's reign comes to a dramatic and ignominious end. Plagued by insecurity over Jerusalem's central place in their nation's religious life, he decides to set up an alternate religious system that was not sanctioned by the Lord. These selfish and fear-driven actions mark the northern kingdom to such an extent that God announces his imminent judgment. National prosperity and security were certainly highly cherished goals for the returning Jewish exiles and those living in postexilic Israel. Would they, like Jeroboam, choose security over obedience? Would they compromise God's law in the interests of self-preservation?

The people of God have faced these kinds of dilemmas quite often throughout history. Of course, the specifics are often quite different. Today, Christians face these types of choices when considering who to support politically. What do we do if the candidate from "my party" espouses unbiblical views and positions? Beyond individual interests, our communities of faith must wrestle with these issues too. Will our church seek the Spirit's leading or will we split into factions that fight over our preferences? Operating by fear and self-interest is a mark that we are living by the flesh. Living that way for very long will inevitably lead to disaster. We can learn from Jeroboam's poor example and do the opposite when we deal with our own insecurities. Following our own rebellious path will only leave us worse off because depravity leads to disaster, no matter the excuses or circumstances. God calls us to live by faith. While his path may be uncertain, he promises that it will not end in disaster.

REGION OF JEROBOAM I (12:25–14:20)

LITERARY STRUCTURE AND THEMES (12:25–14:20)

This section of text focuses upon the exploits of Jeroboam with a particular emphasis upon describing the sin of Jeroboam. There is also lengthy digression that provides a commentary on the prophetic office. The section is subdivided as follows: illegitimate sanctuaries (12:25–33), prophets and prophesies (13:1–34), Jeroboam's indictment (14:1–18), and Jeroboam's death (14:19–20).

- *Illegitimate Sanctuaries (12:15–33)*
- *Prophets and Prophesies (13:1–34)*
- *Jeroboam's Indictment (14:1–18)*
- *Jeroboam's Death (14:19–20)*

EXPOSITION (12:25–14:20)

Jeroboam is the focus in this section of text, with the exception of a passage that focuses on peculiar events surrounding a couple anonymous prophets. Together, they bring the larger section that is concerned with the dissolution of the United Monarchy to a close. One sees how Jeroboam failed to live up to the opportunities offered to him by Ahijah. His own covenantal infidelity secures judgment upon his family.

Illegitimate Sanctuaries (12:25–33)

12:25–33. Jeroboam's endeavors are remembered for the construction of his illegitimate religious system.

One of Jeroboam's first accomplishments was to secure a palace as he developed a national infrastructure. Verse 25 says that Jeroboam "built" (בנה) Shechem and Penuel, but this should be understood in the sense of reinforcing an already existing settlement as critical administrative centers. In the case of

Shechem, it would be his royal residence, and both locations signaled an appeal to the patriarchal traditions associated with the sites (cf. Gen. 12:6; 32:30–31; 33:18–19). At some point during the consolidation and construction of his kingdom, Jeroboam realized that without a religious system his people would return to Jerusalem. This was unacceptable, for Jeroboam feared that such a turn of events would undermine his new kingdom and potentially lead to his death (v. 27). Consequently, Jeroboam created a religious alternative, boasting local worship sites (v. 31), a religious calendar (v. 32), a system of priests (v. 31), and two national shrines located at the northern and southern most reaches of the kingdom: Bethel and Dan (v. 29).

Much has been said about the nature of the two calves erected at Bethel and Dan, including whether the calves represented the Lord. For example, Sweeney (2007, 177) states that the calves did not represent the Lord, but "the mount upon which YHWH rides." DeVries sees them as either ornaments or pedestals (DeVries 2003, 162). What is clear is that Jeroboam's words to the people introducing them to their new alternative system of worship recall Exodus 32:4. In fact, the Hebrew of both passages is identical, save for one initial small particle.

1 Kings 12:28

הִנֵּה אֱלֹהֶיךָ יִשְׂרָאֵל אֲשֶׁר הֶעֱלוּךָ מֵאֶרֶץ מִצְרָיִם

Exodus 32:4

אֵלֶּה אֱלֹהֶיךָ יִשְׂרָאֵל אֲשֶׁר הֶעֱלוּךָ מֵאֶרֶץ מִצְרָיִם

Consequently, the writer connects Jeroboam's actions with one of the great religious failings in Israel's history. And if there was any doubt, an emphatic denouncement of these actions is nestled in the middle of the account (v. 30): "And this matter become a sin" (וַיְהִי הַדָּבָר הַזֶּה לְחַטָּאת). Thus, Wray Beal (2014, 185) says it nicely, "Regardless of Jeroboam's intentions, the act is characterized as wholly sinful."

Prophets and Prophesies (13:1–34)

A prophecy against the altar at Bethel leads to a perplexing encounter between two prophetic figures that speaks to the many dynamics of biblical prophecy. The section can be subdivided threefold (Wray Beal 2014, 190): a prophesy against the altar at Bethel by an unnamed man of God (vv. 1–10), an encounter between two prophetic individuals (vv. 11–32), and further condemnation of Jeroboam (vv. 33–34).

13:1–10. The scene connects with the previous chapter through a smooth syntactical transition. Jeroboam is standing by the altar constructed at Bethel and is confronted by an unnamed "man of God" (אִישׁ אֱלֹהִים). The man proceeds to prophesy against the altar (v. 2), also predicting the rise of Josiah and his definitive religious reforms (2 Kings 22–23). What's more, the verification for this prediction would be that the altar would be torn apart and the dust would be poured out (v. 3).

Predictably, Jeroboam does not receive this word well. Yet when he moves to silence the man of God, the king's hand withers and ceases to function normally (v. 4). This act, in conjunction with the destruction of the altar (v. 5), is immediately understood to be a sign of approval for the man of God and his prophecy. So, Jeroboam seeks healing. The prophet obliges, prays, and Jeroboam's hand is restored. However, the man of God rejects the royal offer to dine, citing a command from the word of the Lord (v. 9). The man of God reveals that he was to deliver his message and immediately return by a different way. He was

also prohibited from eating or drinking water. This command will be the prophet's undoing.

13:11–32. Verse 11 introduces another anonymous character, a prophet (נָבִיא) from Bethel who receives a report of the events of verses 1–10 from his sons. In turn, the elderly prophet saddles his donkey with the intention of meeting the man of God (vv. 12–13). When the two meet under a tree, the elderly prophet solicits him to return with him to fellowship. However, the man of God gives the elderly prophet the same excuse as he gave King Jeroboam (vv. 16–17). The Lord has explicitly commanded him not to eat, drink water, or return the same way. Nevertheless, the elderly prophet persists, even offering a deceitful report (v. 18) that the Angel of the Lord told him via the word of the Lord to bring him back to his house for fellowship, effectively contradicting the man of God's message.

It's not clear why the prophet chooses to deceive the man of God. Perhaps it was his way of determining the legitimacy of the man of God's prophecy. Regardless, in the span of a few verses, an incredible amount of suspense comes to a head in verse 19: "Then the man of God went back with him, and ate food and drank water in his house." The man of God has disobeyed an explicit command given to him.

The results are immediately revealed. While they were at the table, a word came to the elderly prophet that condemned the man of God for his unwillingness to go home immediately (v. 20). Because the man of God disobeyed, insisting on doing the very thing that the Lord told him not to do, his corpse will not be laid in his family's tomb (vv. 21–22). The word for corpse (נְבֵלָה) occurs in contexts describing bodies being left in open fields to be picked a part by wild beasts (e.g., Deut. 28:26; 2 Kings 9:37; Isa. 5:25; Jer. 36:30). Consequently, the price of disobedience is a shameful death. Moreover, disobedience is the pressing issue in this section of text, not the questionable ethics of the elderly prophet and his use of deceit.

When the man of God finished his meal, the elderly prophet provides him with one of his donkeys and he departed (v. 23), only to be mauled to death by a lion that throws his lifeless corpse to the roadside. What's more, the lion stands next to the corpse and the donkey, refusing to molest further either of them (v. 24). As one would image, such a scene catches the attention of those who pass by, including a group of servants who bring the news back to the city. Eventually, the elderly prophet hears of the turn of events and sets out to recover the body. Recovering the body, the elderly prophet laments for the slain man of God and buries him (vv. 29–30). He even expresses solidarity with the dead man, calling him "brother" (אָח), dictating that he be buried in the same burial complex, next to him, upon his death (v. 31). And with one more posthumous praise, the elderly prophet declares emphatically that everything the dead man spoke about will come to pass.

So, what's the purpose of this episode? Is it a scene that puts radical and absolute obedience to the commands of the Lord front and center (DeVries, 171–74)? Is it a commentary on prophecy and its fulfillment (Wray Beal 2014, 195–96)? Is it more symbolic than anything, using events to allude to broad theological issues (Strand Winslow 2017, 119–23; Leithart, 97–102)? Or is it merely an etiological narrative that explains a well-known landmark (2 Kings 23:15–18) and recounts the tensions between the northern and southern tribes (Sweeney 2007, 178–82)? It's my conviction that it's all of these.

This episode speaks to the social, theological, and historical issues that converged to drive the prophetic experiences and the historical contours of Israel and Judah. The prophets were of critical importance within Israelite and Judean culture, and their function was to bring the status of the covenant into clear focus, even if it meant boldly and publicly chastising the monarchy. Such encounters logically produced a critical juncture for the community. Heed the word? Ignore the word? And the response had

far-reaching implications. But it would be incorrect to say that social dynamics did not play a role in prophetic encounters. Certain prophets were viewed with an inherent skepticism because of their place in society. Moreover, there were times when multiple prophetic words were brought to bear upon an individual situation, producing contrasting ways forward. Thus, the community was hard-pressed at times to determine who was correct. In other words, the facts on the ground suggest that the prophetic experience was no simplistic experience.

In this case, there are certain things that are abundantly clear. First, both Jeroboam and the man of God were guilty: Jeroboam for making an illegitimate and heretical religious system, and the man of God for violating his divine command. In each case, there were consequences. Second, the deceit of the elderly prophet from Bethel is not an issue on which the narrative wants to focus. Rather, the focal point is unwavering obedience—no matter what competing words may complicate the situation. Third, while the true word of God may not always be clear, it will be revealed. In the case of the altar's indictment, what happened to Jeroboam's hand authenticated the man of God's authority. In the case of the pronouncement against the man of God, the gruesome death of the man as well as the peculiar action of the lion after its mauling verified that the man of God's command to return home quickly was true. In turn, this consequence validated his prophetic denouncement of the altar at Bethel.

13:33–34. The text returns to focus on Jeroboam's stubbornness. Even after the events between the man of God and elderly prophet from Bethel, Jeroboam did not repent. Instead, he proceeded to construct his alternative and illegitimate religious system, even creating its own priestly system. This suggests that Jeroboam's plea for healing in verse 6 was not made out of genuine remorse. Most importantly, this matter of establishing an illegitimate religious system became the nagging sin that would plague Jeroboam and eventually secure the destruction and expulsion of the tribes of the northern kingdom from the land by the hand of Assyria.

Jeroboam's Indictment (14:1–18)

Jeroboam's inability to rule according to the Lord's standards secured terrible judgment for himself and his family.

14:1–5. Verse 1 opens with "at that time," creating a chronological connection with the events of chapter 13. The issue here is the sickness of Jeroboam's son. Already having a history with Ahijah, the king understandably sends his wife to Shiloh to inquire of Ahijah about their son's fate. However, there is the condition that she wear a disguise, which is never explained. It does create a sense of irony in the narrative. The queen hides her identity when questioning a prophet with failing eyesight (v. 5). Little do they know that Ahijah has been privy to divine revelation and was waiting for the queen's arrival.

14:6–16. As soon as Jeroboam's disguised wife enters the doorway, the prophet engages her. He tells her to come in and even asks about the disguise. More importantly, he informs her straightway that he has bad news: "I am sent to you with difficult things" (וְאָנֹכִי שָׁלוּחַ אֵלַיִךְ קָשָׁה).

Beginning in verse 7, the prophet launches into a speech that flows causatively. Verses 7–9 detail what Jeroboam has done, and verses 10–14 detail the Lord's response. The prophet opens by recalling how the Lord elevated Jeroboam among the populace, making him a leader (דִי נָגִיד) and tearing away a portion of David's kingdom to give to him. Unfortunately, Jeroboam did not respond to the Lord's election in kind. Rather, he failed to act like David. More shockingly, he did more evil than all those who came before him. He provoked the Lord to anger, made idols, and lived a life of blatant disregard for the Lord (v. 9). It goes without saying that judgment was warranted.

Verse 10 emphatically opens (לָכֵן) and reveals the judgment that will transpire. And it's not just punishment. It's the worst kind of punishment—one that affects the people around you as well. It will be a shameful eradication of his lineage. Corpses will be exposed to the natural elements, left to rot, and be scavenged by wild animals. No male shall be left. Moreover, this judgment has already begun to unfold! Ahijah reveals to Jeroboam's wife that when she arrives home, her son will die (vv. 12–13), and the person who will be responsible for silencing Jeroboam's line is already in play (v. 14).

The prophet also reveals something about the distant future. There will come a time when the Lord will root Israel up from the Promised Land and scatter them across Mesopotamia (v. 15). He will give Israel up to exile (וְנָתַן אֶת־יִשְׂרָאֵל בִּגְלַל) because of the sins of Jeroboam and the people of Israel. Jeroboam's wife came to seek a word about her son, only to receive one of the most intense judgments in the Old Testament.

14:17–18. When Ahijah finishes, Jeroboam's wife returns to Tirzah to find that everything that the prophet spoke came to pass. The child died upon her arrival in Tirzah, and all Israel mourned for him.

Jeroboam's Death (14:19–20)

14:19–20. Jeroboam's death notice, which acknowledges other facets of his reign, brings the first literary unit to a close.

Verse 19 references the "book of the annals of the kings of Israel," which was apparently another historiographic resource well-known in the writer's day. Most importantly, it's clear that the writer of Kings did not intend to offer an exhaustive history. Rather, specific events were chosen, correlated, and discussed to accomplish a specific goal or writing purpose.

THEOLOGICAL FOCUS

The exegetical idea (Jeroboam's reign is remembered for the king's construction of an illegitimate and heretical religious system that ultimately secured devastating judgment) leads to this theological focus: The fear and self-preservation at the root of Jeroboam's disobedience is a potentially devastating pair of tendencies in light of humanity's fallen state.

When this section of text closes, Jeroboam's promising future has given way to a bleak one that's already unfolding. How did this happen? Jeroboam was promised a future that would rival David. Yet his future only holds a devastating turn of events.

According to 1 Kings 12:26–27, "Then Jeroboam said to himself, 'Now the kingdom may well revert to the house of David. If this people continues to go up to offer sacrifices in the house of the Lord at Jerusalem, the heart of this people will turn again to their master, King Rehoboam of Judah; they will kill me and return to King Rehoboam.'" Upon realizing this, Jeroboam took advisement, forged two golden calves, and set up an illegitimate and heretical system of worship.

Fear and self-preservation drove Jeroboam to make one of the most egregious mistakes in the history of God's people. Jeroboam's choice to defy God secured judgment upon his family, even becoming a festering wound that would eventually poison the nation. It was a choice driven by fear that undermined a potentially glorious future.

But Jeroboam is not alone. Saul admitted to Samuel that his fear of the people drove him to conscious defiance of the Lord's ordered חֵרֶם on the Amalakites (1 Sam. 15:10–35). The parents of a healed blind man refused to bear witness to the miracle given to their son or to Jesus out of fear for persecution (John 9:13–34). Then in the parable of the tenants (Matt. 25:14–30; Luke 19:11–27), Jesus describes the foolish tenant who decides out of fear to sit on his gift instead of working to ensure that it gains value.

In each case, fear persuaded individuals to make shameful and disobedient decisions.

Despite these negative examples, Scripture also teaches that a crippling fear can be overcome, and it begins with understanding where our fear should be focused. The wisdom literature continuously emphasizes that wisdom for life begins with the person of God and his revelation (Job 28:28; Ps. 19; 27:1; 111:10; Prov. 1:7; 10:9; Eccl. 12:9–14). Jesus would even teach that fearing anything or anyone other than the one who ultimately judges humanity is misguided (Matt. 10:28). Most powerfully, the indwelling of God's loving character perfects us to the point that all unhealthy and misguided fear is driven out so that we may stand confidently at the end of days (1 John 4:16–18).

PREACHING AND TEACHING STRATEGIES

Exegetical and Theological Synthesis

Jeroboam purposefully chooses to rebel against the one who set him on the throne of the northern kingdom. Worried about losing the favor of his people if they worship in Jerusalem, he sets up his own religious centers even featuring idols. This illegitimate and heretical religious system will prove to be a snare and cause of devastation for Israel, given Jeroboam's great evil in instituting this rebellion and idolatry. Despite the Lord's warnings through the words and death of an anonymous prophet, the king is unmoved. God's judgment is subsequently announced through Ahijah, whose pronouncement has devastating short-term and long-term ramifications.

Preaching Idea

Depravity leads to disaster, no matter what.

Contemporary Connections

What does it mean?

What does it mean that depravity leads to disaster, no matter what? It means that even if

169

you think you can get ahead by illegitimate means, it won't pay off. Pete Rose and Barry Bonds were ultimately caught breaking the rules of baseball and have become pariahs in their sport despite their historic records.

Cheaters may get ahead and immoral powers may prosper for a time. Earthly consequences won't always match the offenses committed, but God keeps account. His judgment will mete out true justice, whether in the immediate term like in this passage or in the final accounting of deeds like Matthew 25 and Revelation 18 depict. The ends don't justify the means. And the end will always ultimately be disaster for those who take the path of depravity.

Is it true?

Is it true that depravity leads to disaster, no matter what? As we highlighted under the Theological Focus section, Jeroboam is neither the first nor the last to act out of fear and self-preservation. First Samuel 15, Matthew 25:14–30, and John 9:13–34 all offer examples of others making the same foolish decision. We can even trace this back to Adam and Eve in Genesis 3. Not only does their original sin involve the desire to "be like God," but their subsequent actions of making coverings and hiding from God's presence are also similar to the fear-based behaviors of Jeroboam. Achan keeping some of the plunder of Jericho (Josh. 7) and Ananias and Sapphira lying about their giving (Acts 5:1–11) could also fall under this category.

Romans 6:23 reminds us that all our sin, including our fear-driven disobedience, leads to death. Our depravity will bring disastrous consequences if we let it go unchecked. An athlete who constantly argues with officials will eventually get a technical foul or some other disqualifying violation. When we habitually tell "little white lies," people will realize we can't be trusted. Our depravity fools us into thinking that finding instant gratification is all that matters, whether it is saving face or getting the last word in. It blinds us to the reality that eventually,

consequences will come. God doesn't let sin continue without correction or punishment.

Now what?

If it's true that depravity leads to disaster, no matter what, what should we do about it? Should we just accept our fate and wallow in our sin? Of course not. There is hope. Jeroboam's example is one to avoid, and there are plenty of examples and exhortations that can help us.

One exhortation is, *don't let your sin catch up with you.* Now, admittedly, that sounds strange. But what we mean by that is, confess your sin and get it out in the open. Not repenting of his errors and not reversing course was Jeroboam's biggest mistake. Likewise, we need to take care of our sin immediately to avoid the penalties that will come in the long-term. Find trusted, godly friends who can keep you accountable with your struggles. All sin involves significant cost: porn destroys marriages, anger can derail careers, and bad spending habits can undermine kingdom opportunities that God wants you to be involved in. Confession and repentance will help us avoid the disaster that awaits us.

Another exhortation this section reminds us of is our need to *place our fears and insecurities at the foot of the cross.* Jeroboam was so worried about retaining his own power and keeping his own people in line that he ended up betraying the very God who had put him as king over the northern tribes of Israel. He went so far as to set up a false religious system when that was clearly not God's will and violated His law. We need to instead trust God to preserve, protect, and provide for us. As Jesus said in Matthew 6,

> But if God so clothes the grass of the field, which today is alive and tomorrow is thrown into the oven, will he not much more clothe you, O you of little faith? Therefore do not be anxious, saying, "What shall we eat?" or

"What shall we drink?" or "What shall we wear?" For the Gentiles seek after all these things, and your heavenly Father knows that you need them all. But seek first the kingdom of God and his righteousness, and all these things will be added to you. (vv. 30–33 ESV)

Maybe we need to rethink our plans for building that "Doomsday" bunker in our backyard. Maybe we can trust God when we sense him calling us out of our current job and into an unknown direction. When it comes to our more personal fears and insecurities, maybe we can begin meeting with a Christian counselor who can train us to think and act in a biblically healthy way. Neil T. Anderson of Freedom in Christ Ministries is an excellent Christian author who has written many books, including *The Bondage Breaker*, which can help us focus on our identity in Christ and what that means in our daily lives.

Creativity in Presentation

Few characters in all of literature display the disastrous effects of depravity more than Gollum in the Lord of the Rings series. Gollum, originally named Smeagol, takes possession of the mystical Ring of Power—and then it takes possession of him. His all-encompassing obsession with the ring is vividly described in the books and memorably portrayed in Peter Jackson's movie adaptations. The effect is even more stark when we are given a glimpse of Smeagol before the ring in the trilogy's third film, *The Return of the King*. That scene ends with Smeagol murdering his friend to take the ring. Given that reality, playing the video is probably not advisable for a sermon setting. But merely mentioning his name and projecting his picture will have the right effect for your audience to grasp how our sin and depravity will lead us to ruin and disaster.

Since this pericope covers such a large amount of the text, it's probably wise to pick key parts of each section to read in delivering the sermon, rather than all the verses of all the sections. With the middle passage concerning the prophets, it might be good to share with your audience just how strange this encounter is and how complicated it can be to interpret. We've titled it "No Matter Why You Chose It" in our outline below to highlight how disaster came upon the prophet who "innocently" strayed from God's clear command to him. Even though he may have been tricked by the second prophet, he still should have remained obedient to what God had told him. The apostle Paul offers the proper corrective and perspective on obeying God's commands: "But even if we or an angel from heaven should preach to you a gospel contrary to the one we preached to you, let him be accursed" (Gal. 1:8 ESV). In the end, it will be vital to help your people see how the events with the two prophets in 1 Kings 13 tie back to Jeroboam and how, despite what transpired, he *still* doesn't listen and repent.

The key idea to communicate is that depravity leads to disaster, no matter what. The passage for this preaching unit can be outlined in the following points:

Depravity leads to disaster:

- No matter how you rationalize it (12:25–33)
- No matter why you chose it (13:1–34)
- No matter if you try to avoid it (14:1–20)

DISCUSSION QUESTIONS

1. Why does Jeroboam set up his own religious system (12:25–27)?

2. What other time in Israel's history did the people and their leaders try to represent God with golden calves? What sort of reaction should we have when reading about it here?

3. After properly confronting King Jeroboam, what mistake does the unnamed prophet make (13:11–19)?

4. What unanswerable questions and complicated issues does this episode bring to mind (13:11–32)?

5. How does Jeroboam respond to the Lord's pronouncement of disaster on his family, and what is God's ultimate evaluation of him (13:33–34, 14:7–16)?

6. Taking the opposite approach from Jeroboam, what positive lessons might we learn from the end of his reign?

THE COLLAPSE OF THE UNITED MONARCHY
(1 KINGS 1:1–14:20)

A SUMMARY

As the first fourteen chapters of 1 Kings have unfolded, the first two chapters set the tone. By recounting the tumultuous succession from David to Solomon, a foundational question was introduced: How would the monarchy in the wake of David be defined? Was it going to be just another ancient Near Eastern monarchy, defined by typical obligations, ideology, and mechanisms? Or, was it going to be defined more uniquely by a fierce commitment to the Lord's covenantal ideal? Such questions are laid before the reader in David's final exhortation to Solomon (1 Kings 2:1–9).

Unfortunately, chapters 3–14 suggest that the Israelite monarchy was more typical of ancient Near Eastern monarchies than atypical. The Lord's covenantal ideal would play a role, indeed. However, it's difficult to say that it was a dominant force. Solomon developed political and social policies typical of his day, all in the name of cultural development. His building campaigns required an immense amount of resources, both material and human, and so taxation, conscripted labor, and political wheeling-and-dealing were implemented. Yet make no mistake, Solomon was successful. He channeled his resources to bolster Israelite infrastructure, and most importantly, he brought his father's desire for a temple to fruition. He

was so effective that his administrative and judicial decisions procured unprecedented fame and became paradigms of wisdom.

But when it come to the covenantal ideal and its imprint upon Solomon's methods, there is a palpable elusiveness. Solomon's characterization is shrouded by a certain level of moral ambiguity, and as the reader approaches 1 Kings 11, there is a sense that things are going astray. Various details, dealings, and accounts collaborate to suggest that Solomon's policies flirted with the boundaries of the covenantal ideal. In other words, Solomon did not exhibit a fierce allegiance to the covenant but a comfortable one at best. Ultimately, Solomon's policies undid him and his monarchy. He is judged for his covenantal infidelity, and the kingdom ripped apart. Most importantly, he secured the unfortunate classification that positions him alongside other woeful kings: "Solomon did what was evil in the sight of the LORD" (1 Kings 11:6 ESV).

This first major literary unit in Kings ends with a powerful juxtaposition. Solomon is positioned against Jeroboam, the first king of Israel, who was also offered an opportunity to build a dynasty that would rival David's in the wake of Solomon's sin. All he had to do was what Solomon couldn't: display unwavering covenantal fidelity. Tragically, Jeroboam fell short like Solomon. Moreover,

Jeroboam's chief sin—establishing the two illegitimate religious sanctuaries at Bethel and Dan—would become the festering poison that would continually drag the northern kingdom down throughout their existence in the land. Therefore, obedience, proper worship, and the role of the prophet to educate the community about its status before God, in terms of covenantal behavior or misbehavior, are introduced as this unit closes.

Consequently, the historian has used this first major literary unit (1 Kings 1:1–14:20) to bring into focus the institutions that would dictate the contours of Israel's and Judah's history. Prophets and kings would be at the center, kings with their policies, both good and bad, as well as the prophets with their demands for absolute allegiance to the Lord.

The Divided Kingdom of Israel and Judah
Map by A. D. Riddle

THE DIVIDED MONARCHY
(1 KINGS 14:21–2 KINGS 20:21)

The second major literary unit in Kings is 1 Kings 14:21–2 Kings 20:21, which describes the divided monarchy. This major unit may be divided threefold. The first section describes a period of political upheaval (1 Kings 14:21–16:34). The second section introduces various prophets and kings serving during the divided monarchy period (1 Kings 17:1–2 Kings 13:25). The third section describes yet another period of political upheaval (2 Kings 14:1–20:21).

Across this massive unit, six preaching units have been identified: 1 Kings 14:21–16:20; 16:21–34; 1 Kings 17:1–2 Kings 1:18; 2 Kings 21:1–13:25; 14:1–16:20; 17:1–20:21. Each homiletical unit attempts to harness the most important elements within each subsection.

- First Kings 14:21–16:34 and 2 Kings 14:1–20:21 attempt to develop homiletical ideas from the lessons gleaned from periods of political upheaval that open and close this major literary unit.

- First Kings 17:1–2 Kings 13:25 develops very general homiletical ideas from the stories of Elijah (1 Kings 17:1–2 Kings 1:18) and then Elisha (2 Kings 21:1–13:25). The intention is that these general ideas will be nuanced in accordance with the readers' specific contextual variables.

POLITICAL UPHEAVAL (1 KINGS 14:21–16:34)

The first section of this second major literary unit in Kings is 1 Kings 14:21–16:34, which discusses the political upheaval that develops in the immediate aftermath of the schism. This first section may be divided into two preaching units. First, dynastic stability versus instability characterizes the early decades of the divided monarchy, which are consequently marked by political volatility (14:21–16:20). Whereas Israel exhibits dynastic instability, Judah finds itself on the receiving end of Shishak's military incursion into the region. Second, the Omrides are established through Omri's coup d'état, which stabilizes the region and ushers in a new phase in the history of God's people (16:21–34).

1 Kings 14:21–16:20

EXEGETICAL IDEA

Both Judean and Israelite kings generally failed to honor the Lord and his expectations, yet the intensity of judgment was pacified in Judah because of David's legacy and the occasional good king.

THEOLOGICAL FOCUS

Judgment can only be pacified temporarily, for without complete repentance the root of sin will only grow and consume.

PREACHING IDEA

Half-measures of repentance won't cure full measures of rebellion.

PREACHING POINTERS

Both Judah and Israel find themselves in unstable political circumstances in this section. Unlike Israel, Judah does experience brief eras of positivity, because at times their leadership follows the Lord. The original readers of 1 Kings would have been able to clearly recognize the implications for their context. As they rebuilt their nation, they had two paths to choose from. The first was the path of loyalty and faithfulness to God's law. The second was the path of compromise and rebellion. They could imitate the spiritual reforms like Asa and find national success, or they could tolerate pagan worship in their midst and invite God's judgment. Leaders like Nehemiah and Ezra wholeheartedly served so that the former would be true, not the latter.

Today, living under the new covenant, much has changed in God's equation for dealing with sin. Sacrifices are no longer required, and national prosperity is not on the line. The essential acts of confession and repentance have not changed, however. Jesus's sacrificial death provides forgiveness, but it doesn't give us license to live immorally. James 4:7–10 and 1 John 1:7–9 are just two prominent passages among many in the New Testament underscoring the believer's need to address their sin with God and turn from its enticing grip. But we can't just go halfway in dealing with our sinful habits. The Bible uses commands like "cut it off," "flee," and "put to death" when it comes to sin in our lives (Matt. 5:30; 1 Cor. 6:18; Col. 3:5). This means: Take drastic action now! Don't mess around with sin. Counseling or Alcoholics Anonymous meetings may need to be scheduled. Internet or cable access should be canceled. Quitting a bad habit "cold turkey" may be difficult, but it may be the healthiest way forward. We must deal seriously with our sinful habits and tendencies, whatever they may be. Half-hearted repentance won't fix all-out rebellion.

DYNASTIC STABILITY VERSUS INSTABILITY
(14:21–16:20)

LITERARY STRUCTURE AND THEMES
(14:21–16:20)

This section documents the first Judean and Israelite kings. The Judean monarchy stands in noticeable contrast to its Israelite counterpart, as the latter exhibits significant dynastic instability. Ultimately, a picture is created of a dire situation that incidentally raises the question of whether the fledgling nations can even survive. Yet cutting against the grain of an otherwise worrisome atmosphere are the occasional "good king" of Judah and the promises of God to David (1 Kings 15:4).

- *Judean Kings (14:21–15:24)*
- *Israelite Kings (15:25–16:20)*

EXPOSITION (14:21–16:20)

The period immediately after Rehoboam's failure at Shechem and Jeroboam's theological failures deteriorates very quickly. While Judah's ruling family offers some stability, the southern kingdom is caught up in the political intrigue that dominates the northern kingdom. Violence and subterfuge comes to define the period, and viability of both kingdoms comes to exist on a knife's edge, even though the legacy of David continues to influence the situation.

Judean Kings (14:21–15:24)

The reigns of the Judean kings immediately after Rehoboam were marked by religious decline and geopolitical upheaval, only to be pacified by the legacy of David and the occasional good king.

Shishak

Shishak was the founder of Egypt's twenty-second dynasty. Reigning for just over two decades, his rule was defined by efforts to reassert an Egyptian presence in Syria-Palestine in the aftermath of the Late Bronze Age collapse. His geopolitical efforts are well documented, from harboring political dissidents to erecting Egyptian propaganda (e.g., his stele in Megiddo and inscription at Karnak).

The historical debate around Shishak and the book of Kings revolves around the biblical and Egyptian claims. The former claims a substantial siege of Jerusalem, but the latter makes no mention of Jerusalem. While many people point to the decrepit nature of the Egyptian text, claiming that any reference to Jerusalem has been lost to time, others suggest an answer based more in literary creativity. For example, Finkelstein (2002) argues that the Kings account of Shishak's raid is a literary creation to serve the rhetorical interests of a writer from a later century.

14:21–24. These verses are the introductory comments common to the regnal framework (see "The Framework" section in the Introduction). A peculiar feature here is the description of Jerusalem. It's "the city that the LORD had chosen out of all the tribes of Israel, to put his name there" (14:21). This recalls Deuteronomy's centralization formula and therefore identifies Jerusalem as the central cult site. More specifically, it's the location that uniquely testifies to the Lord's absolute suzerainty over his people (Richter 2002). In turn, its description sets up a contrast with verses 22–24, heightening the egregiousness of Judah's sins. From the very beginning, the historian is proclaiming that religious syncretism, which compromised absolute loyalty to the Lord, developed under Rehoboam, even reaching new heights.

14:25–28. The narrative shifts to the incursion of Pharaoh Shishak, which needs to be understood as punishment for Judah's religious syncretism (Wray Beal 2008, 205; cf. 2 Chron. 12:2). Shishak's incursion did not end with establishing any sort of imperial presence, just the decimation of the royal treasuries. In a concise but hyperbolic statement, the text reveals that "he took everything" (אֶת־הַכֹּל לָקָח), which is particularized in verses 26–27. Wiseman (2008, 164) suggests that the replacement of bronze shields for gold ones reflects Judah's economic decline, which is possible.

In the gate complex of Karnak's temple, Shishak inscribed descriptions of his incursions into Syria-Palestine. Interestingly, while his account references many sites throughout the region, it does not reference Jerusalem. Consequently, there is a debate about the dynamics of Shishak's incursion, including whether he laid siege to Jerusalem (Finkelstein 2002; Levin 2012)

14:29–31. These verses close the reign of Rehoboam and are consistent with the expectations of the regnal framework. Yet they do mention ongoing war between Rehoboam and Jeroboam, which supplements the note of Egyptian incursion. Thus, it was a tense era of political volatility, a theme throughout 1 Kings 14:21–16:20.

15:1–8. Only nine verses are devoted to Abijam's reign. The reader is informed that the conflict that begun between Rehoboam and Jeroboam continued with him. However, the memory of David interjects a positive element into an otherwise short and negative evaluation. According to verses 4–5, judgment is pacified

because of the territorial dominion God promised to David (cf. 11:36 above). Once again, David's legacy dictates the contours of history well after his death.

15:9–24. Asa assumed the Judean throne in the twentieth year of Jeroboam, and he ruled for forty-one years, making his reign the second longest in Judean history. The text reveals that he was a "good king," having done "what was right in the sight of the Lord, as his father David had done" (v. 11). Such categorization is undoubtedly linked to his many cultic reforms. He "put away the male temple prostitutes" (v. 12) and removed the idols made by his ancestors. More provocatively, he removed his mother Maacah from the political scene because of her religious proclivities. She made "an abominable image for Asherah," and so was removed of her duties as "queen mother" (v. 13).

Translation Analysis: The term גְּבִירָה is often translated "Queen Mother," but the semantic range includes the more generic "mistress" (*HALOT*, 2:173). This Hebrew term been related to the Hittite term *tawananna* and the Ugaritic *rbt/rabîtu*, but in Kings it overwhelmingly refers to the mother of a king. Ascertaining the function of the גְּבִירָה has been debated, ranging from no official institutional duty (Ben-Barak 1991) to a sociopolitical role (Andreasen 1983) to a combined cultic and sociopolitical role (Ackerman 1993). Whatever her specific role, 1 Kings 15:13 suggests that it was not absolute.

The Hebrew behind the terms for idols in this passage is interesting. Maacah's idol, מִפְלֶצֶת, comes from a root associated with shuddering horror. In verse 12, the term גִּלֻּלִים comes from a particularly offensive family of words that refers to excrement. We know this because the rabbinical notations dictate that the pronunciation of גִּלֻּלִים was to be replaced by שִׁקֻּצִים, a more sanitized term meaning "abomination." Such a sanitizing tendency is common when dealing which potentially offensive rhetoric, but it does rob the text of its intended effect. Regardless, one can see how the historian slanders pagan religion through a clever use of terms.

However, all was not perfect with Asa's reign. Beginning with a disjunctive clause, the text emphatically states that Asa's reforms were not absolute. Despite all the idolatrous influences that Asa removed, he allowed the "high places" to remain. The term is derived from the Hebrew בָּמוֹת and generally refers to a cultic location that featured worship of some kind. While the exact nature of these locations is elusive, it's clear that the historian perceives them to be an illegitimate influence that compromised proper worship. In fact, the high places will be a common point of criticism by the writer.[1]

Nevertheless, verse 14b prevents any negativity from going too far. Beginning with a contrastive particle (רַק), the text tempers any negative assessment by stating that Asa's heart was at peace (שָׁלֵם) with the Lord. It's as if the historian does not want the reader to dwell too much on the negativity of Asa's reign. Furthermore, there is a possible wordplay between verses 12 and 15, which brackets Asa's regnal summary and playfully focuses upon Asa's commitment to the purity of worship in Jerusalem. Asa removed the "male prostitutes" and brought sanctioned sacrifices to the temple.

In verse 16, the text entertains the conflict between Israel and Judah. In one telling turn of events, King Baasha encroached upon Judean territory by building up Ramah as a strategic location designed to choke Judah out of the geopolitical scene (v. 17). To counter this move, Asa essentially liquidates his assets to entice the Aramean king Ben-Hadad to forsake his standing agreements with Israel and move against Israel's northern border. Apparently, Asa was savvy enough, for verses 19–20 reveal that Ben-Hadad forged a covenant with

---

1   Religious syncretism and its negative impact on the longevity of both Israel and Judah is a dominant theme in Kings. At the heart of it is the term בָּמָה, often translated "high place." The term appears just over one hundred times in the Old Testament, and overwhelmingly refers to places of unsanctioned worship. Yet despite this tendency, there is significant debate around this term.

Etymologically, the Hebrew term is linked to the Ugaritic *bmt* and the Akkadian *bāmtu* or *bāntu*. Semantically, בָּמָה encompasses the idea of the "back part of something" to an elevated place of worship. In the case of the latter range of possibilities, בָּמָה describes both man-made places of worship or naturally occurring, open-air locations. Archaeologically, it's impossible to count all the "high places" that have been identified, but Vaughn has argued that the ubiquitous identification is somewhat problematic (Vaughn 1974). Indeed, Vaughn is correct to point out that no purported "high place" in the archaeological record has been inscriptionally verified as such. Rather, these sites are identified as "high places" based on the profile gleaned from the Old Testament. However, Vaughn's methodological caution ultimately seems too much.

In some cases, scholars have opted for a more generalized approach. Instead of thinking of בָּמָה as a platform or high point, perhaps it's best just to render בָּמָה as "shrine" or "cult complex" (Whitney 1979). Such a suggestion is enticing and does properly represent some of the occurrences of בָּמָה. However, to imply that it always represents a generically defined "shrine" versus an architecturally distinct installation is fallacious (Barrack 1992, 3:198).

In the end, it's best to understand that בָּמָה is an expansive term that can refer to topographical and ecological features as well as diversely styled worship sites. These sites could be in cities or in rural areas. They may or may not be associated with an elevated location. Regardless, the critical feature of Kings is that these "high places" became socially and theologically problematic. According to 1 Kings 3, and other passages in the Old Testament (e.g., 1 Sam. 9–10), the worship of the Lord at a בָּמָה was not illegitimate. However, with the construction of the temple and the centralization of worship in Jerusalem, this changed. And Kings traces how their persistence was a driving force in the religious apathy of Judah and Israel.

Asa and attacked Israel. Predictably, Baasha stopped work on fortifying Ramah in order to reallocate his resources. This, in turn, allowed Asa to seize Israelite resources left at Ramah and use them to build up Geba of Benjamin. Through brilliant political maneuvering, Asa flipped Israelite aggression on its head.

On the one hand, one can't help but marvel at Asa's political maneuvering. On the other hand, Asa's actions are open to notable criticism, criticism which the Chronicler seizes and develops (cf. 2 Chron. 16:7–10). As detailed by Wray Beal (2014, 212–13), Asa responds to the threat of Israel not by trusting in the Lord, but in Aram. Moreover, it's never a good thing to use the temple's resources to secure safety. Consequently, ambiguity surrounds Asa, much like Solomon. Asa values the temple of Jerusalem and successively navigates the political scene. However, those political policies also open the community to negative influences. In the end, Asa is separated from Solomon by his classification as a "good king."

Asa's account closes with a random statement that seems to crave further explanation (cf. 2 Chron. 16:11–14). Yet Kings just reveals that "in his old age he was diseased in his feet" (v. 23). Scholars speculate as to what this refers, and possibilities include gout, vascular disease with gangrene, or a venereal disease (Wiseman 2008, 168–69).

Israelite Kings (15:25–16:20)

The initial years of Israel's rule were marked by short reigns, covenantal infidelity, and dynastic instability.

15:25–32. The dynastic instability that will characterize Israel is put on full display. In just a few verses, Israel will boast three different dynasties, each of which are ushered in by a coup d'état and synchronized with the reign of Asa. But the political instability of Israel vis-à-vis the dynastic stability of Judah is not the only thing that feeds the contrast inherent to 14:21–16:20. All the northern kings are classified as "evil" kings, and in the cases of Nadab, Baasha, and Zimri, their judgment is explicitly linked to the sins of Jeroboam (15:29–30; 16:2–4, 12–13, 19). Thus, a stark contrast is established between Israel and Judah, a contrast that will fundamentally inform the entire literary unit (1 Kings 14:21–2 Kings 20:21).

The account of Nadab is brief, just long enough to give the standard regnal evaluation and a few details of Baasha's coup. Of those details, it's important to note that the coup transpired at Gibbethon, apparently an important border site. According to the account, Baasha killed Nabad while Israel laid siege to the Philistine city. No outcome of this siege is given, but in 1 Kings 16:15 the text reveals that Omri heard of Zimri's usurpation while laying siege to Gibbethon. Secondly, the assassination of Nadab is linked to the judgment pronounced upon Jeroboam by Ahijah (1 Kings 15:29–30). Thus, this destabilizing act is explained in prophetic and theological terms. More importantly, dynastic instability is the righteous outcome of covenantal infidelity.

15:33–16:7. While Baasha's account is short, the historian creates an effective parallel with Jeroboam. Like Jeroboam, a prophetic indictment is leveled at Baasha (16:1–4), and like Jeroboam, Baasha was chosen by the Lord to be the leader of Israel. Unfortunately, Baasha also enticed the nation to sin, incurring the anger of the Lord in the process. And in the end, Baasha's house suffered the same shameful, disgraceful fate as Jeroboam.

16:8–20. Elah is the unfortunate king who is remembered for an ignominious reign cut short by one of his generals. Interestingly, the text reveals that at the time of his death, Elah was in Tirzah "drinking himself drunk." Consequently, Zimri, commander of half the royal chariots, arose against Elah, killed him, and put down the royal family. An implication could be that Zimri was not willing to stand by and watch his king drink himself into oblivion and take his country down with him. Regardless of the reasoning—whether patriotism or raw ambition—Zimri's initiative did not pay off. His reign was only seven days. A week after securing the throne from the Baashite dynasty, the general Omri laid siege to Tirzah. When Zimri realized his imminent demise, he fled to the citadel where he was killed in a conflagration. Strand Winslow argues that Omri's movement against Zimri was out of responsibility and not ambition—that as Zimri's superior he needed to punish him for his usurpation (Strand Winslow 2017, 135). Indeed, Omri was the "commander of the army over Israel" (שַׂר־צָבָא עַל־יִשְׂרָאֵל), which may imply that he was Zimri's superior, and yet there is no explicit statement of conspiracy in the text. But to suggest that his actions were merely those born out of some bureaucratic responsibility seems facile.

THEOLOGICAL FOCUS

The exegetical idea (Both Judean and Israelite kings generally failed to honor the Lord and his expectations, yet the intensity of judgment was pacified in Judah because of David's legacy and the occasional good king) leads to this theological focus: Judgment can only be pacified temporarily, for without complete repentance the root of sin will only grow and consume.

Devoted to discussing the initial reigns after Rehoboam and Jeroboam, this section describes a politically fluid and tumultuous period. It weaves together spiritual and geopolitical upheaval as it juxtaposes the utter failings of the Israelite kings with the general failings of the Judean kings. The only difference between Israel and Judah is the occasional good king and legacy of David.

Asa is one of those occasional good kings. He is said to have done right in the eyes of the Lord, and the text recounts significant reform under his reign. Yet Asa's reforms were not complete. Nestled among the discussion of his reforms, the text explicitly states that the "high places" remained, which is an important qualification. As we shall see, the reforms of Josiah at the end of the seventh century will target these "high places." The high places will come to saturate the nation and become a driving force of pagan and illegitimate worship. In other words, Asa's inability, or unwillingness (it's not clear), to eradicate a problematic feature of Judean culture festered to the point where only the most violent of religious purges could reign it in.

This historical reality sheds light on the gravity of repentance. Repentance must be complete and targeted. It can't be partial or imprecise. Repentance refers to the reversal of a course of action and a return to a certain standard. Consequently, if repentance is not complete, or imprecise, then it's likely that what influences remain will grow and eventually facilitate disastrous circumstances. In a particularly telling example, Hosea laments that Israel's repentance was so lax and imprecise that the pagan influences grew so intense that the nation could not repent and escape judgment even if they wanted to (Hos. 5:4). Here, we see how insufficient repentance grew into destructive habits that sealed judgment. For Kings, the situation will be similar. The inability or unwillingness of certain kings to rid the country of certain negative influences eventually prevented proper repentance and sealed the inevitability of the exile.

PREACHING AND TEACHING STRATEGIES

Exegetical and Theological Synthesis

The further out Judah and Israel get from the glorious days of David and Solomon, the more their kingdoms resemble the frailties of those eras rather than the grandness. This passage documents the various leaders of the divided kingdoms and how they largely failed to live up to the covenant in the ways God desired. Both kingdoms suffer through a great amount of political instability as a result. The rare positive highlights are tied to either God's unmerited favor (Abijam) or seeking his favor through repentance (Asa).

When we contract a serious illness, we are not going to accept a treatment plan that will only partially help us. If at all possible, we will want a plan that leads to a full healing and recovery. No one wants to remain "kind of sick" or "partially cured." If that's true of our physical health, why is that often not reflected in how we view our spiritual health? We cannot take tiny steps to deal with our spiritual struggles when big steps are required to truly fix the problem. Asa's shining example of leading reforms in Judah is tempered with a statement revealing how those steps were incomplete. That is a relevant lesson for our lives. As we have noted in other parts of this story, God desires full devotion and full loyalty. Our sin is an affront to God, and it must be seriously confronted.

Preaching Idea
Half-measures of repentance won't cure full measures of rebellion.

Contemporary Connections

What does it mean?
What does it mean that half-measures of repentance won't cure full measures of rebellion? Under my (Lee's) house is a crawl space where our heating and cooling ducts run from room to room. Recently, almost by accident, we discovered that moisture had rusted out a good-sized hole near the base of the duct where it connected to our furnace. This was beginning to cause our heating and cooling system to inefficiently run for longer and longer lengths of time. Initially, I took some scrap pieces of cardboard and duct-taped them to close the hole. This was a stopgap

measure that didn't perfectly fix the problem—a reality I discovered soon after when I found the duct tape wasn't staying secured. A half-measure solution wasn't good enough; I had to seek out something better. Thankfully, some members of our church had expertise in these kinds of projects and were able to completely replace our ductwork. Only that full-measure solution was able to fix our problem.

That's a good analogy for how we deal with our sinful habits. Dealing with sin in partial ways may work out in the short term, much like Asa's reforms did. But we must deal with all of our sin, its causes, its behaviors, its attitudes—everything in full. The alcoholic will need to become a teetotaler, and may also need to find a social replacement for the bar/party scene if that was part of the draw. The gambler will not just need to cut himself off from the things that feed his habit, but he may also have to do some soul-searching about what is driving him to risk his financial well-being again and again.

Is it true?
Is it true that half-measures of repentance won't cure full measures of rebellion? As this section moves across history from king to king, the repeated pattern certainly makes a compelling case that partial repentance and reforms can't fully counteract long-standing rebellion. Each king is evaluated by his covenant loyalty, and most fail the test. Asa is a bright spot, but even his turnarounds were short-lived. Their temporary nature is connected by the text to the less-than-complete extent of Asa's reforms. His reign is an overall breath of fresh air, but it wasn't without fault. Consider Matthew 12:43–45, where Jesus talks about a demon being cast out of a person and then returning with more demons later on. While the situation of the person described is unusual and thought-provoking, the common understanding is that Jesus is speaking of the need for sinners to completely devote themselves to God and not hold back in the process of repentance.

The theological truth of this is matched by its practical authenticity too. Is it wise for a gambler to visit a casino? Should a recovering alcoholic still visit bars on occasion? The same is true for all sin we may battle with, whether lust, greed, lying, or anger. We cannot experience true freedom and victory without fully divorcing ourselves from the things that tempt us and trigger our sin.

Now what?

If it's true that half-measures of repentance won't cure full measures of rebellion, what can we do to wholeheartedly repent and avoid rebellion like the plague? Do not misunderstand—while Asa's reforms weren't absolute, they did make a difference. His "half-measures" were miles better than what his predecessors, successors, and peers did. The spiritual improvements were good, though they fell short of totally restoring God's people to spiritual vitality.

Some gardening metaphors may help us apply this. First, *weed out sin at its root.* Changing the wrong behaviors is good; changing the wrong beliefs is even better. That's what Jesus is teaching us for a good portion of his famous Sermon on the Mount. In Matthew 5:21–6:4, he steps from one issue to another, sidestepping controversy to get to the heart of each matter. Whether we are counseling our brothers and sisters or dealing with our own problems, we should strive to address the behavior and its root cause. We need to confess our sin to God regularly and transparently, so as not to let any weed grow up in our lives that will cause bigger problems later on.

Second, we must *cultivate a tender heart for God.* Just like plants need good soil to properly grow, our lives will bear good fruit when our hearts are truly aligned with God and his will. Our hearts will flourish when we are worshipping, guided by God's Word, and when we are surrounded by like-minded followers of Christ who will encourage us in our spiritual walk. Paul's parallel passages of Colossians 3:16 and Ephesians 5:18–21 underscore each of these elements for cultivating a faith and life that grows and endures.

Creativity in Presentation

Diaper changing—that unpleasant responsibility that every parent must both embrace and endure. Our struggle with sin can mirror diaper changing in many ways. Sometimes, there's little to no mess, but a change is still needed since rashes and other unpleasantries can develop if a wet or dirty diaper goes unaddressed. That is much like the daily confession that's necessary to weed out sin at its root.

Of course, every parent has had to deal with a "blowout" situation at one time or another. The mess requires extra wipes, additional clothes, special aroma-reducing bags, an unscheduled bath, and plenty of other things that good parents will have on hand for those times when a simple diaper change isn't possible. At times, we can allow our bad habits and sinful tendencies to fester like a messy diaper. And eventually it will require extra effort to clean up if we don't want our lives to stink.

Alternatively, one could use the example of changing clothes after a workout at the gym or after a long day's work. Much like the language Paul uses in Colossians 3, because of the change God brings about internally, we need to be wearing the clothes to match externally.

When it comes to outlining and preaching this passage, it may be simplest to group the pericopes by their clearly identifiable themes. In the suggested outline below, we pair the first and last sections because their content is focused on the sinful rebellion by the leaders and their people. The middle two passages offer glimmers of hope, both with God's gracious decision in 1 Kings 15:4 and Asa's reforms in 1 Kings 15:9–24. One could easily bookend the "rebellion" sections to underscore that the reforms didn't make a lasting difference, because they weren't full-measured.

The key idea to communicate is that half-measures of repentance won't cure full measures of rebellion. The passage for this preaching unit can be outlined in the following points:

- Rampant rebellion leads to chaos and calamity (14:21–30; 15:25–16:20).
- Partial reform leads to temporary relief (15:1–8, 9–24).

DISCUSSION QUESTIONS

1. How are each of the kings in this section remembered? List the positive or negative summaries as they are given by the author:

Rehoboam	Baasha
Abijam	Elah
Asa	Zimri
Nadab	

2. How should Pharaoh Shishak's entrance into this story be interpreted (14:25–28)?

3. What are the reforms that King Asa instituted? What did he fail to reform (15:9–15)?

4. How is Asa's legacy similar to that of Solomon's (15:9–24)?

5. As the focus turns to the northern tribes of Israel, what characterizes these leaders and their reigns (15:30; 16:2, 7, 9, 13, 19)?

1 Kings 16:21–34

EXEGETICAL IDEA
Omride policies brought an aggressive policy shift that sought to stabilize the region but also brought the entrenchment of Canaanite religion.

THEOLOGICAL FOCUS
The egregiousness of Omride sins exists in their high-handedness, which fundamentally undermines the ethos of God's people.

PREACHING IDEA
Prosperity is a tragedy when it comes at the expense of piety.

PREACHING POINTERS
On a strictly historical level, the Omride dynasty was wildly successful. The northern tribes finally found leaders who gave them stability and security. All was not well, however. King Omri and his son Ahab ushered in an era of religious apostasy that God's people had never experienced. The lesson for the readers of 1 Kings couldn't be any clearer: prosperity shouldn't be pursued apart from piety. Throughout history, God's people would have to hold those two factors in tension. The prophets often chastised Israel for defrauding the impoverished and vulnerable. The postexilic, Second Temple, and New Testament periods were all filled with political struggles for various levels of freedom and independence. Israel always had a spiritual conscience, however, and there were many who sought to spiritually discern how best to pursue those marks of success.

The church in the West has faced this balance between prosperity and piety in historically unique ways. Since the dawn of the twentieth century, American Christians have found themselves citizens of an economically flourishing and politically powerful nation. How have we used our strength and influence? The United States has been a global launching point for the gospel. Many ministries have been created that have sought to use material wealth to help the disadvantaged. However, in some cases, Western culture has been promoted itself rather than our Christ. In some cases, especially within North American evangelicalism, the rights and perspectives of women and ethnic minorities have not been fully acknowledged. In some cases, the church in the West has identified with political movements even when they go against Scripture's admonitions. Those compromises result in a diminished witness, which is a true tragedy.

THE OMRIDES ESTABLISHED (16:21–34)

LITERARY STRUCTURE AND THEMES (16:21–34)

The Omride dynasty finally puts an end to the intense political upheaval that characterized the first fifty years of Israel's existence. The dynasty also implemented aggressive policies that ushered in changes and influences that brought Israel's moral and spiritual apostasy to an entirely new level.

- *Omri (16:21–28)*
- *Ahab (16:29–34)*

EXPOSITION (16:21–34)

With his family in power, Omri implements policy shifts. The result was a method of operation that exploited opportunity while opening the nation up to negative cultural influences.

Omri (16:21–28)

Omri's reign was defined by an aggressive policy shift and intense apostasy.

16:21–24. The account of Omri's reign is short but telling. In the aftermath of Zimri's assassination, Israel was divided into rival factions. However, Omri's challenger, Tibni, was overrun when "the people who followed Omri overcame the people who followed Tibni son of Ginath" (v. 22). Thus, Omri's rise to the throne is remembered as a populist movement as much as it was the result of one man's charisma or ambition.

Yet Omri was opportunistic. Kings recalls how Omri purchased a hill from Shemer halfway through his reign to establish a new capital city in the central highlands. Such an effort echoes David's choice of Jerusalem to be his capital, as both sites were free of traditional tribal baggage, and highly strategic. More specifically, Samaria sits on the western slopes of the highlands, west of the watershed, and boasts proximity to roads that easily connect it to the coastal plain and the Jezreel Valley (Rasmussen 2010, 154). Omri's choice sought to make the capital of Israel more accessible to the Via Maris and exploit opportunities for economic advancement that were centered on the coastal plain.

16:25–28. However, the historical account buries any positive spin on Omri's decisions when it emphasizes that Omri "did what was evil in the sight of the LORD; he did more evil than all who were before him" (v. 25). Moreover, "he walked in all the way of Jeroboam son of Nebat, and in the sins that he caused Israel to commit, provoking the LORD, the God of Israel, to anger by their idols" (v. 26). Such a quick shift in the assessment of Omri's reign demonstrates that the significance of any socioeconomic opportunity was dwarfed by the spiritual implications associated with those opportunities.

Ahab (16:29–34)

Ahab further developed the sociopolitical ambitions and policies of his father, bringing with them Canaanite religion.

16:29–33. Ahab goes beyond the actions of his father. Whereas Omri walked in "all the way of Jeroboam" (v. 26), the egregiousness of Ahab's actions are framed by his marriage to the Phoenician princess Jezebel and the institution of full-blown Canaanite religion throughout Israel. According to verses 32–33, Ahab built a temple for Baal, put an official altar in that location, and constructed an asherah, or wooden pole that symbolized the goddess Asherah. Such actions incurred the invective of the historian, who unequivocally stated that Ahab "did more to provoke the anger of the LORD, the God of Israel, than had all the kings of Israel who were before him" (v. 33).

Yet there is another element to Ahab's marriage to Jezebel. It solidified a new trajectory in Israelite foreign policy. Presumably previous alliances were focused on the regions east of the Jordan Valley such as Aram (cf. 1 Kings 15:18–20), but the Israelite-Phoenician alliance sealed through the nuptials of Ahab and Jezebel consummated Omri's efforts. From this point forward, Israel, with its newly accessible capital in Samaria, would focus its economic resources to the west.

Syntactical Analysis:
The phrase הֲנָקֵל לֶכְתּוֹ בְּחַטֹּאות יָרָבְעָם בֶּן־נְבָט *is a dependent interrogative clause*. It therefore urges the reader to consider the magnitude of the king's apostasy. In colloquial terms, verse 31 can be translated, "As if his walking in the sins of Jeroboam son of Nebat was insignificant, it came to pass that he took . . . ".

16:34. This section ends with a peculiar note about Hiel from Bethel. According to the text, he rebuilt the foundations of Jericho as the expense of his children. Apparently, Hiel leveraged the lives of his oldest and youngest sons against revitalization of Jericho. Scholars struggle to explain the presence of this verse. For example, Wiseman ponders if it was sanctioned by Ahab in response to growing Moabite aggression (Wiseman 2008, 175). Clearly, it was added for a reason, but any widely accepted determination is elusive. Ultimately, its function is to serve as a historical anecdote that evidences what happens when ambition is valued above all else, including specifically stated divine decrees.

THEOLOGICAL FOCUS

The exegetical idea (Omride policies brought an aggressive policy shift that sought to stabilize the region but also brought the entrenchment of Canaanite religion) leads to this theological focus: The egregiousness of Omride sins exists in their high-handedness, which fundamentally undermines the ethos of the Lord's people.

What made Omride policies so egregious was not what they tried to accomplish. It's honorable to seek order and stability in the midst of chaos. Rather, it was how their goals were accomplished. Ambition, economic possibility, and social growth were the driving factors while specific expectations of the covenantal ethos were squashed. And when one also realizes from subsequent chapters that there were prophetic voices trying to curb Omride endeavors, one detects a certain level of brazenness to Omride policies.

The actions of the Omrides described in 1 Kings 16:21–34, therefore, echo what is described as "high-handed sin." According to Numbers 15:30, high-handed sin is sin committed with a certain level of blatant disregard for, or cockiness toward, the Lord's known moral and ethical standards. This accurately describes the arrogant policies of Omri and Ahab, as their policies brought with them theological influences that overtly and aggressively sought to suffocate the worship of the Lord. As for the punishment of such a willful violation, Numbers calls out excommunication. Kings, however, will later reveal that Ahab's death on the battlefield will be his punishment (1 Kings 22). In both cases, there is a strong sense of shame that accompanies the punishments.

Undoubtedly, one of the most famous cases of high-handed sin is that of Achan, who willfully violated the חֵרֶם pronounced upon Jericho. And similar to Ahab, his brazen sin resulted in a shameful death. And to be clear, there is no place for brazen, arrogant sin in the life of a Christian. First John makes this very clear. Speaking to children of God, John declares, "Everyone who commits sin is guilty of lawlessness . . . and in [Christ] there is no sin. No one who abides in him sins; no one who sins has either seen him or known him. . . . Everyone who commits sin is a child of the devil. . . . Those who have been born of God do not sin, because God's seed abides in them; they cannot sin, because they have been born of God" (1 John 3:4–6, 8–9). The relevant verbs in this passage appear in the present tense and carry with them a habitual nuance (Wallace 1996, 521). Thus, John is railing against continual sin in the lives of the people who also claim an identify as children of God. In the words of Smalley, John's words imply "not merely breaking God's law, but flagrantly opposing him (in Satanic fashion) by doing so" (Smalley 1984, 155).

PREACHING AND TEACHING STRATEGIES

Exegetical and Theological Synthesis
For all the progress that Omri and Ahab were able to accomplish, those achievements were hollow in God's eyes. Those leaders unashamedly flouted God's standards and allowed wickedness to spread among God's people. Prosperity and success are not bad things in and of themselves. It was the manner in which those things were pursued, the high-handedness of their actions, that incited God's punishment.

This part of Israel's history fits perfectly with what Jesus will teach later on when he states,

> He called the crowd with his disciples, and said to them, "If any want to become my followers, let them deny themselves and take up their cross and follow me. For those who want to save their life will lose it, and those who lose their life for my sake, and for the sake of the gospel, will save it. For what will it profit them to gain the whole world and forfeit their life? Indeed, what can they give in return for their life?" (Mark 8:34–37)

Will it be worth it if we sell out to achieve what the world considers successful? Will I make career advancement my sole priority? Have we even considered if our desire to achieve fame and popularity is at odds with Jesus's call to service and sacrifice? Teens encounter these questions among their peers in high school. College students must wrestle with these things as they consider their profession. Adults have to weigh these choices to balance their work, family, and church commitments and associations. Ministries themselves have to discern if their definition of success is in line with Jesus and his mission. God doesn't want to be a leftover priority, and he is disappointed when we pursue prosperity at the expense of faithfulness.

Preaching Idea
Prosperity is a tragedy when it comes at the expense of piety.

Contemporary Connections

What does it mean?
What does it mean that prosperity is a tragedy when it comes at the expense of piety? It means that any pursuit of success must have moral guardrails. It also means that without moral guardrails, we may career of a cliff as we speed our way toward accomplishing all goals and dreams.

Both churches and individual Christians should take this lesson to heart. Ministries will quickly lose their way if they substitute building programs and flourishing income statements for fruit of the Spirit as markers of true success. Getting recognized for attendance size or cultural influence are meager rewards if they are not accompanied by widespread life transformation. This is the same when one considers the common pursuit of personal success. Achieving one's lofty goals at the expense of family and friends is tragic. Basking in the glow of one's success while ignoring the wants and needs of others is shameful. Both corporately and personally, we have a responsibility to follow God's will, especially when he is blessing our efforts.

Is it true?

Is it true that prosperity is a tragedy when it comes at the expense of piety? Scripture calls us to be excellent in all our endeavors (Prov. 22:29; Col. 3:23–24). Aside from Jesus's teaching, Scripture is replete with examples that express how achieving success is a vain pursuit if it's not done God's way. Joshua 7 records how, in the aftermath of the great victory at Jericho, Achan and his family went against God's orders and selfishly stashed some treasure away for themselves. That secret sin led to an embarrassing defeat and tragic loss of life during their next battle at Ai. Matthew 19:16–30 describes Jesus's interaction with a rich young man who wants eternal life but balks at the call to give up his material possessions. James spends the better part of two chapters to warn his readers against showing favoritism toward the wealthy and buying into their hedonistic attitudes (James 2:1–13; 4:1–10).

Even the secular world recognizes the truth of this principle when given opportunity for reflection. Political activists decry Fortune 500 billionaires when their businesses overwork and underpay their employees as they continue to fill their coffers. Preachers and politicians alike draw the public's ire when their hypocrisy and greed are exposed. Positively, messages like the kind conveyed in the dramatic film *It's a Wonderful Life* (directed by Frank Capra, 1946) are universally celebrated for showing how being a good person is much more rewarding than being a rich person. Who wants to be Mr. Potter when we can be Mr. Bailey? What does being "the richest man in town" really look like? The world does not have the same values we do as Christians, but even they will admit that having some kind of moral compass is needed when chasing success.

Now what?

If it is true that prosperity is a tragedy when it comes at the expense of piety, how do we keep prosperity from becoming a tragedy? How can we make sure our moral compass doesn't break on the path toward success?

First of all, *keep your goals aligned with God's mission.* His Word reveals to us his priorities and his goals. We should make sure ours are lined up with his. Ministers should focus on things other than "buildings, bodies, and bucks" when gauging their church's spiritual well-being. Baptisms and the percentage of people involved in discipleship groups are better numbers to look at. Measuring true spiritual success requires different metrics and narratives than those used to measure success in the world.

Second, *listen to credible critics.* People can and will complain about everything, even when things are going well. But especially when things are going well, it is important to have people who can spot the weak areas and shortcomings. This applies to businesses, churches, and even to our family and personal lives. We need people in and around us who have the freedom to both critique and affirm us, those whom we trust to have our backs but whom we also give permission to call foul on us. And we need to listen to them and heed their advice.

Creativity in Presentation

The Social Network (directed by David Fincher, 2010) is a widely praised movie about the founder of Facebook, Mark Zuckerberg (played by Jesse Eisenberg). As the movie recounts, in his efforts to launch his revolutionary product, Zuckerberg's pursuit of success has cost him dearly, especially in the area of personal relationships. It can serve as a cautionary tale. The final scene memorably observes him, alone in a boardroom staring at his laptop. He begins repeatedly refreshing his own personal Facebook page, hoping his old college girlfriend will respond to his friend request. That scene could effectively introduce or conclude a sermon on this passage.

Besides the other potential illustrations we have cited above, there are other minor ways to illuminate the text. Many are familiar with the one favorable comment earned by Italy's fascist dictator: "Mussolini made sure the trains ran on time." Although an apparent misquotation, this saying is still a relevant metaphor. One could even couple that with touting all of the economic and political success a certain nation in Europe enjoyed before eventually revealing that the country being described was Hitler's Nazi Germany.

This pericope neatly divides in two, between King Omri and King Ahab. Both accounts record similarly negative evaluations. While there is not a lot to differentiate them, we see Omri's reign setting up Ahab's in a very adverse way, as Omri is evil but Ahab is worse than any of his predecessors. Thus, we can see how with Omri, progress is negated. With Ahab, it is accomplishments that are spoiled—especially with the narrator's emphasis on his foreign policy and that unique verse about the rebuilding of Jericho. That last note really punctuates the tragic nature of where God's people were morally and spiritually in that day and how their leadership led them to that place.

The key idea to communicate is that prosperity is a tragedy when it comes at the expense of piety. The passage for this preaching unit can be outlined in the following points:

- Great progress is negated by spiritual compromise (16:21–28).
- Great accomplishments are meaningless if evil is allowed to flourish (16:29–34).

DISCUSSION QUESTIONS

1. What kind of acumen does Omri display that would help the nation of Israel succeed? What decision of Ahab's would have helped his nation politically?

2. What is the spiritual evaluation that 1 Kings gives these men?

3. What specifically does the author cite to make such a verdict?

4. What does this teach us about the leaders we follow?

5. What sort of situations do we encounter where we feel the tension of piety versus prosperity?

PROPHETS AND KINGS
(1 KINGS 17:1–2 KINGS 13:25)

The second section of this second major literary unit in Kings is 1 Kings 17:1–2 Kings 13:25, which describes prophets and kings. This second section may be divided into two preaching units: first, Elijah and the Omrides (1 Kings 17:1–2 Kings 1:18); second, Elisha and kings (2:1–13:25). Together, the passages in this section cover much ground, historically and literarily. Spanning nineteen chapters and approximately one hundred years, this section revolves around royal and prophetic exploits. More specifically, Elijah and Elisha are featured alongside other prophetic figures, some anonymous and some named, to function as checks to royal ambition.

Each passage in this section focuses primarily upon the ministries of Elijah and Elisha respectively, both of which are concerned with solving or combating the theological and social problems that plagued God's people. For example, Elijah's divine encounter at Mount Horeb (or, Sinai) will reveal that the remainder of his ministry, and so much of Elisha's, will be concerned with facilitating judgment upon the Omride dynasty for its egregious apostasy. Similarly, Elisha's ministry will oversee the judgment leveled against Jehu's dynasty in light of their appeasement of Jeroboam's sins. Consequently, 1 Kings 17:1–2 Kings 13:25, perhaps more than any other section in Kings, shows the sometimes untidy convergence of prophecy, history, and geopolitics.

1 Kings 17:1–2 Kings 1:18

EXEGETICAL IDEA
Elijah embodied the prophetic institution, which was defined not by individual personalities but by its theological and social responsibilities.

THEOLOGICAL FOCUS
The essence of the prophetic institution continues when the Lord brings a specific word to a specific situation by means of Scripture.

PREACHING IDEA
God amplifies prophetic voices when we're having trouble hearing him.

PREACHING POINTERS
At this point in Israel and Judah's history, there is a big enough sample size to declare that the office of the king was failing to properly lead the people of God. King Ahab took over for his father, and like many kings before him he has only worsened the spiritual state of his nation. It is at this time that God raised up key prophets to deliver his message and call the people back to their covenant with the Lord. The message and the ministry of the prophets, especially Elijah, represents God's determination to keep his end of his covenant promises. As Walter Brueggemann (2001) puts it, the main function of the prophets was to "criticize" and "energize" God's people. They challenged the spiritually apathetic while encouraging the disillusioned with the hope of God's plan.

The exiled Israelites and those living in the postexilic world dealt with somewhat different circumstances. Their problem was not the presence of evil leadership—their issue was the lack of any internal leadership at all. That's why God raised up men like Ezra and Nehemiah as the people resettled their ancient homeland. Ezra and Nehemiah provided the godly administrative and spiritual leadership the people needed. As a pair, they encouraged the people in God's law and challenged those who doubted or opposed what God was doing. One can debate whether God still ordains prophets in an official, spiritual gift-type capacity. Yet, if one accepts Brueggemann's premise that prophets primarily served to criticize and energize, this author sees no reason to deny that prophetic voices are applicable and necessary for our day. The writings and ministries of those like A. W. Tozer and Dietrich Bonhoeffer certainly were prophetic in their day. The reality is that every generation has its own pockets of spiritual apathy and blindness. And every generation has pockets of faithful but discouraged believers too. It is for those times and for those people that God amplifies prophetic voices, so that those who need it most can hear God's message.

ELIJAH AND THE OMRIDES
(1 KINGS 17:1–2 KINGS 1:18)

LITERARY STRUCTURE AND THEMES
(1 KINGS 17:1–2 KINGS 1:18)

This lengthy portion of Scripture can be broken down twofold by several literary considerations. First, chapters 17–19 feature the prophet Elijah and are connected by several transitional sentences. For example, 1 Kings 17:1–7 is connected with chapter 18 through the issue of drought. Chapter 19 opens with an explicit reference to the events of chapter 18. Indeed, Elijah's interaction with the widow of Zarephath breaks up an otherwise smooth narrative flow. Yet as will be discussed, its function aligns with the function of chapters 17–19 as a whole. Second, in 1 Kings 20–2 Kings 1, Elijah noticeably fades into the background, only to make a few brief appearances. Moreover, the extensive dialogue offered by the prophet in chapters 17–19 is almost completely absent. Elijah is generally more of a passive character in 2 Kings 20–2 Kings 1.

- *Prophets and Problems*
  (1 Kings 17:1–19:21)
- *Wars and the End of Ahab and Elijah*
  (1 Kings 20:1–2 Kings 1:18)

EXPOSITION
(1 KINGS 17:1–2 KINGS 1:18)

This lengthy section details the many interactions between Elijah, Ahab, and Ahab's family. It shows the complex and sometimes intense interaction between prophets, kings, and people. The resulting picture details how the era of Omride rule was a constant battle for the soul of the northern kingdom. Specific followers of the Lord were compelled to stand in the gap and face off against central powers that sought to leverage sociopolitical opportunity against the spiritual vitality of the northern kingdom.

Prophets and Problems (1 Kings 17:1–19:21)

Elijah is shown to be a true prophet of the Lord who is responsible for clarifying the Lord's intentions for his people.

17:1–6. The text abruptly shifts in verse 1, moving from the regnal evaluations to a fully developed narrative. When it opens, Elijah is standing before Ahab, presumably at Samaria, revealing that by the decree of the Lord, precipitation in all forms will cease indefinitely. Interestingly, this proclamation comes in the form of a divine oath (versus a mere statement), giving Elijah, who at this point has only been defined by his home, a certain level of authority. Elijah is a prophet, although not explicitly stated at this point. Moreover, this oath-like pronouncement echoes the curses of Deuteronomy 27–28, revealing that this drought is more precisely understood as a covenantal curse in light of the nation's covenantal infractions (Wray Beal 2014, 231–32).

Verse 2 is equally abrupt as Elijah is told to depart and go east, to the Wadi Cherith, an unknown location that is likely in the immediate vicinity of the Jordan River. There, at this seasonal stream, the Lord miraculously provides for the distressed prophet by means of fresh water and food brought to him by ravens. Sweeney (2007, 21) is correct when he states that such provision recalls the wilderness traditions, in which the Lord provides for Israel by means of quail, manna, and water.

It's not clear where Tishbi was located. The manuscript evidence shows a struggle to make sense of Tishbi, but it's clear that Tishbi was located somewhere in the region of Gilead. Perhaps Tishbi was developed as a play on words to identify people from the "settlers of Gilead" (הַתִּשְׁבִּי מִתֹּשָׁבֵי גִלְעָד; *HALOT*, 2:1712–14). Regardless, the region of Gilead, being east of the Jordan Valley and possessing a relatively narrow strip of fertile land on the edge of the Arabian Desert (Rasmussen 26–28; 161), is the point of emphasis. Elijah, a prophet from a fringe region that borders an inhospitable wilderness, comes to the epicenter of Israelite culture to confront the figurehead of that culture. Elijah brings with him a word of judgment, in this case an indefinite drought. Thus, in the opening verses, Elijah's confrontation is more than a clash of personalities—it's the Lord sending his message to confront the central power structures and their method of operation. Such social dynamics are typical of the way the prophetic office functions (Schreiner 2019, 30–34; also, Introduction above).

Baal

The name Baal refers to an important Canaanite deity who appears throughout the Old Testament as an archnemesis of the Lord (Yahweh). However, there is evidence to suggest that the lines were blurred between Baal and Yahweh in some circles of Israelite and Judean society. For example, some Old Testament texts speak of Yahweh by themes that are also linked to Baal (e.g., Exod. 15; Pss. 29, 74; Dan. 7).

Outside of the Old Testament, Baal first appears in a text from the third millennium BCE. Elsewhere, Baal is copiously referenced in a variety of texts, from a variety of contexts, in a variety of ways. He is the son of El, but is also referenced as the son of Dagan. He is clearly associated with issues of agricultural and reproductive fertility, but there are also other functions attributed to him, such as being the protector of people against cosmic forces. With Asherah, Baal constitutes a force that threatens the religious and ethical systems of the Lord's people (Day 1992, 1:545–49; Herrmann 1999, 131–38).

17:7–16. Most commentators place verse 7 with the previous six verses. However, reading verses 7–24 as a unit has the benefit of including the full introduction of Elijah's sojourn into Phoenician territory (Wray Beal 2014, 232). Verses 7–16 continue the miraculous provision of food (cf. v. 4 with v. 9), and verses 17–24 demonstrate the Lord's (Yahweh's) rule over sickness and death. Together, chapter 17 initiates the Lord's challenge of Baal, which will reach a climax on Mount Carmel. The Lord is operating on Baal's turf and he (not Baal) is in control of the heavens. It's the Lord who is providing sustenance in the middle of catastrophic drought, not to mention resurrecting people. As Sweeney (2007, 209) says, the Lord is confronting certain aspects of Baal's power: his control of nature, his home in Phoenicia, and his ability to sustain life.

Having received the word of the Lord, Elijah obediently goes into Phoenician territory to find a widow appointed by the Lord. At the city gate, the customary congregating point for travelers in search for provision, the prophet finds the widow "gathering sticks." He calls out to her, rather bluntly, urging her to bring him some water. She complies, only to find that the prophet then asks for food. Initially, the widow deflects. With an emphatic pronouncement, by an oath addressed to the Lord (v. 12), she testifies that her intentions are to return home, fix one final meal, and die in peace (v. 12). All of this creates a gut-wrenching scene; she has resigned herself and her son to death. Consequently, the commands of the prophet (vv. 10–11) initially strike the contemporary reader as insensitive. Yet there are larger issues in play.

In addition to the anti-Baal polemic, Elijah, as a sojourner, is assuming longstanding social

Elijah Receiving Bread from the Widow of Zarephath by Giovanni Lanfranco. Public domain.

17:17–24. The moral obligations associated with hospitality and sharing meals can explain the emotional accusations of verse 18. Sometime after the miraculous provision of food, the son of the widow, who is called the "mistress of the house" in verse 17 (בַּעֲלַת הַבָּיִת), falls seriously ill. The text tells us that "there was no breath in him" (לֹא־נוֹתְרָה־בּוֹ נְשָׁמָה), but some scholars ponder if he had actually died (e.g. Sweeney 2007, 215). While reasonable, such a position relegates the woman's accusation to mere rhetoric and does not consider the implications of נְשָׁמָה, the word for "breath." It occurs twenty-five times in the Old Testament, one of which appears in Genesis 2:7 as the "breath of life" that God breathed into Adam at creation. Thus, while there is no explicit statement that the son died, the reader could infer as much. Most importantly, the woman understands this turn of events to be a personal punishment for her sins (1 Kings 17:18). According to her, Elijah is no longer the agent of provision. Rather, he is a harbinger of judgment. She is distraught and understands her hospitality to have been worthless.

Elijah's response is immediate. Like the previous command for her to bring him a small cake (v. 11), Elijah again issues a command—to give him her son. The prophet then takes the son to his quarters in the "upper room," where he lays him upon his bed, prays to the Lord, and stretches himself over the son three times (vv. 19–21). The content of the prayer is quite bold. It's a rhetorical question that places the onus on the Lord. I (David) translate the Hebrew of verse 20 as follows: "O Lord, my God! Even to the widow, with whom I am staying as a sojourner, will you act terribly by killing her son?" With such a statement, Elijah is highlighting what's at stake for her future (the killing of her only means of provision as she gets older) and the unfairness of the turn of events (her moral uprightness for allowing Elijah to stay as a foreigner). Righteousness is not supposed to secure calamity.

customs. He proceeds to the city's gate complex (פֶּתַח הָעִיר) because as the city's place of public assembly, travelers sought provision and lodging there (cf. Judg. 19:15). Elijah is also appealing to the social norms of hospitality, which mandated that people were obligated to offer provision and safety to travelers (King and Stager 2001, 61–63, 234–36). As for the sharing of food, it signaled an intensification of the relationship. By sharing a meal, the two parties would have effectively ratified a set of moral obligations between them. Nevertheless, the woman is a widow and the situation dire, which explains the widow's initial desire to pass Elijah along. How can she be expected to honor such expectations when she is on the precipice of death? This is why Elijah must be forceful and encourage her not to be afraid (v. 13). It's not insensitivity. Rather, it's a call to look beyond the tragedy of her current context and fulfill moral and social responsibilities. If she can do that, the prophet declares that she will be repaid with a perpetual supply of bread. Ultimately, the widow obeys, and, according to verse 16, she is repaid accordingly.

The prophet apparently did not wait for an answer. He quickly performs an action over the limp body three times, but the precise nature of it is elusive. Theories include a medical procedure, ritual purification, or sympathetic magic (Kiuchi 1994, 74–75, 78; Lasine 2004, 123–25; Sweeney 2007, 215n26). However, Davis has argued on linguistic and comparative grounds that Elijah's action was not stretching but some type of shaking to diagnose a probable coma (Davis 2016). Regardless of the exact action, the text reveals that "the LORD heard the voice of Elijah," which produced the resuscitation of her son. This is significant, as it represents a focal point of the episode. The prophet of the Lord not only has the privilege of bearing the divine word and being the facilitator of divine action, but he also has a relationship that is so close that he can boldly intercede and influence the actions of the

Elijah Raises the Son of the Widow of Zarephath by Gustave Doré. Public domain

Lord. Or, as Davis says, the prophet can mediate the power of the Lord (Davis, 481).

Upon the son's healing, the prophet brings him downstairs and hands him to his mother. His response is concise, "See, your son is alive" (17:23). And the woman's response constitutes an emphatic conclusion to verses 7–24: "Now I know that you are a man of God, and that the word of the LORD in your mouth is truth." This confession is also literarily important, because the legitimacy of Elijah's ministry and the deity whom he represents will be challenged publicly in the next section of text. Thus, these verses establish the prophet's credibility and the Lord's global power in anticipation of the showdown on Mount Carmel.

18:1–2. Chapter 18 opens with an imprecise chronological marker. The question is whether it refers to the point when the drought began (17:1–7) or after the resuscitation of the Phoenician boy. Given that what transpired happened in the third year of the drought, "after many days" (v. 1) likely refers to the elapsed time between Elijah's new command and the resuscitation of the Phoenician boy. Regardless, the command is clear. Elijah is to return to Ahab so that the Lord can send rain. Based on the syntax of the Hebrew, there is a causative relationship here; the obedience of the prophet will result in precipitation. Moreover, the syntax shows that Elijah's return to Ahab was foremost about alleviating the severe famine (v. 2).

18:3–16. Verses 3–16 switches focus to Obadiah, the individual in charge of the palace (lit., the one "who was over the house"). This switch constitutes a digression from the main thrust of the narrative, which is about bringing back precipitation (see above). Obadiah has been zealous, covertly defying Queen Jezebel. While she was hunting down the prophets of the Lord, Obadiah boldly hid one hundred prophets of the Lord in two caves and provided them with sustenance (v. 3). Indeed, the daily provision of one hundred mouths is no small feat, but as the chief administrator of the palace, he would have had access to the necessary goods. Moreover, this continues the theme of unlikely provision observed throughout chapter 17.

At some point not disclosed by the text, Ahab conscripted Obadiah's help to find resources for the royal equine herd, which was not only a valuable commodity in the Iron Age but also a defining characteristic of Ahab's rule. The Kurkh Monolith gives an account of the Battle of Qarqar (853 BCE) and testifies to the potency of Ahab's army, which featured a sizable chariot corp (*COS*, 2.113A).[1] Yet most importantly, there's something poetic here. Obadiah is smuggling food for one hundred mouths while the royal equines are starving.

Eventually, Ahab and Obadiah split (vv. 5–6), and it's when they split that Obadiah meets Elijah. The precise location is not revealed, but Obadiah is overwhelmed at the sight of the prophet. He falls prostrate and addresses him deferentially, "Is that you, my lord, Elijah?" Elijah responds in the affirmative and then sanctions the palace supervisor to reveal the prophet's location to the king. Interesting, Elijah's expectation is that Ahab would come to him. However, Obadiah is skeptical, not to mention fearful. Based on Obadiah's testimony, Ahab had begun to deploy search parties across the region in search for the prophet. Apparently these were serious endeavors, indicative of an obsession. Obadiah recounts how any unsuccessful effort had to be verified under an oath. Consequently, Obadiah was

keenly aware that any false alarm would result in his death.

Obadiah is convinced that the prophet's transient nature was problematic. He feared that as the message made its way to the king, the prophet would move on from that location, resulting in a royal waste of time. Most importantly, such a waste would likely get Obadiah killed (v. 12), and such an ignominious death would not align properly with the expected result of his fierce defiance and faithful service to the prophets of the Lord. So, to calm Obadiah's anxiety, Elijah counters with his own oath. He swears by the Lord that he would seek an audience with Ahab on that very day (v. 15). This was apparently satisfactory. Verse 16 reveals that Obadiah returned to Ahab and revealed that he located Elijah.

18:17–19. Ahab meets Elijah with an accusation. However, most translations fail to communicate the intensity of the interrogation. The sense of the Hebrew is, in fact, more accusatory than inquiry-based. The phrase (הַאַתָּה זֶה עֹכֵר יִשְׂרָאֵל) is properly translated, "Is that *you*, O troubler of Israel?!" In response, Elijah is just as forceful. First, he clearly throws the blame back upon the Omride dynasty by calling out their apostasy, specifically their allegiance to "the Baals." Next, he proposes an ultimatum, a showdown that will pit the Lord (Yahweh) and Elijah against the prophets of Baal and Asherah. It will happen on Mount Carmel and take place in full view of the public (v. 19). Yet most interesting is the logic behind the challenge. Verse 19 opens with the particle

---

1   The battle of Qarqar (853 BCE) must be understood against Iron Age imperial ambitions of the Neo-Assyrian Empire. The Assyrian desire to claim Egypt into their empire ensured that Israel and Judah, along with their neighbors, would come under siege. During the campaign of Shalmaneser III, a coalition of nations met the ambitious Neo-Assyrian army near the Orontes River where the exact outcome is difficult to understand. The account of the battle is commemorated upon the Kurkh Monolith, a limestone monument reaching over seven feet discovered by British archaeologists in the middle of the nineteenth century. What is clear is that the Assyrians did not recall any further advancement in the immediate aftermath of the battle, suggesting that the coalition, which included King Ahab of Israel, successfully hindered the Assyrian advance.

עַתָּה, which suggests that this turn of events is in response to the specific accusation of verse 17. In other words, it's possible to understand the showdown on Mount Carmel as a spontaneous challenge.

Syntactical Analysis:

The Hebrew phrase הַאַתָּה זֶה עֹכֵר יִשְׂרָאֵל in verse 17 displays two important features. The interrogative particle and the demonstrative pronoun combine to intensify the clause. And given the demands of the context, the intensity of the interchange focuses upon the accusation versus whether Ahab recognized Elijah.

18:20–29. Regardless of whether the showdown was planned or not, Ahab accepts. He, the people of Israel, and the prophets gather on Mount Carmel, a strategic choice. Geographically, it highlighted the Mediterranean coast and controlled the north/south movement along the Coastal Plain into the Jezreel Valley. It received ample rain, making it a lush environment and symbolic of agricultural fertility. If there was any place in the region where Baal should have had the upper hand, it was here. And as a mountain, it possessed conceptual significance, as mountains were perceived to be places where the heavenly and terrestrial realms met (cf. 1 Kings 8). Consequently, Mount Carmel was the ideal location to see a religious and political ultimatum play out.

Once all parties were assembled, Elijah opens with a simple question designed to force the nation of Israel to consider their indecisiveness and waywardness: "How long will you go limping with two different opinions? If the LORD is God, follow him; but if Baal, then follow him" (v. 21). The Hebrew is more colorful. It literally reads, "How long with you limp upon two crutches?" Moreover, the word for "limp" in verse 21 plays off verse 27, where the same verb (פסח) denotes the ritualistic action of the pagan prophets. Thus, Elijah begins his address by insulting the pagan practitioners and the nation

as a whole by associating their ritualistic actions and indecisiveness with chronic disability.

Israel doesn't respond to Elijah's initial question. Elijah then proceeds to detail the dynamics of the contest. He calls for two bulls, one of which will be sacrificed. On the one hand, one will be prepared by the prophets of Baal. It will be cut into pieces and set upon an altar prepared for a sacrifice. On the other hand, Elijah will do the same. However, in both cases, the fires shall not be lit. The god who proves himself to be indeed God will light the fire. With this explained, the people finally answer and accept the conditions (v. 24). Elijah allows the prophets of Baal to go first (v. 25).

The text discloses that the prophets of Baal called upon Baal for hours but with no answer. They shouted and danced, but no answer. Then at noon, Elijah began to mock them (v. 27). As if Baal could not hear, he told them to shout louder. He questioned whether Baal was preoccupied or even on holiday. In response, the prophets shouted louder, continued their ritualistic dancing, and began to customarily gash themselves as a display of their commitment to the deity (v. 29; Roberts 1970). The text even recounts how "blood flowed." To the reader, this situation is appalling. Yet as time passed, and Baal remained silent, the prophets of Baal became more desperate. But this is the point. The frenzied actions of the prophets of Baal are set in stark contrast to the calm actions of Elijah. Whereas the prophets yell, dance, and cut themselves, Elijah calmly prays to the Lord to decisively show himself mighty (vv. 36–37).

18:30–40. All this proceeds past midday, until the time of the evening sacrifice (vv. 29, 36). At this point, Elijah gathers the populace around him where he begins to rebuild a decrepit altar. Of particular importance is the use of twelve stones, representative of the twelve tribes. Moreover, Elijah proceeds to make some upgrades to his altar in comparison to the one constructed by his opponents. First, he cuts a trench around the base of the altar. Then, he orders twelve jars of water to be poured over the sacrifice. It's difficult to know precisely how much water was used, but it's telling that the description emphasizes that the wood and offering were drenched. According to verse 35, "the water ran all around the altar, and filled the trench also with water." This is particularly striking, given that this showdown takes place in the context of a crippling drought.

With the soaked offering prepared, "at the time of the offering of the oblation" (v. 36), Elijah prays and asks God to reveal himself in a mighty way. The Hebrew is a bit vague with this chronological marker, and so there is some debate on precisely when this sacrifice took place. According to Pentateuchal legislation, there were daily sacrifices in the morning and the evening (cf. Exod. 29:38–42; Num. 28:3–8). However, later Jewish traditions speak about a daily sacrifice earlier in the day as well. If the sacrifice happened in the evening, at sundown, how would there be enough time for Elijah to round up the prophets and execute them? However, DeVries correctly emphasizes the positioning of "today" in the Hebrew syntax (230). In other words, the immediacy of events is the point of emphasis. *Today* the ultimatum is realized.

The brevity and logic of the prophet's prayer is telling. Foremost, it's short, contrasting with the long affair of the prophets of Baal (Wiseman 2008, 182). Also, Elijah's prayer appeals to the patriarchal traditions, defining God by his historical relationship with Abraham, Isaac, and Jacob. Most importantly, Elijah prays that two things are revealed: first, that the people of Israel would know that the Lord is God in Israel; second, that the people realize that Elijah has been a faithful servant of the Lord, faithfully doing his bidding (v. 36). Then there is the emphatic call to action. "Answer me, O Lord, answer me" (1 Kings 17:37), which brings bring the focus of the prayer back to the Lord's revelation of his power. It's an emphatic plea, not to be silent like Baal has been to his prophets. And if the Lord answers, the prophet is confident that it will result in the nation returning to the Lord.

The intensity of the Elijah's prayer is matched by the intensity of the Lord's answer. As if on cue, the "fire of the Lord" instantaneously consumed everything—from the stones to the wood to the sacrifice, even the water that had spilled into the trough (v. 38). The reaction of the people was, of course, predictable. They fell upon their faces and twice declared, "The Lord indeed is God; the Lord indeed is God." But the prophet was not satisfied with a mere declaration. He wanted the pagan influence purged from society, not to mention evidence of the people's newly found commitment. Therefore, Elijah commanded that the people to round up the prophets of Baal in order to be executed. The people complied and took them to banks of the Qishon, a major river that flows through the Jezreel valley at the base of Mount Carmel.

It's a disturbing and violent scene, one that invokes modern images of prisoners being placed before a firing squad. But it must be understood in context. The verb used to denote the rounding up of the prophets (תפש) is often used in military contexts (Deut. 20:19; Josh. 8:23; 1 Sam. 15:8; *NIDOTTE*, 4:326–27). And the verb for "killing" the prophets (שחט) exhibits a broad usage in sacrificial contexts (*NIDOTTE*, 4:77–80). Consequently, the picture created is that of a religious battle being fought for the soul of the nation. It was a desperate time that called for extraordinary measures. Nevertheless, the responsibility for the killing action was that of the prophet, for וַיִּשְׁחָטֵם exists as a masculine singular verb.

18:41–46. The text does not reveal how Elijah found himself in front of Ahab again, but in verse 41 the prophet is again a part of a royal audience. In this instance, contrary to previous encounters, the meeting is positive. Elijah encourages him to "eat and drink," a call that has important covenantal connotations. As Roberts

(2000) argues, this simple statement shows Ahab's admission of the Lord's superiority and officially signals the country's recommitment to Yahweh as God. It's more than a meal for sustenance after a long and trying day. It's a meal that highlights a covenantal renewal ceremony, which is also the reason why the prophet can anticipate the approaching storm (הֲמוֹן הַגֶּשֶׁם).

What follows is a bit peculiar. Ahab obeys, taking part in a covenantal ceremony, but Elijah proceeds to ascend to the top of Mount Carmel. There, he bends down and places his face between his knees. It's possible that this signifies a praying posture (DeVries 2003, 217), but the text does not demand such an interpretation. It could be a sign of physical and emotional fatigue, which would make his epic run to Jezreel all the more impressive (v. 46). Nevertheless, Elijah urges his servant to look for rain. The servant initially sees nothing. But after returning six more times, he sees the tiniest of clouds on the horizon. This is all the prophet needs. He commands the servant to instruct Ahab to make haste toward his home so that the rain will not overtake him. And the rain was intense. The sky darkened and the clouds surged. Finally, there was a "great rain."

The peculiar element comes next. As Ahab rides to Jezreel, "the hand of the LORD came upon Elijah." In turn, he girded his loins and proceeded to run ahead of the king until he reached Jezreel. Running ahead of a king was often a show of public support (cf. 1 Kings 1:5), which suggests that this twenty-seven kilometer run was more than a divinely initiated workout. Rather, it was a show of respect, divine approval, and prophetic support (Sweeney 2007, 230). The Lord's prophet runs ahead of Ahab as a downpour follows. To those in Jezreel who saw this, it could only be understood as an emphatic statement of divine alignment.

The girding of one's loins is a phrase that denotes "a preparation for physical action . . . to secure or safeguard one's genitals by wrapping a cloth between one's legs and around one's waist, and, also, to encircle one's waist with a garment that can hold a weapon, such as a belt" (Low 2011, 4).

19:1–18. If we understand Elijah running ahead of Ahab as a show of divine approval and prophetic support, then Jezebel's murderous threats are even more shocking. Moreover, it's telling that her threats are punctuated by an oath. Jezebel is so impassioned about her desire to kill Elijah that she subjects herself to divine curses and death if she fails (v. 2).

In response, Elijah runs. He heads south to the southernmost reaches of Judah, in Beersheba. Yet when he gets there, he leaves his servant and goes further, into the wilderness (v. 3). This retreat is telling. First, the fact that Elijah felt compelled to go beyond Beersheba, one of the southernmost cities in Judah, testifies to the political reach of the Omrides. Apparently, Elijah was not convinced that the king of Judah could protect him. Second, the fact that Elijah flees deep into the wilderness suggests that he is trying to find something more than safety. The "wilderness" was an important concept within the biblical worldview, a location that brought one to the precipice of the divine realm. It was a place of terror and awesomeness (Schreiner 2020). Consequently, Elijah flees to the borders of the earthly realm, presumably to encounter the Lord in addition to securing his safety. These are the actions of a deeply frightened man.

In the midst of Elijah's escape, he is again provided by the Lord. One day past Beersheba, Elijah resigns and wishes for death (v. 4). Then, when sleeping under a solitary tree, he is visited by an angel. The angel doesn't even entertain his request, but instead exhorts the prophet to eat (vv. 5–6). This happens a second time, and with the second course the angel reveals that the food was necessary because of his pending journey (v. 7). Forty days and forty nights was the length of Elijah's journey, taking him to the region of Mount Horeb, also known as Mount Sinai, "the mountain of God" (v. 8).

The encounter with the Lord revolves around a simple question, "What are you doing here, Elijah?" (vv. 9, 13). The question is asked twice, and in both instances the prophet answers in the same way: "I have been very zealous for the Lord, the God of hosts; for the Israelites have forsaken your covenant, thrown down your altars, and killed your prophets with the sword. I alone am left, and they are seeking my life, to take it away" (vv. 10, 14). The prophet is looking for sympathy. He's making an emotional appeal to his piety and commitment. He wants encouragement, and a pat on the back. Unfortunately, he gets none of this. Instead, the Lord gives two responses. First, the Lord declares he will be passing by (v. 11). In many ways, this is what was expected for the mountain of God. Windstorms, fire, and earthquakes are the hallmarks of a theophany. Ironically, however, the Lord appears in none of them. Rather, he appeals in just a sound, asking the same question as before, "What are you doing here, Elijah?" (v. 13). After Elijah responds in the same way as before (v. 14), the Lord moves to give the prophet some new perspective. The Lord tells the prophet to leave the relative safety of the wilderness and carry out three specific actions. He is to anoint Hazael as king over Aram, Jehu as king of Israel, and Elisha as his successor (vv. 15–16).

Indeed, such an exhortation not only continues to ignore what the prophet wants, but also adds to the animosity already existing between Elijah and the royal family. Yet in sidestepping the immediate desires of the prophet, the Lord does something more enriching: he begins to recalibrate the prophet's perspective. The prophet sees the issue as an emotional and personal one; but in turning inward in the way he has, the prophet has skirted his social responsibilities. This command to return to his homeland and to initiate sweeping social change essentially tells the prophet that any clarity over his recent experiences will come as he carries out his daily responsibilities. And as if the prophet still needed more nudging, this encounter closes with the Lord revealing to him that he has completely misread the situation: there are seven thousand in Israel who have remained faithful.

19:19–21. When Elijah comes upon Elisha, he is working in the field. The text reveals that Elisha had twelve oxen with him, which may be indicative of a family with substantial resources (Wray Beal 2014, 255).[2] Elijah "passed by" and threw a garment over him." This action appears odd, but Elisha clearly understood its value. Elisha runs after Elijah only to ask to say goodbye to his family. Elijah's response initially appears harsh, but Wray Beal (2014, 255) is certainly correct when she states that it's an answer that puts the onus back upon Elisha: "Elijah's 'What have I to do with you?' places responsibility for a response solely upon Elisha, with no manipulation by the prophet. The call is uncompromising: Elisha must choose, but in choosing he becomes committed."

Such an ultimatum clarifies the meal given by Elisha. Verse 21 recounts how Elisha used the farm equipment to build a fire for the slaughtered oxen in order to provide a meal for his family. It's a declaration of a complete shift in Elisha's identity. No longer will he be known as the son of Shaphat, a farmer. Rather, he would be known as Elisha, the servant of Elijah.

Wars and the End of Ahab and Elijah (1 Kings 20:1–2 Kings 1:18)

The prophets were defined not by individual personalities but by their theological and social responsibilities. First Kings 20 begins a section that reveals the details of the sweeping changes that Elijah will facilitate (cf. 2 Kings 19:15–16). However, it also introduces one of

---

2   However, DeVries (2003, 239) interprets this as evidence of a communal venture.

the most complicated historical debates associated with Kings. In short, many scholars believe that chapters 20 and 22 are traditions originally from later in Israelite history but were used in this context to bolster an anti-Omride agenda.[3] However, further complications are almost always associated with proposals of large-scale reordering of the text.

Indeed, there are historical difficulties associated with chapters 20 and 22. However, their difficulties do not justify a notion that these chapters were originally about some other Israelite king and only attached to Ahab to further some agenda. The anonymity often highlighted is best understood as a literary convention and rhetorical effort, and the conflict between Israel and Aram is best understood as a perpetual reality that defined, in part, the Iron Age.

First Kings 20 through 2 Kings 1 brings Elijah's ministry to a close. In these four chapters, Ahab and his son Ahaziah will die, and Micaiah the son of Imlah will join Elijah in prophesying against Ahab. There is also the familiar episode of Naboth's vineyard. The section ends in a manner similar to the way it started—Elijah proving himself to be a legitimate man of God.

20:1–12. Sweeney (2007, 237–38) is right to highlight how chapter 20 progresses by specific syntax. In verses 1, 13, 23, and 35, the introduction of a new character is shown through a disjunctive clause, and when these introductions are considered with the anonymity of certain characters, this chapter focuses the reader's attention upon the actions of the characters, versus the characters as people. Thus, it's a section that highlights the egregiousness of disobeying specific commands given by the Lord.

The scene opens with the king of Aram leading a coalition (thirty-two kings) in the siege of Samaria (v. 1). As was typical with such warfare, the king of Aram offers the king of Israel a deal. It's important that Ahab is mentioned here, for in the remainder of the scene, except for verses 13–14, Ahab is not mentioned. Overwhelmingly, the title "king" is preferred, and such anonymity parallels the anonymity of the Aramean king[4] and other characters throughout the narrative. Nevertheless, what is not cryptic is the price the Aramean king places upon Samaria. He asks for money and people (v. 3), which by the presence of the suffixes refers to the financial and personnel resources of the royal house. This price is accepted by the king.

However, the king of Aram gets greedy. He wants more. He resends his messengers and demands more plunder. This is no small request, for the archaeological record of Samaria suggests that the palaces were lavishly decorated. What's odd is why the Aramean king did not demand such plunder initially. Regardless, the king of Israel seeks counsel, who promptly advise him to reject the second request (vv. 7–8).

When the words of the Israelite king's rejection reach the Aramean king, he reacts passionately, responding with an oath that binds him to killing the Israelite king (v. 10). In turn, the Israelite king insults the Aramean, who in turn responds—while intoxicated—with a call to arms.

20:13–22. At this point, an unnamed prophet appears to counsel the king further. First, the prophet draws the king's attention to the opposing forces (v. 13). He does this to heighten the stakes and create a context in which the Lord's salvation will occur. According to the prophet, the king of Israel is to marshal the

---

3   This historical issue is covered in detail in Kyle R. Greenwood and David B. Schreiner, *Ahab's House of Horrors* (2022, forthcoming).

4   Ben Hadad, which means "son of Hadad," is used throughout. This may be a throne name and not a personal name, although the discussion is difficult (Younger Jr. 2016, 249).

"young leaders of the provinces," for they will deliver Israel (v. 14). The anticipated victory will result in the recognition of the Lord's power and salvation (v. 13).

The king obeys. He marshals 232 "young leaders of the provinces" to lead the army in battle (vv. 15, 19). When they appear on the battlefield, the opposing coalition observes them and the Aramean king issues an order to take the Israelites alive, regardless of their motives (v. 18). This is an odd command, and perhaps this has something to do with the inebriation of the Aramean coalition (v. 16). Regardless, the youths routed the Aramean kings, chasing the coalition away (vv. 20–21). Yet any joy is short-lived, as the prophet reveals to the king that the Aramean king will return during next year's campaign season.

Who were these "young leaders of the provinces"? The Hebrew reads נַעֲרֵי שָׂרֵי הַמְּדִינוֹת, which literally translates to, "by the young men of the commanders of the provinces." It seems then that victory over an intimidating coalition would come through capable, trained, but unproven men from the administrative districts of Israel. They would lead a general fighting force against a prominent coalition, which bodes well for the intentions of the battle—to secure an awareness of divine power and protection (v. 13).

20:23–35. Verse 23 begins with another disjunctive clause, like verses 1 and 13. The servants of the king are highlighted as well as their advice to the king. They argue that the Lord is "a god of the hills," and so to ensure victory, any military strategy needs to account for this variable. Instead of fighting them in an area that played to those strengths, the Arameans need to draw the Israelites out. They reorganize and restock (v. 25), but the difference will be the location of battle. Instead of the central highlands, the plains, where the power of the chariot can be utilized to great effect, would be the site of conflict.

Such advice betrays the Aramean religious perspective. They assumed that the Lord ruled

a particular region and to battle against him in that region would ensure defeat. Thus, the trick was to lure Israel, who were perceived to be an extension of the deity, away from that region. Of course, all of this is part of the lesson to be learned. "Because the Arameans have said, 'The LORD is a god of the hills but he is not a god of the valleys,' therefore I will give all this great multitude into your hand, and you shall know that I am the LORD" (v. 28). The Lord intends to show that he is not confined by any geographic boundary or topographic feature. He exercises his lordship over all the earth and over every country. This is a lesson that Egypt learned previously (cf. Exod. 14–15), and Assyria will learn later (2 Kings 18–19).

The king of Aram agrees to the advice and begins to marshal another army. When spring arrived, he marched to Aphek, a (multisite?) city that sat along a regional highway that connected the Kings Highway with the Via Maris just east of the Sea of Galilee in the region of Bashan (Rasmussen 2010, 34–35; 155–57). The one who controlled Aphek controlled entry into the Israelite hinterland.

In response, Israel marched to Aphek, desiring to meet them on the open field of battle. Open-field warfare normally happened when each side perceived themselves to be on par with their opposition, and in this instance, this reality makes the descriptions of verse 27 very intriguing. Israel's army is described as "two small flocks of goats," while the Aramean armies spanned the countryside. The descriptions, therefore, envision a clear difference between the Israelite and Aramean armies. The writer wants the reader to imagine Israel as the clear underdog, for such an emphasis reinforces the point: the Lord will achieve victory so that all will know.

Very little text is devoted to the battle itself—just two verses (vv. 29–30). But within these verses, casualties and escapes are described. The Aramean infantry and the Aramean king find themselves cornered inside Aphek. With nowhere to go, the Arameans decide to test a rumor, that the Israelites are "merciful" (v. 31). This does not imply that Israel exhibited a tendency to "forgive" their enemies, as if they would merely let them go. Rather, it meant that there was precedent for installing defeated enemies as vassals. Consequently, the Arameans clothed themselves with sackcloth and ashes and put ropes around their necks as a sign of full surrender. Yet what transpired was so shocking that it became the basis for the Israelite king's judgment pronounced just a few verses later.

The king of Aram directly appeals to Ahab. He asks that he might live (v. 32). He is fearful and hoping that the rumors would prove to be true. Ultimately, it was his lucky day. The king of Israel accepts him as a colleague, not a subordinate. He publicly addresses him as "brother," a sign of political comparability and acceptability, and allows him to ride in the royal chariot (vv. 32–33). Indeed, Israel dictates a treaty that will define their future relationship, including territorial and economic concessions (v. 34), but it's clearly not in line with the intentions of the Lord.

20:35–43. In verse 35, the scene again shifts to another anonymous prophet. He was commanded by the Lord to give a particular word to the king of Israel, but interesting is the method by which the divine word is to be revealed. First, he needs to look the part. So, he asks a fellow prophet to strike him (v. 35). The fellow prophet, unfortunately, balks at this exhortation, which incurs the indignation of the prophet and secures his death for disobedience (v. 36). The first prophet eventually finds a companion who does strike him voluntarily (v. 37). Then, the prophet disguises himself and waits for the king (v. 38).

When the king passes by, presumably in a royal processional celebrating his recent victory, the prophet calls out for the king and proceeds to recount a concocted scenario designed to set up the king (vv. 39–40). This recalls Nathan's concocted parable given to David in the wake

of his sin with Bathsheba (2 Sam. 12), and the result is the same. The disguised prophet recalls how he was to watch a prisoner of war upon the punishment of death. Yet as he was "doing this and that," the prisoner escaped. Thus, the set up uses an appeal for clemency as the king has the power to grant a pardon. However, the king brushes aside the request, essentially confirming that the victim must bear the responsibility.

Once the king pronounces his verdict, the prophet reveals himself and pronounces the divine verdict (v. 41). The king was tasked with carrying out a particular task, which was fulfilling the Lord's חֵרֶם, or total victory, against the Aramean coalition (v. 43). Instead, he allows the king to live so that Israel could reap the economic and political benefits. And just as the hypothetical scenario demanded the death of the absentminded military guard, so too is death demanded of the king.

The king, like David, is publicly shamed. However, whereas David immediately confesses his sin, we are merely told that the king of Israel goes home to Samaria "resentfully sullen" (סַר וְזָעֵף). There is no hint of remorse or contrition for his infraction, just angry emotion for his chastisement. But there's more. This scene also recalls Saul's violation of the חֵרֶם against the Amalekites, and it fits the larger theme of obedience to the word of God, which is the focal point around which this chapter revolves. No matter how extreme or unorthodox the commands of the Lord may sound, people—kings, prophets, and the general populace—are judged by their willingness to obey divine decrees.

21:1–7. The events of chapter 21 transpire sometime after the battle with the Arameans at Aphek. The reader is immediately introduced to Naboth, who is a Jezreelite with a vineyard adjacent to the royal palace (v. 1). According to verse 2, Ahab wants to acquire the vineyard in order to make a vegetable garden (גַּן יָרָק). Initially, Ahab offers a fair price, perhaps even a generous price (v. 2), but he comes up against something beyond any price tag. Naboth reveals how this plot is part of his family's inheritance, and by responding with an oath, he effectively ends the conversation. Ahab understands the situation, although it puts him in a sour mood. The king returns home "resentful and sullen" (v. 4) in order to lay down, pout, and go on something akin to a hunger strike (v. 5).

The interaction between Naboth and Ahab shows that there were limits on royal power in ancient Israelite society (Sarna 1997, 119–20). However, the limits on royal power were sometimes ignored when a certain level of ambition entered the equation. When Jezebel arrives, she immediately takes charge, displaying a posture that contrasts with the king. Whereas the king is moping around, she perceives an opportunity and pounces. After asking the king about his problem, she essentially insults Ahab and demands that he pull himself together and allow her to take care of things. Important is the syntax of verse 7 (אֲנִי אֶתֵּן לְךָ אֶת־כֶּרֶם). The emphatic first-person form clearly shows that she intends to oversee the situation and expects a particular chain of events to unfold. What is unclear is just how much Ahab knew about the specifics of her plan of action.

21:8–16. Jezebel manipulates the legal system (Sarna 1997, 122). Her play is to use two shady characters (בְּנֵי־בְלִיַּעַל) to publicly accuse Naboth of blasphemy, which would be done when he was part of a banquet featuring the elite of Israelite society (v. 12). Thus, this takedown effectively had all the elements of a juicy scandal: conspiracy, power, deception, and the highest of stakes.

Apparently, the "sons of Belial" played their parts well. According to verse 13, their public testimony resulted in the quick and shameful death of Naboth. "So they took him outside the city, and stoned him to death" (v. 13). With Naboth gone, and with the penalty being blasphemy, the king was free to annex the land. Consequently, Jezebel sends a message to Ahab urging him to seize the property. Ahab responds immediately.

21:17–29. The word of the Lord then comes upon Elijah, and the prophet is commanded to again publicly confront Ahab. Here, the punishment is twofold. It targets not only Ahab, but also Jezebel. In both instances, their deaths will be public and shameful, a fitting response to what happened to Naboth. Moreover, Ahab's punishment will extend to his descendants, and Jezebel's corpse will be eaten by wild animals.

The interaction between Elijah and Ahab is intense. Elijah starts it off when he asks, "Have you killed, and also taken possession . . . ?" (v. 19). This question, obviously, doesn't need an answer as it alludes to the corrupt action of the king in the Naboth affair. And the king knows it. Therefore, he attempts to deflect and downplay the Naboth affair in his response. However, Elijah will not let the king off the hook. Brilliantly, the prophet inverts the deflection by playing off the king's hostility toward the prophet. And in the end, Elijah makes it clear that the real enemy is the king himself, sealed by his propensity to do evil.

This judgment oracle recycles elements of Jeroboam's judgment (cf. vv. 21–22 with 1 Kings 14:7–11). Just as Jeroboam's sin negatively affected the longevity of his dynastic line, so too will Ahab's sin. And to twist the knife a bit, 21:25 contextualizes the sins of Ahab historically. He was unparalleled, one of a kind. His willingness to sell himself to evil and paganism, and to allow his malicious wife to influence him, solidified a legacy that was worse than the indigenous peoples of Canaan who were subjected to חֵרֶם. But, ironically, this damning indictment is not the final word. Against all odds, Ahab displays humility and repentance. Taking up the official posture of mourning, he exchanged his royal garb for sackcloth and fasting (v. 27). Consequently, the king once again finds himself depressed. Yet in this instance it's due to remorse over his actions. The result is the postponement of judgment—not the absolution of judgment. Judgment will be realized in the days of his children (v. 29).

This scene recalls two other scenes in Israel's historical literature that connect public admission of sin with the modification of judgment. In 2 Kings 22:11–20, Huldah proclaims that Josiah will be gathered with his ancestors and will not see the judgment of Judah. In 2 Samuel 12:13–16, David's public confession seals his salvation from death. Furthermore, the postponement of judgment to the succeeding generations reminds the reader of Ahijah's oracle given to Jeroboam in response to Solomon's sins. All these scenes testify to the conviction that the Lord's determinations may not be beyond modification.

22:1–28. Chapter 22 opens with a recognition that Aram-Israelite relations had enjoyed peace for three years, a statement that effectively intensified the significance of what transpires. The king of Israel wants to violate a treaty (cf. 1 Kings 20:34), move against Aram, and plunge the region into war once again. The rationale? He wants Ramoth Gilead back, and he summons King Jehoshaphat of Judah to consult in the decision. Nevertheless, this meeting is about pressing Judah into military service. Consequently, the king's questions (vv. 3–4) intend to declare intention and secure allegiance rather than solicit advice.

In this process, it's Jehoshaphat who insists that the Lord be consulted (v. 5), an insistence that establishes him as the positive character and foil to the anonymous "king of Israel." Moreover, Jehoshaphat's character is further defined when he balks at the unanimity of the prophetic voices, realizing that unanimity in a situation as complex as breaking a treaty for land strains credibility. In the end, under the pressure of Jehoshaphat, the king of Israel concedes to consult Micaiah ben Imlah, who happens to be a prophet with a history. The Israelite king "hates" him, "for he never

prophesies anything favorable" about him (v. 8), which appears to be a sentiment shared by many. As Micaiah is ushered into his royal audience, the messenger urges him to speak with the other prophetic voices (v. 13).

Micaiah appears in the midst of a circus. Jehoshaphat and the king of Israel are sitting in Samaria's gate complex, a place of public gathering, with Zedekiah son of Chenaanah and the other prophets doing their business in very flamboyant ways (vv. 11–12). Shockingly, Micaiah initially echoes their advice, telling the king to go to war with confidence (v. 15). However, the king of Israel immediately realized that such a statement was too good to be true. So, he presses the prophet to be more forthcoming (v. 16). In response Micaiah relays an ominous vision that predicts defeat. The prophet sees Israel without a leader.

Micaiah's second response is accepted by the king of Israel, although the king brushes it aside with an "I told you so" response aimed at Jehoshaphat. Yet, as if to double down and combat the lackadaisical response toward his prophecy, Micaiah emphasizes the validity of his message by appealing to his opportunity to watch the divine council unfold. Micaiah paints a picture of tense deliberations among the heavenly hosts that ultimately ends up with the Lord's sanctioning Ahab's deception by means of false prophecy.

Predictively, this message is not well received by the other prophets. In turn, Zedekiah assaults Micaiah as a public sign of shame and rebuke. Nevertheless, Micaiah digs in his heels and further fights for the truth of his prophecy. While Zedekiah appeals to emotion in his defense, Micaiah appeals to the authoritative traditions of Israel when he tells Zedekiah to allow events to unfold. In good Deuteronomic fashion (Deut. 18:21–22), Micaiah knows that his words will come to pass and put his legitimacy beyond question.

Admittedly, the vision of the divine council is initially theologically disturbing. The syntax clearly communicates that the Lord is seeking to dupe Ahab for the purpose that he might die in battle (v. 20). Moreover, the spirit (הָרוּחַ) volunteers to go out and be a deceptive spirit (רוּחַ שֶׁקֶר) in the mouths of the prophets. In other words, the Lord is sanctioning false prophecy to secure the downfall of Ahab. However, this all must be understood in context. Ahab is already under the hammer of judgment for willfully disobeying the commands of the Lord (ch. 20), and the Naboth conspiracy only complicated things further (ch. 21). Thus, the divine council does not represent the machination of a malicious God. Rather, the council was convened to bring necessary judgment.

Syntax: The Hebrew in question reads: מִי יְפַתֶּה אֶת־אַחְאָב וְיַעַל וְיִפֹּל בְּרָמֹת גִּלְעָד. Important are the three verbs, יְפַתֶּה, יַעַל, and יִפֹּל, which cooperate to produce a nuance of finality. The Lord is asking for a volunteer to act in a way that will bring the specific result of Ahab's death in battle. And in verse 22, it will come to pass by means of false prophecy.

Micaiah is imprisoned, as the king is confident that he will return "in peace" (v. 27). The prophet, however, does not share such optimism. As the king readies himself and the prophet is taken away to jail, Micaiah calls out one last time, pitting his reputation as a legitimate ambassador of the Lord against the ego of the king.

22:29–40. These verses recount the battle of Ramoth Gilead. Jehoshaphat is told to wear his royal garb while Ahab enters battle in disguise (v. 30). Such a plan would dictate that Jehoshaphat be the focal point of the opponent's effort, thereby shedding light on the hierarchy between the Israelite and Judean kings.

Ivory House

Ahab's "ivory house" refers not to a house constructed of ivory, but likely a building or room decorated with ivory overlays. Evidence of ivory production and trade has been discovered all throughout the ancient Near East, exhibiting ebbs and flows consistent with the general economic trends of the region. In every case, the presence of ivory is indicative of affluence and prominence. Specific to Ahab's ivory house, excavations at Samaria uncovered a large cache of ivory reliefs. And the prophet Amos (3:15) targets the ivory of Samaria in the context of its judgment (Hays 2016).

Initially, the plan works for the Israelite king. According to verses 32–33, the Arameans tore off after Jehoshaphat. However, upon closer examination, Jehoshaphat's pursuers realized that it was not Ahab. In turn, they broke off the pursuit. Eventually, the Aramean army found its mark. Yet the death of the Israelite king appears to come in a seemingly random and unlucky fashion. An unnamed Aramean randomly shot an arrow that, of all places, penetrated the weak spot of the king's armor. Yet when does bad luck become something else? Consequently, this episode is not merely an unlucky turn of events. Rather, it's a fitting end for the Israelite king who was responsible for so much disrespect toward the Lord. His death is doubly shameful (death on the battlefield and the dogs that later lick up his blood) in fulfillment of prophecy uttered long ago.

Verses 39–40 round out the account of Ahab, who was known for much more than what is covered in Kings. In particular, he is remembered for his building projects, including the famed "ivory house." When he died, the reigns of the Israelite kingdom were peacefully given over to Ahaziah.

22:41–53. First Kings closes with a brief evaluation of Jehoshaphat and Ahaziah. Jehoshaphat is remembered positively, being one of the few kings who did good in the eyes of the Lord—although, like Asa, he did not deal properly with the high places. Also, Jehoshaphat was apparently politically savvy, securing a treaty with Israel and successfully engaging in battle. However, the Judean king also suffered a failed business venture, although he was wise enough to cut his losses (vv. 48–59).

The chapter closes with the brief regnal evaluation of Ahaziah. He did evil in the eyes of the Lord, enticed Israel to sin, and provoked the Lord to anger. Ahaziah carried forth the commitment to religious syncretism consistent with his predecessors.

2 Kings 1:1–4. This chapter opens with an imprecise chronological marker—after Ahab's death but within the timeframe of Ahaziah's reign. In addition, the scene is also introduced with a reference to Ahaziah's injury. According to verse 2, the king had fallen through an opening and severely injured himself, enough to cast doubts on his recovery. Thus, the king dispatches an entourage to the Philistine city of Ekron to inquire about what will happen. This is the problem. The king of Israel decided to solicit Baal-Zebub of Ekron and not the Lord (Yahweh). Consequently, the Lord dispatches his own messenger to head off the royal messengers. And the message is simple. Essentially, "Why Baal? Do I not exist? Because of all this, you will die!"

1:5–16. The messengers eventually return to the king, who is perplexed. So, he asks why they returned (v. 5). In response, they describe their encounter, including the statement of judgment (v. 6). Naturally, the king is inclined to ask a follow-up question, and in the process of answering that question the men describe Elijah by his distinctive appearance. Apparently, the prophet's reputation preceded him only in certain circles. Nevertheless, Ahaziah realizes whom they met and immediately responds. However, it's not a response of acceptance or reverence. Rather, the king dispatches an entire military unit of fifty men. Such an action can only be interpreted antagonistically. The king wanted to force the prophet to come back to Samaria in order to answer directly to the king.

Elijah responds in a way that puts his prophetic authority on full display: "If I am a man of God, let fire come down from heaven and consume you and your fifty" (v. 10). Then, similar to what happened to the altar of the Lord on Mount Carmel (1 Kings 18:38), fire descended from heaven and consumed the force intent on coercing Elijah to come back to the capital. But what's more, the king sends two more military units. The second ends with the same result (2 Kings 1:13), but the third attempt is more successful thanks to the leader, who wisely pleads with the prophet.

Syntax

The syntax of 2 Kings 1:16 makes it clear that Ahaziah's death sentence is linked to his attempts to solicit Baal-Zebub. The construction יַעַן אֲשֶׁר functions in tandem with the particle לָכֵן. In addition, the infinitive construct לִדְרֹשׁ makes it clear that the solicitation of news from Baal-Zebub was the specific action in question

The commander of the third unit greets Elijah not with arrogant confidence but with a humble awareness of who Elijah is. Apparently, he was able to learn the lessons his predecessors could not. Falling on his knees, the third commander appeals to the sanctity of life and an awareness of what just happened (vv. 13–14). Such a posture, in turn, secures the compliance of the prophet, but not before the Lord's sanction (v. 15). Consequently, the prophet proceeds to return to the king. There, in the presence of the king, Elijah declares the verdict against the king, which is also explicitly linked to Ahaziah's inquiry of Baal. "*Because* you have sent messengers to inquire of Baal-Zebub, the god of Ekron . . . *therefore* you shall not leave the bed to which you have gone, but you will surely die" (v. 16).

Important to note is the absence of any response by the king when Elijah personally delivers the oracle of judgment. This establishes

2 Kings 1 to be a counterpart to 1 Kings 17. Both narratives are concerned with Elijah's authority as a prophet, and both focus upon Elijah hearing and obeying the word of the Lord. There's also an explicit recognition that he is a "man of God" (1 Kings 17:24; 2 Kings 1:13). Such connections establish an inclusio for the Elijah cycle, suggesting that the entire section of text (1 Kings 17:1–2 Kings 1:18) is concerned with the prophet's function in Israelite society. Legitimate prophets enjoy the protection and provision of the Lord and are responsible for disseminating the word of the Lord, exhorting covenantal faithfulness.

1:17–18. The final verses of the chapter recount the death of Ahaziah, which is explicitly linked to the fulfillment of Elijah's prophecy. In his stead, Jehoram becomes king of Israel.

THEOLOGICAL FOCUS

The exegetical idea (Elijah embodied the prophetic institution, which was defined not by individual personalities but by its theological and social responsibilities) leads to this theological focus: The essence of the prophetic institution continues when the Lord brings a specific word to a specific situation by means of Scripture.

This lengthy literary section juxtaposes the prophetic institution with the monarchy. Whether it was Elijah, Micaiah ben Imlah, or some anonymous prophet, the prophets brought a specific word of God to bear upon a certain situation, urging those who were listening to uphold the covenant and the lifestyle it espoused. In certain circumstances, the prophets brought the words of judgment. In total, then, this section suggests that the prophetic office was critical to keeping the royal institution and society at large in line.

Yet this section also showed the difficulties inherit to the institution. In short, there were many prophets saying many different things. Recall that just as Micaiah ben Imlah proclaimed judgment against Ahab, Zechariah son of Chenaanah proclaimed Ahab's victory. Consequently, the question of verification always followed closely behind any prophetic utterance.

Nevertheless, we can't allow the difficulties associated with the prophetic office to overwhelm the beauty of the office. The very notion of a prophet, one who brings God's specific word(s) to a situation in life, demonstrates the intimacy and accessibility that the Lord desires for his people. The Lord *wants* to guide his people in complex and difficult situations. And he wants this so much that he will send personalized messages to help secure the proper outcome.

For Christians, all of this remains true. The Lord still wants to guide us and encourage us through personalized communications. However, the way this transpires is different from what we see in Kings. Instead of people coming with those messages, the Lord's direction often comes through Scripture. Why? Jesus.

The incarnation of God and his word in the person of Jesus ushered in a new era for the people of God, fulfilling the Law and the Prophets (Matt. 5:17) in the process. And because Jesus's death on the cross initiated the new covenant (Luke 22:20), Jesus's life and the teachings associated with his ministry are a part of the covenantal standard by which the Lord's people are to order their lives. Scripture as a whole, therefore, tells us how to confront the unrighteousness and immorality we may encounter. Scripture encourages us and guides us in times of transition and crisis.

PREACHING AND TEACHING STRATEGIES

Exegetical and Theological Synthesis

As 1 Kings ends and 2 Kings begins, God raises up Elijah to confront the corrupt king and stir up a spiritual revival among his people. Speaking and acting on God's behalf, Elijah calls the people to recognize two general truths about

Yahweh: his unmatched ability to provide and his unrivaled supremacy as Lord of all.

Those general truths concerning God's provision and supremacy are not distant and unrelatable to us. God's ability to provide is dearly cherished by the churchgoer who just got laid off. A reminder of God's sovereignty offers balanced perspective for the politically active Christian who is passionate about their party. The implications of these truths may not always be welcomed. But prophetic voices are often meant to challenge calloused hearts just as much as comfort the struggling.

Preaching Idea
God amplifies prophetic voices when we're having trouble hearing him.

Contemporary Connections

What does it mean?
What does it mean that God amplifies prophetic voices when we're having trouble hearing him? Sometimes we have let our spiritual ears get plugged up or we get distracted listening to other voices telling us what to do. Sometimes the burdens of life drag us down and we have a hard time keeping up a hopeful perspective. It is in those kinds of moments that God faithfully reaches out to remind us of who he is and what he desires of us.

This does not need to drift into the magical or mystical side of spirituality. We don't have to visit some Christian guru in the mountains to discover God's prophetic voice. In fact, it does not even need to be a speaker, teacher, or prophet at all.

For four years, I (Lee) worked at my alma mater heading up seminary admissions. I was still serving in my local church, as well as serving a school whose mission I believed in. Eventually I felt a "spiritual itch" tugging at my heart to pursue the pastoral call I knew God had placed on my life. The problem was, I never acted on that prompting. Then almost

out of the blue, the school eliminated my job due to budget cuts. All of the sudden I was completely free to seek out pastoral positions. As it turned out, I ended up getting hired at a nearby church that had posted their opening with our school only a few months before. Ironically, I had been responsible for posting it to the school website. I wholeheartedly believe that losing my job was God's prophetic voice forcing me out of my cautiousness and into the path he wanted me to take.

Is it true?
Is it true that God amplifies prophetic voices when we're having trouble hearing him? Much ink has been spilled over the nature, purpose, and present relevancy of the *charismata* gifts (gifts of grace from God's Spirit). Prophecy of course falls under this category, as Paul outlines in 1 Corinthians 13–14. This is not the proper place to rehash those complex arguments, though there are a few resources that make good starting points (e.g., Fee 2014, 692–731; Gaffin and Grudem 1996). For our purposes here, it is this author's (Lee's) opinion that the office of prophet is not applicable in this age *like it was in 1–2 Kings*. However, prophets and prophecy certainly are pertinent to us today. If we presuppose that prophecy isn't about fortune-telling as much as it is criticizing and energizing, then we can recognize how God might speak to us through his Spirit, through his Word, and through his messengers in those ways. God may prompt one of our good friends to call us out on some blind spots in our character and actions. God may convict us of some unaddressed sin as we take some time to listen to the Spirit in prayer. God may also inject some hope and encouragement into our hearts by providentially having us read some "perfect verses" in our devotions that relate to what we are going through that week. God has a way of amplifying his message to make sure we cannot miss it.

Now what?

If it's true that God amplifies prophetic voices when we're having trouble hearing him, what can help us hear and respond to his message? Israel and its kings were spiritually deaf, so God raised up Elijah and other messengers at key times to get their attention and call them back to righteousness. Similarly, when we are hard of hearing, what should we do?

First, *we can pray for provision as a top priority*. Elijah's words and actions pointed people to God's infinite ability to provide. The God of Elijah has not changed and still delights to provide for his people. Whether it was a famine, illness, spiritual conflict, or just our strength to serve, God provided again and again in Elijah's day, and nothing has changed about his desire to help us in those ways either.

A second way we can apply this passage is to *obey God in whatever he calls us to do*. He may lead us to have a hard conversation with someone dear because we see them straying from the right path. He may ask us to offer some hopeful reassurance to someone we barely know. Likewise, when he chips away at our calloused hearts and deaf ears, he will expect us to take hard steps to make sure we can still hear his voice. Those hard steps might mean cutting off unhealthy relationships, switching jobs, or changing your daily routine to make your walk with Christ more of a priority.

Third, this passage invites us to *assess where our loyalties lie*. Do we serve Baal or Yahweh? Is our allegiance to the king or Jesus? Am I totally sold out to the political party that puts immigrant children in cages or the party that sees nothing wrong with killing the unborn? The reality is, we are citizens of heaven. No political party, cause, or movement should rival our commitment to living for Jesus.

Creativity in Presentation

When considering God using his prophets to *amplify* his message to his hard-of-hearing people, some easy illustrations present themselves quite naturally. The preacher's microphone, for instance, serves essentially the same purpose—to amplify one's voice so that all can hear clearly. One might try whispering, yelling, or adjusting the mic to audibly emphasize this point. Hearing aids and megaphones would also similarly work as metaphors for this idea.

The authors of this commentary are aware that this particular section covers a lot of ground in the text. Many preachers break up Elijah's life up into its very own series. We've divided it up in this way to keep the larger context in view. To do so, though, will require adjustments homiletically. Preaching it as we've outlined it below will prevent one from diving too much into the specific stories. It would be wisest to read only the key verses of each story and summarize the rest for the audience. Doing so can allow the "forest" of the message not to get lost in all the "trees" of specific stories. One possible alternative would be to break this up into two sermons, since there seem to be two distinct truths that the prophetic voices are reminding us of God's powerful provision and his unrivaled sovereignty.

The key idea to communicate is that God amplifies prophetic voices when we're having trouble hearing him. In this passage as a preaching unit, we hear prophetic voices that remind us of two truths involving God's provision on the one hand and God's supremacy on the other:

- How God powerfully provides like no other (1 Kings 17–19)
  - Nourishment in a famine (17:1–16)
  - Life despite death (17:17–24)
  - Vindication over opposition (ch. 18)
  - Strength in our weakness (ch. 19)
- How God righteously reigns like no other (1 Kings 20–2 Kings 1)

- ◦ Prophetic voices call for obedience in light of God's sovereignty (ch. 20)
- ◦ Prophetic voices confront brazen sin in light of God's righteousness (ch. 21)
- ◦ Prophetic voices get confirmed by God's intervention (1 Kings 22–2 Kings 1)

DISCUSSION QUESTIONS

1. What are the ways God provides in 1 Kings 17–20?

2. How does God undermine the validity of Baal and establish his own supremacy in 1 Kings 17, 18, and 20:13–30?

3. In the epic showdown at Mount Carmel, what are the major contrasts of the story (1 Kings 18)?

4. How might we understand King Ahab's sin, repentance, and ultimate downfall (1 Kings 21:25–29; 22:29–40)?

5. Elijah's ministry highlighted God's powerful provision and unrivaled sovereignty. How might those realities challenge us? How can they encourage us?

2 Kings 2:1–13:25

EXEGETICAL IDEA

As a prophet, Elisha served all levels of society to provide social, theological, and political insight, but Jehu's coup inaugurated a period where the basic vitality and effectiveness of God's people, including the continued existence of the Davidic line, were being compromised by internal and external pressures, which were all linked to shortsighted decisions and covenantal unfaithfulness.

THEOLOGICAL FOCUS

God's grace offers hope in life's precarious situations.

PREACHING IDEA

Desperate times call for divine measures.

PREACHING POINTERS

Turmoil and unrest mark this period of Israel's history. This larger unit is loosely tied together by Elisha's prophetic ministry, as he succeeds Elijah during a tumultuous time for both Israel and Judah. Elisha is described serving in a wide variety of situations, from helping commoners in crisis to advising kings regarding their military campaigns. Besides the prophet, several other leaders are noted for their activities. Some are graded positively, others negatively. What seems clear is that all aspects of life during this time were fraught with instability and anxiety. The Jewish people of the exilic and postexilic periods could relate all too well as they studied this part of their history. Disagreements, conflicts, and uncertainty were the norm as they resettled their homeland. Their one hope would be to follow godly servants and leaders like Elisha and trust the Lord to bring order to their chaos.

We do not lack turmoil in our world today, nor do we have to look very far for reasons to be anxious. Job layoffs, Wall Street fluctuations, and contentious political developments can all directly impact our lives and catch us unprepared. When desperate times arrive, it is natural to wonder what God is up to or even where he is. One helpful response is to take Mr. Rogers's classic advice and "look for the helpers." Has God raised up some individuals or groups that are providing support and service to those in need? Are there leaders who are embodying a response of steadfast faith when others are acting out of fear? Church work teams that help clean up in the aftermath of natural disasters exemplify this, as are Christians who volunteer at homeless shelters or with Big Brothers Big Sisters of America. The common saying is, "Desperate times call for desperate measures." But for people of faith, desperate times call for *divine* measures. We can be the hands and feet of Jesus and make an incredible impact, especially in times of turmoil and unrest.

ELISHA AND KINGS (2:1–13:25)

LITERARY STRUCTURE AND THEMES (2:1–13:25)

This section of text can be divided in two given a couple of considerations. First, the first subsection (2:1–8:29) opens and closes with notations of transition. A prophetic transition (2:1–18) looks toward a political transition (8:7–29). Second, of the fifty-nine occurrences of the name "Elisha" in 2 Kings 2–13, there are only seven after 2 Kings 8. Moreover, six of those seven occurrences appear in Elisha's death notice (13:14–21). Therefore, while the ministry of Elisha provides coherence for this entire section (chs. 2–13), with the onset of 2 Kings 9 the prophet recedes into the background in the second subsection (9:1–13:25).

Within the first subsection (2:1–8:29), two narrative cycles follow after a scene of prophetic transition. Within each narrative cycle, a scene (or scenes) features Elisha's performance of a food-miracle. This gives way to a scene (or scenes) involving Israel's hostile interaction with its neighbors, Moab and Aram, respectfully. The narrative cycle ends with a scene (or scenes) that features the prophet dealing with an economic obstacle. Cumulatively, this section intertwines the prophetic office with politics and social issues.

- *Elisha's Ministry (2:1–8:29)*
- *Internal and External Threats (9:1–13:25)*

EXPOSITION (2:1–13:25)

One of the foci of this lengthy section of text is Elisha. The successor to Elijah, Elisha further develops their ministry of accountability. Interestingly, Elisha appears to have a more active role in the politics of the region. The other focus falls upon the tumultuous events of the northern and southern kingdoms. Jehu's dynasty comes after the deposed Omride, and after a lengthy period of rule, Jehu's family yields to a series of unstable ruling families that ultimately lead the region into the clutches of the Neo-Assyrian army.

Elisha's Ministry (2:1–8:29)

Elisha's ministry addressed all levels of society to provide social, theological, and political clarity during the tense period of Iron Age II.

2:1–18. The first eighteen verses of this first subsection are concerned with a prophetic transition. The ministry of Elijah gives way to the ministry of Elisha, and it's accomplished in a magnificent way. When the scene opens, Elijah and Elisha are on their way from Gilgal to Bethel. On the one hand, Elijah attempts to break away from Elisha by urging him to stay as he proceeds to their sanctioned destination. However, Elisha digs in, going so far as to invoke an oath (v. 2). Such defiance contributes to the suspenseful tone, which was established immediately in verse 1 (Sweeney 2007, 272).

The suspense of this scene is furthered by two other realities. First, this cycle of Elijah proposing that Elisha stay behind only to be countered by Elisha's emphatic refusal recurs two more times (vv. 4, 6). Second, at every stop Elisha is met by members of the prophetic guild (lit., "sons of the prophets"; בְּנֵי־הַנְּבִיאִים) who ask him if he is aware of the worst-kept secret in the region—this is the day that the Lord plans to take Elijah away. In each case, Elisha acknowledges the inevitable but effectively tells the group to shut up (הֶחֱשׁוּ v. 3), as if he does not want to think about what is bound to happen.

Consequently, a peculiar picture is created of Elijah's successor. Clearly, he has taken his calling to forsake his previous way of life seriously (cf. 1 Kings 19:19–21). Yet his insistence that he keep Elijah close, and his refusal to entertain the implications of Elijah's impending departure, suggests both a close connection between the two and a certain level of anxiety for Elisha. In patriarchal societies, a double portion of a family's inheritance was given to the firstborn because he would eventually bear the responsibility of provision for the *bêt 'āb*, literally, "house of the father" (Strand Winslow, 168; Sweeney 2007, 272; Wiseman 2008, 208). Could it be, then, that Elisha realized that he was going to bear the responsibility of taking over Elijah's ministry, which spurred him to ask for a double portion of Elijah's spirit (v. 9)?

Elijah's ascension into the heavens happened in an instant. The text reveals that as Elijah and Elisha were "walking and talking" (הָלוֹךְ וְדַבֵּר), a chariot of fire separated the two and allowed the whirlwind to scoop Elijah heavenward. Apparently, the experience was completely unsettling, for Elisha was capable only of shouting barely coherent phrases and ripping his clothes in two: "Elisha kept watching and crying out, 'Father, father! The chariots of Israel and its horsemen!' But when he could no longer see him, he grasped his own clothes and tore them in two pieces" (v. 12).

The only thing left behind was Elijah's garment, which becomes symbolic of the prophetic transition. Taking up the cloth that signified Elijah's choice of Elisha (1 Kings 19:19), Elisha reenacts the actions of Elijah

Elijah Taken Up in a Chariot of Fire by Giuseppe Angeli. Public domain.

(v. 8), striking the Jordan River. And just as the river parted for Elijah, so too did it part for Elisha. According to verse 15, a company of prophets watched from a nearby distance and interpreted the Elijah-like events definitively: "The spirit of Elijah rests on Elisha" (v. 15). However, their awkward insistence that they look for Elisha to ensure that he was indeed gone raises the question of whether the company wanted to verify the prophetic transition or was trying to hang on to the past. Regardless, Elisha was convinced, and after three days of futility searching for Elijah, Elisha reminds company of his suggestion not to go search.

2:19–22. The first of two narrative cycles begins here with Elisha's first significant miracle at Jericho. According to the inhabitants, the city was is good order (טוב), but its water source was compromised. The people describe it as "bad," but the Hebrew word choice conveys something more malicious and diabolical (רע). Moreover, the tainted water has proven to be agriculturally disastrous. The water is "evil," and "the land is unfruitful." Naturalistic explanations have varied, including a temporary burst of naturally occurring radioactivity (Blake, 1967) or the onset of schistosomiasis (Hulse 1970), and all remain conjectural.

The prophet plays the hero by performing a ritual involving an action and a corresponding pronouncement. First, Elisha demands a "new bowl" filled with salt (v. 20), which is then emptied at the water's source. Once completed, the prophet proclaims, "I have made this water wholesome; from now on neither death nor miscarriage shall come from it" (v. 21). In the end, the city's water source was fixed permanently.

Interestingly, the NRSV translates the same word in verses 19 and 21 differently (תְּלַכֵּשְׁמ). It's a term often associated with biological infertility or the loss of children (Hamilton 1997, 4:105–07; cf. Hulse 1971,

382–83). Consequently, it's possible to see a subtle polemic against Canaanite fertility religion. The Lord's prophet, not Baal or Baal's prophet, cures the infertility of the land. This implies that this short account continues the polemic against Baalism and Canaanite fertility religion so prominent in Kings, as well as lends further credibility to the prophet and prepares the reader for what happens next.

2:23–25. The reader assumes that Elisha headed up to Bethel once his business at Jericho's water source was finished, and some have argued that this route is a deliberate retracing of Elijah's final journey (Strand Winslow, 170). While on the road, he is hassled by an unknown-size group of men. And what happens constitutes a morally difficult scene that clashes with many modern sensibilities.

According to the text, the prophet responds to the group's insults by turning, looking, and then cursing them by the name of the Lord. Immediately, two bears sprang from their normal habitat to maul forty-two members of the group, "splitting some of them open" (וַתְּבַקַּעְנָה מֵהֶם). In response to such a grotesque turn of events, the prophet merely proceeds on to Samaria by way of Mount Carmel (v. 25).

Lexical Analysis: Much has been said about the description of this group of adversaries. The noun is נַעַר, which manifests a very broad semantic range. It can refer to boys of a certain age, even young ages, but also specific classes of people, such as servant (cf. Gen. 18:7). Understanding its related terms in other languages, the broad semantic range is reinforced. Consequently, it's a word that demands clarification and qualification from its context.

In this passage, נַעַר is immediately qualified by the semantically broad adjective קָטָן, referring to a young age or social insignificance.

Consequently, the sense in verse 23 is notoriously ambiguous. It could refer to a group of young boys or physically capable men who are carrying a certain social stigma.

Nevertheless, verse 24 later describes the mauled forty-two as "boys" (יְלָדִים), suggesting that younger rather than older is the intended meaning (Hamilton 1997, 3:124–27; Carroll 1997, 3:910–12).

Other than the insults hurled at the prophet by the group of men (v. 23), there is a dearth of verbal interaction in this scene. This, coupled with the string of short clauses and the intended inference that the prophet's curse incited the animals to attack, creates a less than desirable image of the prophet. Elisha looks morally detached from his surroundings, vindictive, and emotionally unphased by the brutal scene that just unfolded in front of him. However, despite the difficulties of this scene, the reader must remember that this scene functions to simultaneously define and defend the prophetic office. The prophet of the Lord can bring death just as well as he can bring life (Cogan and Tadmor 2008, 39). Moreover, as the mouthpiece of the Lord, the prophet enjoys protection. Bluntly stated, "Don't mess with Elisha" (Strand Winslow, 170)!

3:1–3. The regnal introduction of Jehoram introduces the next phase of the first narrative cycle. Coming to power in the eighteenth year of Jehoshaphat, he reigned twelve years. While he was not as bad as his father and mother (Ahab and Jezebel), as he removed Baal's pillar, he did evil in the eyes of the Lord (v. 2) and clung to the sins of Jeroboam (v. 3). This means that he perpetuated the unsanctioned worship at Bethel and Dan.

3:4–27. In verse 4, the reader is introduced to Mesha, the king of Moab. He is described

as a *nōqēd* (נֹקֵד), which is often translated as something like a "sheep breeder." Yet to be more precise, this title refers to a manager and marketer of large herds of sheep (Craigie 1983, 71–73). This implies, then, that Moab's chief contribution to the economy of the region was through its sheep husbandry. In addition, Mesha is described as a vassal of the Omride dynasty, owing a yearly tax of one hundred thousand "lambs" (כַּר) and wool of one hundred thousand rams (אַיִל). This was a substantial burden, and so it makes sense that Mesha rebelled upon hearing of Ahab's passing (v. 5).

This notification adds to the interesting relationship among kings. Just as Mesha was subordinate to Israel, so too was Jehoshaphat and Judah, for Jehoram's question to Jehoshaphat in verse 7 was not really a question at all. It's a command veiled as a question, demonstrated by the Judean king's formulaic response (v. 7). Yet there's another layer to these relationships. Edom is apparently a vassal of Judah (cf. 2 Kings 8:20). Thus, Israel sees an opportunity to catch Moab off guard. Instead of attacking Moab from the north, having come through Ammonite territory, Israel ambitiously sought to exploit the Judah/Edom relationship so to unexpectedly attack from the south, by way of the "Desert Edomite Road" (v. 8).

Unfortunately, the plan ran into serious problems. Seven days in, the coalition found itself out of water (v. 9). Such a turn of events caused the Israelite king to become anxious and dejected, to the point where he openly pondered the likelihood of ignominious defeat (v. 10). But similar to 1 Kings 22, Jehoshaphat stands as the voice of reason and spiritual maturity. He suggests consulting a "prophet of the Lord," with the hope being, of course, to gain clarity and insight during this time of crisis.

Elisha's name is floated by an unnamed member of Israel's royal court (v.

11). Moreover, Elisha's history as Elijah's apprentice (lit., "he used to pour water on the hands of Elijah") is emphasized. For Jehoshaphat, this was apparently enough, immediately accepting that "the word of the LORD is with him" (v. 12). Yet Elisha did not share Jehoshaphat's enthusiasm. He needed convincing. Initially Elisha rebuffs the coalition, urging them to consult the illegitimate prophets so often pursued by Jehoram's predecessors (v. 13). Only when the king of Israel appeals to an oracle supposedly offered by the Lord (but not recounted in Scripture) does Elisha consent. Nevertheless, Elisha makes it clear that Jehoshaphat's character and presence secured the deal.

Elisha prophesies under the influence of the harp (v. 15), and his words are somewhat cryptic. He predicts that a dry riverbed, probably the Wadi Zered, will be filled with pools of water without the onset of rain (vv. 16–17). Although this sounded unbelievable, Elisha emphasizes that even this event is nothing to the Lord. More importantly, this miracle will be linked to a successful campaign against Moab. The nation will be defeated, cities destroyed, and the land decimated (vv. 18–19). The very next day, suddenly, water flowed from the direction of Edom to fill the land (v. 20).

In verse 21, the scene shifts to Moab. At the report of the imminent invasion, every able-bodied person, regardless of age, was marshalled to battle. However, what the Moabite army saw early in the morning set into motion a series of events that would result in their country's decimation. The pools of water that were created by the sudden rush of water appeared "red as blood" (v. 22). Likely caused by the red sandstone of the region, this natural phenomenon was erroneously interpreted as a sign of the coalition's infighting. Thus, the Moabite army heads directly to the camp of their enemies hoping to loot what remained in the camp.

Unfortunately for them, they were greeted by a camp filled with a capable army eager to pursue them.

Naturally, the Moabite army retreated, but the Israelite coalition attacked (v. 24). And as the Israelite army pursued, they left a wake of destruction. Cities were "overturned" (הרס) and arable fields were rendered useless by littering them with stones. In addition, springs were stopped up and trees cut down (v. 25). Such action was typical practice in ancient warfare, designed to cripple the economic and ecological possibilities of the nation, although Deuteronomy 20:19–20 imposed restrictions on such actions. The exception to such devastation was Kir-Hareseth, the city where Moab made their last stand.

Mesha attempted to break through the coalition's line with seven hundred infantrymen, but when this failed he chose to sacrifice his heir, the crown-prince, "his firstborn son who was to succeed him" (v. 27). In turn, a "great wrath" (קֶצֶף־גָּדוֹל) descended upon Israel and forced them to withdraw from the battle. This constitutes one of the most perplexing scenes in Kings as many questions persist. Clearly, the crown-prince was the sacrifice; the grammar makes this clear. However, what was the nature of the sacrifice? Moreover, what are the dynamics of the "great wrath" that fell upon Israel? Whence does the wrath originate? Moab's god, Chemosh? Israel's God, Yahweh?

Wiseman (2008, 214) proposes three options to make sense of this scene. First, the "great wrath" is better understood as a "great anger" that is felt by Israel in response to witnessing such a horrific event. It was so horrific that they could not compel themselves to finish the attack. Rather, they left for home. Several commentators hold to this position (e.g., Strand Winslow, 173–74; Sweeney 2007, 284). Second, the "great wrath" is Moab's reaction to the desperate situation, and it frightened Israel into retreat. Third,

221

the "great wrath" comes from the Lord and turned against Israel because the intensity of their attack crossed some moral line. All these options are left wanting. An alternative proposal has been offered by Drew Holland (2020). He argues, based on intertextual references throughout the Old Testament and a consideration of ancient Near Eastern culture, that the "great wrath" was from the Lord and was imposed on Israel for their willingness to take part in a child sacrifice offered as penance by a vassal (Moab) for their rebellion against their suzerain (Israel). Thus, the Israelite coalition forfeited their divinely ordained victory by yielding to their tendency to engage in inappropriate sacrifices.

4:1–7. In verse 1, the reader is introduced to a significant socioeconomic problem. An unnamed widow from the company of prophets (בְּנֵי־הַנְּבִיאִים) is confronted with the reality that her two sons will be taken from her to pay off an outstanding debt. Such a scenario was not uncommon in antiquity, even in ancient Israel, although biblical legislation sought to restrict the practice of selling people into slavery to pay off debts (cf. Exod. 21:7; Lev. 25:39–42). Nevertheless, the servitude of her two sons would leave the widow without a source of steady provision and thus relegate her to the fringes of society. Thus, the widow's crying out (צְעָקָה) to Elisha implies a sense of urgency and desperation.

In a way that recalls the actions of a willing kinsmen to redeem a family member, Elisha confronts the situation, although Cogan and Tadmor (2008, 56) suggest that the phrasing of the initial question implies a sense of pessimism: "What shall I do for you? Tell me, what do you have in the house?" (v. 2; cf. Gen. 27:37; 1 Sam. 10:2). There's not much—only a small jar of oil (אָסוּךְ שָׁמֶן). But apparently, that's enough. Elisha instructs the widow to go home and borrow as many empty jars as she can. Then, she is to shut the door and start pouring. She is obedient, and when she starts pouring the oil into the empty jars, the oil does not stop until the last empty jar is filled (v. 6). In turn, the woman returns to Elisha to share the news and seek further guidance. Elisha encourages her to sell the oil in order to pay off the debt and live on what's left.

This scene recalls Elijah's miracle of provision for the widow at Zarephath (1 Kings 17:14–16) and the miraculous feedings of Jesus in the New Testament (see also Strand Winslow, 175). In each case, very little food is miraculously multiplied to satisfy an overwhelming need. In the context of Kings, Elisha continues the prophetic function of miraculous providing for those who find themselves in compromising socioeconomic situations.

4:8–37. Verse 8 introduces the reader to a prominent Shunammite woman (אִשָּׁה גְדוֹלָה), who according to the text struck a relationship with Elisha during his itinerancy. Beginning with a meal, the woman saw an opportunity to ensure that Elisha would stay with her and her husband when he was in town. However, the text does not explicitly say why she decided to renovate her house on behalf of Elisha. It does say that she was convinced of his prophetic standing and that he would stay if she built the room.

There are social elements in play here. The Shunammite woman displays hospitality toward Elisha, and given Elisha's query in verse 13 it's possible to understand that there were expectations of reciprocity. In addition, Elisha's question implies that he enjoyed a certain amount of social influence. And that she responded to Elisha's question with a "thanks, but no thanks" not only reinforces her description as a "great woman" but also suggests that she does not suffer from any adverse social stigma. Yet Gehazi's observation about her elderly husband and lack of children (v. 14) hints that a stigma may lay on the horizon (Strand Winslow, 176). Interestingly, this is what Elisha seizes upon, in turn forecasting the delivery of a son within approximately one year, despite her protests not to falsely get her hopes up (v. 16).

In this interaction, we can hear faint echoes of the birth proclamation of Isaac. While this woman did not laugh like Sarah (Gen. 18:12), and there is no notation of any genetic obstacle to fulfilling a pregnancy, the news of the miraculous birth of the Shunammite boy (v. 17) is not only greeted with skepticism but also framed with the same approximate chronological marker (cf. Gen. 18:10, 14). Literarily, the birth constitutes narrative material that's critical for what unfolds.

Verse 18 continues the account of the Shunammite woman, although one should assume a fairly lengthy span of time between the events of verses 1–7 and verses 18 and following. The boy has grown (וַיִּגְדַּל), enough to accompany his father in the fields. Yet his work was cut short due to an incapacitating headache (v. 19). It was serious enough to send the boy home, but interestingly there is no indication that the father attended to his ill-affected child.

The mother took the child on her lap only to watch him expire around noon (v. 20). At this point, the Shunammite woman steps into action. She places her dead son on Elisha's bed (lit., the bed of the man of God) and sets out to confront the prophet (vv. 21–22). At this point, her husband appears, but not with support. Rather, he questions her decision to seek out the prophet, for there apparently was a custom to seek prophet advice during a new moon festival. Nevertheless, this confrontation enhances the woman's characterization. She is the dominant character, not afraid to push past social norms when certain variables exist.[1] Not

Prophet Elisha and the Shunammite Woman on Mt. Carmel by Gerbrand van den Eeckhout. Public domain.

only does she effectively shrug off her husband (vv. 22–24), but she also lies to Gehazi, Elisha's mediator, in order to secure an audience with Elisha (v. 26), and then presses the prophet into personally dealing with the situation (v. 30).

Eventually, Elisha sends Gehazi with specific instructions, which lend credence to the urgency of the situation (Wiseman 2008, 217). He is to take the prophet's staff and not be sidetracked along the way. However, in a way that recalls the inability of Jesus's disciples to drive out evil spirits (Matt. 17:14–20; Mark 9:14–29, 37–43a), Gehazi was unable to resurrect the boy (v. 31). Therefore, Elisha enters the room and closes the door behind him and proceeds to pray (v. 33). What follows is a scene that's remarkably similar to 1 Kings 17:17–24. Just as Elijah prayed, stretched himself over the child, and revived the dead child, so too did Elisha. Yet the Elisha account offers more details. Elisha twice places his face and hands evenly over the dead boy's face and hands. In response, the child

---

1   The characterization of the woman is partially determined by the characterization of her husband. It's possible to understand the husband as a foil, but Strand Winslow (2017, 176–77) understands him in a less hostile and more ignorant way.

sneezes seven times and then opens his eyes (v. 35). When Gehazi brings the Shunammite woman in, her response is predictably that of respect and reverence for the prophet. She falls at Elisha's feet and then leaves with her son.

There are two important historical questions associated with Elisha's resurrecting the Shunammite boy. First, what did Elisha actually do? As mentioned above, Davis (2016) suggests that Elijah's mysterious actions were a ritualistic diagnosis that involved shaking a body. Is it possible, then, that Elisha is also performing some diagnostic ritual by spreading his body evenly over the boy's? Or, were Elisha's actions more therapeutic, given that the "flesh of the child became warm" (v. 34)? Second, what is the historical relationship between 2 Kings 4:18–37 and 1 Kings 17:17–24? Did both prophets encounter similar situations and thus employ essentially the same ritualistic action? Or are the striking similarities between the accounts indicative of a literary relationship—that is, in order to stress the connections between Elisha and Elijah, a literary scene was used to give the impression that they performed essentially the same miracle in the same way? Many scholars believe that one scene is fashioned after the other.

All things considered, the burden of proof exists with those who insist that one scene was fashioned after the other, implying that one of the two prophets (or both, for that matter) did not perform this feat. Given the prophetic texts found throughout the ancient Near East, prophets used a diverse arsenal of rituals to diagnose and treat certain conditions. Thus, the reason the scenes appear so similar is that Elijah and Elisha employed similar (not identical) rituals in response to similar situations.

4:38–41. Verse 38 begins the next cycle. But where the first cycle began with one food miracle (2:19–22), this cycle begins with two. The first involves a stew that was inadvertently cooked with poisonous vegetation. The terms that describe the vegetation are difficult, but the effect is clear enough: there was death in the pot! Important in this scene is the lexical and syntactical overlap with 2:19–22 as well as the general sequence of events. This suggests that Elisha used a similar ritual in response to a similar situation. In the context of Kings, this again testifies to Elisha's ability to provide on behalf of fellow prophets, particularly in times of need.

4:42–44. The second food miracle also echoes in Scripture. Yet in this case, Christians hear the echoes of Jesus most loudly. Miraculously multiplying a relatively small amount of food to feed a sizable group of people, even resulting in leftovers, anticipates Jesus feeding the multitudes (with Wiseman 2008, 218). Thus, Jesus and Elisha exist in the same family of prophetic miracle workers. In the context of Kings, Elisha is again proven to be a prophet who shows a deep concern for the populace as well as geopolitics. This scene also continues the extensive polemic against Baalism (Strand Winslow, 178; Sweeney 2007, 287–88).

There is significant syntactical and lexical overlap between 2 Kings 2:21 and 4:41. In both instances, there is a command to throw a counteragent into the source of poison followed by a pronouncement. In addition, the verb שָׁלַךְ features prominently.

2 Kings 2:21:

וַיֵּצֵא אֶל־מוֹצָא הַמַּיִם וַיַּשְׁלֶךְ־שָׁם מֶלַח וַיֹּאמֶר כֹּה־אָמַר יְהוָה רִפִּאתִי לַמַּיִם הָאֵלֶּה לֹא־יִהְיֶה מִשָּׁם עוֹד מָוֶת וּמְשַׁכָּלֶת

2 Kings 4:41:

וַיֹּאמֶר וּקְחוּ־קֶמַח וַיַּשְׁלֵךְ אֶל־הַסִּיר וַיֹּאמֶר צַק לָעָם וְיֹאכֵלוּ וְלֹא הָיָה דָּבָר רָע בַּסִּיר

5:1–27. Chapter 5 introduces the reader to a new character. Naaman is a revered foreign military general, known for his divinely sanctioned victories on the battlefield (v. 1). However, Naaman also suffered from a skin condition that tarnished his social stature (v. 1; מְצֹרָע). While many translations render the description of his condition as leprosy (e.g., NRSV), it's not clear from what condition Naaman suffered. The term מְצֹרָע, with its related terms, refers to a wide variety of skin conditions, all of which are not Hansen's disease (Hulse 1975; Johnson 2003, 534; Wright and Jones 1992, 4:277–81). The description does recall conditions that rendered Israelites cultically impure (e.g., Lev. 13–14), but it's not clear if this condition prevented Naaman from participating in the Aramean cult (cf. Cogan and Tadmor 2008, 63, who ponder a lesser severity). Regardless, his condition constitutes an important characteristic, and poses the problem within the narrative that craves a solution (Strand Winslow 2017, 179–80).

The solution to Naaman's problem begins to appear with one of his wife's servants, a young girl who had been displaced from Israel during an Aramean raid (1 Kings 5:3). She references Elisha with confidence, assuring her mistress that Naaman's hope for healing lay in a foreign land and with a foreign prophet. Apparently, this is enough, for verse 4 discloses how Naaman requested permission to enter Israel and find the venerated prophet.

With permission granted (v. 5), Naaman sets out with an "enormous sum" as payment for the prophet's services, which also points to the gravity of this personal crisis (Sweeney 2007, 299). However, this scene shows how Naaman's efforts are compromised by faulty assumptions. The first was the incorrect assumption *where* the prophet could be found. When he arrives at the Israelite court, in fact, the Israelite king interprets Naaman's visit conspiratorially, as an effort to reinvigorate the Aramean/Israelite conflict (v. 7). Fortunately, Elisha gets wind of Naaman's visit and dispatches a message to

Elisha Declining Naaman's Presents
by Abraham van Dijck. Public Domain.

temper the volatility and urge Naaman to come to him.

When Naaman arrives, Elisha does not even rise to meet him, highlighting the power structure that is governing this interaction. Instead, a messenger comes with instructions to wash seven times in the Jordan River (cf. Lev. 13–14). Naaman is, in turn, offended, so much so that he initially chooses to return to Aramean territory in a flurry of anger (1 Kings 5:11–12). However, unnamed servants again weigh into the situation, essentially pointing out the faulty logic of the general's tantrum (v. 13). Naaman eventually yields, washing himself in accord with the prophet's instructions. In turn, he's healed (v. 14).

The second faulty assumption of Naaman's journey was *how* he was to be healed. Clean water was assumed to be a vital ingredient, but aided by the wisdom of his subordinates, Naaman eventually realized that the mechanisms of healing sometimes confront one's assumptions. Wiseman (2008, 220) offers insight here: "The aim was to teach him humility and faith . . . the great man may expect some great thing while God often tests us with small things." Most importantly, the second faulty assumption leads into the third: *how the Lord is to be worshipped.* Naaman assumes that healing requires payment in response. This is quickly rebuffed by Elisha (vv. 15–16), clarifying that "Elisha doesn't need anything from Naaman" (Sweeney 2007, 301). What is expected, however, is allegiance, an implication that Naaman anticipates. The difficulty is that the solution to his problem inevitably creates another problem (Wray Beal 2014, 335): How can Naaman live out his monotheistic confession (v. 15) when his social prerogatives will require that he be present in pagan worship ceremonies?

It's interesting, given all the hostility in Kings to improper worship, that significant ambiguity remains in this scene (cf. Wray Beal 2014, 336). Not only does Naaman request what's essentially a free pass for participating in pagan worship, but he assumes that a couple cart loads of dirt—perhaps to construct some type of "mini Israel" (Wray Beal 2014, 335)— would allow the Lord to function within Aramean territory. Naaman's monotheistic confession is hampered by what appears to be lingering henotheistic ideas. As stated by Wiseman (2008, 220), "Naaman's knowledge of God was as yet weak." Ultimately, Elisha responds with a simple, "Go in peace." Thus, Naaman's confession and Elisha's rejection of payment, not the general's actions after the fact, are the focal point of the episode.[2]

Initially, this may seem odd. However, the ending sets up nicely verses 19–27 wherein one sees a different side of Gehazi. The trusted associate of Elisha usurps Elisha's decision not to accept any gift in response to Naaman's

healing, which eventually seals his lot for the rest of his life.

Gehazi takes it upon himself to chase down the Aramean after he "had gone from him a short distance" (v. 19b) in order to obtain at least a portion of the offered payment (v. 20). Gehazi believes that Elisha has been foolish, and to accomplish his goal, he fabricates a need involving a couple prophets looking for some supplies. Initially, Gehazi only requests a reduced portion of the initially offered payment. Yet there's some irony here, for Gehazi solicits one talent of silver and some clothes (v. 12).[3] Nevertheless, after some arm-twisting by Naaman, Gehazi opts for two talents of silver (v. 23).

Gehazi is aware of his actions, for upon approaching the interior portion of the city he relieves the load from those who helped him in order to hide it (v. 24). Nevertheless, Gehazi's chicanery is not missed by Elisha. As soon as Gehazi returns to tending to Elisha, the prophet pointedly asks him about his whereabouts (v. 25). Gehazi can't hide at this point, and his deception is exposed as Elisha claims to have observed the entire transaction in spirit (v. 26). In turn, Elisha's final rebuke takes the form of a rhetorical question that places the onus squarely on Gehazi and highlights his greed and selfishness in the process (v. 26). It suggests a time where basic sustenance was difficult to achieve, and extravagance offended the majority of the populace who were barely scrapping by. Ultimately, Gehazi assumes Naaman's impure condition, thus banishing him to the fringes of Israelite society (v. 27).[4]

---

2   Strand Winslow (2017, 182–83) links these two points. She argues that the rejection of payment reinforces the essence of Naaman's confession: that the Lord and his prophet is superior—and will always be superior—to everyone else. Wray Beal (2014, 332) also emphasizes the centrality of the confession.

3   One talent weighs approximately seventy-five pounds and, depending on the quality of the silver, could be worth tens of thousands of dollars.

4   Naaman and Gehazi are more than two people whose paths cross at a certain moment in time, for their characterization suggests a deeper function. Specifically, one can see them representing two paths in life, divergent choices that can be made in response to the word of God. Moreover, the paths represented are often played out on personal and corporate levels.

6:1–7. The miracle of the ax head is an interlude in the Elisha cycle (Wray Beal 2014, 340), although some commentators note the connections between 6:1–7 and those previous by means of the Jordan River (e.g., Cogan and Tadmor 2008, 70; Sweeney 2007, 301). These verses recount how Elisha accompanied a host of prophets in their pursuit of building supplies. According to verse 1, the prophetic group had grown too large for their current space, and so after securing the blessing of Elisha, which again demonstrates his leadership over the group, they travel to the vicinity of the Jordan River to gather timber. Unfortunately, in the process of their work, an ax head is dislodged from its shaft, sinking to the bottom of the river. This was significant. According to biblical legislation (Exod. 22:14), full restitution was required for the loss or death of borrowed property. Therefore, this unnamed prophet incurred a significant debt, which was clearly a cause for concern (1 Kings 6:5).

When Elisha hears of the problem, he attends to the situation. He finds the spot and performs a miracle that brings the ax head to the surface of the water, where it can be

---

The debate of what disease Naaman had notwithstanding, the general was chronically sick. Moreover, the situation was urgent, for his request for permission to seek healing abroad is met with an official correspondence and an astronomical sum of payment. However, when arriving in Israel, Naaman immediately confronts preconceived ideas about how his healing will play out. He assumes that he will find Elisha in the royal court. He assumes a certain protocol for his healing. And he assumes that a price be paid. He's wrong on all accounts. Instead, Naaman learns that the Lord's salvation defies preconceived notions but is always definitive. In fact, it's these realizations that compels Naaman to declare, in a very Israelite way, that "there is no God in all the earth except in Israel."

Juxtaposed to Naaman is Gehazi, Elisha's servant. When Gehazi appears in the narrative he is wrestling with what he believes to be the stupidity of Elisha. In response to Naaman's insistence to pay the prophet, Elisha had flatly refused, likely to ensure that the relationship between parties is understood. There must also be no hint that Naaman's salvation was purchased. Gehazi fails to grasp this lesson because his greed is crouching at the door. And it was his greed that encouraged him to chase the Aramean general down and fabricate a scenario to procure a small amount of the proposed payment. To be clear, the issue is Gehazi's deception and blatant disobedience. Even when he can come clean, Gehazi doubles down, sadly deepening his deception. In the end, Gehazi inherits Naaman's condition and is therefore banished to the fringes of Israelite society.

On a personal level, Naaman and Gehazi show how choices can affect our standing within God's community. Naaman is the "outsider" who becomes an "insider," and Gehazi is the "insider" who becomes an "outsider." While Naaman's skin condition is his immediate problem, he finds a more significant problem when pursuing physical healing. In other words, his physical ailment is the mechanism that allowed him to realize his spiritual ailment. His confession of faith, therefore, is the climax of the scene, not his ascent out of the waters of the Jordan. Conversely, Gehazi's problem is completely spiritual. It's disenfranchisement and greed, and both sentiments fuel his deceptive and disobedient actions. Whereas Naaman is ultimately able to see his shortcoming, Gehazi can't. And tragically, Gehazi's attitude ensures that he is banished from the community.

On a national level, Naaman demonstrates how the Lord should and can be acknowledged by all nations. The Lord is not restricted by geography, and he orchestrates the actions of all nations, including Israel's enemies. He is "God alone in all the earth." This means that Israel does not have a corner on the market when it comes to the worship of the Lord. Gehazi demonstrates the premium of obedience and the recognition of God's word through his prophets, two messages that were particularly important for Israel. Yet perhaps most interestingly, the Naaman/Gehazi dynamic is mirrored elsewhere in Scripture. In Joshua 2–7, Rahab, the Canaanite designated for חֵרֶם, who exists outside the Israelite community, switches places with Achan, the Israelite from Judah, because of her action and confession and conversely his blatant violation of חֵרֶם. There too, the insider assumes the stigma and punishment of the one initially outside the community.

retrieved. Interesting are the use of a new piece of wood (v. 6) and the explicit command for the anonymous prophet to do something in response (v. 7). Both elements recall previous miracles. In 2:20, a new bowl is used to clean Jericho's spring, and virtually all of Elisha's documented miracles involve the prophet commanding people to do something. Yet certain mechanisms of this event are not clear. Indeed, the iron ax head is brought close enough to the surface to be grabbed. But the word often rendered as "float" (וַיָּצֶף) is difficult, and it's not clear whether the new wood was thrown on the top of the water or thrown into the water (v. 6). Regardless, this is another example of Elisha bearing responsibility for the social well-being of all people, not just the upper echelon of society. Perhaps then this is another reason why this scene is juxtaposed to the healing of Naaman.

6:8–23. The Elisha cycle resumes in verse 8, and it continues to display the extraordinary abilities of Elisha as well as his intimate connection with the heavenly realm. However, the message of this particular episode goes beyond Elisha's prophetic abilities.

The scene opens with a note of contextualization: "Once when the king of Aram was at war with Israel" (v. 8). And as should be the case with all good military preparation, advice is solicited. The text does not specify the content of the advice, but that's not the point (v. 8). Rather, the point is the ability of Elisha to intercept the information and warn the Israelite king in a way that defies reason (v. 9). In this narrative, the Israelite king heeds the prophet's warning and again warns the unspecified location of the imminent attack. Of course, this perturbs the Aramean king, who becomes convinced that he has a spy in his ranks (v. 11). Yet after some explanation by his servants, he realizes that the prophet, while not present, is somehow privy to the words he speaks behind closed doors (v. 12). Consequently, the

Aramean king's response is predictable—eliminate the threat. He first seeks intelligence as to Elisha's location, and upon obtaining that information he dispatches a "great army" (חַיִל כָּבֵד) to Dothan by the cover of darkness.

Surprise is the goal, and Elisha's attendant was certainly surprised. According to verse 15, the attendant wakes the prophet in a fit of despair, essentially lamenting, "Oh no! What are we going to do?" The attendant lacks hope, but Elisha confronts it with a bold but simple statement, "Do not be afraid, for there are more with us than there are with them" (v. 16). Such a comment echoes so many other passages throughout Scripture that reveal how God wants to comfort his audience when they are faced with an overwhelming situation (e.g., Jer. 42:11; Matt. 17:7; Luke 1:30; Acts 8:9). Elisha also prays that his attendant's eyes are opened so he can see the truth of the situation. The Lord hears and opens his eyes, and what the attendant sees changes his perspective. A fiery chariot force encircles Elisha, proving to the attendant who really has the upper hand. But Elisha prays again, this time to strike the foreign army with "blindness" (1 Kings 6:18) so that he could lead them into a trap (cf. LaBarbera [1984, 184, 643] argues for a figurative blindness). The Lord responds, and Elisha leads the Aramean army into the interior of Samaria. Then Elisha prays a third time, to open the eyes of the hostile military force. When their eyes are opened, they find themselves in a corner, inside Samaria with nowhere to go.

Given that the words עַיִן (eye) and ראה (to see) appear four times and six times, respectively, in 6:8–23, this scene plays off what it means to "see" and understand. Both the Aramean king and Elisha's servant misunderstood their situation, and both the Aramean army and Elisha's servant needed to have their eyes opened to properly understand their reality. This episode is suggesting that there is more than meets the eye, and left to one's own skewed, restricted perspective, people sometimes miss out. Moreover, some understand 6:8–23 with 6:24–7:20 to be a satire aimed at the general ineptitude of Israelite monarchy (LeBarbera 1984, 184).

Most importantly, this scene is building to one of the great acts of mercy in the Old Testament. Moreover, the conclusion of this scene starkly contrasts with what was recounted in 1 Kings 20:35–43. There, Ahab is chastised for being gracious to his enemies, but here the Israelite king, who desperately wants to strike down the Aramean army, is redirected. Instead of slaughter, there will be a feast, which may allude to some covenantal agreement (Wiseman 2008, 223). Instead of a display of power and dominance, Israel will show mercy, sending the Aramean force home with a full stomach (2 Kings 6:22–23). To his credit, the Israelite king obeys, but questions persist for the reader. Why the difference? While both episodes emphasize the importance of obedience, the situation in 1 Kings 20 involved a command to subject the adversary to חֵרֶם (v. 42). Moreover, the lesson here is also about how one's perspective, one's ability to "see," may fail them. And particularly appropriate for geopolitics, sometimes mercy may de-escalate tensions.

Ben-Hadad

Identifying Ben-Hadad is incredibly problematic. There is attestation of a Ben-Hadad in Syrian and Assyrian inscriptions, but those witnesses don't alleviate the problems associated with the biblical witness. Kings references a Ben-Hadad, son of Tab-Rimmon, son of Hezion (1 Kings 15:16–22) and a Ben-Hadad, son of Hazael (2 Kings 13:3–7). Together, these passages suggest the existence of two Aramean kings with the same name. However, due to the characterization of the Aramean Ben-Hadad in 1 Kings 20–2 Kings 8 in relation to the Omride kings, some scholars have pondered whether there was a third Ben-Hadad.

Ultimately, the question of Ben-Hadad, even the number of Ben-Hadads, remains unsolved. The present state of the evidence simply does not allow for any definitive conclusion. Ben-Hadad means "son of Hadad," which suggests the possibility that it is a royal title rather than a personal name. However, the same usage of the phrase in the Zakkur inscription suggests otherwise (Pitard 1992).

6:24–7:20. In verse 24, it's revealed that Israel and Aram are again fighting. Yet in many ways, this situation ratchets up the intensity. There is a lengthy siege that has impressed a most desperate situation upon Samaria (Sweeney 2007, 311–12). Animal excrement was being sold for fuel and (cultically impure) mutilated animals for food (Lev. 11; Deut. 14). Moreover, cannibalism was taking hold, a widely attested reality of siege warfare (Wiseman 2008, 224). One day while the king was "walking on the city wall" (2 Kings 6:26), an unnamed woman cried out for justice. According to her story, an acquaintance reached an agreement. One day they would eat her son, and on another day the two would eat the other son. Apparently, primal urges of self-preservation had overrun familial instincts. However, when it came time to eat the second son, the other woman balked. In other words, the woman crying out to the king had been duped into killing and eating her son.

As one would expect, this news of such an appalling situation sent the king into a frenzy, publicly tearing his clothes and vowing to kill Elisha (v. 31). And there's a terrible irony here. Justice would require killing (and eating) of an innocent child (Strand Winslow, 189). As for why Elisha is blamed, the reader is not told specifically, but it certainly adds another level of tension to an already tense situation. In turn, the king dispatches what can only be understood as a hatchet man. However, before he could arrive, Elisha explains to the elders that a man approaches with explicit directions to decapitate him (v. 32). He therefore exhorts his audience to lock him in a room in anticipation of the king's arrival (v. 32).

The situation does not get that far. Upon his arrival, the messenger lashes out at Elisha, pressing him to explain what appears to be an unjust situation (v. 33).[5] In response, Elisha offers an oracle of prediction. In about twenty-four hours the economic situation of Samaria would return to its pre-siege state (7:1). Unfortunately, the advisor to the king (lit., "the captain upon whom the king leaned") doesn't believe the prognostication, and his obstinance secures another prediction. However, this time it's one of death and judgment. All that Elisha predicted will happen, but the messenger will not see it (v. 2).

What begins in verse 3 is how Elisha's prediction came to pass. It began with a group of four lepers wrestling with the inevitabilities of their situation. Ultimately, they decided that there was more hope in switching sides, a shameful and treasonous act. It would be better to take their chances with the Aramean camp than sit outside of Samaria. Even if they were allowed to seek shelter in the city (Lev. 13:11, 46; Num. 12:14–16), they would eventually die of starvation. It's a classic lose-lose situation. However, when they came upon the Aramean camp, they found it abandoned. Apparently, the Arameans had fled so quickly that they left their animals, tents, and possessions. Consequently, the lepers began looting.

After two trips, the lepers developed a moral crisis that was likely rooted in some unstated social norm (Wiseman 2008, 225). Eventually they informed the king (v. 9), but their message was initially received with intense skepticism. It was even mocked. It's interpreted as a classic "too good to be true" scenario. Instead, the king offers an alternative narrative to the situation that they describe. It's a ruse, a trap, designed to entrap the Israelites (v. 12). Nevertheless, the king is convinced to dispatch a small reconnaissance force to check out the report. What was found verified the testimony of the lepers, and the group retraced the path of retreat all the way back to the Jordan River thanks to the trail of plunder that littered the ground. According to verse 6, the Lord "caused the Aramean army to hear the sound of chariots . . . the sound of a great army." The sound evidently threw the army into a panic and convinced them that Israel had purchased reinforcements.

When the news reached Samaria, the inhabitants responded with riotous fervor. They rushed out to the camp to partake in the plundering that the lepers had begun, and in the process, they trampled the messenger against whom Elisha had prophesied (v. 17). They killed him on the spot, fulfilling the prophecy, and the text doesn't want the reader to miss this. Verses 18–20 are devoted to reiterating the prophecy of verses 1–2 in detail as a way to emphasize his death.

It's worth noting the differences in Elisha here versus the other episodes that feature him. Here, Elisha does nothing to facilitate the salvation of God's people. He only offers prophetic explanation. Moreover, this scene anticipates another episode in Kings where a besieging army will be miraculously devastated overnight (cf. 2 Kings 18–19).

8:1–6. Chapter 8 reintroduces the reader to the Shunammite woman (cf. 4:8–37). While there is a debate as to the literary relationship between these two passages, here Elisha warns her of a pending famine. It's coming, and it will be severe. The prophet, therefore, encourages her to resettle, but he does not dictate where. Nevertheless, this was no small request. Recall that she was adamant that she lived among her people, and any move away would have a negative impact on her ability to retain the land.

---

5   Some translations read in 2 Kings 6:33 that the king came to the city, because reading "the messenger" here introduces a tension in the direct discourse that immediately follows. However, the first-person form of the quotation can be explained if one understands that the messenger is adopting the actual words of the king.

Nevertheless, for seven years she lived in Philistine territory, a region whose coastal climate insulated them from the ravages of famine.

Literary Observations

At the conclusion of chapter 5, Gehazi inherits Naaman's ailment in response to his disobedience. This turn of events implies that Gehazi was banished to the outskirts of Israelite community (Lev. 13–14). In chapter 8, Gehazi is enjoying royal company. Either Gehazi's condition did not preclude him from keeping royal company, possibly because he had been healed, or this scene is placed out of order to fit the historian's historical presentation. Sweeney (2007, 316), notes several connections with 2 Kings 4, including the famine and the statement that the Shunammite woman took her son and left after he was resurrected. Wiseman (2008, 225) says 8:1–6 is a continuation of 2 Kings 4:8–37.

When the seven years conclude, she returns to Israel. Unfortunately, she returns to find that her past problem of provision persists, just in a different form. Her home and land, her source of provision, is gone. It's unclear why, exactly, but one should assume that there were social and legal expectations regarding how land rights could be forfeit (Cogan and Tadmor, 88; Fritz 2003, 273). Her only recourse is to make an appeal to the king.

Again, the Shunammite woman shows initiative. She seeks an audience with the king, which further suggests a certain social status for the woman. Most critical for the narrative is how she arrives at the perfect time. As she approaches the court, Gehazi happens to be entertaining the king with tales of Elisha, particularly how he resurrected the Shunammite's son (vv. 4–5). Some may call it coincidental, or even serendipitous, but the sense of the narrative is that it was providential. What's more, the mere reputation of Elisha is powerful enough (also Wray Beal 2014, 360). The prophet does not even have to be on site to sway royal decisions.

In this case, the woman's appeal is not only granted, but she is to receive the revenue from the land while she was away (v. 6).

8:7–15. The cycles devoted to Elisha's ministry began with a prophetic transition. Here they conclude with political transitions, which is particularly appropriate given how so many of the preceding scenes showed Elisha's association with the geopolitical developments in the region. The first political transition involves the ascension of Hazael.

The scene opens with word reaching Elisha that Ben-Hadad, king of Aram, had fallen ill (v. 7). Interestingly, Elisha heads to Damascus, where he is received warmly. There is no hostility over the fact that he's a prophet from Israel, and this scene again testifies to Elisha's international prestige. Moreover, the prophet receives a well-endowed royal emissary, which happens to be headed by Hazael—forty camels' worth, with "all the goodness of Damascus" (כָּל־טוּב דַּמֶּשֶׂק), to be precise.

Textual Ambiguity

Verses 10–11 are ambiguous. While English translations are uniform in their reading of verse 10, the Hebrew is difficult. The phrase in question, "to him," is written in a peculiar but not unprecedented manner (GKC, 103g). It's possible, however, to understand a negation opposed to a prepositional phrase. Thus, one could read, "Say, 'You will certainly not live,'" which would take away the theological conundrum of prophetic falsehood that's imported into this scene when Elisha tells Hazael that Ben Hadad will be cured but later die (cf. Deut. 18:17–22). Nevertheless, the Masoretes believe that the prepositional phrase "to him" was the intended sense.

In 2 Kings 8:11, it's unclear who stood silent and who was embarrassed at the silence. The subjects of the verbal forms וַיַּעֲמֵד and וַיָּשֶׂם are not specified. However, given that "the man of

God" is the explicit subject of the next clause, וַיֵּבְךְּ, it's likely that Hazael is the one who stared to the point of embarrassment.

Hazael obediently asks Elisha about the fate of his king, but things quickly get weird. Elisha responds, but cryptically. It seems that the king will heal, but he will also die, a shocking pronouncement that is also reflected in the emphatic syntax of verse 10 (חָיֹה תִחְיֶה vs. מוֹת יָמוּת). What's more, an awkward stare-down ensues, which was only broken by the prophet's weeping ("He fixed his gaze and stared at him, until he was ashamed," v. 11). And when Hazael inquiries about the emotional outburst, Elisha reveals to Hazael the future horrors that he will perpetuate against Israel, describing in terrible detail the carnage of war and collateral damage (v. 12). At first, Hazael is dismissive of the proclamation, saying, "What is your servant, who is a mere dog, that he should do this great thing" (v. 13)? However, Elisha verifies his vision with an appeal to the Lord. This appears to be enough, for Hazael breaks off the encounter and returns to Ben-Hadad. When asked, Hazael tells Ben Hadad that he will recover (v. 14), but the next day, with the words of the prophet firmly entrenched in his mind, the aide suffocates the king with a wet rag, usurping the throne in the process (v. 15).

This scene brings to fruition the proclamation given to Elijah long ago when he was seeking refuge at Sinai (1 Kings 19:15–16). It was proclaimed that Hazael, Elisha, and Jehu would be anointed to oversee a critical geopolitical transition. However, Elijah was only able to anoint Elisha before he ascended to heaven. As for Jehu's prophesied role, his anointing as king will become the focus of the account in 2 Kings 9.

8:16–29. The political transition in Aram is juxtaposed with two transitions in Judah. In verses 16–24, the reign of Jehoram of Judah is recounted. [6] The son of the righteous Jehoshaphat, Jehoram's reign conversely resembled the reigns of the Israelite kings. In fact, the historian calls out the close similarity with the Omride dynasty, a particularly damning criticism borne out of his marital relationship with the Israelite dynasty (v. 18). However, the historian pacifies his harsh criticism by drawing the reader's attention to the promise of land given to David (v. 19; cf. 1 Kings 11:36; 15:4; Schreiner 2014). In addition, Jehoram's reign was also defined by the rebellion of Edom (2 Kings 8:20). Apparently, Jehoram attempted to coerce them back into the fold of Judean influence, but he failed (v. 21), a failure that was also

---

6   If there is one situation that puts the difficulties of establishing a chronology for Kings on full display, it's the issues associated with the reigns of Jehoram. Traditionally, the spelling "Jehoram" is understood to be an alternative form of "Joram," and that there were two kings, one in Israel and one in Judah, that had the same name. Sharing names is not a problem, but the discrepancies about when each Jehoram arose (cf. 2 Kings 1:17 and 8:16) can't be explained by assuming there were two kings with the same name.

Solutions have ranged from textual-critical, arguing that the discrepancies are the result of intentional and unintentional corruptions, to the historical. For example, several scholars have considered variations of the reality that there was only one Jehoram who reigned in both Israel and Judah. In every case, explanations and reconstructions are extremely speculative, assuming many important details not in the text (Barrick 2001). Nevertheless, these reconstructions rightly point to the close sociopolitical connection between the Judean and Israelite kings during the Omride era. Moreover, they rightly emphasize the sociopolitical turmoil that plagued the region in the era of Jehu's coup, even threatening the viability of the Davidic dynasty.

Presently, it seems wisest to accept the fact that any precise chronology or reconstruction of the Omride and Davidic lines is unobtainable. There are significant textual and historical difficulties, but radically emending the text or postulating a sweeping historical reconstruction based on debatable assumptions is no better.

understood to be as a watershed moment in Judean history. The historian felt the need to clarify that from that point on, Edom had been in revolt. Libnah, a site in the Shephelah, also seceded. So while Judah persisted, largely due to the legacy of David, her geopolitical influence was being pulled back.

Verses 25–29 recounted the rule of Jehoram's successor, Ahaziah. He reigned only a year, and his mother was the infamous Omride Athaliah (2 Kings 11:1–21). As the granddaughter of Omri (2 Kings 8:26), she likely ensured that Omride policies and practices remained front and center in the Judean court. Consequently, it comes as no surprise that the historian's criticism of Ahaziah emphasizes Omride-influenced practices (v. 27). Also of note is the close political relationship that persisted between Israel and Judah during his reign. According to verse 28, Ahaziah accompanied the Israelite king Joram to war against Hazael and Aram at Ramoth Gilead. This joint endeavor was the context where Joram suffered his wound, which required him to return to Jezreel to heal. Unfortunately for Ahaziah, his visitation of Joram there ended in his assassination by Jehu (cf. 9:27–29).

The Black Obelisk

Standing just above two meters in height, and made of black alabaster, the Black Obelisk was discovered during the earliest excavations of Mesopotamia by Austen Layard in 1846. It recounts the imperialistic exploits of Shalmaneser III across twenty panels. One of those panels has traditionally been understood to feature "Jehu, from the House of Omri," paying homage and tribute to the Assyrian king.

However, the description "from the house of Omri" appears to conflict with Kings, which implies that Jehu was not from the Omride family. In turn, scholars have discussed the content of the inscription, suggesting that the Assyrians were in error, that Jehu was a distant relative in Omri's line (Schneider 1996), or that not Jehu but Jehoram is represented on the monument (McCarter 1974) (*ANET*, 281; *COS* 2.113F).

Neo-Assyrian Black Limestone Obelisk of Shalmaneser III, Nimrud, 825 BCE. Public domain.

Internal and External Threats (9:1–13:25)

Jehu's coup instituted a period where the vitality and effectiveness of God's people, even the longevity of the Davidic dynasty, was compromised by internal and external pressures as well as the implications of shortsighted decisions.

Second Kings 9:1–10:36 recounts in vivid detail Jehu's rise to the Israelite throne. Given in distinct movements, the account as a whole bears witness to the elements in a successful coup d'état. First, one must take out the ruler (9:14–29). Then, the immediate (9:30–37) and extended families (10:1–17) must also be neutralized in order to reduce the possibility of any lingering blood vengeance. Finally, a successful coup always deconstructs the supporting social infrastructures (10:18–31).

9:1–13. The account of Jehu's coup begins in 2 Kings 9:1. In the preparatory verses of 1–13, we're told that Jehu's actions are encouraged by no less than two factors. First, Elisha the prophet urgently dispatches "a member of the company of prophets" (v. 1) to Ramoth Gilead with the expressed purpose of anointing Jehu as the new king. Moreover, Elisha gives him specific directions how this the encounter was to play out. The young prophet, who is never named, complies and confronts Jehu while he is among his commanders, eventually anointing him in a back room (vv. 4–10). As this happens, the prophetic delegate reveals that Jehu's rise to the Israelite throne will also constitute divine judgment of the Omrides for their infractions against the prophets and servants of the Lord (vv. 7–10). In other words, Jehu's coup enjoyed divine stimulus and theological reasoning, which was critical for any validation of royal succession that defied an expected order.

Second, Jehu's colleagues also facilitated Jehu's rise to power. Through their emphatic proclamation of him as king, they overwhelm what appears to be a preliminary lethargic attitude toward the news. Initially, Jehu downplays his prophetic encounter, responding to the sarcastic inquiry of his colleagues with deflection. Many English translations don't do justice to the dynamics of this interaction. Thus, I translate verses 11–12 as follows:

> When Jehu went out to the servants of his lord, they asked him, "Is it okay? Why did this crazy guy come to you?" He said to them, "You know those guys and their crazy talk." But they said, "Liar! Tell us!" He responded, "He said this and that to me, saying 'Thus says the LORD, I have anointed you as king over Israel.'"

In response, his fellow commanders quickly move to symbolically and publicly proclaim him as king. This means that Jehu has secured a capable military force to support his movements, which is another critical variable for securing power—muscle.

9:14–29. With the die cast, Jehu sets his eyes to Jezreel, an Omride center of power and the location where Joram was recovering. However, before Jehu sets out, he gives strict orders not to allow anyone to leave Ramoth Gilead. Jehu's departure would have raised eyebrows and almost certainly produced some sort of dispatch. So, to ensure his approach was as controlled as possible, he seals the city (v. 15).

Apparently, Jehu drove his chariot like a madman (v. 20), and so a sentinel of Jezreel was able to see Jehu and his company approaching from a distance. In response, the city predictably dispatches a messenger to ascertain the nature of Jehu's visitation. But when the messenger arrives with the question of intention (v. 18), he's met with a sarcastic scoff that incriminates him merely based on his association with the royal family. Ultimately, the messenger gets the hint, realizes the inevitability of what's coming, and falls in line with Jehu's company.

The same scenario plays itself out a second time (vv. 19–20), and with the assimilation of the second messenger, Joram knows he must meet the company personally. So, he readies his chariot and rides to meet Jehu with Ahaziah by his side. When he arrives, Joram asks the same question as his previous messengers. "Is it peace?" However, Joram is met with even more disdainful sarcasm, particularly when Jehu clarifies the irony of the question. Essentially, Jehu asks how Joram can even *think* that peace is a possibility given the theological atrocities Jezebel continues to perpetuate. As alluded to by Wiseman (2008, 235), there can be no political peace without religious peace.

At this, Joram commands Ahaziah to flee. He also accuses Jehu of treason (v. 23), and retreats to the safe confines of Jezreel. However, Joram only gets so far. He is quickly shot by Jehu, pierced between the shoulders and cutting into his heart (v. 24). To add insult to this mortal blow, Jehu shames the dead man when he commands that Joram's body be dumped on the ground in fulfillment of the prophecies made against the Omride line, specifically against Ahab for the Naboth affair (1 Kings 21:19; 21–22; 26). Unfortunately, Ahaziah gets caught up in Jehu's zeal. He is shot as well, and eventually he expires while at Megiddo (2 Kings 9:27). Eventually, his body is taken back to Jerusalem and given an honorable burial (v. 28), unlike Joram.

Verse 29 repeats 2 Kings 8:25 with only a minor variation between the synchronization.

9:30–37. With the king of Israel dispatched, Jehu moves to target Jezebel. When Jezebel hears of Jehu's arrival, she donned special attire and proceeded to watch the general as he entered the city (v. 30). The nature of her clothing is not specified, and some have linked it to burial clothes (Strand Winslow, 204), coquettish activity, or official attire that signals a willingness to negotiate (Sweeney 2007, 335; Wiseman 2008, 236). Regardless, she eventually repeats the question of the messengers, asking about his intentions (v. 31). However, given that she calls Jehu "Zimri," she clearly understands Jehu's usurping

and murderous intentions (cf. 1 Kings 16:8–14; Strand Winslow, 204; Sweeney 2007, 336).

Jehu brushes aside Jezebel's question and plays to his position of strength. He calls out to whoever is in earshot to have them declare their allegiance to him (2 Kings 9:32). Two or three eunuchs respond merely with eye contact, which in turn encourages Jehu to call for Jezebel's body. Obediently, the two eunuchs cast her body from the upper-story window, securing their place in biblical history as the anonymous assassins of Queen Jezebel. However, the narrative is focused on the violence of the situation. The reader is told that blood spattered on the buildings and that horses trampled her corpse (v. 33). What's more, her corpse was consumed so voraciously by the dogs there that by the time Jehu enjoyed his victory meal (v. 34), the only part of her body left was her skull, her feet, and her hands (v. 35). The cumulative effect of such gruesome detail is to not only to paint a shameful picture of her death, but also draw attention to the fact that the details of her death fulfilled prophecy (vv. 36–37).

It's interesting to note that up to this point in the narrative, Jehu is shown to be a very charismatic person. His colleagues didn't hesitate to blow the trumpet and proclaim him king when they heard of his secret appointment. His army rushed to Jezreel with him and dispatched the Judean king upon command. The army discarded Joram's corpse, and Jehu convinced two eunuchs to throw Jezebel out a window. In fact, while Jehu is credited for killing "all who were left in the house of Ahab" (10:11; 17), the text only credits the death of Joram to the hand of Jehu. In this way, Jehu's charisma and persuasion are unmatched.

10:1–17. The next phase of Jehu's coup affected the larger Omride family. According to verse 1, Ahab had seventy sons, which could be a stylized number (Wiseman 2008, 238). But as long as a member of the royal family lived, they would have a claim to the throne (Strand Winslow,

205–6; Wiseman 2008, 237–38). To combat this, Jehu again wields his extraordinary persuasion. He sends an official correspondence to all the social elites, encouraging them to present the next would-be Omride ruler, undoubtedly to identify another Omride to fight (v. 3).

At this point, Jehu is oozing with confidence, particularly since he realizes that he has all the momentum. And the elites understand this dominance. So, they decide to cast their lot in with him. It's an emphatic plea, designed to signal immediate capitulation (v. 5). In return, another letter is dispatched from Jehu, in which he requests the heads of all the sons (v. 6). This is a call not only to purge Israelite society of the entire family, but it's also a statement of brutal violence that forces them to demonstrate their allegiance. Ultimately, the elders comply, decapitating the sons, putting their heads into baskets, and shipping them off to Jehu (v. 7).

When Jehu receives the gift, he commands that his people pile the heads in public. Why? Because large piles of heads can be a particularly effective deterrent. As Strand Winslow (2017, 206) says, it's a "thinly veiled threat." Moreover, it was a deterrent popularized by Assyrian monarchs (Wiseman 2008, 239). However, there is a theological element to all of this. Jehu's public explanation of this grotesque visual is contextualized by an appeal to Elijah's prophecy. Jehu justifies his actions by an appeal to divine sanction.

In verses 12–17, Jehu proceeds to Samaria. Along the way, Jehu encounters two parties. The first are those who are related to the recently slain Ahaziah. This group also constitutes a threat to Jehu. So, Jehu ushers them to the Pit of Beth Ecked, where they are slaughtered, all forty-two of them (v. 42). Again, the rationale for such actions is to shut off any avenue where blood vengeance may develop. Yet in this context, Jehu also encounters Jehonadab, the Rechabite. The Rechabites were an obscure but unique element within Iron Age Israelite society. According to 1 Chronicles 2:55, their lineage reached back to the Kenites, and Jeremiah 35 reveals that their identity was tied up with a nomadic and sober way of life (vv. 6–7). More importantly, Jehu's encounter with Jehonadab bears witness to the religious zeal of the Rechabites. When Jehu offers his hand, Jehonadab accepts and rides with Jehu (2 Kings 10:15) to witness Jehu's "zeal" for the Lord (v. 16). In other words, Jehonadab publicly declares his support of the new regime.

10:18–27. The last phase of Jehu's coup was to destroy the infrastructure that supported the previous dynasty. Therefore, the official Baal cult fell into Jehu's crosshairs. Baalism embodied so much of Canaanite paganism, and ever since Elijah's encounter with Baalism on Mount Carmel, the books of Kings has made it a point of emphasis, particularly linking it to the shortcomings of the Omride dynasty. However, Jehu's efforts are not telegraphed. According to verses 18–22, Jehu addresses the worshippers of Baal and brags how his piety toward Baal will surpass that of Ahab's. However, the reader knows that this is a ruse, an effort to gather all the proponents of Baalism in one location to expedite the purge.

When the assembly gathered, packing the temple of Baal "from wall to wall" (v. 21), Jehu called for the full trappings of worship to be brought out. And after one last sweep through the sanctuary was conducted to ensure that there would be no collateral damage (v. 24), Jehu sets his violent plan into action.

He initiates sacrifices and offerings, but all this was to deflect any attention from what was about to transpire. Jehu then commanded the eighty men stationed outside the sanctuary to slaughter the worshipers of Baal (v. 25). From there, the hit squad proceeded into the temple's stronghold, forcibly removed the sacred pillars, and burned the temple (v. 26). Furthermore, the site was desecrated by making it into a public restroom.

10:28–31. Verse 28 begins the summarization of Jehu's reign. But in these verses, the focus is upon assessing the actions of 2 Kings 9:1–10:27. Indeed, Jehu is credited with wiping out Baalism from Israel (שמד), undoubtedly a braggadocious claim that needs to be understood for its rhetorical effect. However, there is a sense of irony that settles on these verses.

Wray-Beal (2014, 372–73) has emphasized the collaboration of the root שׁלם, the verb נכה, and the intimate association between the judgment of the Omrides and the judgment of Baalism within 2 Kings 9–10. Channeling Saul Olyan (1984), Wray-Beal points out that the noun שָׁלוֹם occurs ten times in 2 Kings 9–10 (2 Kings 9:11, 17–19, 22, 31; 10:13) while its related verb appears in 2 Kings 9:26. This recurrence constructs an overwhelming sense of irony in the narrative: Jehu's violent and inherently non-שָׁלוֹם actions are intended to reinstitute a שָׁלוֹם.[7] Similarly, the use of the verb נכה carries a sense of irony. Recurring ten times in 2 Kings 9–10 (2 Kings 9:7, 15, 24, 27; 10:9, 11, 17, 25, 32), this verb functions as the passage's technical term of judgment. However, in 10:32 Hazael strikes Israel, hence the sense of irony. Consequently, Jehu goes from striking down God's adversaries to having his nation struck. The rationale for this turn of events? Jehu was not willing to eliminate Jeroboam's illegitimate worship centers (vv. 28–31).

In Hosea 1:4, judgment is linked to Jehu's bloody actions at Jezreel. Traditionally, this tension has been explained in several ways: (1) Jehu went beyond the expectations of the command and killed too many; (2) Jehu's actions were essentially selfish and self-aggrandizing; (3) Jehu's actions at Jezreel did not result in a greater, nationwide spiritual reform; (4) Jehu involved innocents in the affair (Wiseman 2008, 237).

10:32–36. These verses conclude the summarization of Jehu's reign. The reader is told that the remaining exploits of his reign are documented in typical royal fashion (v. 34) and that his death was honorable and characterized by a peaceful transition (v. 35). He reigned twenty-eight years. However, the historian notes that "the LORD began to trim off parts of Israel" by means of Hazael (v. 32). Such a comment implies a systematic and slow progression toward 2 Kings 17. Strictly speaking, the geopolitical footprint of Israel reached its apex under Jehu's dynasty (Rasmussen 2010, 162).

11:1–3. In 2 Kings 11, the narrative focus switches to events in Judah, where the dynastic turmoil is similar to what is seen in Israel. Moreover, both series of events are related, historically and textually. As stated by Sweeney (2007, 342), the syntax of verse 1 suggests that chapter 11 can be understood as an appendix to all that preceded it.

It is difficult to determine to whom Athaliah was born. Clearly, she was a member of the Omride royal family, but 2 Kings 8:26 calls her a "daughter of Omri" (בַּת־עָמְרִי) while 2 Kings 8:18 describes her as a "daughter of Ahab" (בַּת־אַחְאָב). Some have explained the issue by appealing to the semantic ambiguity inherent to "daughter," that 2 Kings 8:26 could mean "granddaughter of Omri" or "descendent of Omri" (Cogan and Tadmor 2008, 98). Adding to the problem, however, is the chronological problems created if one assumes that she was Ahab's daughter. One could speculate that while Athaliah was Ahab's sister, perhaps a very young sister, Ahab was responsible for her upbringing (Katzenstein 1955, 197). So, she just assumed the description as Ahab's daughter.

---

7   Wray Beal relies upon Saul Olyan, "Hăšālôm: Some Literary Considerations of 2 Kings 9," *CBQ* 46.4 (1984): 652–68.

Beyond question is that Athaliah was given by the Omride royal family in marriage to Jehoram, sealing a fledgling political relationship between Jehoshaphat and Ahab. Thus, the Omride line was fused with the Davidic dynasty in the person of Ahaziah in an attempt to appease political tensions. Unfortunately, such an effort almost destroyed the Davidic dynasty (Brewer-Boydston 2016; Thiel 1992).

Athaliah was the member of the Omride royal family who married into the Davidic family and gave birth to Ahaziah. When he was killed by Jehu during the Omride purge, Athaliah quickly saw Judah as her only hope for perpetuating Omride influence in the region. To accomplish this, the Davidic line had to be eradicated. Consequently, her actions rival those of Jehu in enacting a systematic purge of a sitting dynasty.

As this was transpiring, and in a way that echoes Exodus 1–2, Ahaziah's sister Jehosheba heroically snatched up Ahaziah's infant son (גנב; Exod. 20:15), Joash, and smuggled him, with his nurse, into the interior of the temple, where he stayed for six years (2 Kings 11:3). Then, when he was seven years old, Jehoiada the priest organized his own coup d'état to reestablish a proper Davidide on the throne.

Virtually nothing is said about Athaliah's six-year reign. However, based upon the reform and purification efforts after the disposal of Athaliah, it's reasonable to conclude that she encouraged the pollution of the national cultic system. This is further supported by the testimony throughout 2 Kings 11:4–21[12:1], which theologically justifies the coup.

11:4–12. The architect of the coup, the priest Jehoiada, initially summons Israel's elite mercenary corps in order to secure their allegiance (Cogan and Tadmor 2008, 126). The sequence is interesting. That the legitimate Davidide is only brought forward after the covenant was enacted suggests that the situation may not have been that desperate. If the situation was widely recognized as dire, would a covenant have been necessary? Regardless, with the covenant binding, Jehoiada is free to carry out his well-coordinated coup, which involved a very public coronation scene.[8]

11:13–21[12:1]. The commotion of the coronation scene was enough to get the attention of Athaliah (v. 13). She quickly proceeds to the temple to ascertain the nature of the celebration, and when she arrives, she clearly understands the implications of what she sees. "Treason!" she

---

8   Second Kings 11, along with the testimony of other cultures, offers an opportunity to reconstruct the contours of a Judean coronation ceremony. However, any reconstruction must remain general.

The coronation took place at the temple. In addition, it appears to have included several critical actions. First, 2 Kings 11 suggests that the king was crowned by a priest with some type of headpiece. The word used is הַנֵּזֶר, which signifies the dedication of the king under the authority of the Lord and was akin to a headpiece worn by the priest (Exod. 29:6). It's not clear what the diadem looked like, but it clearly symbolized the monarchical institution. Second, the king was also given the עֵדוּת. According to the syntax, the נֵזֶר and the עֵדוּת are essentially two sides of the same coin, but the עֵדוּת appears to represent a set of expectations and responsibilities. Third, there was an official installation consummated by a physical anointing, presumably with oil. Finally, there was a public proclamation, "May the king live!" At some point, the newly installed king was ushered out to the large pillars that Solomon constructed to highlight the temple's entrance. This action was a presentation of the new king to the populace.

Second Kings 11 also speaks to a covenantal ceremony between the king, the people, and the Lord. The intention, according to verse 17, was to renew public allegiance to the Lord. However, it's difficult to see this particular action as being typical. Rather, it's better to see verse 17 as recalling a specific ritual deemed necessary by specific implications of Athaliah's reign.

cries, but to no avail. She is then quickly ushered away at the command of Jehoiada, paraded out of the temple, and eventually executed just outside the royal residence (vv. 15–16).

The overthrow of Athaliah is not complete with her death. Just as Jehu understood the need to cripple any lingering social support, so too does Jehoiada. Thus, the overthrow quickly moves to decimate the pagan cult. Baal's temple is destroyed alongside Baal's iconography, pillars, and even the chief priest of Baal, Mattan (v. 18). Interestingly, the overthrow of Athaliah is conducted by a diverse group, comprised of members from the priestly faction, elements of the military, and a distinct group within Israelite society, "the people of the land" (Cogan and Tadmor 2008, 129–30). Thus, the resetting of a proper Davidic king on the throne is recognized as a benefit to the totality of the society. This conviction also informs the community-wide covenant enacted (v. 17).

12:1–16[2–17]. The account of Joash's reign continues in 2 Kings 12, and it's given in three distinct sections that initially appear only roughly connected (vv. 1–16[2–17]; 17–18[18–19]; 19–21[20–22]). However, upon further inspection each section of chapter 12 builds into the next, eventually bringing the account to a logical conclusion.

Joash's reign is predominately defined by the temple repairs he facilitated. Yet what's critical in the account is the inversion of major characters from the previous chapter. In chapter 11, Jehoiada is the active character, while Joash sits in the background. However, in 12:1 Joash is set off as the dominant character and the priest becomes passive. This development is critical to the narrative as it focuses upon how Joash's plan for reconstruction will rely upon the priestly faction.

Joash initially rolls out a plan that encourages discretion and initiative among the priests. According to verses 4–5[5–6], the priests were to divvy out the necessary funding for temple repairs. Funding was to come from "all the money offered as sacred donations" (v. 4; כֹּל כֶּסֶף הַקֳּדָשִׁים), which is then further specified by a series of explanatory clauses. It was to be the money taken from individual assessments and offerings. In other words, the funds for the repairs were to come from the priestly revenue. However, by the twenty-third year of Joash's reign, it was clear that the plan had failed (v. 6[7]). Consequently, Joash was forced to implement a contingency plan.

Plan B took priestly discretion and initiative off the table. When appropriate, the funds would go directly to the laborers themselves as a donation box was placed "beside the altar on the right side as one entered the house of the LORD" (v. 9[10]; cf. vv. 10–11[11–12]). And in the end, the secondary plan was successful. However, it's curious that so much space is devoted to explaining the flow of funding. The details suggest a controversy among Jerusalem's institution, perhaps even the possibility that the priests had misappropriated funds (*contra* Sweeney 2007, 351; with Wiseman 2008, 250–53). What's more, the Chronicler testifies to this possibility when he recounts a rift that developed between Joash and the priests (2 Chron. 24:17–22).

12:17–18[18–19]. In the first sixteen verses of chapter 12, Joash is presented as a leader with clarity and control. However, in verses 17–18[18–19], the script is flipped when Joash performs actions that are legitimately described as hypocritical. In order to alleviate the pressure from Hazael's incursion into Judah, Joash raids the temple treasuries to pay off the Aramean king. In other words, he depletes the very treasuries that he had worked so hard to rebuild. This course of action sheds light on an observable inconsistency in the actions of Joash.

12:19–21[20–22]. The logical outcomes of this inconsistency play out in the final verses of chapter twelve (*contra* Strand Winslow 2017, 215; with Sweeney 2007, 349; 353). After beginning the conclusion of Joash's account with a familiar formula, verses 20–21[21–22] recount how Joash was eventually assassinated by his servants Jozacar and Jehozabad. Virtually nothing is known about these two, but the Chronicler identified the mothers as Ammonite and Moabite, respectively (2 Chron. 24:26).

13:1–9. There are four distinct sections in 2 Kings 13, but they are all associated by a concern with the Aramean and Israelite conflict. In the midst of these sections, the death of Elisha and Aramean transition of power is documented.

The pace quickens beginning in 13:1, shifting from detailed accounts to concise evaluations and brief discussions of important events. For Jehoahaz of Israel, elements of his reign are recounted in a way that recalls the cycle ubiquitous to Judges (sin, oppression, cry for help, and deliverance). According to verse 3, the Lord's anger "was kindled against Israel" because of their apostasy. In turn, the Lord "gave them repeatedly into the hand of King Hazael of Aram, then into the hand of Ben-hadad son of Hazael" (v. 3). However, verse 4 reveals that Jehoahaz "entreated the LORD" (חלה) and the Lord "heeded him" (ראה). In turn, the Lord sent a "savior" (מוֹשִׁיעַ) to facilitate the alleviation of oppression (v. 5). Sweeney (2007, 355) believes that the "savior" was Jehoahaz's son, but Strand Winslow (2017, 216) identifies the difficulty with this. Wiseman (2008, 255) believes it was the Assyrian king Adad-nirari III. Regardless of who it was, the savior was apparently successful, after which the Israelites "lived in their homes as formerly" (v. 5). Nevertheless, and perhaps in the most significant parallel to the Judges cycle, salvation brought no fundamental change to Israel's spiritual state. According to verse 6, Israel persisted in their apostasy.

This raises the question of purpose. Why the allusion to the Judges cycle? In Judges, each individual cycle contributes to a larger

movement that not only ushers in social chaos (Judg. 17–21), but they also speak to the bankruptcy of the institution. By the conclusion of Judges, the reader realizes that the judge, while important within a certain era, was ultimately not able to lead the community through the social, political, and theological developments of Iron Age I (Stone 2012, 197–203). Similarly, the historian is subtly criticizing the northern king, suggesting through an analogy that the monarchy was unable to lead the community through the social, political, and theological developments of Iron Age II.

Kings offers one final note on Jehoahaz. During his tenure, the Israelite army was decimated by continuous conflict with Aram. While it's impossible to know the amount lost, the figures given in 2 Kings 13:7 are small and somewhat shocking. In particular, the number of cavalry and chariot units is noteworthy. But in the end, Jehoahaz transitioned peacefully to his son Joash.

13:10–13. The reign of Joash of Samaria is very brief. It's introduced (v. 10), he is quickly evaluated (v. 11), and his reign closed (vv. 12–13). In each section, the phraseology is typical of what one has seen in Kings, and the most important realization about Joash of Samaria was that he perpetuated the sins of Jeroboam I.

13:14–21. These verses bring the life and ministry of Elisha to a close. And in the process, we see an interaction that is representative of so many things previously seen in the Elisha narratives. The king seeks out Elisha, and the prophet offers advice that speaks to a pressing sociopolitical situation. In addition, Elisha tells Joash that he needs to perform an action that will function as a symbolic representation of what is about to unfold. Unfortunately, the king fails to meet the expectations of the Lord and therefore experiences divine chastisement. In sum, Elisha continues a contentious relationship with the monarch, even to the point of his death.

When the scene opens, the reader is told that Elisha had fallen ill, and it would eventually overtake him to the grave. Therefore, Joash's grievous cry makes sense. However, it is complicated. "My father, my father" suggests that the king respects the prophet's position of intimate authority. Yet this coupled with the following phrase, "the chariots of Israel and its horseman," repeats what Elisha said as he watched Elijah get taken away (2 Kings 2:12). A cry of respect and authority is paired with a militaristic allusion. Thus, Joash, like Elisha before him, is lamenting the passing of a divinely sanctioned voice that had worked with the monarchy to navigate the tense geopolitical situation (Wray Beal 2014, 410).

The action that Elisha commands Joash to perform attempts to alleviate the king's concerns. The king is to grab a bow, with some arrows, open the westward facing window (the general direction of Aram), and fire. With the prophet's hands on the king's to symbolize cooperation (Wiseman 2008, 257), the king obeys, and the prophet in turn offers an utterance that anticipates victory at Aphek (13:17). Then, Elisha tells the king to fire more arrows and "strike the ground with them" (v. 18). No further explanation, just to fire them into the ground. But when the king obeys and strikes the ground thrice, Elisha becomes angry (v. 19). Unbeknownst to Joash, three strikes were too few. Instead, five or six times was the desired amount. Consequently, Israelite victory over Aram will not be absolute but only temporary (v. 19).

Such chastisement initially appears harsh. The command to strike the ground was open-ended. So, if there was no specific command, why was Joash ridiculed? It's all about the impression our actions give. If Joash was thoroughly committed to definitively dealing with the Aramean threat, then his actions would have left nothing to chance.

The final picture given of Elisha demonstrates how his capabilities as a life-giving miracle worker extend beyond his life (vv. 20–21). According to the account, one of the men responsible for burying the prophet was killed by a random Moabite raiding party. However, when he fell into the open grave and touched the bones of Elisha, he was resuscitated (cf. 1 Kings 17:17–24; 2 Kings 4:8–37). What a final and emphatic statement about the prophet's abilities.

Hazael

Hazael was one of the greatest Aramean rulers. According to 2 Kings 8:7–15, he usurped the throne, a reality that is independently verified by the record of Shalmaneser III when he refers to him as a "son of nobody." However, his rise to prominence was not immediate.

When Hazael assumed the throne, the regional coalition that worked to fend off the Assyrian advance since the Battle of Qarqar in the middle of the ninth century disbanded. This allowed Shalmaneser III to raid the region, enacting heavy tribute in the process. Hazael was forced to retreat into Damascus and helplessly watch Shalmaneser's efforts from confinement.

When Shalmaneser retreated to Mesopotamia shortly after, the Assyrian Empire went into a period of decline, which allowed Hazael to rebuild his reputation and extend his dominance over the region. It was also during this period when Hazael pressed upon Israel and Judah most intensely. In fact, his grip over the region was so famous that later Assyrian inscriptions referred to Aram as a product of the "House of Aram."

When Hazael died, his son Ben-hadad took over, but he was not as successful as his father (Younger 2016, 249–55; Pitard 1992, 3:83).

13:22–25. The final verses of chapter 13 bring to fruition the prophetic words of

Elisha given to Joash (vv. 15–19). Importantly, the alleviation from Aramean oppression was rooted in divine grace and the patriarchal promises, the latter being uncommon in Kings. But the syntax makes this clear. Verses 22–23 juxtaposes a statement of Aramean oppression (v. 22) to an explicit statement of the Lord's graciousness and compassion for his people, which is immediately followed by a clause that causally links divine favor to "his covenant with Abraham, Isaac, and Jacob" (v. 23). Thus, the Lord is compassionate and he remembers.

Upon Hazael's death, Aramean kingship was passed to Ben-hadad (v. 24). Yet in this context, Joash reclaimed land that had been taken by Aram during the reign of his father Jehoahaz. Moreover, verse 25 explicitly identifies three victories, in accordance with Elisha's prophecy. Such notification arises from the period before the exile, as the final clause of verse 23 speaks of Israel remaining in the land.

THEOLOGICAL FOCUS

The exegetical idea (As a prophet, Elisha served all levels of society to provide social, theological, and political insight, but Jehu's coup inaugurated a period where the basic vitality and effectiveness of God's people, including the continued existence of the Davidic line, were being compromised by internal and external pressures, which were all linked to shortsighted decisions and covenantal unfaithfulness) leads to this theological focus: God's grace offers hope in life's precarious situations.

The absence of Elisha in 2 Kings 2:1–13:25 after the opening verses of chapter 9, save for his death notice (13:14–21), is noteworthy. What's more, the impact of Jehu's coup quickly expands, even producing an existential threat for the Davidic dynasty. Even when there is positivity with Joash's reforms, there is still an undercurrent of factionalism within Judean society that complicates the Aramean threat. Consequently, when Elisha recedes to the background after the onset

of 2 Kings 9, Kings allows the reader to see just how precarious the situation was.

Yet even as the situation in Israelite and Judean societies continued to erode because of internal and external pressures, God's grace is still observable. God anointed bold people to carry out his will. He inspired people to defy the central power structures on behalf of a society's most vulnerable. He brought saviors to give the community reprieve from oppression. Consequently, it should come as no surprise when this unit of text ends with a few verses that emphasize the grace and compassion of the Lord alongside his willingness to remember his covenant with the Patriarchs. For an Iron Age Israelite or Judean, the patriarchs may have been no more than legacies of a distant past. However, the writer realized that godly legacies continue to affect the contours of history as the Lord continues to honor them.

PREACHING AND TEACHING STRATEGIES

Exegetical and Theological Synthesis

Second Kings 2–13 is a goldmine for historians, especially religious historians. It is filled with several intriguing historical figures as well as dramatic highs and lows of Israel, Judah, and surrounding entities.

The typical treatment for studying this large section would be to break it up and look at each unique story in depth. There is a tremendous advantage to working with this unit of text as a whole, however. Taking these twelve chapters as a whole allows the reader to better assess both the arc of Israel and Judah's decline and God's continuing faithfulness toward his people. Sometimes we get so focused on the small snippets of time that we forget the larger work that God has done in our lives. Sometimes we let the tyranny of the urgent control us, and fail to consider the greater purpose God wants us to live for.

Christ-followers are never going to be immune to difficult trials or desperate times. But we can respond differently from those around us who are not yet trusting the one true and living God. We can be like Elisha and offer godly service and godly insight to those in need. We ought to be first in line to supply and serve at food banks when the economy goes in the tank. We can fund the adoption process for the couple who is seeking to provide a home to the orphan. Desperate times take many forms, but God's people can embrace them by taking divine measures to live out God's purpose.

Preaching Idea

Desperate times call for divine measures.

Contemporary Connections

What does it mean?

What does it mean that desperate times call for divine measures? "Desperate times call for desperate measures" is the well-worn cliché that describes going all-in when you have nothing left to lose. Diligence and perseverance are certainly good qualities. Yet there are some circumstances that require more than human effort to climb out of.

Desperate times can come in different forms. Our bills pile up as our paychecks are going down. The doctor gives us grim news about our latest rounds of tests. Our kids start making poor choices and developing bad habits. There are wise steps we should take to help deal with these kinds of things. The wisest course of action would be to seek God's help in prayer and be ready for him to provide what is needed.

Is it true?

Is it true that desperate times call for divine measures? Pastor Jack Graham is credited with saying, "Sometimes God has to put us

flat on our back before we are looking up to him."[9] That idea certainly fits with this section of 2 Kings. Yet within these desperate circumstances, God extends his gracious provision. There is certainly a fair share of fools who attempt to navigate their troubles on their own. But those who seek the Lord experience his divine favor in amazing ways.

Sometimes God must humble us and put us in desperate circumstances so that we will actually pay attention to what he's trying to do. A financial crisis can be an opportunity to evaluate the wisdom (or lack thereof) of using our credit cards. Marital conflict can be God's way of adjusting our selfish mindset and to teach us what sacrificial love is. Receiving a serious medical diagnosis can literally put us flat on our back so we can watch God's immeasurable power go to work. Desperate times are chances to see God's divine measures accomplish incredible things.

Now what?

If it's true that desperate times call for divine measures, what should we take away from this passage? Desperate times come in many shapes and sizes. This passage shows that they can be individual or nationwide. They can be related to our health, threaten our relationships, or involve military conflict. So whenever and however we find ourselves at the end of our rope, what does this passage teach us?

One undeniable lesson we should take away is to *seek God's help first*. Everyone from long-time friends to antagonistic kings recognized that Elisha was God's messenger and could give divine aid and insight if approached. The exact methods will be different for us, but we still need to promptly seek godly counsel and God's direct help. Prayer, for example, should be a first priority, not a last resort. If our child falls ill, shouldn't we pray for God's help as we take him or her to the

---

9   Quoted in Ron Rhodes, *1001 Unforgettable Quotes about God, Faith, and the Bible* (Eugene, OR. Harvest House Publishers, 2011) 65.

doctor? When news breaks of our government making a particular decision that seems unwise or even unrighteous—will we complain, type an all-caps opinion on social media, or will we take the issue to God? If we lose our job, there's nothing wrong with immediately searching out other openings. But couldn't it make a difference if we asked our pastors or church small group to pray for our situation?

Another application from this passage comes from the other end of the spectrum. We certainly need to seek God's help when we are desperate, but we also need to *seek to be God's help* for the desperate. In early 2020, the COVID-19 pandemic disrupted "normal life" not just in the United States but around the world. Businesses, schools, and churches were all impacted. My (Lee) church complied with the guidelines, though we were determined not to shut down our ministry just because our services were canceled. We connected with a local graphics company, who made a giant sign for us that simply said "NEED HELP? CALL US" with our phone number. We also supported our local food bank and food pantry. Our deacons began regularly calling all of our people to make sure everyone had the help they might need. Desperate times call for divine measures—and we can be the instruments God uses to make a difference.

Creativity in Presentation
The David Tyree "Helmet Catch" in Super Bowl 42 would make for a great illustration of how desperate times call for divine measures.

The New York Giants were trailing the undefeated New England Patriots 14–10 with less than two minutes to go in Super Bowl 42. On third down and five, quarterback Eli Manning dropped back to pass and was quickly forced to scramble as multiple Patriots defenders closed in on him and nearly sacked him. Evading their grasp for an instant, Manning looked downfield and launched a pass toward little-used wide receiver David Tyree. Tyree was not wide open by any means and as he caught the pass, All-Pro safety Rodney Harrison jumped with him and tried to wrestle the ball out. When the players hit the ground, Tyree maintained control of the ball and secured it by holding the ball between his hand and his helmet. Watching Manning's scramble, commentator Troy Aikman remarked that "I don't know how he got out of there." NFL Films founder Steve Sabol called it "the greatest play the Super Bowl has ever produced." Adding to the mystique of the play was the later revelation that during a pre-game prayer, Tyree had been told by a teammate's mother that he'd make a key play in the game.[10]

We're not here to suggest that God had a direct hand in who won the Super Bowl in January of 2008. But the play itself shows how when desperate times come, we need extra help to make the improbable or even impossible happen. The Giants needed Manning to escape a couple sure tackles. Manning needed Tyree to make an incredible effort to catch the ball. Tyree needed Harrison not to hit the ball as they collided.

Video clips and still photos of this play are natural visuals to accompany a description of this play that will be remembered by the fan and non-fan alike. Sometimes in sports we see "divine interventions" play out. These examples can serve to point to actual divine measures where God works in and through his people to provide in our distress.

Much like the previous preaching unit (1 Kings 17–2 Kings 1), we are covering a lot of textual ground here in this preaching unit of 2 Kings 2–13. It is perfectly logical to break up Elisha's ministry, but by tackling this unit of text as a whole we are hoping to keep the

---

10   "My Big Game Moment: Tyree Relives That One Amazing Catch," Fox Sports, December 16, 2013, https://www.foxsports.com/nfl/story/my-big-game-moment-tyree-relives-that-one-amazing-catch.

larger context in view. Within this larger swath of history, we see both specially chosen servants and specifically appointed kings being the divine measures used to work out God's purposes throughout these events.

The first half is mostly focused on Elisha. The stories fall into one of several categories, including God's confirmation of his authority, God's provision of basic necessities, God's provision of relief in dire circumstances, and God's intervention within political conflicts. The second half is more focused on the key political leaders than on the prophet Elisha. While these leaders are appointed by God, they often fall into one of two categories. Some go too far with their power, and others don't go far enough in leading their reforms. (See proposed outline below.) Like the previous preaching unit, this preaching unit could easily be split into two messages to avoid overwhelming the audience with the amount of context we are trying to cover. But it will be important not to lose sight of the overarching theme.

The key idea to communicate is that desperate times call for divine measures. The passage for this preaching unit can be outlined as follows:

- Divinely empowered servants are called to provided divinely arranged assistance (2:1–8:29).
  - God confirms his special servants in special ways (2:1–18, 23–25).
  - God's provision comes in the form of basic necessities (2:19–22; 4:42–44).
  - God's provision comes in the form of critical relief (4:1–7, 8–37, 38–41; 5:1–27; 6:1–7; 8:1–6).
  - God's provision comes in the middle of political conflict (3:1–27; 6:8–23; 6:24–7:20).
- Divinely appointed leaders are called to pursue divinely ordained outcomes (9:1–13:25).
  - Divinely appointed leaders can go too far (8:7–15, 16–29).
  - Divinely appointed leaders may not go far enough (chs. 9–10, 11–13):
    - In leading revolution (10:28–36)
    - In leading reform (12:17–21)
    - In leading recovery (13:14–19)

DISCUSSION QUESTIONS

1. Second Kings 2:19–25, especially verses 23–25, is one of the most interesting and difficult passages in the Old Testament. What does this passage convey, and how can we faithfully explain the ambiguity of the events to our audience?

2. The previous question can also apply to 2 Kings 3. How should we understand the ultimate ending at the end of the chapter, as God's wrath falls on his victorious people?

3. What are the surprising and remarkable elements of Naaman's healing in 2 Kings 5?

4. How does God deliver his people from hopeless situations in 2 Kings 6–7? What can we learn from these miracles?

5. What are the reforms that King Joash leads (2 Kings 12)?

6. As Elisha's life concludes, what lessons stand out to you about his life and the circumstances he found himself in (2 Kings 13:14–25)?

POLITICAL UPHEAVAL
(2 KINGS 14:1–20:21)

The third and final section of the second major literary unit in Kings is 2 Kings 14:1–20:21, which describes yet another period of political upheaval. This third section may be divided into two preaching units. First, there is the arrival of Assyria (14:1–16:20). This first passage resumes the fast pace of 1 Kings 14:21–16:34 and recounts the tumultuous geopolitical landscape of late Iron Age II. Second, there is Samaria versus Jerusalem (17:1–20:21). This second passage features a contrast between Israel's capital city of Samaria and Judah's capital city of Jerusalem. Both capitals were subjected to devastating Assyrian sieges, but the outcomes were very different.

This section also functions with 1 Kings 14:21–16:34 to bracket 1 Kings 17:1–2 Kings 13:25, creating a literary inclusio that establishes a hermeneutical lens for understanding the divided monarchy (Bauer and Traina 2001, 117–18). According to Kings, the period of the divided monarchy existed on a knife's edge, and there was a fine line between relative prosperity and devastating chaos. The difference between the two outcomes was dictated by several factors converging upon each other, including external pressures, the sitting dynasty, the relative piety of the sitting dynasty, as well as a general willingness to yield to the word of the Lord given by the prophets.

2 Kings 14:1–16:20

EXEGETICAL IDEA
After the departure of the prophets Elijah and Elisha, this period of the divided monarchy reverted to instability while the presence of the Neo-Assyrian Empire redefined the geopolitical landscape, putting Israel and Judah in potentially compromising situations.

THEOLOGICAL FOCUS
Poor choices that produced a spiritually compromised existence for God's people is a symptom of the fall, yet this situation need not persist.

PREACHING IDEA
Sinful choices lead to serious catastrophe that only God's grace can rescue us from.

PREACHING POINTERS
Political turmoil continued for Judah and Israel, only now those kingdoms were without the divinely empowered prophetic presence of Elijah and Elisha. The focus is primarily on the numerous kings who rise and fall. Almost without exception, these kings stumble into trouble because of the decisions they make as they lead. As the record of 1 and 2 Kings advances closer and closer to the period of exile, the mistakes of their ancestors would become more and more relevant to Israel as they reestablished themselves as a people. Spiritually faithful leaders bring security and stability. Otherwise, this is what happens when rulers rule poorly: political infighting and external pressure from world powers.

As Christians today, we need to be careful about drawing too many political conclusions, as we are no longer identified by ethnic or political traits (Rom. 4; Gal. 3:28; Phil. 3:17–20). We will still struggle with these kinds of sins, however. The temptation to act out of ambition, pride, and selfishness is ever present for us as individuals and groups. Should I push hard for my preferred building proposal rather than wait for a consensus to settle on one of the options? Will my social media presence be driven to enhance my personal brand or for other more worthy causes? Will we do whatever it takes to get our church attendance up, even if it sacrifices some biblical principles? Will we sell out to support a political party or candidate because it will make our lives "easier"? Sinful choices will lead us straight into trouble, whether making decisions about how to lead our church, corporation, research group, family, or just our own lives. God's grace can temper the consequences at times, but catastrophe awaits those who lead by their own sinful desires.

THE ARRIVAL OF ASSYRIA (14:1–16:20)

LITERARY STRUCTURE AND THEMES (14:1–16:20)

This section reverts to quick alterations between the reigns of Judean and Israelite kings. However, the precariousness of the geopolitical situation is intensified with the arrival of Assyria under the leadership of Tiglath-pileser III (cf. 15:19, 29; 16:1). Moreover, the text suggests a watershed moment in the history of God's people during the reign of Ahaz (16:1–20). Consequently, this section can be subdivided into a period without Assyrian presence and a period with Assyrian presence as follows:

- *Before Assyria (14:1–15:16)*
- *Assyrian Presence (15:17–16:20)*

EXPOSITION (14:1–16:20)

Both Israel and Judah find themselves plunged back into sociopolitical instability. However, now the turn of events is linked to the imperial agenda of the Neo-Assyrian Empire. The effect is an unpredictable scene where kings in the north rule for short periods of time and then are deposed by violent actions. In Judah, there is dynastic stability, but the Davidic kings are increasingly making decisions that continue to compromise the spiritual viability of Judah.

Before Assyria (14:1–15:16)

Both Israel and Judah plunge back into a period of sociopolitical instability.

14:1–22. Amaziah succeeded Joash when he was twenty-five years old. He enjoyed a lengthy reign of twenty-nine years and a relatively positive evaluation. According to verse 3, he did "right in the sight of the Lord, yet not like his ancestor David." Such a qualification is the same

as Joash and therefore suggests that he allowed worship at the high places (2 Kings 12:3). Also of note, Amaziah took measured vengeance upon those who assassinated his father (v. 5). His acts of retributive vengeance were focused upon the perpetrators only and not extended to the extended family (v. 6), which contrasts with the rampant actions of Jehu and Athaliah. The impetus for such restraint? The teaching of Moses, particularly the Deuteronomic command to restrain one's vengeance, which is quoted in Kings (Deut. 24:6).

> **Samaria Ostraca**
>
> Found in 1910, this collection of ostraca number sixty-six potsherds with ink writing. They are one of the most studied collections of preexilic Hebrew inscriptions, and they offer important linguistic, administrative, and social information during the reign of Jeroboam II. Wiseman (2008, 263–64) argues that the receipts on the ostraca show an "increasing royal income" that ended up fueling the prophetic critique. In 2020, a team of scholars subjected the handwriting of the ostraca to an algorithmic analysis and determined that the sherds were composed by two scribes and represent a key moment in the development of literacy in Israelite culture (Faigenbum-Golovin 2020).

However, while Amaziah exhibited restraint in his actions toward those responsible for killing his father, he showed no restraint in his efforts to reassert Judean influence in the region. According to verse 7, Amaziah sanctioned military maneuvers against Edom at two unknown locations. The "Valley of Salt" may have been near the Dead Sea, and whatever happened at Sela was apparently intense and overwhelming.

Ten thousand Edomites were reportedly killed, which may be a stylized number. From there, Amaziah rode this wave of victory and fixated upon Israel. Whether it was to "renegotiate" a political relationship, to play the bully, or to force reunification (cf. 2 Chron. 25:6–16; Strand Winslow, 222), Amaziah challenged Jehoash of Israel to open conflict (2 Kings 14:8). This was a bold move, and it was one that would have disastrous consequences.

When Amaziah's dispatch reached Jehoash, the Israelite king tried to deescalate the situation by sending an allegorical reply that creatively encouraged the Judean not to "poke the bear" (vv. 8–9). In the allegory, Amaziah is the worthless thorn brush who seeks a biological absurdity—becoming like a majestic cedar. Moreover, in its insistence to accomplish what can't be done, it refuses to acknowledge the imminent danger to its existence. Therefore, it's trampled by an animal. Unfortunately, this warning falls on deaf ears, and Amaziah refuses to be content with his victories over Edom.

Eventually, Israel and Judah meet in open warfare at Beth-shemesh, which is deep in Judean territory in the Sorek Valley. There, the Judean army was forced to flee, and king Amaziah was captured by Jehoash in the process (v. 12). However, he was not executed. Rather, something arguably worse happened to Amaziah. He is escorted to Jerusalem where he is forced to watch the Israelite army break down approximately six hundred feet of the city wall, plunder Jerusalem's precious metals and valuables, and take away hostages (vv. 13–14). It was a public shaming that was made worse by the fact that Amaziah remained king after the fact. He was left to rule Judah bankrupt and with a giant hole in Jerusalem's wall. It's no wonder that a faction within Judean society

conspired to kill him (v. 19). He was forced to flee to Lachish, Judah's major administrative city, where he was eventually killed. Ironically, the men who killed him also brought his body back so that he would be given an honorable burial. Moreover, Ahaziah, the rightful heir, assumed the throne (vv. 20–21). Thus, it appears that this conspiracy can be interpreted as an effort to rid the throne of a king who had long outlived his effectiveness and constantly reminded the community of the shameful defeat by Israel born out of childish aggression, although some interpreters do not link the assassination of Amaziah to his defeat by Jehoash (Wray Beal 2014, 419).[1]

14:23–29. Jeroboam II ruled Israel after the death of Jehoash. Jehoash's reign was largely defined by his conflict with Amaziah of Judah, and he died approximately halfway through Amaziah's reign. Jeroboam's ascension was peaceful, and he enjoyed a very long reign, forty-one years (v. 23). Geopolitically speaking, the reign of Jeroboam II represented the apex of Israel's territorial footprint (Rasmussen 2010, 162). According to verse 25, Jeroboam restored the border of Israel, wrestling territory from Damascus and Hamath and extending the border from Lebo-hamath to the Sea of the Arabah (i.e., the Dead Sea). Such an extent rivaled the borders celebrated during Solomon's reign and was apparently foreseen by Jonah the prophet. However, Jeroboam is remembered as an "evil king" because he perpetuated the sins of Jeroboam I (v. 25). Consequently, this creates a theological difficulty for Kings and its governing theology. If Jeroboam was an evil king, why did his reign see so much geopolitical success? The answer is: divine grace and prophetic prophesy in response to the distress of the people (v. 26). Jeroboam II

---

1   The text notes in 2 Kings 14:17 that Amaziah "lived" after the death of Jehoash, which is not to say he "ruled." Wray Beal (2014, 419) interprets this as an allusion to a co-regent ruling with Amaziah. This is an important observation, but it could be interpreted as a subtle criticism that acknowledges a deepening disenfranchisement within the public vis-à-vis Amaziah.

died peacefully and handed his kingdom to his son Zechariah.

15:1–7. Azariah is also known as Uzziah (2 Kings 15:30–34; 2 Chron. 26; Isa. 1:1, 6:1), and he continues the trend of his father and grandfather (Jehoash). He did good in the eyes of the Lord, but not completely. He did not eradicate the high places, and the people continued to worship there (vv. 3–4). Most importantly, "The LORD struck the king, so that he was leprous to the day of his death" (v. 5). Kings is not clear about the events that led the Lord to strike him with leprosy, but the Chronicler offers an extended account of Azariah's reign (2 Chron. 26). There, the Chronicler recounts Azariah's arrogance that grew out of his geopolitical and social successes. At one point, Azariah inappropriately offered a sacrifice in the temple and refused to yield to the priests who tried to stop him. At this moment, the king was struck with leprosy and was therefore banished to isolation (2 Chron. 26:16–21). Jotham, his son, ruled as co-regent until Azariah's death.

Why does the author of Kings omit the detail that the Chronicler chooses to include? Was the Chronicler privy to more information than the writer of Kings? The scenario of ignorance is unlikely. What's probable is that Kings intentionally omits these details out of historiographic intention. For example, Wray Beal (2014, 427) argues that the brevity of the Kings account is due to a desire to emphasize the grace of God and the relative stability of the Judean monarchy vis-à-vis the Israelite monarchy. In addition, the brevity of the account aligns nicely with the pace and function of this subunit, which seeks to end the second major literary unit with a return to political instability.

15:8–12. Zechariah succeeds his father Jeroboam II, and his reign was vastly different. Whereas Jeroboam's reign was long and geopolitically successful, Zechariah did evil in the sight of the Lord, perpetuated the sins of Jeroboam I, reigned six months, and was assassinated and succeeded by Shallum. Zechariah's assassination is explained as the fulfillment of prophecy leveled against Jehu for his apostate actions (2 Kings 10:30–31).

15:13–16. Shallum's reign was even shorter that Zechariah's. He reigned only one month (v. 13) and apparently didn't reign long enough to even garner an evaluation. He was assassinated by Menahem during his brutal campaign through the Israelite heartland and, according to the text, his sacking of Israelite cities was punctuated by the mutilation of pregnant women (v. 16). A disturbing image, for sure, that also recalls and surpasses the picture of Israel immediately before Omri's rise to the throne. The difference here is that the usurper Menahem did not offer the political charisma and relative stability that Omri offered. As one will see, the stability that would offset Israelite instability would come in the form of Neo-Assyrian imperialism.

Assyrian Presence (15:17–16:20)
The presence of the Neo-Assyrian Empire redefined the geopolitical landscape of Syria-Palestine and put Israel and Judah in potentially compromising situations.

15:17–22. The account of Menahem's reign is brief. Ruling a decade, he did evil in the eyes of the Lord by not turning from the sins of Jeroboam. Nevertheless, his reign was defined by his association with Assyria. According to verses 19–20, Menahem colluded with Assyria to solidify his political position. However, this was accomplished with a substantial tribute, which the king squeezed from the populace in the form of taxation. Only after tribute was paid did Pul and his Assyrian army return to Mesopotamia. Menahem passed away peacefully and left the throne to his son Pekahiah (v. 22).

Tiglath-pileser III

Tiglath-pileser III, also known as Pul in 2 Kings, was one of the most famous warrior kings of the Neo-Assyrian Empire. Assyrian records attest to his brutal battlefield tactics and methods of exile and forced migration. Although Tiglath-pileser was most likely royalty, there is reason to believe that he was not in direct line to secure the throne.

According to Kings, Tiglath-pileser invaded Israel twice, and both times were related to his efforts to extend the Assyrian Empire to Egypt. The second invasion was in connection with the Syro-Ephraimite War, which was a conflict that featured a coalition of Syro-Palestine polities against Judah. Judah resented the Syro-Palestinian push to expel Assyrian imperialism, which secured Jerusalem's siege by members of the coalition to force Judean capitulation. As a response, Ahaz, king of Judah, requested the help of Tiglath-pileser III, a move that solidified Judah's status as a vassal to the Assyrian Empire (Cazelles 1992; Dubovsky 2006; Galil 2000; Kitchen 2003, 38).

15:23–26. Like his father, Pekahiah did evil in the eyes of the Lord by allowing the sins of Jeroboam to persist (v. 24). But unlike his father, Pekahiah did not enjoy a peaceful death. He was ultimately assassinated by Pekah, one of his military officers, along with fifty Gileadite men. According to the text, the mob stormed the palace citadel and eventually killed the king.

15:27–31. When Pekah usurped the throne by assassination, he continued in the ways of Pekahiah and Menahem. He did evil in the eyes of the Lord and did not curb the sins of Jeroboam. It's also during this reign that Tiglath-pileser III (aka Pul) returned to Samaria. In this instance, however, he didn't return home with just tribute.

The Capture of the City of Astartu by the Assyrian King Tiglath-Pileser III. Public domain.

Rather, according to verse 29, Tiglath-pileser III deported portions of the populace as he took over several cities. Pekah was ultimately assassinated by Hosea (v. 30).

15:32–38. In these verses, the focus shifts to the Judean king Jotham. He did right in the eyes of the Lord, which contrasts with Menahem, Pekahiah, and Pekah. Jotham also rebuilt the "upper gate of the house of the Lord" (v. 35). However, the high places remained—a qualification that blemishes an otherwise positive record (vv. 34–35). Most importantly, the Syro-Ephraimite War began during his reign. Presented as an event orchestrated by the Lord (v. 37), it would come to define the reign of his son Ahaz.

16:1–20. Ahaz assumed the Judean throne in the seventeenth year of Pekah's reign (v. 1). He was twenty and reigned sixteen years (v. 2), and is remembered negatively. He did not do as David did, but was like the kings of Israel (vv. 2b–3). Moreover, "he even made his son pass through fire" like the nations expelled from the Promised Land, and he sacrificed and made offerings virtually everywhere (vv. 3b–4). In other words, Ahaz was the antithesis of the ideal ruler in 1–2 Kings, and by associating Ahaz with the infractions of the populace, the indigenous Canaanites, and impious Israelite kings, Ahaz's condemnation is not only beyond question, but also becomes paradigmatic (Strand Winslow, 228; Sweeney 2007, 381–82).

Verse 5 begins the account of the Syro-Ephraimite War (735–732 BCE), a regional crisis that dictated the sociopolitical dynamics of the region for the next 150 years and solidified the negative perceptions surrounding Ahaz (cf. 2 Chron. 28:1–27; Isa. 7:1–8:15). During this crisis, Aram and Israel applied pressure to Judah, threatening siege while Edom reclaimed strategic territory at Elath, south of the Dead Sea (vv. 5–6). Ultimately, Ahaz buckled under the pressure, for according to verse 7 the Judean king initiated official correspondence to Tiglath-pileser III in order to appeal for support. This required monetary enticement, and so Ahaz raided valuables housed in Judean storehouses, the temple, and other institutions to bribe (שֹׁחַד) the Assyrian king and demonstrate just how serious the request was.

Textual Analysis: The consonants in the Hebrew text of verse 6 clearly states that Rezin, the Aramaic king, returned Elath to Edom. בָּעֵת הַהִיא הֵשִׁיב רְצִין מֶלֶךְ־אֲרָם אֶת־אֵילַת לַאֲרָם

However, the Masoretic notations suggest that the consonantal text be emended because of a probable scribe error. In place of "Aram," Edom is read by many scholars and all English translations.

There is substantial debate about whether an imperial relationship had been in place between Judah and Assyria prior to the events of the Syro-Ephraimite War. For example, Sweeney (2007, 380) argues that a Judean/Assyrian relationship existed previously because of Judah's relationship with Israel. In other words, because Judah was a vassal to Israel, and because Israel was a vassal to Assyria, Judah was by default a vassal to Assyria. If this is correct, then Ahaz's appeal was not required but deepened Judah's imperial association with Assyria, leaving Ahaz "obligated" to Tiglath-pileser III (Sweeney 2007, 380). Regardless of any previous relationship, it's clear that the Assyrian king took the opportunity to move against Damascus and Rezin, sacking the city and deporting some of the city's population (v. 9).

At some point, Ahaz met Tiglath-pileser III in Damascus to pay homage. While there, Ahaz became fixated on a certain, vaguely defined altar. What is clearly described is how Ahaz commissioned Uriah the priest, who incidentally was a valuable and respected colleague of Isaiah (Isa. 8:2), to reproduce the altar down to the last detail before the king returned (2 Kings 16:10–11). The priest played his part well, for according to verse 12, when Ahaz returned to Jerusalem, he officiated an elaborate worship ceremony by offering the necessary lot of sacrifices (v. 13). Wiseman (2008, 279) cites the scope and nature of the sacrifices and connects Ahaz's ceremony to Solomon's temple dedication ceremony. Thus, Ahaz's celebration was the antithesis of Solomon's celebration. Yet perhaps more importantly, Ahaz was inspired to reorganize the temple complex and institute a new worship program, and Uriah obeyed (vv. 14–16).

Early commentators argued that these reforms were directly commissioned through Assyrian imperial policy. Yet in recent memory, scholars have opted for a different interpretation, particularly since studies have shown that the Assyrian modus operandi required significant monetary payment, not religious worship (Cogan 1974; McKay 1973; Sweeney 2007, 384). Yet in the midst of this, Kings makes an important comment: "He did this because of the king of Assyria" (v. 18). Kings creates the impression that Tiglath-pileser III was dictating and Ahaz was his puppet, which exists in stark contrast to the ideal of the historian. Expectations of worship, sociopolitical policies, and so many other things were to be dictated by the Lord. Instead, it appears that a pagan Assyrian monarch was firmly entrenched in the affairs of Judah—a situation which was the logical result of increasing Assyrian presence.

THEOLOGICAL FOCUS

The exegetical idea (After the departure of the prophets Elijah and Elisha, this period of the divided monarchy reverted to instability while the presence of the Neo-Assyrian Empire redefined the geopolitical landscape, putting Israel and Judah in potentially compromising situations) leads to this theological focus: Poor choices that produced a spiritually compromised existence for God's people is a symptom of the fall, yet this situation need not persist.

The sections builds as the geopolitical situation deteriorates and Assyria becomes more of a dominant force, further complicating an already delicate situation. It boils over with the onset of the Syro-Ephraimite War, and in particular the fight over Judah's role. Interestingly, Kings recounts no real struggle for Ahaz. Simply, Kings reveals that Ahaz chose to bribe Assyria and pronounce his servitude and sonship to Tiglath-pileser III (2 Kings 16:7). With this choice, and the anti-reforms that follow, Ahaz effectively makes his bed with the Assyrian Empire. Essentially, the Judean king proclaims, "The Lord doesn't matter as much as the Assyrians." The result is that Judah becomes spiritually compromised to a degree that has not been experienced up to this point.

Spiritual compromise is something about which the Bible has much to say. Even specific to Kings, the writer shows in the life of Solomon, Ahab, or others that there are varying degrees and varying manifestations of spiritual compromise. But here the picture is rather specific. The choices of Ahaz resulted in a level of spiritual compromise that would transcend his generation by drastically altering the status quo. Put another way, his choice led to the spiritual compromise, not the other way around. In a sense, this specific manifestation of spiritual compromise echoes the choices of Adam and Eve.

When the first couple chose to disobey in Eden, they fundamentally altered the status quo and spiritually compromised all who followed them. As discussed in Romans 5, with Adam's actions sin and death entered the world, and from that point on death exercised dominion. Nevertheless, it's also true that death no longer reigns supreme thanks to the righteous action and choice of Jesus of Nazareth. Consequently, the example of Ahaz need not be lived out in perpetuity. Generations need not be bound by the errors of previous generations, which is a reality that one sees play out in the life of Hezekiah.

PREACHING AND TEACHING STRATEGIES

Exegetical and Theological Synthesis

A series of kings come and go in both Israel and Judah during this period of instability during the divided monarchy, and while there are a few bright spots, they cannot stop the slide of compromise for God's people. The author of 2 Kings puts the responsibility on the leaders for their poor choices.

It is not one awful decision that makes everything fall apart. Neither is there one specific repeated mistake that is made over and over. This is a period of history where an amalgam of bad decisions leads to certain inevitabilities. The kings made various poor choices based on pride, foolishness, and spiritual apostasy—among several other things—and those bad calls produced bad results, further entrenching the moral and political decline of God's people.

The only surprising result coming from this string of bad leadership is that the devastation and catastrophe isn't worse or didn't come sooner. Indeed, the Babylonian exile lies ahead, but for now God graciously gives the people more time. Only God's mercy prevents Judah and Israel from feeling the full weight of their sin. They experience their share of misery and trouble, but the worst is still to come.

Preaching Idea

Sinful choices lead to serious catastrophe that only God's grace can rescue us from.

Contemporary Connections

What does it mean?

What does it mean that sinful choices lead to serious catastrophe that only God's grace can rescue us from? This passage teaches a theme that is common within Scripture: God reserves harsh punishment for blatant sin. It offers glimpses of grace too, where God withholds his punishment at times and blesses the rare faithful king.

One of the blessings of being involved in ministry is discovering the variety of stories people have of coming to faith. Some are "lifelong" believers who trusted Christ as children. Others convert much later in life. The latter can be a source of profound perspective about this subject. Many will express regret at the past lives they led and the mistakes they made that still affect them in different ways. Those saints often understand God's amazing grace in a deeper way because they have dealt with the heavy physical, emotional, and spiritual toll that their choices have taken on them. There is both a warning call and an invitation to worship within this passage. The warning is about the serious consequences our selfish choices have. The invitation to worship is based on the reality that God offers his grace to us no matter the hole we have dug ourselves in.

Is it true?

Is it true that sinful choices certainly lead to serious catastrophe? As Paul says in Romans 6:23, "the wages of sin is death." Thankfully, the rest of this verse speaks to our hope for rescue by God's grace: "but the gift of God is eternal life through Jesus Christ our Lord." This Old Testament history actually foreshadows the gospel in a sense. To put it another way, it exemplifies the "dark side" of the gospel. As Paul outlines the gospel in the first few chapters of Romans, humanity's common problem is and has always been choosing the creation over the Creator (e.g., Rom. 1:18–3:20). We embrace what we want over what God wants. Over and over again in this pericope, these kings are choosing what they think is best rather than considering what God might want them to do.

There is a common plot device in sitcoms, shows, and movies where a character gets themselves into trouble by telling a lie and then attempts to cover it up with more and more lies.[2] Eventually the jig is up, the offender is caught, and lessons are learned. While it may be a silly trope, it demonstrates that even the nonbelieving world recognizes how easy it is to compound mistakes by doubling down on bad choices. Though most anyone can recognize the dangers of outright lying, blatant cheating, or engaging in addictive behaviors, the Christian should live with the perspective that *any* choice that is not in line with God's will has potentially catastrophic consequences. Gluttonous diet choices can lead to medical problems. Shrugging off studying can lead to failing grades. Regularly yelling at your kids can lead to a fractured or antagonistic relationship as they grow up.

Now what?

If it's true that sinful choices lead to serious catastrophe that only God's grace can rescue us from, what choices can we make to apply or respond to the lessons we can learn from these chapters? The main characters and the main developments in this part of Old Testament history are clear. Kings wield their power in foolish ways and those unwise decisions have large-scale ramifications. Most of us reading this some 2,500 years later are not going to enjoy the same level of clout no matter what we accomplish. Even if our influence falls woefully short of an ancient Middle Eastern monarch, we should still take heed of this passage's lessons. The decisions you make as a parent, branch manager, teacher, counselor, or pastor can still have significant impact on individual lives both positively and negatively.

Given that we want to avoid the sinful choices and negative consequences pictured in these chapters, three choices stand out as we look for applications or ways to respond.

First, *choose God's way especially when it is hard.* God's way is often hard because it does not come naturally to us. We naturally want to cut down others when they disrespect us. The world tells us to indulge in whatever sexual pleasure appeals to us. Our employer might not see anything wrong with cutting corners and expect us to follow along with the rest of our coworkers. The people of God need to see through those pressures and realize that God calls us to a better way. Even if it is harder, it will be more rewarding and we will avoid serious catastrophe.

Second, *choose humility to keep a level head.* When we are in positions of influence or authority, it is all too easy to let it feed our egos. Instead of making the kinds of mistakes these kings do, we ought to look for opportunities to serve. Popular reality TV show *Undercover Boss* (created by Stephen Lambert, 2010–) disguises various CEOs and plants them within their own company doing various menial jobs. Without exception, these privileged higher-ups come away from the experience with a greater appreciation for their employees and how the work of others contributes to their own success. Those superiors embraced lessons in humility and in turn worked to bless others.

Third, *choose to listen to the right voices.* It matters little whether the title of "parent" is the only authority you have. You do not need to be in control over a Fortune 500 company to realize what kind of catastrophe can come from our sinful choices. Therefore, we should listen to God through his Word and his Spirit. God has provided those two points of access so we can discern how to make the most honoring decisions that please him. We also need to listen to godly advisors. A healthy faith community should offer plenty of good examples for new parents to connect with as they seek to raise their kids. As you step out in faith in a new career venture, the *New York Times*

---

2   "'Faulty Towers' Plot," TV Tropes, accessed May 21, 2020, https://tvtropes.org/pmwiki/pmwiki.php/Main/Fawlty TowersPlot.

best seller on the subject is a fine place to start. But have you also made sure to find resources that incorporate sound spiritual principles into their views?

The bad choices we make can send us straight into trouble. But if we make sure to choose God's way, choose to embrace humility, and choose to listen to the right voices, we will find success.

Creativity in Presentation

In the late 2010s, the Museum of the Bible was opened to much fanfare within the American evangelical world. It enjoyed an impressive facility in Washington, DC, and proudly marketed its collection of ancient manuscripts and artifacts.

Before long, however, the Museum found itself in the middle of international controversy. They were widely criticized for breaching accepted ethical practices in procuring some of their documents. They got financially entangled with trusted experts who led them astray. Ultimately they have had to publicly admit their failings on a number of fronts and returned many documents that had been stolen or fraudulently obtained.[3] The Museum of the Bible has unfortunately become a cautionary tale of how ambition can blind even well-intentioned leaders. It led them to compromise their decision-making and resulted in professional disgrace. Their story, at least in their early history, fits with the arc of this passage. Sinful choices will lead to serious catastrophe. Just as God's grace was still present with his people in 2 Kings 14–16, God can certainly still be honored by this museum. Yet this early part of its story provides this passage with a modern-day illustration for comparison. Featuring the museum's website or promotional videos would be a way to enhance the story with visuals.

With the overarching, central truth being about the bad choices these rulers made, the following outline features five sinful choices that led to disaster of various proportions. God's grace is still present in different ways and could be cited within the first two sections (King Amaziah, Jeroboam II) and the last section (King Jotham). I (Lee) did combine 2 Kings 14:23–29 and 15:8–16 because of the lineage of kings and how all three achieved, inherited, or obtained a politically successful situation but abused grace by using their power for evil.

The key idea to communicate is that sinful choices lead to serious catastrophe that only God's grace can rescue us from. The passage for this preaching unit can be outlined in the following points:

- Foolish ambition will lead to catastrophe (14:1–22).
- Abusing grace will lead to catastrophe (14:23–29; 15:8–16).
- Pride will lead to catastrophe (15:1–7).
- Ill-advised alliances will lead to catastrophe (15:17–31).
- Outright rebellion will lead to catastrophe (16:1–20).

---

3 There have been several good write-ups in secular and Christian media. This one is as comprehensive and detailed as any: Ariel Sabar, "A Biblical Mystery at Oxford," *The Atlantic*, June 2020, https://www.theatlantic.com/magazine/archive/2020/06/museum-of-the-bible-obbink-gospel-of-mark/610576.

DISCUSSION QUESTIONS

1. King Amaziah is viewed as a "good king" for the most part but ultimately slips up as he tries to conquer not only Edom but Israel as well. Have you ever seen good leaders "bite off more than they can chew"? How can we prevent our own ambition from getting the best of us?

2. How are we to explain the long and successful reign of Jeroboam II despite his wickedness (14:23–29)?

3. Where else does Uzziah/Azariah show up in Scripture, and how does that add to our understanding of this point in history?

4. What empire is entering the picture in 2 Kings 15–16? How do Israel's and Judah's kings handle it?

5. Looking at these various sinful choices, which of them have you struggled with? How did you combat them? In your failures and successes, what have you learned that helps you spiritually moving forward?

2 Kings 17:1–20:21

EXEGETICAL IDEA

The Assyrian Empire's swift invasion and destruction of Samaria and Israel demonstrated Judah's relative superiority over Israel, yet King Hezekiah's decisions with the Babylonian envoy tempered any unqualified praise and foreshadowed the demise of Judah.

THEOLOGICAL FOCUS

The portrayal of Hezekiah testifies that the success of one's faith journey and legacy for the next generation is contingent upon one's consistent commitment to Christ.

PREACHING IDEA

The difference between victory and defeat is a lived-out faith.

PREACHING POINTERS

This section is a study in contrasts. The Assyrian Empire swiftly conquers the northern tribes of Israel, while the southern kingdom manages to survive that threat. The record of 1–2 Kings has transparently shown all the failings and flaws of both groups as the harsh reality of exile loomed larger and larger over Israel's history. The unwritten question that the author seems to be posing for his readers is, "What is the difference between the two?" or more specifically, "Why did the exile come in stages?" Second Kings 17–21 offers an explanation. More than Israel, Judah maintained at least a semblance of faithfulness to the covenant—and under Hezekiah's leadership, it was more than a semblance. He led significant reforms and remained faithful to the Lord even when his enemies were at his doorstep.

We are not facing an actual military conquest, yet we are engaged in warfare. As Paul describes in Ephesians 6:10–18, Christ-followers must be prepared for spiritual battles by putting on the armor of God. While there is much to say about that passage, what is generally obvious is that the illustration is meant to encourage believers to understand who they are in Christ and "fight" (i.e., live) accordingly. The student who faces antagonistic peers at school can maintain a strong witness by starting each day in the Word and prayer (Eph. 6:17–18). The housewife can parent her young kids with confidence by seeking the Lord's help daily with each parental challenge and difficulty that arises (Eph. 6:16). The aging grandparents can influence the next generation by imparting godly advice, sharing honestly about their own mistakes and successes and how God's grace saw them through it all (Eph. 6:14). Spiritual victory comes when we live out our faith. Defeat follows when we make our own choices and do our own thing no matter what God has said.

SAMARIA VERSUS JERUSALEM
(17:1–20:21)

LITERARY STRUCTURE AND THEMES (17:1–20:21)

Chapter 17 is a critical chapter in 2 Kings. It not only begins a contrast between Samaria and Jerusalem, but it also explicitly links the destruction of the northern kingdom to the nation's perpetual spiritual shortcomings. It explains what happened to Israel and why, ultimately painting a tragic picture of a land populated by foreigners who permanently installed a culture of syncretism.

Chapters 18–20 offer a different tone. While these chapters also discuss a national crisis brought on by Assyrian imperialism, they ultimately celebrate a national salvation. In the face of a siege, Jerusalem remains intact, functioning as a tangible point of the Lord's presence on earth. This is a powerful statement that closes a unit that featured the paralleled existence of Israel and Judah as a divided monarchy. Thus, Judah is demonstrated to be superior, particularly since its dynasty and capital remains. In addition, these chapters hearken back not only to 1 Kings 8 with its understanding of Jerusalem as the cosmic mountain but also to the exodus tradition and the Sea of Reeds (Schreiner 2018). However, these chapters simultaneously create a theological conundrum. With the exception of a handful of "good" kings, the Davidic dynasty has been shown to be relatively unfaithful to covenantal expectations—a lingering reality that is reinforced by Hezekiah's lapse in judgment (2 Kings 20), and which will be front and center in the final unit of Kings.

- *Samaria Sacked and Israel Exiled (17:1–41)*
- *Jerusalem Saved and Judah's Continuation (18:1–20:21)*

EXPOSITION (17:1–20:21)

The stingy indictment of Israel that opens this section gives way to the account of how Jerusalem escaped the clutches of Sennacherib when he approached Jerusalem on his third military campaign. Together, these chapters bring the importance of Jerusalem and the relative superiority of Judah into sharp focus. However, as quickly as this picture is brought into focus, the final, tragic phase of this history is anticipated through the foolish actions of Hezekiah.

Samaria Sacked and Israel Exiled (17:1–41)

Due to perpetual covenantal unfaithfulness, Samaria is sacked and Israel is deported, resulting in an imperially sanctioned repopulation program that only intensified the tragic circumstances.

17:1–6. The opening verses are concerned with what happened to Samaria and Israel in its final days. Hoshea was the last king, and he came to the throne in the twelfth year of Ahaz. His reign, predictably, is negatively evaluated but relatively qualified through a "faint praise" of comparison to other Israelite kings (Strand Winslow, 231; v. 2). Most importantly, these verses recount how Shalmaneser V reinforced vassalage upon Israel at some point in his nine-year reign, enacting tribute and forcing service to the Assyrian Empire. Yet Hoshea rebelled by colluding with Egypt and withholding tribute, two of the cardinal sins one could commit against the Assyrian Empire (v. 4). These infractions resulted in a three-year siege of Samaria that eventually ended with the imprisonment of Hoshea, the destruction of the city, and the deportation of the populace (vv. 4–6).

Historical Problem

There is a lingering question regarding Samaria's destruction. Essentially, who was responsible? Was it Sargon II, or was it Shalmaneser V?

According to 2 Kings 17:1–4, Shalmaneser sieged Samaria. And this is reinforced by certain Mesopotamian witnesses. However, the extrabiblical claims are varied. The Babylonian Chronicle and Shalmaneser's Eponym List credit him with sieging Samaria. However, Sargon II claims several times that he was responsible for the sacking of Samaria.

Ultimately, there are several possibilities. But the possibility that best accounts for the most data is the likelihood that both Shalmaneser and Sargon sieged the city and subjected the regions to repopulation campaigns. Therefore, the biblical witness likely telescopes an otherwise lengthy process (Elayi 2017, 45–61).

17:7–23. The explanation of Samaria's destruction begins in verse 7 (וַיְהִי כִּי). According to the historian, the deportation of Israel and destruction of Samaria can be explained simply by the accusation that the Israelites "sinned" against the Lord their God, who is then defined by his actions during the exodus. This creates an ironic atmosphere. The Lord saved his people from imperialistic hegemony (יַד פַּרְעֹה מֶלֶךְ־מִצְרָיִם) generations before, only to later give them up to another imperialistic force because of their perpetual rebellion.

The indictment begins generally, for the accusation of "sin" (חטא) invokes a broad range of possible infractions. However, the subsequent verses particularize the indictment through specific infractions, many of which can be categorized as idolatry and improper worship practices. Yet verse 13 interjects a change of pace by recalling the Lord's periodic exhortation to Israel to abandon their waywardness and return to a way of life marked by obeying the entire body of Israel's authoritative teaching (וְשִׁמְרוּ מִצְוֹתַי חֻקּוֹתַי כְּכָל־הַתּוֹרָה). Nevertheless, the indictment is clear. Israel was condemned for a complete collapse of their social and theological order through syncretism and covenantal infidelity. In short, Israel was judged because of their brazen apostasy.

Syntax: The culpability of Jeroboam I to Israel's history of illegitimate worship is communicated by specific syntax. Jeroboam is the subject of the verb חטא, which appears in a causative stem (*hiphil*) with Israel as the expressed direct object. Thus, "Jeroboam *caused* Israel to sin" by means of the unsanctioned altars at Bethel and Dan.

Another feature of verses 7–23 is the corporate emphasis. The verbal forms of these verses are overwhelmingly plural, demonstrating that the nation as a whole is being chastised. That is, the sacking of Samaria, the deportation of its inhabitants, and the eradication of the nation was due to a systemic national failure. Only in verses 21–23 is Jeroboam called out specifically, which incidentally brings to fruition a thread that has appeared consistently throughout Kings: the decision of Jeroboam I to construct altars at Bethel and Dan caused Israel to sin (1 Kings 14:6; 15:26, 30, 34; 16:26; 22:53; 2 Kings 3:3; 10:29–31; 13:2, 6, 11; 14:24; 15:9, 18, 24, 28).

Yet Jeroboam I and Israel are not the only condemned parties in these verses. Judah is mentioned in passing (2 Kings 17:19), but by doing so the historian anticipates the ending of Kings (Sweeney 2007, 391). Moreover, by equating Judah's national infraction with those of Israel, the historian alludes to the question that is informing this entire presentation: If Judah was guilty of the same infractions, why was the Judean exile realized so many years later?

17:24–41. The final verses of this chapter move away from explanation back to describing the events surrounding Assyria's sacking of Samaria. More precisely, the verses describe Assyrian resettlement efforts. Imperial policy dictated that people were imported from all parts of the empire, and for Samaria this resulted in people from Mesopotamia and beyond. They came to repopulate the cities (v. 25), and, unfortunately, resettlement efforts also brought further spiritual corruption and entrenchment in syncretism, which would eventually incur the wrath of the Lord. According to verse 25, the Lord sent lions to kill a significant portion of the populace. While it's difficult to determine the exact details of this event, including the species, there is precedent in Kings for using lions as mechanisms of judgment (1 Kings 13:24; 20:36). Moreover, mauling by lions recalls specific curses invoked when covenants were violated (Cogan and Tadmor, 210). This image emphasizes not only that covenantal expectations continued to order the events of the land but also the conviction that the Lord's judgment is decisive, absolute, and does not discriminate.

To his credit, the Assyrian king eventually acknowledged what was revealed—this tragedy was the result of offending the Lord by means of unsanctioned worship practices syncretism (2 Kings 17:26). However, royal efforts to pacify the situation failed to be effective. The king dispatched priests "from Samaria" back to Bethel to "teach them the law of the god of the land" (v. 27). While this may reflect specific Sargonic policy (Paul 1969), the historian emphasizes that the people persisted in their syncretism (vv. 29–31). The result was a gross amalgamation of Yahwism and paganism, which ultimately creates a tragic picture for the end of the chapter. The Lord's people have been exiled,

their has been city destroyed, and the new inhabitants of the land have suffocated any hope for legitimate Yahweh worship.

In the midst of these verses, there is also a recollection of the exodus and the Sinaitic covenant (vv. 35–40). Interestingly, it appears as a digression. The notification of syncretistic practices allowed the historian to engage an impassioned tangent and remember covenantal expectations and infractions. This effectively intensifies the tragedy of this chapter, firmly framing the fall of Samaria in terms of disobedience, covenantal infidelity, and a shameful disregard for expressing appreciation for God's saving actions. Importantly, this digression sets up a contrast that will feature the salvation of Jerusalem from the hand of the same imperial force.

Jerusalem Saved and Judah's Continuation (18:1–20:21)

In the context of the Assyrian Empire's swift invasion and destruction of Samaria and Israel, chapters 18–20 bring certain ideas to culmination and demonstrate Judah's relative superiority over Israel. However, Hezekiah's foolishness in the wake of his healing simultaneously tempers any praise and foreshadows the demise of Judah.

18:1–12. The chapter opens with the customary formula of introduction. In the third year of Hoshea, when he was twenty-five years old, Hezekiah began a twenty-nine-year reign. "He did what was right in the sight of the LORD" (v. 3), but Hezekiah is also explicitly compared to David (כְּכֹל אֲשֶׁר־עָשָׂה דָּוִד אָבִיו). This praise is then explained by noting his reform efforts (v. 4) and his unwavering trust in the Lord (vv. 5–6). Moreover, Hezekiah is praised for his rebellion against Assyrian imperialism and his defeat of the Philistines (vv. 7–8). The ultimate result of such praise is a pronouncement that "there was no one like him among all the kings of Judah after him, or among those who were before him" (v. 5). More than any other king up to this point, Hezekiah is presented as the proper successor of King David.

Verses 9–12 recount what was already discussed in chapter 17. Shalmaneser began a three-year siege of Samaria that ultimately led to the destruction of the northern kingdom and the deportation of its populace to Mesopotamia because of their rebellion against the Lord's covenantal ideal. Yet these verses are more than a simplistic reiteration. Rather, they reiterate to make clear the contrasting fates of Samaria and Jerusalem, the latter of which is discussed in what follows.

Hezekiah's reforms sought to end unsanctioned and pagan worship throughout Judah through a destructive process called centralization. The high places, which were constant sources of criticism for the historian, were removed (סור), asherah poles were cut down (כרת), pillars smashed, and even the bronze snake (called Nehustan) that God used to save the wilderness generation from serpents was broken (cf. Num. 21; כתת). Only the temple in Jerusalem remained.

Such centralization efforts allude to Deuteronomic legislation (cf. Deut. 12–26). However, the historicity of such efforts is perpetually questioned by scholars. In short, the lack of definitive archaeological evidence continues to push some scholars to ponder whether the event of 2 Kings 18:4–5 is the product of a postexilic ideology retrojected back onto the text. Such revisionism is not necessary, but the historical realities of this period urge the consideration of several factors when trying to reconstruct Hezekiah's centralization, including the idea that it may have been a lengthy and sophisticated process (Moulis 2019).

18:13–16. Jerusalem's siege account is lengthy, and it's complicated by verses 13–16. Cutting against the larger narrative, which celebrates Judean defiance of Assyria, these verses detail how Hezekiah raided the royal treasuries

and stripped (קצץ) the gold from the doors of the temple and palace property to pay tribute to Assyria. In fact, these details have encouraged some to reconstruct a second siege during Hezekiah's day (Bright 2000, 298–309). However, such a reconstruction is problematic for several historical reasons (Young 2012, 66–73; Elayi 2018, 85–87).

Ultimately, Kings presents the account of Sennacherib's siege in a way that is consistent with rhetorical features of ancient Near Eastern historiography. It honors the historical realities of Sennacherib's siege while emphasizing the important and shocking reality that Jerusalem was not burnt to the ground. Therefore, verses 13–16 need not be understood as a contradiction to the verses that follow. Rather, they recount one element within a complicated outcome to a complicated situation (Schreiner 2019, 106–10). The negative outcome of the events—a payment of tribute—is presented immediately so as to make way for the positive outcomes—the salvation of Jerusalem against all odds.

18:17–19:37. Sennacherib made his camp at Lachish, and from there he dispatched three officials to the capital. It's not immediately clear if the envoy also included a military force, but based on 19:35 the army arrived at some point. Regardless, a "powerful team" of three Assyrian officials are met by three Judean officials: Eliakim, the official "over the palace"; Shebna, the royal secretary; and Joah, the recorder (Wiseman 2008, 294). The place of negotiation was "the conduit of the upper pool," next to "the highway to the Fuller's field" (18:17), which is also the location where Isaiah met Ahaz to counsel him during the Syro-Ephraimite War. It's proven difficult to determine where this location is, but it must have been within earshot of the city wall, given that the Judean delegation would eventually request that all discourse take place in Aramaic.

Eventually, the Rabshakeh speaks, bringing a terrorizing speech of "deception and psychological warfare" (Wiseman 2008, 295). Driven by rhetorical questions, the Assyrian targets two objects of Judean confidence. Egypt is mocked (18:21), equated with a useless, broken reed. Regarding any confidence in the Lord (Yahweh), the Rabshakeh publicly suggests that the reforms of the current administration angered the Lord. Hezekiah's pious actions, according to the Assyrian, made things worse. The proof? The Assyrian army up to this point had utterly devastated the Judean countryside. And as if this were not enough, the Rabshakeh fused his chastisement with insults. He proposes that if Judah can provide enough men, Assyria would actually supply them with horses (18:23). Most egregiously, the Rabshakeh maintains that he—not Hezekiah—enjoys the Lord's sanction and that he is the obedient one (18:25).

Lachish

Ancient Lachish, a thirty-one-acre site strategically located approximately forty-five miles southwest of Jerusalem, is identified as modern Tel ed-Duweir. While the site exhibits evidence of occupation spanning from the Neolithic to Hellenistic periods, the Late Bronze and Iron Ages were high points of occupation and influence. The site was first excavated in the 1930s, but most systematically by David Ussishkin from 1969–76.

Stratum IV, which can't be dated precisely, shows evidence of systematic fortification. It was destroyed by an unknown means, but it served as the foundation for Stratum III's reconstruction. The city of Stratum III was an important administrative center for Judah during the Iron Age, and this city suffered a massive conflagration at the hands of Sennacherib in 701 BCE. Lachish was quickly rebuilt in Stratum II, but it suffered a similar fate as the city of Stratum III, but this time by Nebuchadnezzar.

There is a consensus among scholars that Sennacherib decorated his palace with depictions of Lachish's siege, but there is a debate as to the extent that the Assyrian wall depictions accurately reflect the details of the siege (Shea 2005). However, there is no controversy surrounding the importance of the Lachish Letters. This cache of ostraca were found in a gate room immediately beneath a destruction layer dated to 587 BCE. These letters offer an important window into Judean culture immediately before the Babylonian Exile. Letter 4 has drawn parallels to the book of Jeremiah by mentioning the signal fires of Azekah (Hadley 2018, 139).

The Rabshakeh's discourse is a sustained attack on Judean political policy and theology. Consequently, the despair inherent to verse 26 is not unexpected. So, to minimize the devastating effect of Assyrian rhetoric, Judean officials request that talks take place in Aramaic and not Hebrew. The former became Assyria's imperial language, and the populace would have struggled to understand the Assyrian threats. Yet Assyria knows that such capitulation would have undermined their psychological warfare. Therefore, Rabshakeh persisted, beginning with a sarcastic bit (18:27).

In his second discourse (18:28–35), the Rabshakeh addresses the populace more directly (18:28). In doing so, the Assyrian pits Hezekiah and the Lord against Sennacherib, highlighting the futility of the Judean king and the limitations of the Lord. It's a blunt chastisement that is designed to infuse doubt into the Judean psyche by pointing out the obvious: "Has any of the gods of the nations ever delivered its land out of the hand of the king of Assyria? Where are the gods of Hamath and Arpad?" (18:33–35). But in the midst of this, the Assyrian gives the Judeans an option: if they abandon the city and "make peace" with Assyria, they will be able to enjoy their land until they are departed to a land like Judah (18:31–32). Essentially, the choice is theirs, but in the Assyrian scenario their salvation from death exists with Assyria and not with Hezekiah and the Lord.

The text reveals that "the people were silent," for there was to be no answer per the command of the king (18:36). Instead, the three Judean officials took the word to Hezekiah with their clothes torn, thereby setting the stage for a showdown. The tension is palpable, and national despair could not be any higher. Like his father, Hezekiah faces a decision that will have tremendous implications upon Judah's existence and vitality moving forward.

Hezekiah's response is telling. According to 19:1, his immediate action was to intercede on behalf of his country. Dawning sackcloth, the king went into the temple to pray while he dispatched Eliakim, Shebna, and the priestly leadership to seek the counsel of Isaiah the prophet (19:2). The king approached the divine throne in the temple, while his leadership approached the Lord's spokesman. Thus, Hezekiah responded to the Rabshakeh's taunts with a two-pronged appeal.

With respect to Isaiah, the request is that of intercession. The king wants the prophet to directly appeal to the Lord on behalf of the remaining Judeans. And the prophet's response is somewhat cryptic but authoritative. Speaking on behalf of the Lord, the prophet essentially communicates, "Fear not. I've heard all the Assyrian's taunts, and I am already working behind the scenes. He will die when he's back in Assyria" (19:6–7). It's a call to continue to trust and be patient. Yet the problem with such a word is that the Rabshakeh is still on Jerusalem's doorstep, and the Assyrian official has proven to be quick to emphasize Jerusalem's precarious position, even if Assyria's focus would be temporarily shifted from the city. And according to 19:10–13, the Rabshakeh appears to have anticipated any words of prophetic encouragement. He doubles down on flaunting what he believes to be the quintessential proof of Assyrian superiority. No one else's gods saved them. Why would Judah be any different?

Upon receiving a second correspondence, Hezekiah returns to the temple to intercede on behalf of the city. Laying the document "before the Lord," Hezekiah employs a known practice of worship and appeals to the cosmic authority and power of the Lord (Na'aman 1974, 29–31; Wiseman 2008, 299). He's the one enthroned in the cosmos and its Creator. Moreover, Hezekiah makes monotheistic claims and then entreats the Lord to act so that all will know that he is, in fact, the Lord alone: "Incline your ear . . . open your eyes . . . and see . . . hear the words of Sennacherib. . . . So now, O LORD our God, save us . . . from his hand, so that all the kingdoms of the earth may know that you, O LORD, are God alone" (19:16–19).

Syntax: The syntax of the clause אַתָּה־הוּא הָאֱלֹהִים לְבַדְּךָ *in 19:15 is important.* The third personal masculine personal pronoun functions as a copula, creating a predicate nominative. Addressing the Lord, Hezekiah emphatically states "You are God." The presence of the adverb לְבַדְּךָ, however, imports a level of exclusivity. Thus, "You are God alone." And when verse 15 is coupled with clause כִּי לֹא אֱלֹהִים הֵמָּה in 19:18, a monotheistic statement is created.

According to 19:20, Isaiah responds to the king a second time, but this time with a fully formed oracle of judgment aimed at Sennacherib. It draws attention to the Assyrian's imperialistic hubris by recognizing Assyrian mockery and arrogant rhetoric (19:23–24). Yet this is countered by an appeal to divine determinism. According to 19:25–26, the Lord has allowed this to happen, and nothing that the Assyrian does or spouts is surprising (19:27). In fact, it's because of all this arrogant raging that the Lord will subject the Assyrians to their own devices (19:28). The Lord will force Assyria to return shamefully and painfully in the direction whence they came. And the proof of this will be experienced in the local agriculture. Jerusalem will not go hungry. Instead, the aftergrowth from the seeds scattered by Assyrian devastation (versus intentional sowing and harvest) will nourish Jerusalem and Judah for two years. A miraculous turn of events, indeed! But such a miracle was necessary for Judah to survive and thrive in the wake of Assyrian devastation.

The thrust of this oracle is simple enough. Not one element of this crisis has surprised the Lord. In fact, the Lord has allowed Assyrian arrogance to swell so that their fall would be that much more dramatic. And when they fall, they will fall so hard that Judah will patiently rebuild their crops and infrastructure while the Lord miraculously provides for them out of the ravages of the siege. Not one Assyrian will enter Jerusalem, and no offensive maneuver will be put forth. The Lord (Yahweh) *himself* will defend the city and send Assyria home, both for his sake and the sake of David (19:34).

Second Kings 19:35–37 quickly recounts the conclusion of the crisis. That night, according to 19:35, the Angel of the Lord (Yahweh; מַלְאַךְ יְהוָה) swept through the Assyrian camp. The devastation was so quick and so intense that after everything settled, the bodies of the dead Assyrians littered the ground. Sennacherib was not one of the dead, but his demise came soon enough. Upon his return to Assyria, he was assassinated while worshipping one of his gods. His son Esarhaddon succeeded him, all of which are facts verified by Assyrian records (Wiseman 2008, 303).

The salvation of Jerusalem echoes with Exodus 14 (Schreiner 2018). The accounts of the annihilation of the Egyptian and Assyrian armies exhibit several points of contact and collaborate to establish a literary and historical connection. The message declares that the Lord continues to save his people against all odds, even from the greatest imperial forces. There exists, then, a pattern of salvation for the sake of his people and for the sake of his glory. In this context, the salvation of Jerusalem stands in stark contrast with the destruction of Israel and Samaria. Where one city survived with its dynasty intact, the other was fully consumed by the Assyrian Empire,

repopulated by foreigners, and enjoyed no sanctioned king. Most importantly, the salvation of Jerusalem proved the Lord's approval of Judah and the Davidic monarchy relative to Israel and its numerous dynasties more than any other historical event. Sennacherib's failure proved Jerusalem's superiority.

20:1–21. Chapter 20 moves on from Sennacherib's siege through a general chronological marker ("In those days . . ."; בַּיָּמִים הָהֵם). The Babylonian envoy apparently arrived at the same general time as Sennacherib's siege. At some point, Hezekiah became sick to "the point of death" (v. 1). Again, Isaiah appears, although it's not clear if the king summoned the prophet or if Isaiah sought out the king. Regardless, the initial message is concise and clear: "Set your house in order, for you shall die; you shall not recover." In response, the king rolls over to face the wall to pray. In doing so, the king asks the Lord to remember the manner by which he lived his life. That is, the king makes one last appeal to his piety to save his life (v. 3).

This was enough. According to verse 4, Isaiah was not even able to leave the palace complex before he was impressed to return to the king and offer an alternative pronouncement. Another oracle is delivered, this time disclosing imminent salvation. The Lord heard his prayer, observed his tears, and so chose to heal him—a remarkable turn of events. The passionate pleas of God's people can persuade him to alter his determinations! In three days, Hezekiah will be well enough to worship. More importantly, he will also be given fifteen more years to live and a renewed commitment that the Lord will protect Jerusalem and the Davidic dynasty (vv. 5–6). Consequently, what started as a depressing encounter ended up as a celebratory one.

The chronological relationship between verse 7 and what follows is difficult. Many translations anticipate Hezekiah's recovery when they read "so that he may recover" (e.g.,

NRSV). However, the Hebrew suggests a past tense, "and he recovered" (וַיֶּחִי). Such a reading therefore renders the request for a sign (v. 8) as an awkward one. Interestingly, Isaiah's account (Isa. 38) does not testify to such a sequential conundrum when it recounts the application of the figs at the conclusion of the interchange. Nevertheless, the reader should understand the application of the fig poultice as the therapeutic mechanism that facilitated the king's healing and the sign of the shadow as the psychological mechanism employed to reduce the king's anxiety. Isaiah's account may testify to the sequence of events, while Kings is not as concerned with strictly minding the sequence.

The characterization of Hezekiah in verses 12–19 constitutes a notable departure from that up to this point. The wise and faithful king switches places with an egotistical and shortsighted one. At some point, literally "at that time," Hezekiah welcomed a Babylonian envoy from Merodach-baladan, king of Babylon (v. 12). Bearing official correspondence and gifts, the envoy was shown the full glory of the Judean monarchy. From its infrastructure to its commodities and resources, "there was nothing in his house or in all his realm that Hezekiah did not show them" (v. 13).

These actions eventually produced another meeting between the king and Isaiah, and the atmosphere of the second meeting was very different. Isaiah interrogates the king, seeking clarification on the envoy's origin and intentions (vv. 14–15). To his credit, the king is truthful, and there is no hint of elusive behavior. Yet honesty is not enough. Eventually, Isaiah predicts a moment when the same group will return, but not in peaceful diplomacy. Rather, they will come to plunder, destroy, and cart away. In short, Isaiah predicts the Babylonian exile.

Hezekiah's response is rather shocking. Essentially, the king shrugs his shoulders and concedes, unconcerned with what his descendants will face (v. 19). Such a "cavalier and selfish" attitude stands in stark contrast to the passionate king who intensely interceded on behalf of his people (Strand Winslow 2017, 250), although there are some who question whether Hezekiah was apathetic (Wiseman 2008, 307–8). Nevertheless, this scene is a bucket of cold water poured on a very positive portrayal of Hezekiah. Even the best Judean kings were susceptible to lapses in piety as well as making shortsighted decisions that had devastating consequences, and coming at the end of the Hezekian material, it leaves the reader with a sour taste. Later, we will see similar phenomena play out in the life of Josiah.

Verses 20–21 close the reign of Hezekiah. Despite his shortsightedness, he is remembered positively, particularly for his upgrades to Jerusalem's water system. He died and peacefully passed on his throne to Manasseh.

THEOLOGICAL FOCUS

The exegetical idea (The Assyrian Empire's swift invasion and destruction of Samaria and Israel demonstrated Judah's relative superiority over Israel, yet King Hezekiah's decisions with the Babylonian envoy tempered any unqualified praise and foreshadowed the demise of Judah) leads to this theological focus: The portrayal of Hezekiah testifies that the success of one's faith journey and legacy for the next generation is contingent upon one's consistent commitment to Christ.

This final subunit of the central literary unit in Kings is action-packed and theologically informative. The reader is told why an entire nation is lost while another nation is saved. Amid this stands Hezekiah, the Judean king who is celebrated for his trust, piety, and reforms. Yet Hezekiah's characterization in these chapters is not without blemish. In fact, the final picture of the king is rather sobering. Second Kings 20 reveals how Hezekiah exhibited a shortsighted perspective at a very strategic moment, a posture that had far-reaching consequences.

Such a juxtaposition testifies to lessons that are central to one's spiritual maturation. First, living faithfully requires continual commitment. One's spiritual success is never the result of a one-time commitment or decision, because believers are bombarded daily by new variables and new experiences that create moments of renewed allegiance to the Lord. Second, there must be a premium put on the legacy one leaves behind, as well as a commitment to set the succeeding generation up for success. Hezekiah's anemic response to Isaiah's prophetic declaration suggests a remarkable amount of apathy toward the next generation.

The apostle Paul seems to have been keenly aware of his responsibility to the next generation of believers. The Pastoral Epistles, in part, served as his final act of investment into Timothy and Titus to ensure that they were given the tools and advice necessary for success as young leaders in the Christian movement. And the epistle of James famously advocates for continual submission to God and resistance of the devil in the context of a believer's daily life (James 4:7–10). What's more, the gospel of Luke suggests that Jesus's repulsion of Satan was a continual feature of the Messiah's ministry (cf. Luke 4:13). Ultimately, this suggests that one's journey toward spiritual maturation is neither predictable nor consistent. Rather, that journey is dynamic and erratic. Success, therefore, is contingent upon consistently renewing one's commitment to Christ.

PREACHING AND TEACHING STRATEGIES

Exegetical and Theological Emphasis
The reason why the southern tribes of Israel were able to escape the fate of their northern counterparts is clear. King Hezekiah led his people to inward and outward faithfulness. When the crisis of the approaching Assyrian army hit, God honored that faithfulness and delivered his people in a surprising way. God rescued the king in a personal way as well, healing him from a sickness. In both cases, Hezekiah earnestly sought the Lord's help. These incidents show that his earlier reforms were more than just rote performances; they were driven by a heart for God, echoing his ancestor David. Like David, Hezekiah's record was not perfect (18:13–16; 20:12–21) but the arc of his life was clearly directed by his commitment to God. His lived-out faith made all the difference as he led God's people.

Preaching Idea
The difference between victory and defeat is a lived-out faith.

Contemporary Connections

What does it mean?
What does it mean that the difference between victory and defeat is a lived-out faith? Spiritual victory is simply the result of living out our faith and committing ourselves afresh to following God's will in all our decisions and actions over time. Failure to do that can result in spiritual defeat. This kind of commitment can flesh itself out in something as basic as developing the habit of waking up early to spend time praying and reading Scripture. It can be as advanced as a church starting up a food pantry in its community for those affected by economic downturns. Our faith should be reflected in how we spend our money—am I keeping it all for myself or generously supporting charities?

As James make so clear in his letter, it is not enough to carry a spiritual label or merely identify as a Christian. Those claims and labels must be backed up by good deeds (James 2:14–26). A sports team can prepare 24/7 for their opponent. They can make all the bold predictions in the world about the imminent victory. But unless they follow their coach's instructions and execute what they practiced, all the talk is hollow and all the preparations are for naught. Likewise, we will only find victory in life when we live out our faith.

Is it true?

Is it true that the difference between victory and defeat is a lived-out faith? Spiritually speaking, yes, it makes all the difference. Of course, in arenas like athletic competition or military conflict, outcomes often result from a combination of a variety of factors. Turnovers, proper technique, and injuries often factor in who wins or loses in sports. General strategy, supply chains, weapons technology, and allied support can all make or break military campaigns.

Spiritual victory is much simpler. God determines success and failure. He pronounces the winners and losers and it is those who live out their faith whom he rewards. People who obey him, stay committed to His will, and choose to do what is right are those who God honors. Hezekiah's life depicts this in positive and negative ways. To the extent that he was a faithful king, he and his kingdom flourished. When he took the wrong path, God pronounced judgment on his people.

Now what?

If it's true that the difference between victory and defeat is a lived-out faith, what is important to put into practice in order to ensure spiritual victory? Mark Twain tells of a conversation he had with a businessman who had a well-earned reputation for being ruthless in his dealings. This man told Twain, "Before I die, I mean to make a pilgrimage to the Holy Land. I will climb Mount Sinai and read the Ten Commandments aloud at the top."

"I have a better idea," Twain replied. "You could stay in Boston and keep them."[1]

We often think making grandiose gestures or attempting great feats will bring God's approval. The God of the Bible makes it simpler than that. He's looking for heartfelt devotion and consistent faithfulness. This is not about earning his approval or manipulating God into doing what we want. Make no mistake, it is out of his grace that he grants us victory and success. Yet we see his favor fall on those who only seek to do his will.

Since this passage demonstrates just how crucial it is that we are living out our faith, we should *make sure we seek God's direction in every situation*. When our grades are struggling, have we examined our hearts and habits to evaluate whether we are giving our best efforts in class? When our friends start in with off-color jokes, will we speak up, stay silent, or join in? When that family member keeps pushing our buttons, will we just "let them have it" or ask God to provide us with Christlike love and patience instead?

This passage also shows how important it is that we strive to *leave a legacy of faithfulness*. King Hezekiah has a sterling reputation in comparison to almost every other king in these two books of Kings. His reign was certainly a bright spot. Yet it ends on a down note. His foolish interactions with the Babylonians lead to a prophetic pronouncement that his success will die with him. Judah's good fortune does extend longer, but eventually Babylon does conquer the southern kingdom. Through the methods of donations, endowments, and inheritances, there are plenty of ways to leave a legacy of monetary and material resources. But while "moth and rust destroy and thieves break in and steal," Christ-followers need to prioritize leaving a faithful spiritual legacy. Have our kids and grandkids grown up understanding what it means to know and serve Christ? Serving in an older church, I (Lee) have found myself officiating the memorial services for twelve different people over the

---

1   "Obedience Is Better than Sacrifice", *Ministry 127*, accessed July 2, 2020, https://ministry127.com/resources/illustration/obedience-is-better-than-sacrifice.

past two years as of this writing. There is a special joy when we can celebrate the life of a faithful saint. It is never "easy," and yet those services are always healthy reminders about leaving a legacy of faithfulness whenever the Lord calls us home.

Creativity in Presentation

The corporation Blockbuster will not ring any bells for younger people, but for the Gen X and older crowd that video store was an entertainment staple for quite a long time. At their peak, they had nine thousand stores and raked in just under $10 billion in revenue. In 2000, Blockbuster executives had a meeting with a new company named Netflix, which was sending subscribers DVDs through the mail. Netflix sought to merge with Blockbuster for $50 million. Blockbuster declined the offer, reportedly laughing their upstart competitor out of the meeting. That turned out to be a pivotal moment for both companies. Within ten years, Blockbuster had filed for bankruptcy and Netflix had emerged as the leader in the new industry of online streaming entertainment. Twenty years after that fateful meeting, Netflix was valued at $194 billion.[2]

Whether it was hubris, greed, or lack of business vision, that unfortunate business decision led to the demise of a once-great company. It illustrates how the difference between victory and defeat can often come down to a specific meeting, one particular decision, a single fatal flaw, or a unique strength.

There is one important decision that determines each person's destiny—and that of course is one's decision to trust Christ as Lord and Savior. While our capital *V* Victory may be assured, whether we are victorious in the day-to-day aspects of life depends on if we are living out our faith or not. If we want to avoid having our lives fade away like Blockbuster, we should commit ourselves to the way of Christ each and every day in each and every decision.

This passage begins and ends with failure, as disobedience and complacency are the main causes for the downfalls recorded in those passages. The bulk of the attention and the message can be given to the middle portion and the incredible events in King Hezekiah's life. His story is one of God rewarding faithfulness even when defeat seems inevitable.

The key idea to communicate is that the difference between victory and defeat is a lived-out faith. The passage for this preaching unit can be outlined as follows:

- God doesn't take disobedience lightly (17:1–41).
- God honors faithful devotion (chs. 18–19).
  - God blesses his faithfully devoted people (18:1–12).
  - God delivers his faithfully devoted people (18:13–19:37).
- God doesn't take complacency lightly (20:1–21).

---

2   Dave Roos, "10 Worst Business Decisions Ever Made," *How Stuff Works*, updated May 26, 2020, https://money. howstuffworks.com/10-worst-business-decisions3.htm.

DISCUSSION QUESTIONS

1. What are the ways that Israel strayed from the right path? What sins are listed in 17:7–17?

2. How are the above sins contrasted with King Hezekiah? What are the specific reforms that are recorded (18:1–8)?

3. What are some common idols that Christians tolerate and accept in our present day?

4. What stands out to you in the back-and-forth between the Assyrians and Hezekiah's leaders (18:19–37)?

5. How does Hezekiah respond to the crisis caused by Assyrian "deception and psychological warfare" and his own health crisis (19:1–4; 20:1–4)? How can that be instructive to us in our own crises?

6. What was Hezekiah's mistake that concludes the account of his reign (20:12–21)? What should we learn from it?

THE DIVIDED MONARCHY
(1 KINGS 14:21–2 KINGS 20:21)

A SUMMARY

At the conclusion of the first major literary unit (1 Kings 1:1–14:20), the historian brought into focus the institutions that would dictate the contours of the history of Israel and Judah moving forward. Prophets, with their voices of critique and support, were discussed alongside kings and their governing policies. In addition, the first unit clarified the quintessential choice that the kings of Israel and Judah would face—whether or not to be faithful to the covenant. And intimately connected to this choice is the existence of competing centers of worship. Judah enjoyed Jerusalem, with its temple, and Israel possessed two sites situated at the northern and southern ends of its territory, Bethel and Dan. Consequently, when the first unit concluded, there were two kingdoms, once united, that were poised to exist side by side in the southern Levant. What remained unanswered was how everything would unfold.

The second literary unit (1 Kings 14:21–2 Kings 20:21) brought clarification to this lingering question. It showed that the two major social institutions were complex realities. There were kings who did good in the sight of the Lord and kings who did evil. And in the case of the good kings, there was a continuum upon which that king was situated. On one extreme there was Hezekiah, who was uniquely Davidic-like and better than all the others. On the other end, there were kings like Jehoshaphat whose "goodness" was qualified by his inability to remove the high places. The bad kings were constant in Israel and widespread in Judah, but even the bad kings of Judah were pacified by the lasting legacy of King David (e.g., 1 Kings 15:4; 2 Kings 8:19). The prophets, similarly, were a complicated institution. There were true prophets and false prophets, demonstrating that the word of the Lord was not unopposed even within the prophetic institution itself! The prophets were also involved in the political developments of the era, and their ministry was not restricted to either Israel or Judah. The result is a literary unit that defies any simplistic generalization.

The second literary unit also showed that the historical contours of Israel and Judah were determined by a sophisticated interaction between people's choices, divine determinations, and national forces. For example, Ahab's choice to violate the demands of the חֵרֶם leveled at the Arameans (1 Kings 20) secured his judgment and, ultimately, the judgment of his dynasty. To bring about that end, Jehu was anointed to facilitate their dynastic fall, but Jehu's movements against the Omrides engendered a devastating set of circumstances that almost brought an end to the Davidic dynasty. Of course, all of this was predicted well before it transpired (1 Kings

17:15–17). Regarding the national forces, Edom, Moab, Aram of Damascus, and, most importantly, Assyria and Babylon are discussed. Each one—to varying degrees—influenced the contours of Israel and Judah's history. In the case of the latter two, both would be instruments of national judgment, although in this second literary unit Assyria is the dominant force.

Nevertheless, despite this historical complexity, the message at the end of the second literary unit is clear enough. Israel's propensity to continuously disregard the covenantal ideal, a characteristic inaugurated during Israel's first dynasty, secured its destruction. In contrast, Judah enjoyed the Davidic dynasty, whose founder cast a positive shadow long after his death, providing a legacy that would continually fend off the full force of judgment for so many years. Moreover, Judah boasted of Jerusalem, with its temple. And if there were any questions about Judah's relative superiority, they were answered in the events at the end of the eighth century. Whereas Samaria and Israel were destroyed by the Assyrians, Jerusalem with its sitting dynasty was saved. Yet Judean superiority—linked to its capital and dynasty—was not to be absolute. The second literary unit ends with an anticipation of the Babylonian exile.

JUDAH ALONE
(2 KINGS 21:1–25:30)

The third major literary unit in Kings is 2 Kings 21:1–25:30, which describes Judah alone after Assyria's devastation of Samaria and Israel. It is divided into two sections: 1) the good and the bad (21:1–23:30); and 2) the end (23:31–25:30). Together, these two sections include three preaching units: 21:1–26; 22:1–23:30; 23:31–25:30.

THE GOOD AND THE BAD
(2 KINGS 21:1–23:30)

The first section of the third major literary unit in Kings is 2 Kings 21:1–23:30, which discusses the good and the bad—or to be more precise, the bad and the good. First, Manasseh and Ammon (21:1–26) are the bad. The unraveling of Judah begins with, and is secured by, Manasseh, the Judean king who dramatically reneges on virtually everything that his father Hezekiah had accomplished. Ammon follows suit. Second, Josiah (22:1–23:30) is the good. In contrast to Manasseh and Ammon, Josiah's reign offers a moment of reprieve but only a glimpse of restoration. Sadly, Josiah's spectacular reforms do not last, neither are they enough to undo Judah's descent toward the exile.

2 Kings 21:1–26

EXEGETICAL IDEA
Manasseh undermined the reforms of his father and secured the destruction and judgment of Judah, while Ammon's reign intensified the sociopolitical tensions.

THEOLOGICAL FOCUS
Past faithfulness is no guarantee of future faithfulness, but focused engagement on the Lord's teachings increases the likelihood of future faithfulness.

PREACHING IDEA
Legacies are dismantled much more easily than they are constructed.

PREACHING POINTERS
After the godly reign of King Hezekiah, Judah experiences spiritual whiplash when his son and grandson take over the throne. His son Manasseh seems especially dedicated to reversing the progress and reform Hezekiah had instituted. He leads the nation headlong back into flagrant idolatry. It was at this point that God announced his coming judgment of exile on Judah—the exile that the first readers of 2 Kings would have been all too familiar with. After reestablishing themselves in their homeland, the Jewish people returning from exile now reading this account would have been reminded that all the work they had done could be fumbled away by those who came after them. The only way forward would be to spiritually invest in the next generation, to ensure that their sons and grandsons remained faithful to Yahweh.

Many Christians have lamented the direction of Western culture in the twenty-first century. Few have thought to consider whether Western Christianity is at least in part to blame. For much of the late twentieth century in the United States, conservative Christians sought to carve out cultural influence through political means, by forming the Religious Right voting bloc. Might the results we decry in the 2000s and following decades be a direct consequence of previous generations of Christians pursuing political power at all costs? Subsequent generations seem to be disillusioned by that quest. Many have rejected the faith altogether. The positive legacies of twentieth-century Western Christianity—global missions, scholarship, musical worship, humanitarian aid, civil rights progress—are often disregarded because of the way Christian leaders put the emphasis on the wrong pursuits. Some Christian legacies of recent times need dismantling. But the world around us is increasingly dismissive of the whole, not just the particulars. The Western church needs to move ahead with a greater desire to leave a legacy that is faithful to the gospel. That will entail raising up disciples and leaders who will follow in our faithful footsteps, instead of walking away disappointed by the failings of their spiritual forebears.

MANASSEH AND AMMON (21:1–26)

LITERARY STRUCTURE AND THEMES (21:1–26)

These few verses are historically critical. Manasseh's reign undoes everything that Hezekiah accomplished, and does so in dramatic fashion. In fact, the judgment of Judah is secured because of his apostate actions. Ammon continues in his father's footsteps, but he is assassinated by factions within his inner circle. Together, these kings plunge Judah back into social and political degradation as well as moral and spiritual apostasy.

- *Manasseh's Apostasy (21:1–18)*
- *Ammon's Death (21:19–26)*

EXPOSITION (21:1–26)

Immediately on the heels of Hezekiah come the reigns of Manasseh and Ammon. Both are bad kings, and the former is credited with securing judgment upon Judah. In other words, all Hezekiah's advances were undone in less than one generation.

Manasseh's Apostasy (21:1–18)

Manasseh undoes all the reforms of Hezekiah and secures the judgment of Judah.

21:1–18. Manasseh's reign begins the final major literary unit of Kings, and with his reign the negativity of 2 Kings 20 that looms on the horizon comes more clearly into view. Generally, Manasseh's reign is defined by his reversal of Hezekiah's reforms and the revival of traditional Canaanite cultic practices (Cogan and Tadmor 2008, 272). Indeed, Manasseh did evil in the sight of the Lord, but the text is very clear that Manasseh's reign was theologically and historically devastating. He followed the "abominable practices of the nations that the LORD drove out before the people of Israel" (v. 2). He rebuilt (בנה) the high places (הַבָּמוֹת) Hezekiah tore down (עבד; v. 3), and erected altars to Baal and Asherah in the temple, which is where the Lord chose (בחר) to "put [his] name" (vv. 4, 7). He shed innocent blood (v. 16), and engaged in prohibited sorceries, even making his son pass through the fire (v. 6). He is linked overtly to Ahab (v. 3) and implicitly to Jeroboam I while being considered worse than the Amorites (v. 11). As summed up by one commentator, Manasseh is described as "an enthusiastic idolater, wholly bent on abandoning the Mosaic Law. . . . [a]n inveterate sinner" (Cogan and Tadmor 2008, 270).

Child Sacrifice?

The question whether Manasseh engaged child sacrifice stems from several factors, including different terminology in Scripture. Certain places use different phrases, which has caused some to question if the accusation of "causing their sons and daughters to pass through the fire" (2 Kings 16:3; 21:6) is more figural than "burning their sons and daughters" (Deut. 12:31; 2 Kings 17:31). It is noteworthy that the indictment of Manasseh strongly echoes Deuteronomy 18:9–12, a passage that uses the idea of causing one's children to pass through the fire (Cogan and Tadmor 2008, 266; Strand Winslow 2017, 253).

In 1975, Morton Smith responded to Moshe Weinfeld's argument for a figural understanding of Manasseh's indictment. According to Smith (1975, 267), there is insufficient comparative and textual evidence to conclude that the king "purified" and dedicated his children to service of a pagan deity. Yet while Cogan and Tadmor correctly point to the lack of any distinction in the prophetic texts, there is legal evidence from Mesopotamia that filicide could be circumvented by dedicating one's child to a life of service. In the end, it's possible that Manasseh did the unthinkable.

Most importantly, it was because of Manasseh's actions and policies that the judgment of Judah was secured. The syntax of verse 11 and the form of verses 11–15 are clear: "Because [יַעַן אֲשֶׁר] of these evil abominations that Manasseh king of Judah did," judgment will fall. Verses 12–15 then detailed the pending judgment, which is described in vivid terms similar to the judgment of both Samaria and Ahab (v. 13) as well as being tied to the people's habitual rebellion since the exodus (v. 15). Moreover, as pointed out by Wray Beal (2014, 491), the images of judgment eventually recall images of disorder prior to creation. Thus, Judah's judgment will be definitive and leave no doubt. The Lord will take away his protection, offering Judah up to their enemies (v. 14) and allowing disorder to reign as they are wiped clean.

All of this presents a significant question: If Manasseh was so bad, why was his reign so long? Reigning fifty-five years in Jerusalem (v. 1), his reign constitutes the longest of any Judean king. According to the theological paradigm assumed by Kings, such evil should not have translated into such a lengthy reign. The Chronicler would later address this issue, recounting how Manasseh ultimately repented during a period of Assyrian captivity (2 Chron. 33:10–13), even though the destruction of Judah was the result of "the sins of an entire generation" (Sweeney 2007, 427–28). Yet Kings does not dwell upon the issue. Instead, Kings focuses on the egregious actions of the king and their nationalistic implications, emphatically pinning the reality of the Babylonian exile on him and his policies.[1]

Importantly, Manasseh's reign also looks forward to the next great Judean reformer. As one will see in the reform account of Josiah (chs. 22–23), the cultic elements that Manasseh constructed and/or revived will fall firmly within the crosshairs of Josiah's violent reform. Cultic vessels and altars made for Baal, Asherah, and the hosts of heaven, which stood in the temple, will be burned in

---

1   The memory of Manasseh as presented in Kings is extremely negative. He had no redeeming value as he coordinated a reversion back to indigenous paganism and, most egregiously, secured the path to the Babylonian exile. However, the Chronicler's account tempers this overwhelming negativity. Indeed, the Chronicler recognizes that Manasseh resurrected the paganism stamped out by his father, but Manasseh apparently learned the error of his ways while in exile. There, he repented and was eventually restored (2 Chron. 33:10–13). Moreover, the Chronicler suggests that Manasseh's restoration facilitated a new level of spiritual and theological awareness. But perhaps most telling about the Chronicler's account is the strategic ignorance of Manasseh's role in securing the Babylonian exile. According to Cielontko's (2019, 243) summary, Kings emphasizes Manasseh's role in national judgment while the Chronicler emphasizes the king's repentance.

So which memory is best? Can they both coexist, and if so, which one is preferred? In answering, it's important to realize that the Bible's diverse testimony is one that was not explained away. Rather, it established a trajectory that was eventually played out in Jewish and Christian traditions across the centuries and millennia that followed. On the one hand, Manasseh is remembered as an archvillain, even as the killer of the prophet Isaiah. On the other hand, Manasseh is remembered as the paradigmatic repenter. Consequently, the traditions of Judaism and Christianity apparently were comfortable with accepting such a complex memory and using it as a way to advance their theological message. Thus, this diversity is something that should be embraced, particularly for historical reasons. The memory of Manasseh is not only a vivid case study in how memories are formed and disseminated but also how complex memories are affected by textual genre and geopolitical contexts.

the Kidron Valley. The high places throughout Judah will be profaned, and other actions will be taken. Manasseh ultimately died peacefully, was buried with honor, and was succeeded by his son Ammon.

Ammon's Death (21:19–26)
Ammon's short reign intensifies the sociopolitical tensions of the era.

21:19–26. Not much is recounted about Ammon. After the typical introduction (v. 19), he is remembered in "the shadow of his father" (Wray Beal 2016, 492). The mantra "like father, like son" comes to mind as the reader is told that Ammon continued the apostate actions and policies of Manasseh (vv. 20–22). However, in contrast to his father, Ammon is assassinated for reasons that while still remaining elusive almost certainly were political in nature (Cogan and Tadmor 2008, 275–76; Wray Beal 2014, 492). According to verse 23, royal servants conspired and killed him in his royal residence. Yet this action produced more violence. In response to Ammon's death, factions within the ambiguous group "the people of the land" (עַם־הָאָרֶץ; Cogan and Tadmor 2008, 275) killed the conspirators and installed their man upon the throne—Josiah. Much to his chagrin, the most enduring elements of Ammon's reign were linked to his death.

THEOLOGICAL FOCUS
The exegetical idea (Manasseh undermined all the reforms of his father to the point that he secured the destruction and judgment of Judah, while Ammon's reign intensified the sociopolitical tensions) leads to this theological focus: Past faithfulness is no guarantee of future faithfulness, but focused engagement on the Lord's teachings increases the likelihood of future faithfulness.

Kings has recognized that past faithfulness is not a guarantee of future faithfulness, particularly in times of communal transition.

In particular, the transitions between Jehoshaphat and Jehoram as well as between Jotham and Ahaz proved to be very informative. Jehoram solidified Omride policies in Judean affairs (2 Kings 18:17–18), and Ahaz permanently opened the door for Assyria to dominant the region until its demise at the end of the seventh century (2 Kings 16:1–20). Both kings rejected the policies of their fathers. Similarly, but more egregiously, Manasseh's actions secured judgment, thereby completely undoing the pious reforms of his father.

In the New Testament, the phenomenon of future faithfulness in light of times of transition appears in relationship with congregational health after the initial phase of evangelization. The initial acceptance of Paul's message and ministry by the Galatians did not translate to subsequent spiritual health. Rather, it translated into short-term illness, as the congregation quickly adopted an unhealthy reliance upon traditions linked to a false gospel (Gal. 3). Similarly, in Corinth Paul's congregation quickly allowed factionalism and other internal tensions to foster division and strife.

More positively, the transition within the ranks of the disciples in the wake of Jesus's resurrection and ascension eventually produced an emboldened group of men who would produce congregations and fellow believers throughout the world. The difference? According to Acts 1, the disciples gathered together, as a group, and devoted themselves to prayer (Acts 1:12–14). In addition, they encouraged each other through the exposition of Scripture. Consequently, this suggests that a continual and focused engagement of the Lord's authoritative teachings dramatically increases the likelihood that past faithfulness will translate into future faithfulness. This, in fact, was precisely what Joshua had been commanded to do centuries earlier (cf. Josh. 1:7–9).

PREACHING AND TEACHING STRATEGIES

Exegetical and Theological Synthesis

The positive spiritual momentum Judah experienced under Hezekiah only lasts for a generation. By the time his son takes over, idolatry and apostasy are allowed to flourish once again. The faithfulness of the father did not get passed down to the son. Adding further insult to injury, the faithlessness of Manasseh gets passed on to his son Ammon.

Constructing a good legacy is a lot like constructing a building. It takes time, careful planning, discipline, and the proper tools and materials. Likewise, destroying a good legacy is similar to destroying a building. All you need is a wrecking ball operated by a machinist intent on demolishing it. In this case, the wrecking ball is a king who wants nothing to do with following the Lord. Dismantling legacies is much easier than creating them. If we intend on leaving a legacy that truly lasts, we will put great effort into molding those who will succeed us, imparting to them the spiritual values and practices of biblical discipleship.

Preaching Idea

Legacies are dismantled much more easily than they are constructed.

Contemporary Connections

What does it mean?

What does it mean that legacies are dismantled much more easily than they are constructed? Even based just on experience or the witness of history, we know that constructing something (a house, a city, a nation) requires far more time and effort than dismantling it. Given how much easier it is to dismantle legacies than it is to create them, one might question whether it is even worth it. Scripture certainly warns us about what kind of legacy we pursue. Just because legacies can be dismantled is not to say that all legacies are meaningless. Paul uses a building metaphor to define what a meaningful legacy looks like in 1 Corinthians 3:10–14 (NIV):

> By the grace God has given me, I laid a foundation as a wise builder, and someone else is building on it. But each one should build with care. For no one can lay any foundation other than the one already laid, which is Jesus Christ. If anyone builds on this foundation using gold, silver, costly stones, wood, hay or straw, their work will be shown for what it is, because the Day will bring it to light. It will be revealed with fire, and the fire will test the quality of each person's work. If what has been built survives, the builder will receive a reward.

The key he identifies is that any legacy we pursue needs to be founded on Christ. That means we should put all our energy into discipling and preparing those who will succeed us. Churches can create internship programs for those aspiring to vocational ministry. We can personally volunteer as youth leaders or coaches invest in the next generation. Serving with the Big Brothers Big Sisters of America program is another way to make a real legacy difference in our community in this way. If the legacy we leave does not involve encouraging the spiritual growth of others, it will not last.

Is it true?

Is it true that legacies are dismantled much more easily than they are constructed? The entire history of Israelite kings serves to demonstrate in general what we see here specifically. Namely, legacies are rapidly ruined when subsequent leaders do not follow the same path. While 1–2 Kings deals with royal legacies for a people group, we see the same principle play out with the reputations of high-profile individuals in our day.

Alex Rodriguez was hailed as one of the all-time great baseball talents until he was caught using performance-enhancing drugs. Lance Armstrong was admired not just for his Tour de France victories but also for his work on behalf of cancer charities. Few celebrities experienced a steeper downfall than when it was proven he had been doping all along. This kind of downfall happens when a CEO turns over the keys to his incompetent son, or the long-time pastor fails to prepare his ministry for his retirement. Legacies and reputations are built over time but are often dismantled quickly. In some cases, reputations are ruined before careers are over. In other cases, legacies get lost after people pass away.

Now what?

If it's true that legacies are dismantled much more easily than they are constructed, what can we do about it? How should we respond? This passage records quite a historical letdown after the righteous reign of King Hezekiah. If he failed to establish a lasting legacy, what hope is there? What can we do to avoid our legacies from being torn down after we are gone? If prioritizing discipleship is important, how might we go about doing that?

Prayer is a great place to start. We need to pray for people to whom we can "pass the baton." We might be pleasantly surprised who God brings across our path when we ask him for these opportunities. On the flip side, young people should also pray for God to provide godly mentors who can help direct and prepare them.

Once those opportunities have presented themselves, a simple combination of *personal relationship* and *proven resources* will allow for this kind of legacy-making discipleship to occur. Each of these parts of the equation are essential to the process. Gifted mentors might be able to exclusively utilize their relational skills to equip their mentees. For the rest of us, we can take advantage of the large amount of books and materials that can help. Of course, one should not fully depend on resources without the personal touch of a relationship.

When it comes to resources, *Respectable Sins* by Jerry Bridges (2007), *Disciplines of a Godly Man* by Kent Hughes (2001), and *The Tech-Wise Family* by Andy Crouch (2017) are recommended. Those works cover different areas and are intended for different audiences. All three are theologically grounded, practically oriented, and offer godly life guidance.

Creativity in Presentation

Anyone who has babysat, parented, or just observed toddlers knows two incontrovertible truths. Toddlers like blocks, and they love to topple whatever construction piece is in front of them. A parent can help them put the pieces together and even follow the directions for a special project. But does the child admire the beauty of this creation? No! It is all negated in mere seconds, given the young child's proclivity to topple stuff.

This is a perfect picture of what happens when these evil kings follow Hezekiah. His son and grandson both demonstrate a depraved proclivity to destroy all the good spiritual progress he made. A video of the above situation or even a live demonstration by the pastor or a child on stage would certainly drive the preaching idea home.

Another illustrative option would be the song "Legacy" by Nichole Nordeman. While the song may not be familiar to contemporary audiences anymore, the lyrics powerfully express the desire to leave the right kind of legacy that pleases God first and foremost.[2]

Under this chapter's "Contemporary Connections" we have emphasized optimistic, positive applications that represent the opposite of the obvious negative implications that stem from 2 Kings 21. The outline below reflects the

---

2   Nichole Nordeman, "Legacy," track 4 on *Woven & Spun*, Ariose Music, 2002, compact disc.

negative tone of the passage itself. We must be aware of how easily things can fall apart. In the end, there is hope that God is still in charge and will not tolerate those who dismantle godly work. Clearly there is a tension here, and there is nothing wrong with letting the audience feel that pull. Both hope and fear can spur us on to faithfully invest in our relationships with others, in order to leave a legacy that isn't quickly dismantled, including disciples who in turn continue to do the same.

The key idea to communicate is that legacies are dismantled much more easily than they are constructed. The passage for this preaching unit can be outlined in the following points:

- Our depravity can quickly ruin positive spiritual growth (21:1–9, 19–22).
- God's consequences can be, but are not always, immediate (21:10–18, 23–26).

DISCUSSION QUESTIONS

1. How specifically did Manasseh roll back the reforms Hezekiah had enacted (21:1–9)?

2. What was God's decision resulting from all these evil acts (21:10–18)?

3. How can we reconcile Manasseh's long reign, his pervasive wickedness, and God's goodness?

4. How does Ammon's rule compare to his father and grandfather (21:19–22)?

5. How does Ammon's reign end (21:23–24)?

6. Who have you seen leave faithful legacies? What allowed some to last, while others didn't?

2 Kings 22:1–23:30

EXEGETICAL IDEA
King Josiah's extensive spiritual reforms throughout the land of Judah and Jerusalem, while intensely focused on pushing the nation back to the Lord, could not sway the determinations of the Lord.

THEOLOGICAL FOCUS
In certain instances, no amount of repentance will alter the determinations of the Lord.

PREACHING IDEA
God's Word is final.

PREACHING POINTERS
Looking back, Judah's exile was inevitable. Even though King Josiah led extensive spiritual reform, it was not enough to avert God's coming judgment on his people for centuries of sin. As the people returned from this exile and studied this history, they would learn a double-sided lesson. Yes, the Babylonian exile was deserved. The nation's continued faithlessness earned that punishment that God had announced. Yet this period also offers a positive lesson, especially to the original audience of Jews returning from exile to resettle their homeland: Josiah's reign is an example to follow as they rebuild their society. His reforms followed God's Word, thus giving the people one final peaceful era before the end came. God's word of judgment could not be avoided, but it served as the template for a good king leading his people in repentance.

It is in that latter lesson where we find points of relevance for our lives today. Is God's Word our template, our compass that guides our lives? When a classmate stumbles upon essays online that fit the assignments for the class we are taking, will we cheat or will we let God's Word determine what we do? Scripture clearly tells us to "pray continually" in all circumstances and situations. Do we? Or do we try to figure out our own solutions to the issues in front of us? Like a fresh-faced cadet following the orders of his drill sergeant, we need to follow God's Word as our final authority in what we say, think, and do.

JOSIAH (22:1–23:30)

LITERARY STRUCTURE AND THEMES (22:1–23:30)

King Josiah is another bright spot in the history of God's people. He was unrivaled in his zeal for purging from Judah any hint of unorthodox worship. From inside the temple to the Judean countryside to the priests involved, even into the territory to the north as far as Bethel, Josiah systematically and violently pushed Judah back to true worship of the Lord. However, his spiritual reforms were ultimately futile, as they did not change the determinations of the Lord—and his untimely death seemed to accelerate that outcome. This section of text breaks down nicely threefold: finding the Torah (22:1–20), futile reforms (23:1–27), and Josiah's tragic death (23:28–30).

- *Finding the Book of the Torah (22:1–20)*
- *Futile Reforms (23:1–27)*
- *Tragic Death (23:28–30)*

EXPOSITION (22:1–23:30)

Josiah is the next great reformer of Judah, and his exploits are detailed in these chapters. His actions were intense, focused, and inspired by Judah's sacred traditions. However, as great as those reforms were, they could not sway the impending judgment. Moreover, the full effect of the reforms were never realized. The account of Josiah's reign ends with his tragic death, which made way for Judah's rapid demise.

Finding the Book of Torah (22:1–20)

The prophetess Huldah verifies that the disaster described in סֵפֶר הַתּוֹרָה would come to pass, but that Josiah would not witness it because of his emphatic response to the words.

22:1–7. After a quick introduction to Josiah's reign (vv. 1–2), where the reader is told that Josiah was installed at eight years old and that he did right in the Lord's sight by living like David and not turning "aside to the right or to the left" (v. 2; cf. Deut. 17:20), the account fast-forwards to his eighteenth year. During that year, the then twenty-six-year-old king dispatched his secretary, Shaphan, to Hilkiah, the priest, with the expressed instruction to appropriate tax revenue directly to the supervisors and their workers facilitating temple renovations (2 Kings 22:4–6). In a move that recalls Jehoash's administrative method during a reform (12:9–16), oversight was cast aside as the workers were honest (בֶּאֱמוּנָה הֵם עֹשִׂים; 22:7).[1]

---

1 When did Josiah institute his reforms? According to Kings, it was during his eighteenth year as king after the book of the Torah was discovered. However, according to 2 Chronicles, his reforms preceded finding the book of the Torah, and began in his twelfth year. Both cannot be true. However, Wray Beal (2014, 502) is certainly on target when she emphasizes that the differences between Chronicles and Kings is linked to each's historiographic intentions. By contextualizing the discussion of Josiah's reforms in the immediate context of finding the book of the Torah, Kings emphasizes Josiah's pious zeal and singular focus to facilitate a spiritual reset for the nation. In fact, a similar rationale can explain the differences in the death account of Josiah. While Chronicles seeks to flesh out the theological reasoning behind such a tragic death vis-à-vis his pious zeal, Kings emphasizes the abruptness of Josiah's death, as it led to the quick demise of the nation.

What Did Hilkiah Find?

The phrase סֵפֶר הַתּוֹרָה is often translated as "the book of the law." Both words individually exhibit very broad semantic ranges, but as a construct chain, the reference is to a collected body of authoritative teaching. Many English translations display a preference for rendering תּוֹרָה as "law," but such a decision imports some restricting connotations.

This phrase appears elsewhere (Deut. 28:61; 29:20; 30:10; 31:26; Josh. 1:8; 8:34; 2 Chron. 34:15; Neh. 8:3), and in each case the phrase refers to an authoritative document that articulated the covenantal ideal governing the relationship between the Lord and his people, including expectations in light of obedience or disobedience. However, many scholars assume that what was read to Josiah was either Deuteronomy or some form of it. Yet Arnold (2020) has shown that the Deuteronomic occurrences of the phrase assumes a widely attested convention that refers to some text-object more than written content. And since all the references cataloged above are influenced by Deuteronomy's occurrences, the most one should say is that the priest found a text-object that was likely very similar to Deuteronomy. We just can't determine with certainty if it was a copy of Deuteronomy.

22:8–13. But interestingly, Hilkiah's documented response has nothing to do with the appropriation of funds or general finances. Rather, it was the revelation that the "book of the Torah" had been discovered (סֵפֶר הַתּוֹרָה). Clearly, the finding of this document is of the utmost concern here, and the shifting of focus from the finances and logistics of the ongoing renovations constitutes a critical development in the account (Cogan and Tadmor 2008, 293; Wray Beal 2014, 502). These verses set the stage for what follows. In other words, highlighting the discovery of an authoritative body of teaching justifies what follows. Thus, Josiah's forthcoming actions transcend any royal decree or simplistic political power play. Instead, his drastic reforms are rooted in divine sanction and authoritative teaching.

Josiah's reaction upon hearing the content of the book of the Torah intensifies the scene. The syntax of verse 11 emphasizes that Josiah's reaction was both immediate and intense, tearing his clothes as the words were being read to him (וַיְהִי כִּשְׁמֹעַ הַמֶּלֶךְ אֶת־דִּבְרֵי סֵפֶר הַתּוֹרָה וַיִּקְרַע אֶת־בְּגָדָיו). Moreover, dispatching his administrative leadership to "go, inquire of the LORD for me" (v. 13), specifically to determine what the content of the document meant for the current state of affairs, adds another layer to the gravity of the situation. A picture is painted of a king shocked into action.

22:14–20. A five-member delegation is dispatched to consult the prophetess Huldah. The wife of Shallum, keeper of the wardrobe (שֹׁמֵר הַבְּגָדִים), she is also described as a נְבִיאָה, which is the feminine form of the *terminus technicus* for a prophet. Huldah, therefore, was a recognized prophet who lived inside the city, likely in the western portion that had been enclosed by Hezekiah (Sweeney 2007, 445). Moreover, her husband may have been a priest related to the prophet Jeremiah (cf. Jer. 32:7). More interestingly, that she is the only female prophet mentioned in Kings raises the question of why Judean leadership would have consulted her. It's hard to know definitively, but Cogan and Tadmor (2008, 283) raise an interesting possibility when they cite Neo-Assyrian oracles of salvation uttered by women in the courts of Assyrian kings. Sweeney (2007, 445) cites rabbinical interpretations that voice a similar opinion. Could it be that Judean leadership sought out Huldah because they believed her utterance would be a more positive understanding of the text just read? If so, the delegation was unquestionably disappointed. Huldah's oracle is explicit—both negative and positive. The disasters referenced in סֵפֶר הַתּוֹרָה were coming (v. 16) precisely because of Judah's religious apostasy

(v. 17). The only redeeming value in this situation was that Josiah would not witness the tragedy. Huldah prophesies that he would die and see his kingdom peacefully passed to his successor because of his reaction to the reading of the סֵפֶר הַתּוֹרָה (v. 19). Yet, as we shall see, this prophecy will raise some theological questions.

Futile Reforms (23:1–27)

While Josiah's reforms were intense and comprehensive, they were ultimately futile as they could not deter imminent divine judgment.

23:1–3. Verses 1–3 constitute the introduction for one of the more memorable chapters in the Old Testament: Josiah's great, but short-lived, reform. Central to this introduction is the covenantal ceremony that involved the entire country. According to these verses, elders, priests, all the people—from the least to the greatest—not only observed the covenantal ritual but sanctioned it (v. 3). Such a notation is important, for while specific details about the ceremony are withheld, Josiah's reforms sought to embrace even leadership structure held over from pre-monarchical times (Cogan and Tadmor 2008, 284; Sweeney 2007, 446). Nevertheless, the reader should not dwell here, but rather proceed with the chapter's flow. There will be details when recounting the reforms, for that is the passage's focus. What follows is a communal endeavor that is exhaustive in its focus, not merely the pious zealotry of just one man (Winslow 2017, 262).

In addition, there is a crucial sequence established by these verses. The reforms are instituted after Huldah's oracle, which has clearly revealed impending judgment. Thus, the impression is created of a king whose commitment to installing the Lord's sanctioned way of life at the national level will not be swayed.

23:4–20. All the actions recounted in verses 4–20 must be understood in terms of centralization, a governmental prerogative that reached well beyond Jerusalem. Moreover, according to verses 15–20, Josiah's reformations went past the borders of Judah into what used to be Israelite territory. Verses 19–20 recount how Josiah targeted the shrines and high places of Samaria, and verses 15–18 detail how the king fixated on Jeroboam I's altar in Bethel. In both cases, those inappropriate worship centers were desecrated and violently destroyed. In the case of Samaria, verse 20 reveals how Josiah "sacrificed" (זבח) the priests associated with the sites. Indeed, this is a violent image, but it should be understood as proof of Josiah's zeal and awareness of how problematic the religious influences of the north have been. Moreover, it places Josiah in line with Elijah, who slaughtered the prophets of Baal in the wake of the Mount Carmel showdown (1 Kings 18:40).

Josiah's intensely violent reforms were also comprehensive. Verses 4–11 offer a laundry list of desecration aimed at people, places, and instruments of worship condemned by Deuteronomy. Illicit priests, whether idolatrous or illegitimate (הַכְּמָרִים [v. 5]; הַכֹּהֲנִים [v. 8]), all over Judah were disposed of authority. Vessels of Asherah and Baal were burned in the Kidron Valley outside Jerusalem. Pagan statues were taken from the temple, pulverized into dust, and then cast to the wind over known burial sites—another sign of complete desecration. Josiah even defiled the Topheth, the place where people "would make a son or a daughter pass through fire as an offering to Molech" (v. 10). Not even animals were exempt, as the king removed valuable horses from service because they were dedicated to astral deities. Yet Josiah's reforms also specifically targeted the influence of a few kings in particular. In addition to Jeroboam's legacy by means of the altar at Bethel (vv. 15–18), Solomon (v. 15) as well as Manasseh and Ahaz (v. 12) are specifically referenced. Such specificity suggests a perception that the reigns of these three Judean kings constituted critical junctures in the spiritual corruption of Judean society.

All things considered, Josiah's reforms were both symbolic and practical. Symbolically, they targeted important hubs and focal points of apostate activity. However, such strategic warfare would have been futile if it were not for the systematic disruption and deconstruction of religious infrastructure. The desecration of locations, the removal of authority, and the displacement of priests and officials accomplished this. The result was a total spiritual reset for Judah. Yet interestingly, there are important anecdotes that appear in the midst of an otherwise intense series of events.

First, verse 9 reveals that some priests "ate unleavened bread among their kindred." This suggests that Josiah's reforms were not without some form of grace. The illegitimate priests were not necessarily killed (as were some at Samaria) but could be allowed to resume a place among their kin. Second, in the process of defiling Jeroboam's worship precinct at Bethel, Josiah's men discovered the grave of the unnamed prophet who predicted the demise of that sanctuary before his untimely death (1 Kings 13:1–34). His grave was spared any desecration. Therefore, while violent, Josiah's reforms manifested a certain degree of perspective.

Neco

Pharaoh Neco, or Neco II, was a member of the (twenty-sixth Egyptian) Saite dynasty. He ruled from 609 to 595 BCE, which represented a time of complicated Egyptian resurgence when the Neo-Assyrian empire was retracting. Eventually, to combat the surge of the Media/Babylonian alliance, Neco sided with Assyria.

While there are biblical, Mesopotamian, and Greek sources that speak to his reign, no Egyptian sources exist. Nevertheless, there is enough to (generally) reconstruct Neco's geopolitical role during the final decade of the seventh century. He seems to have been a significant player in the region. He engaged in infrastructure repair, fostered trade relations with the Greeks, orchestrated periodic raids into Syria-Palestine, and even dictated regime changes. As mentioned in kings, he deposed Jehoahaz in favor of a king who would be more favorable to Egyptian ambitions. Moreover, according to Mesopotamian sources Neco was integral in delaying the eventual Babylonian occupation of Syria-Palestine (Higginbotham, 2006–9, 4:247; Hobbs, 1992).

23:21–23. The catalog of reforms pauses at verse 21 to recount the Passover celebration. The brevity in the Kings account is expanded by the Chronicler (2 Chron. 35:1–19), but 2 Kings 23:21–23 does enough to establish the Passover as a central feature in Josiah's reforms and that the fervency of Josiah's celebration set him apart. According to verse 22, "No such Passover had been kept since the days of the judges who judged Israel, even during all the days of the kings of Israel and of the kings of Judah." Moreover, as a national celebration mandated by Pentateuchal legislation (Exod. 12:1–20; 23:14–19; 34:18–26; Num. 9:1–14; Deut. 16:1–8), the celebration functioned in support of Josiah's nationalistic reassertions. Yet the reader must not forget that the Passover is not the focal point of the larger presentation (*contra* Winslow 2017, 267). Because it disrupts the flow of the catalog of reforms it should be understood more as a historical anecdote that further defines Josiah's superiority as the paradigmatic Judean king.

23:24–27. The catalog of reforms resumes in verse 24, where it's declared that Josiah expelled all the sources of unsanctioned divination. Importantly, this expulsion is linked syntactically (לְמַעַן) to the king's obedience to the book of the Torah found by Hilkiah. Moreover, such syntax suggests that the phrase "so that he established the words of the law that were written in the book that the priest Hilkiah had found in the house of the LORD" (v. 24) functions as a final statement for the entire catalog of reforms. Each individual action has been working toward a specific outcome—the establishment of a way of life defined by the Lord's authoritative teaching.

Verse 25 offers an explicit statement of incomparability inspired by Deuteronomy's *Shema* (Deut. 6:4), implying that Josiah sits alone atop of the echelon of Judean kings: "Before him there was no king like him, who turned to the LORD with all his heart, with all his soul, and with all his might, according to all the law of Moses; nor did any like him arise after him." Tragically, however, such praise is immediately tempered by one of the most intense statements of divine rejection found in the Old Testament. Consequently, the account does not let the reader revel in Josiah's success. In 2 Kings 23:26–27, the reader is reminded not only of imminent judgment that lay on the horizon, but also that the Lord stands to reject (מאס) his people—a statement that is intensified by the memory the Lord's choice of Jerusalem, the establishment of Jerusalem as the place of the name, and shameful comparison to Israel (v. 27).

Tragic Death (23:28–30)
Josiah's tragic death halts his promising reforms and inaugurates a rapid decline toward the Babylonian exile.

23:28–30. The account of Josiah's reign ends with a brief account of his ignominious death. The Chronicler also recounts the king's death, but with more

The Death of King Josiah by Antonio Zanchi. Public domain.

explanation (2 Chron. 35:20–36:1). However, the brevity of the account in Kings is the point. The fact that the reader is simply told that Josiah met Pharaoh Neco (וַיֵּלֶךְ . . . לִקְרָאתוֹ) and was killed by him at Megiddo, and the further fact that the reader is not told why Josiah confronted Neco nor about the details of the confrontation—only that the royal servants took the corpse of Josiah from Megiddo to Jerusalem, where he was buried in his tomb (2 Kings 23:28)—prevents the reader from lingering.

The Chronicler's account contains more detail, including the reason behind Neco's march, why Josiah confronted the Egyptian, and even why and how Josiah died. This is not surprising. The Kings account produces historical and theological questions that crave answers, and so it's logical that the Chronicler attempts to answer them. Yet fundamental to the Chronicler's pursuit for clarification is a question of compatibility. Simply, is Josiah's death compatible with the prophecies presented to him by Huldah (cf. 2 Kings 22:16–20)? The prophetess anticipated on the one hand that the king would not see the forecasted judgment. Certainly, this element of the prophecy is compatible with the Kings account. Yet the circumstances surrounding Josiah's death seem to contradict the prophesied gathering of the king to his ancestors in peace (cf. 2 Kings 22:20). To be sure, this is a difficulty that is not easily explained, and the nature of the Chronicler's account proves the community's struggle with it. Yet if one recognizes the relative peace of Josiah's reign and the peaceful transition to his son Jehoahaz (23:30), as well as the fact that his body was returned to Jerusalem, one can see the success of Huldah's oracle. Nevertheless, it must be emphasized that the main function of Josiah's tragic death in the context of Kings is to show that it inaugurated a rapid decline that would ultimately end in Jerusalem's sacking and the deportation of the Judean populace.

THEOLOGICAL FOCUS

The exegetical idea (King Josiah's extensive spiritual reforms throughout the land of Judah and Jerusalem, while intensely focused on pushing the nation back to the Lord, could not sway the determinations of the Lord) leads to this theological focus: In certain instances, no amount of repentance will alter the determinations of the Lord.

Wray Beal (2014, 500) has argued that chapters 22–23 are organized in a chiastic pattern, featuring the reforms of Josiah.

Regnal summary (22:1–2)
　Discovery and response to the book of the Torah (22:3–20)
　　Ceremony (23:1–3)
　　　Reforms (23:4–20)
　　Ceremony (23:21–23)
　Final notation of response to the book of the Torah (23:24)
Regnal summary (23:25–30)

While the chiasm is not precise, it does rightly emphasize that Josiah's reforms are the focal point of the chapters. And given a precedent within Kings to highlight the appeasement of judgment in light of repentance (e.g., Hezekiah's reforms in 2 Kings 18–20), one would logically hope that the judgment pronounced by Huldah would be modified. Yet, this is not what happens. Rather, the account ends with one of the most emphatic statements of rejection in the Old Testament. In other words, there is a palpable irony in these chapters. Josiah's intense reforms are ultimately remembered for their futility.

Consequently, Strand Winslow (2017, 269–70) is surely correct to point out the canonical awkwardness of this passage, particularly when one considers the role of repentance in Jesus's messages. She ultimately, and properly, states, "For Josiah, doing God's will was the reward in itself. May he be a model for us all" (270). Yet perhaps an equally important lesson is to realize that sometimes the interplay between humanity and God is one-directional. Much has been said in this commentary that Kings acknowledges a mysterious interplay between the determinations of the Lord and humanity's choices in the context of history. But here one sees that in certain circumstances even the most pious actions cannot sway the Lord's determinations. The die has been cast—a lesson intimately experienced by Jeremiah when he was commanded not to intercede on behalf of Judah (Jer. 7:6; 11:14).

PREACHING AND TEACHING STRATEGIES

Exegetical and Theological Synthesis

King Josiah leads widespread repentance in the kingdom of Judah. He ushers in societal reforms and a renewed commitment by the people to the covenant. Sadly, his positive example is a last gasp for God's people before the exile. Too much damage had been done, and God had given them many "second chances." Judgment was about to arrive in the form of Babylon.

God's word is the last word. Sometimes he extends grace. But not all consequences can be avoided. A teacher may overlook one instance of tardiness. If it turns into a pattern, no amount of apologizing will allow the guilty student to sidestep their punishment. The class rules cannot be disregarded. Likewise, God was compelled to discipline his people so that they would understand the seriousness of their perpetual rebellion.

Preaching Idea

God's Word is final.

Contemporary Connections

What does it mean?

What does it mean that God's Word is final? There is a double meaning to this passage's central idea. God's Word is final in that his announced judgment is unavoidable. God's Word is final also in the sense that it is the final authority for the spiritual reform Josiah initiates. Not only are there two sides to that idea, but they offer a pretty stark contrast to each other.

As referenced earlier, Josiah's story evokes the common debate over divine determinism and humanity's free will. The author of Kings indicates that there is a limit to how much we can change or effect certain outcomes. So given that conclusion, are Josiah's reforms drained of all meaning and importance because they didn't prevent the exile? Not necessarily. He certainly made a difference within his generation, and was given high marks for it.

This reminds us that doing the right thing is still important—even if it does not alter the course of history. The oft-tardy student ought to still come to class on time even if detention awaits them at the end of the week. They do it not just to avoid worse consequences but also realizing it is part of their personal maturing process. The employee who finds out they have a pink slip coming can still honor God and their employer by faithfully carrying out their duties until the end. God's Word should still be final even when His word is final and the results are set.

Is it true?

Is it true that God's Word is final? The hit Broadway musical *Hamilton* features a number of powerful themes in its retelling of the life of American founding father Alexander Hamilton. One of the main conclusions is captured in the song "Who Lives, Who Dies, Who Tells Your Story." The song (in George Washington's voice, later joined on the chorus) opens by lamenting the lack of control we have in how we are remembered and how our legacies live on.[2] The

---

2   L. Miranda, "Who Lives, Who Dies, Who Tells Your Story," *Hamilton: An American Musical*, track 46, Atlantic Records, 2015, compact disc.

song recognizes that history is usually written by those who survive and come out on top. It laments that as much as we may try, we do not have full control over the narrative of our lives.

While some may question or even deny that God is in control of human history, Scripture demonstrates again and again that God is orchestrating earthly events toward his divine purposes. He is the one who gets to tell The Story. His approval and his will should be what matters most to us (see Matt. 10:26–28). It is his evaluation that matters. God's Word is final and he will have the final word.

Now what?

If it's true that God's Word is final, how should we respond to outcomes or trajectories that seem inevitable today? Given that God's Word is final, should we retreat into robotic passivity if we have no say in matters? Of course not. To borrow a much-used statement, "When the Bible is clear, be clear. When it is silent, be silent." I (Lee) would even add—"and be charitable in between."

We should *be clear when God's Word is clear*. Interpretive issues can certainly muddy the waters at times. That should not distract us from what is obviously and consistently stated in Scripture. There is no ambiguity on issues like stealing, drunkenness, helping the poor, or even the centrality of faith in Jesus Christ.

Yet to *be silent when the Bible is silent* is likewise important. Issues such as what retailers a person shops at, music preferences, and Bible translations are all outside the purview of direct statements of Scripture. Biblical principles need to inform our choices. But we cannot declare God's will to be on a certain side of an issue when it is not addressed in the text.[3]

This is where the additional statement *be charitable in between* comes into play. God's Word is final, and in places like Romans 14–15, it directly tells us to accept and love each other when we have differences. It is unfortunate when we do not live into that calling. The "Worship Wars" that marked many Western churches in the late twentieth century caused much division because people insisted on their preferences over the essentials of unity, love, and charity.

Creativity in Presentation

"If the world was ending tomorrow, how you would spend today?" While on the surface that is a morbid question, it is an effective icebreaker that people often give interesting and entertaining answers to. It is a perfect lead-in to this passage. You might ask people in your audience that question or even record a "man on the street" interview and play the video in your service, revealing the answers that members of the general public gave.

The people of Judah living through this part of history were about to have their world end, figuratively and literally. Judgment hung over King Josiah and his kingdom, and they were directly confronted with it when they discovered God's Law in the temple. How did they respond? They responded with repentance and spiritual reformation.

Following the major units as we have outlined above in the exegetical section, three key points emerge related to God's Word being final. It is the final *solution* for Josiah who is trying to renovate and rebuild his city. It is the final *authority* that determines the direction and nature of the reforms. It is the final *destiny* for the people—and ultimately all people.

The key idea to communicate is that God's Word is final. The passage for this preaching unit can be outlined as follows:

---

3   See this blog article for additional wisdom on this idea: Wes McAdams, "Speak Where the Bible Speaks; Be Silent Where the Bible Is Silent," RadicallyChristian.com, December 23, 2015, accessed August 11, 2020, https://radicallychristian.com/speak-where-the-bible-speaks-be-silent-where-the-bible-is-silent.

- God's Word is the final *solution* for those seeking true success (22:1–20).
- God's Word is the final *authority* for those who seek to please God (23:1–27).
- God's Word is the final *destiny* for humanity who must submit to their Creator (22:14–20; 23:28–30).

DISCUSSION QUESTIONS

1. How does Josiah's focus change after they find the book of the Law in the temple (22:1–13)?

2. What significance is there that the king's delegation seeks out the prophetess Huldah to better understand the Law and God's will (22:14–20)?

3. What actions did Josiah take to demonstrate his loyalty to the Lord (23:4–20)?

4. What are some ways we can follow that example in our lives?

5. Second Kings 23:24–27 describes some distinct contrasts between Josiah's faithfulness and the Lord's decision to punish Judah. What does this tell us about Judah's history of failures?

6. What lessons about God and his Word do we learn from King Josiah's life?

THE END (23:31–25:30)

The third and final section of the third major literary unit in Kings is 2 Kings 23:31–25:30, which describes the end—namely, the fall of Jerusalem to Babylon. This third section features one preaching unit to conclude, which is due to the fast pace and connectedness of the narrative.

2 Kings 23:31–25:30

EXEGETICAL IDEA

The dethronement of King Jehoahaz plunged Judah into a turbulent period defined by new suzerains, rebellion, political gambling, and a tragic end in exile, yet the release of Jehoiachin from prison presented hope.

THEOLOGICAL FOCUS

The hope represented at the end of Kings manifests the grace of God.

PREACHING IDEA

The hope of God still flickers in our darkest days.

PREACHING POINTERS

Even as the tragic end of Judah is vividly depicted, the author of Kings leaves his readers with the faintest glimmer of hope. A king still lives. He is a vassal of a foreign empire, but one who enjoys a modicum of honor and favor. His status is symbolic of the people corporately. While they have been forcefully subjected to a foreign power, they would eventually emerge from their darkest days with their national identity intact. The flicker of hope that Jehoiachin represents would turn into a full-blown flame as God would restore his people to their land.

Since the earliest settlers and the later founding of our nation, Christians have enjoyed a great amount of privilege and freedom in the United States of America. There have not been many prolonged "dark days" for Christians in the West. We can learn a lot from our brothers and sisters in other contexts in this sense. They have much to teach us about holding on to hope, no matter the darkness. We should also be able to relate to this on a personal level. When a health crisis hits and the medical bills pile up, where do we find hope? There are few days as dark as when a marriage falls apart. Christians are also not immune to stressing over political developments. What if churches lost their tax-exempt status? What if our religious freedoms were taken away by the government? Trials have a way of exposing where our hope lies. And if it is set on Christ, we can be confident that we will not be disappointed.

THE FALL OF JERUSALEM TO BABYLON
(23:31–25:30)

LITERARY STRUCTURE AND THEMES
(23:31–25:30)

Jerusalem finally falls, but the lead-up to that moment is not simple. In the span of approximately twenty years, Judah will go through four kings and be under the influence of one regional power and one empire. However, despite the geopolitical mess, hope remains. Thus, the fall of Jerusalem, the Lord's chosen place, is a tragedy that is tempered by grace of God.

In this subunit of the final chapters of Kings, the historical account comes to a dramatic end. The final kings are recounted in rapid succession as the text builds toward a fairly detailed account of Jerusalem's sacking. In addition, events subsequent to Jerusalem's sacking are briefly recounted, including a cryptic notification that Jehoiachin is released from prison. This section can be subdivided according to the final kings of Judah, as follows:

- *Jehoahaz (23:31–35)*
- *Jehoaikim (23:36–24:7)*
- *Jehoiachin (24:8–17)*
- *Zedekiah and the End (24:18–25:26)*
- *The Release of Jehoiachin (25:27–30)*

EXPOSITION (23:31–25:30)

The final decades of Judah were a whirlwind. Kings were deposed and policies were dictated by major political powers, all with the haunting realization that the end was coming. Moreover, the demise of the final Judean king happens with a painful echo to the book of Joshua. Zedekiah is caught and led off to exile on the same plains across which Israel marched when they came to take the Promised Land centuries earlier.

Nevertheless, the book ends with the release of Jehoiachin, who had been exiled in 597 BCE.

Jehoahaz (23:31–35)

The dethronement of Jehoahaz plunges Judah into a turbulent geopolitical context.

23:31–35. Jehoahaz, whose original name was apparently Shallum (Jer. 22:11) and was not the oldest of Josiah's sons, is remembered for two things: (1) he did evil in the sight of the Lord, failing to secure anything close to the positive evaluation of his father (23:32); and (2) he was deposed by Neco during his third month of rule. According to the Kings, Neco first imprisoned Jehoahaz in Riblah in the land of Hamath, which was a well-known administrative center used by several forces during their military campaigns through Syria-Palestine (Cogan and Tadmor 2008, 303); and then in Egypt, where he later died (v. 34). The reason for Neco's regime change is almost certainly linked to Jehoahaz's older brother "being a complaisant and accommodating vassal" (Honeyman 1948, 18). Originally named Eliakim, he was enthroned by Neco and promptly given the name Jehoiakim. According to verse 35, Jehoiakim capitulated to Egyptian demands and taxed the land and the people of the land in order to accommodate Egypt's hegemonic burden, although he was apparently engaging in a dubious building campaign at the same time (Jer. 22:13–19).

Jehoiakim (23:36–24:7)

When Babylon assumes control over Syria-Palestine, Judah becomes a Judean vassal.

Eventually they rebel and are invaded by Babylon, which is presented as a mechanism of judgment.

23:36–24:7. Jehoiakim's reign lasted eleven years, and he is remembered negatively. He did evil "just as all his ancestors had done" (23:37). However, his reign is remembered more for the imperialistic shift that occurred. In the years subsequent to the Battle of Carchemish (605 BCE), Babylon had taken control of Syria-Palestine, effectively establishing Judah as a Babylonian vassal. For three years Judah and Jehoiakim functioned as faithful vassals, but they eventually rebelled (24:1) under the influence of Egypt and the results of an Egyptian/Babylonian conflict along the coastal plain. Naturally, this rebellion incurred the wrath of the Babylonian Empire and its king Nebuchadnezzar. So, in the third year of Jehoiakim's reign, the Babylonian army moved toward Jerusalem to engage in its first siege of the Judean capital. Jehoiakim, however, would die before the siege began, handing the throne to his son Jehoiachin.

The invasion of Babylon, which included the help of the Arameans, Moabites, and Ammonites as Babylonian vassals (24:2), is presented as divine judgment. The Lord is the subject of 2 Kings 24:2, and the expressed purpose of the action was to "destroy" Judah (אבד) in fulfillment of the prophetic word uttered in response to "the sins of Manasseh" and the innocent blood that Manasseh spilled (24:3). Consequently, one begins to see how the legacy of Manasseh dictates the contours of history. The threat that has been lingering on the horizon is now coming into full view.

Nebuchadnezzar

Nebuchadnezzar was the oldest son of Nabopolassar, considered the founder of the Neo-Babylonian Empire. Before becoming king, Nebuchadnezzar proved himself a very effective general, in particular at Carchemish in 605 BCE,

when he secured the defeat of the Egyptian/Assyrian alliance. He became king when his father died while he was away projecting Babylonian ambitions.

While named after Nebuchadnezzar I (ca. 1100 BCE), Nebuchadnezzar saw himself in the likeness of Hammurabi. He had great imperialistic ambitions, subjecting the peripheries of his empire to crippling polices for the benefit of Babylon.

In 598–97, he subjected Jerusalem to a first siege, eventually forcing the city to surrender in March of 597. About a decade later, Nebuchadnezzar sieged Jerusalem again in response to Zedekiah's rebellion. In the summer of 586, Jerusalem was overrun again, but this time the city and temple were destroyed and the vast majority of the remaining populace was exiled (Roberts 2006–9, 4:245–46).

Jehoiachin (24:8–17)

Nebuchadnezzar's first siege resulted in the exile of the royal family, the best of Judean society, and the installation of another vassal king.

24:8–17. Similar to Jehoahaz, Jehoiachin reigned only three months before he was deposed by a foreign king. Moreover, he is also evaluated negatively. However, Jehoiachin is deposed in the context of a siege, which happened in 597. According to verse 12, Jehoiachin "gave himself up" along with the totality of his court. It is unclear how long the siege lasted, but it's clear that Jehoiachin was exiled to Babylon in the eighth year of Nebuchadnezzar's reign, fulfilling Jeremiah's prophecy against him (Jer. 22:24–27).

Along with personnel, Nebuchadnezzar relieved Jerusalem of its treasures, not only from the royal residence but also from the temple—from the instruments of worship to artisans and craftspeople to warriors to the elite of the land and beyond. According to verse 14, "no one remained, except the poorest people of the land."

Surely this is a rhetorical exaggeration, but the intention is clear enough. Nebuchadnezzar sought to enact a stiff penalty that would simultaneously cripple Judean society and suffocate any further thought of insurrection. In an attempt to ensure this, Jehoiachin's uncle Mattaniah, who was renamed Zedekiah, was installed as a vassal king (v. 17).

Zedekiah and the End (24:18–25:26)
Zedekiah's reign brings the occupation of the Promised Land to a tragic end.

24:18–25:26. The account of Zedekiah's reign is defined by its echoes with other portions of Kings. On the one hand, so many of the experiences of the kings subsequent to Josiah were experienced by Zedekiah. Like Jehoiakim, he reigned eleven years but rebelled against Babylon under the influence of Egypt (23:36; 24:1 vs. 24:18–20). Like Jehoahaz, Zedekiah was eventually taken to Riblah to face condemnation by a superior king, although Jehoahaz faced Neco the Egyptian, whereas Zedekiah faced Nebuchadnezzar of Babylon (23:33 vs. 25:6). The exiles of both Jehoiachin and Zedekiah were punctuated by a deportation of the populace and the leaving of the poorest of Judean society (24:13–16 vs. 25:7, 12). Yet there are other echoes as well. The descriptions of how the Babylonians plundered the temple (24:13–17) "parallels" the vivid details of the temple's construction in 1 Kings 6–7 (Strand Winslow 2017, 280), symbolically demonstrating that the Lord has removed any semblance of protection. More precisely, the looting of the temple suggests that Jerusalem could no longer be understood as the cosmic center of the universe—a reality also communicated by the fact that this event represented the seventh time a king entered the temple to remove its treasures (Leithart 2006, 274).

There is another echo—more subtle, but discernible—when one considers where Zedekiah was finally overtaken by the Babylonian army after fleeing through a gate near the royal precinct (25:4). According to 2 Kings 25:5, Zedekiah was abandoned by his army and captured on the plains of Jericho (עַרְבוֹת יְרֵחוֹ), which is the general location of Israel's entrance into the Promised Land. The reader, therefore, is invited to make a connection back to the earliest period of Israel's occupation and realize that the community has failed. Their final king flees for his life and is finally taken captive by the Lord's instrument of judgment at the place where Israel entered the land. The Lord's people were promised that covenantal faithfulness would translate into keeping the Promised Land. Yet because the country and its leadership failed to honor the covenant, they flee by the same direction in which they entered.

Kings presents the sacking of Jerusalem with a fair amount of detail, likely due to the historian's reliance upon personal testimony and official records. The siege that preceded the razing of the city lasted approximately one and a half years, and it ended when a breach was made in the wall (25:4). In turn, much of the city fled, with the royal administration fleeing by way of a gate between the walls near the king's garden. By the end of the siege, Kings also notes that the famine was severe (25:3), and that the Babylonian army pursued the fleeing Judeans as they scattered in all directions (25:4–5). Zedekiah's family was eventually killed in front of him just before his eyes were gouged out (25:7). Thus, the final Judean king was taken into exile a maimed and shamed man. At the hands of Nebuzaradan, whose title paranomastically means "chief slaughterer" (Strand Winslow 2017, 280), the city was systematically burned, the walls destroyed, and a majority of the populace deported (25:8–11). And in the process of all of this, a relatively small group of important officials were executed at Riblah, perhaps in response to some undescribed zealotry or as a deterrent (25:18–21; Wiseman 2008, 335).

In the aftermath of this, Nebuchadnezzar appointed Gedaliah, the grandson of Josiah's secretary Shaphan (22:3), as the top political leader over the people who remained in Judah (v. 22). While the original Hebrew does not specific the role of Gedaliah—merely stating that Nebuchadnezzar appointed (פקד) him over the people that remained—it's clear that he was appointed because of his willingness to toe the Babylonian line. According to 2 Kings 25:23, the other communal leaders assembled at Mizpah, just north of Jerusalem, where Gedaliah exhorted them to "not be afraid because of the Chaldean officials; live in the land, serve the king of Babylon, and it shall be well with you." However, such exhortation fell on deaf ears. In the seventh month of his tenure, a group of ten, led by Ishmael of the royal family, conspired and assassinated Nebuchadnezzar's chosen leader. Such an action may have ridded the community of Gedaliah, but it produced another exodus toward Egypt out of fear of Babylonian retaliation (cf. Jer. 41–43). Indeed, a poetic ending to a national tragedy. The Lord's people were led out of Egypt, only to flee back to Egypt out of fear (Strand Winslow 2017, 282).

The Release of Jehoiachin (25:27–30)
Jehoiachin's release from prison and favorable position in the Babylonian court symbolizes an unrealized and undefined hope for the Lord's people.

25:27–30. Kings ends with a historical notification. At the very end of his thirty-seventh year of exile, Jehoiachin was released from prison by the Babylonian king Evil-Merodach during the king's ascension year. Evil-Merodach corresponds to Amel-Marduk, who was the son and successor of Nebuchadnezzar (Cogan and Tadmor 2008, 328). Interestingly, Kings recounts the favorable disposition between Jehoiachin and Evil-Merodach. The Babylonian king restored Jehoiachin (literally "lifted the head of

Jehoiachin"; נָשָׂא...אֶת־רֹאשׁ יְהוֹיָכִין), spoke kindly to him, and gave him a seat next to the other kings in Babylon. Consequently, the Judean king symbolically changed out of his prison garb and dined regularly with the Babylonian king, even receiving a "regular allowance" (אֲרֻחַת תָּמִיד) of provisions. Many scholars are even of the opinion that this historical reality is preserved in the Babylonian record (Alstola 2019, 58–78).

Ultimately, the interpretive question that must be answered is whether this notification is merely there for historical purposes or whether it is indicative of something else. Is this merely the historian recognizing a fact of history? Or, is the historian ending the historical work with a note of undefined hope? I (David) am of the opinion that it's the latter.

THEOLOGICAL FOCUS
The exegetical idea (The dethronement of King Jehoahaz plunged Judah into a turbulent period defined by new suzerains, rebellion, political gambling, and a tragic end in exile, yet the release of Jehoiachin from prison presented hope) leads to this theological focus: The hope represented at the end of Kings manifests the grace of God.

The emotion and tension of the final chapters in Kings is palpable. The reader knows that the Lord has taken his hand of protection away from his people, and as each new Judean king is met with more complications, the reader also wonders what may have been going through the mind of God. At this point, the prophets, namely Jeremiah and Habakkuk, are instructive. Both prophets ministered in the final years of Judah, and both prophets reveal a divine disposition that is very matter-of-fact. Habakkuk is told that judgment is imminent, though maybe not immediate. Jeremiah is told that any intercession will be futile. Instead, both prophets are to focus their messages upon the facts of history—judgment is coming.

Yet among these prophets, hope is not dead. Jeremiah, for example, emphasizes the future beyond the exile. He is told to purchase land as a symbol of restoration (Jer. 32:1–15). He speaks of a righteous branch (33:14–26), a new covenant (31:31–34), and more. Habakkuk speaks hopefully about the future when he faithfully declares that he will rejoice in the Lord as his salvation and strength despite his society collapsing around him (Hab. 3:17–19). Consequently, the final lesson of Kings is simple, but very profound: there is still grace and provision; there is still hope, even when the people of the Lord maneuver themselves into a corner where the Lord has no choice but to permit the full force of judgment to fall.

PREACHING AND TEACHING STRATEGIES

Exegetical and Theological Synthesis
Like dominoes falling one right after the other, the last kings of Judah give way to one another as Babylon threatens then invades their land. They each try their best to remain on the throne, but one after another fails to prevent what God had declared to be certain. After all the conflict and destruction, a short note of positive news ends the historical account: Jehoiachin is released from Babylonian prison and given favorable standing in the royal court.

This judgment was never the ultimate end for God's people. He was not going to abandon them during or after their exile. Hope was never lost and it will never be lost. We may have to deal with the consequences of our own actions—or the actions of others in some cases. The hope of Christ's return should be enough to guide us through any dark time, whether it be personal or societal.

Preaching Idea
The hope of God still flickers in our darkest days.

Contemporary Connections

What does it mean?
What does it mean that the hope of God still flickers in our darkest days? With God there is hope. We can know that the hope of God still flickers because our hope is in our faithful God. He has promised us that "his mercies never come to an end; they are new every morning" (Lam. 3:22–23) and that "my grace is sufficient for you, for my power is made perfect in weakness" (2 Cor. 12:9). Even if the short-term outlook is bleak, our long-term hope is sure.

In October 2011, Theo Epstein signed on to be the president of baseball operations for the Chicago Cubs baseball organization. The Cubs had a well-earned reputation as "lovable losers" and always seemed to find a way to fail even when on the brink of success. As Epstein took over, the franchise was in pitiful shape, with a bad major league team and little talent in the minor league pipeline. From the beginning, Theo and his team set out on a long-term rebuild that would see worse results before it got better. Eventually savvy trades, wise drafting, and an immense amount of patience paid off. In 2015 they made the National League playoffs, and the next year they won their first World Series in 108 years. Throughout the five-year process, there were many losses and disappointments. Those provided plenty of opportunities for doubters and critics to take their shots. Soon enough, players began emerging, improvement occurred, and hope began to grow. All along the way, Epstein preached patience and confidence in the team's vision. Hope was a mere flicker early on, but it paid off in the end.

Is it true?
Is it true that the hope of God still flickers in our darkest days? It may not seem like it some days, but Scripture informs and encourages us to answer with a resolute, "Absolutely!" God's revealed plan in His Word has an unmistakable

ending. Jesus is the hope of the world, and all who commit to him in faith will not be disappointed.

Passages like this one point us ahead to Revelation 21–22, which describe for us how we have a new creation coming. No matter how harsh or difficult our current reality is, the future is still bright. Disease cannot extinguish it; death cannot bury it. Trials will come, Satan may seek to discourage us, and our kingdoms may fall. But we have a Savior who has conquered the grave and defeated our enemies for us. We do not have to fear dark days; God's hope remains for all in Christ.

Now what?

If it's true that the hope of God still flickers in our darkest days, what can we do in response to what may be the darkest days of our culture and times? The final chapters of 2 Kings contain the final record of the unraveling of the nation of Israel as represented by the kingdom of Judah. Their society is upended, their security overthrown. Their people have been killed, deported, or left in misery. Only the releasing of a former king in the foreign capital is offered to symbolize the potential of hope for the future.

No one would ever choose for their nation to be conquered. No one would ever choose to receive a cancer diagnosis. There is never a "good time" for a loved one to pass away. Businesses institute layoffs. Investment markets crash. Dark days come in many forms, and the people of God are not exempt from them. Thankfully, our hope and confidence are not founded on those temporary things. Even if our hope seems small, we can be steadfast as long as it is fixed on the enduring promises of our Creator, who directs history toward his redemptive purpose.

With that in mind, what can we do? For starters, *never give up hope*. We do not have to force ourselves to "be happy" at all times. Instead, we can hold on to hope by letting our long-term perspective guide our short-term emotions. We can encourage others with our hope too, even if it is faint. Those who are hurting or struggling with despair need to hear that God loves them, and they need to see it through our compassionate service too. Hosting a baby shower for the new single mom can be that kind of compassionate service. Even just providing a dish for a funeral meal can offer the blessing of hope to those who are hurting.

It is also important that we *never tire of doing good*. Even if hope seems lost, there is value in doing what's right. The film *A Hidden Life* (directed by Terrence Malick, 2019) portrays the true story of Franz Jägerstätter. Franz was a simple Austrian farmer who refused to fight for the Nazis in World War II because of his Christian beliefs. His life didn't alter the course of history, but the film makes a powerful case for the significance of remaining committed to righteousness no matter what. We should always seek to do what is right even when it "won't change anything." We are not responsible for outcomes, only for what is within our control. May we never tire of doing good.

Creativity in Presentation

To introduce this passage, plan ahead of time to have the sanctuary lights dimmed as you begin your message. Have a lighted candle on stage along with a flashlight. Pose a question along the lines of, "How would you rate your hope? Would it compare more to the candle, flashlight, or these stage lights?" You could have your tech people turn on the room/stage lights at that point for effect. You may even want to get specific and ask people to rate their level of hope about their family life, career, the political climate, etc.

Connect people's responses to this story by having the lights dimmed again and describing how Judah's hope is a mere flicker in this passage. Be sure to call attention to the fact that even though their hope seemed to be waning, it was not permanently extinguished. God still had redemptive plans for them and still has similar purposes for us, no matter how dark our days might seem.

For the most part, this passage is comprised of brief accounts of the final failing kings of Judah. God has determined to judge his people, but these leaders are not helping matters by making shortsighted decisions. Highlighting those aspects of these accounts should be kept simple. Pivoting to the final note of hope can direct the audience to consider the larger story of Scripture and how this portion of history fits into God's grand plan.

The key idea to communicate is that the hope of God still flickers in our darkest days. The passage for this preaching unit can be outlined in the following points:

- Dark days grow darker when we try to go our own way (23:31–25:26).
- Hope is found in the gracious purposes of God (25:27–30).

DISCUSSION QUESTIONS

1. What are some of the foolish political decisions that these kings make to try to avoid their own demise (23:31–24:7)?

2. To what extent does Babylon penalize Judah? What was the purpose behind these punitive actions (24:8–17)?

3. What are the final shameful consequences that Judah experiences when Zedekiah was reigning (24:18–25:26)?

4. How do the final few verses cast some hope in the midst of all of this devastation (25:27–30)?

5. What does this passage communicate about God's judgment and his grace?

6. Considering both this passage and 1–2 Kings as a whole, what are some ways that Jesus's arrival as Messiah relate to this part of Israel's history?

JUDAH ALONE (2 KINGS 21:1–25:30)

A SUMMARY

At the end of the second major literary unit, the atmosphere of the account is, by and large, positive. Sure, the northern kingdom of Israel had been sacked because of their habitual sin. However, Jerusalem and the Davidic dynasty had just experienced not only one of the greatest moments of national salvation but also one of the greatest kings in their history. In fact, comparison was made to the great King David! Up to that point, that had yet to happen. Nevertheless, there were subtleties that seemed to cut against the positive atmosphere. Chapter 20 offered a different picture of Hezekiah, presenting him more as a foolish king who lacked insight than as a great reformer who stood defiantly for the Lord.

Sadly, chapter 21 is the wet blanket that suffocated the flames of positive renewal. Manasseh, due to political pressure, instituted policies and effectively undermined all the policies of his father. And at this point, the Lord had enough! The text tells us that during the reign of Manasseh judgment was sealed. In fact, not even the greatest reforms in Judean history, those of Josiah, could undo the pronouncement of judgment. Huldah is there to tell Josiah's men, essentially, "This is great! But it's just not going to matter for the nation in the end."

That tragedy comes quickly. Josiah dies in battle as he foolishly tries to head off Pharaoh Neco at the Megiddo Pass. And on the way back to Egypt, Neco deposes the sitting Judean king (Jehoahaz) to put a pro-Egyptian Judean in place (Jehoiakim). When Jehoiakim dies, Jehoiachin rules for just long enough to surrender Jerusalem to Nebuchadnezzar in 597 BCE. Jehoiachin is ushered off the Babylon and Zedekiah is put in his place. Finally, about a decade later, Zedekiah angers Nebuchadnezzar one time too many, resulting in the tragic sacking of Jerusalem. At that moment, the city is burnt to the ground, the best of what remained was taken to Babylon, and God's people entered into a period defined by theological dissonance. Yet cutting against all of this are the final verses of the book. The reader is told that Jehoiachin is released to eat at the king's table. This short notice offers a glimpse that God's people still have a future, albeit undefined.

And so the book of Kings ends. It's tragic, for sure. But perhaps the full brunt of the tragedy can't be fully understood until we look back, standing at the end of the story. When we do this, we see harmful tendencies established early on in systems and methods of operation. We see great opportunities for spiritual renewal and reform flipped aside by a myopic pursuit of influence. We see blatant apostasy left unchecked because those guilty of the apostasy had the benefit of the central power structures. And perhaps most troubling, we see how perpetual actions can put us, and those around us, on a path to judgment that cannot be avoided. We see that there comes a breaking point for the Lord, where judgment *must* fall before his grace can be allowed to grow again.

REFERENCES

Ackerman, Susan. 1993. "The Queen Mother and the Cult in Ancient Israel." *Journal of Biblical Literature* 112: 385–401.

Alster, Bendt. 1975. *Studies in Sumerian Proverbs*. Copenhagen Studies in Assyriology 3. Copenhagen: Akademisk Forlag,

Alstola, Tero. 2019. *Judeans in Babylon: A Study of Deportees in the Sixth and Fifth Centuries BCE*. Culture and History of the Ancient Near East 109. Leiden: Brill.

Anderson, Neil T. 1990. *The Bondage Breaker*. Eugene, OR: Harvest House.

Andreasen, N. A. 1983. "The Role of the Queen Mother in Israelite Society." *Catholic Biblical Quarterly* 45: 179–94.

Arnold, Bill T. 2020. "Deuteronomy's Book and Hammurapi's Stela: The Referent of 'This *Sēper*' in Deuteronomy 28:58." *Vetus Testamentum*.

Arnold, Bill T. and John H. Choi. 2018. *A Guide to Biblical Hebrew Syntax*. 2nd Edition. Cambridge: Cambridge University Press.

Arnold, Bill T. and David B. Schreiner. 2017. "Graf and Wellhausen, and Their Legacies." Pages 252–73 in *A History of Biblical Interpretation, Volume 3: The Enlightenment through the Nineteenth Century*. Edited by Alan J. Hauser and Duane F. Watson. Grand Rapids: William B. Eerdmans.

Arnold, Patrick M. 1992. "Gibeon (Place)." Pages 1010–12 in vol. 2 of the *Anchor Bible Dictionary*. Edited by David Noel Freedman, Gary A. Herion, David F. Graf, John David Pleins, and Astrid B. Beck. 6 vols. New York: Doubleday.

Averbeck, Richard E. 1997. "שָׁחַט." Pages 77–80 in vol. 4 of the *New International Dictionary of Old Testament Theology and Exegesis*. 5 Vols. Edited by Willem VanGemeren. Grand Rapids: Zondervan.

Baker, David W. 1992. "Ophir (Place)." Pages 26–27 in vol. 1 of *Anchor Bible Dictionary*. Edited by David Noel Freedman, Gary A. Herion, David F. Graf, John David Pleins, and Astrid B. Beck.. 6 vols. New York: Doubleday.

Barré, Michael L. 1992. "Treaties in the ANE." Pages 653–56 in vol. 6 of *Anchor Bible Dictionary*. Edited by David Noel Freedman, Gary A. Herion, David F. Graf, John David Pleins, and Astrid B. Beck. 6 vols. New York: Doubleday.

Barrick, W. Boyd. 2001. "Another Shaking of Jehosphat's Family Tree: Jehoram and Ahaziah Once Again." *Vetus Testamentum* 51.1: 9–25.

Bauer, David and Robert Traina. 2011. *Inductive Bible Study: A Comprehensive Guide to the Practice of Hermeneutics*. Grand Rapids: Baker Academic.

Ben-Barak, Zafrira. 1991. "The Status and Right of the גְּבִירָה." *Journal of Biblical Literature* 110: 23–34.

Bhattarai, Abha and Todd C. Frankel. 2018. "Walmart Said It's Giving Its Employees a Raise. And Then It Closed 63 Stores," *Washington Post*, January 18. https://www.washingtonpost.com/news/business/wp/2018/01/11/walmart-to-raise-starting-hourly-wage-to-11-offer-paid-parental-leave/?utm_term=.19ae6c5f33f6.

Bin–Nun, Shoshana R. 1968. "Formulas From Royal Records of Israel and of Judah." *Vetus Testamentum* 18.1: 414–32.

Biran, Avraham and Joseph Naveh. 1993. "An Aramaic Stele Fragment from Tel Dan," *Israel Exploration Journal* 43.2–3: 81–98.

_____. 1995. "The Tel Dan Inscription: A New Fragment." *Israel Exploration Journal* 45.1: 1–18.

Blake, Ian M. 1967. "Jericho (Ain Es-Sultan): Joshua's Curse and Elisha's Miracle—One Possible Explanation." *Palestine Exploration Quarterly* 99.2: 86–97.

Breech, John, 2021. "Urban Meyer Fired by Jacksonville Jaguars as Controversies Rock His First Season as Head Coach." CBS News, December 16. https://www.cbsnews.com/news/urban-meyer-jacksonville-jaguars-fired-controversies-first-season-head-coach.

Brewer-Boydston, Ginny. 2016. "Athaliah, Queen of Judah." In *The Lexham Bible Dictionary*. Edited by John D. Barry, David Bomar, Derek R. Brown, Rachel Klippenstein, Douglas Mangum, Carrie Sinclair Wolcott, Lazarus Wentz, Elliot Ritzema, and Wendy Widder. Bellingham, WA: Lexham Press.

Bridges, Jerry. 2007. *Respectable Sins: Confronting the Sins We Tolerate*. Colorado Springs: NavPress.

Bright, John. 2000. *A History of Israel*. 4h Edition. Louisville: Westminster John Knox.

Brueggemann, Walter. 2001. *The Prophetic Imagination*. 2nd Edition. Minneapolis: Fortress Press.

Carroll, M. Daniel. 1997. "קָטֹן." Pages 910–12 in Vol 3 of *New International Dictionary of Old Testament Theology and Exegesis*. Edited by Willem VanGemeren. 5 Vols. Grand Rapids: Zondervan.

Cazelles, Henri. 1992. "Syro-Ephraimite War." Pages 282–85 in vol. 6 of the *Anchor Bible Dictionary*. Edited by David Noel Freedman, Gary A. Herion, David F. Graf, John David Pleins, and Astrid B. Beck. 6 vols. New York: Doubleday.

Cielontko, David. 2019. "Two Faces of Manasseh: The Reception of Manasseh in the Early Jewish Literature." Pages 239–260 in *The Last Century in the History of Judah: The Seventh Century BCE in Archaeological, Historical, and Biblical Perspectives*. Edited by Filip Čapek and Oded Lipschits. Atlanta: SBL Press.

Clifford, Richard J. 1972. *The Cosmic Mountain in Canaan and the Old Testament*. Harvard Semitic Monographs 4. Cambridge, MA: Harvard University Press.

Cook, John A. and Robert D. Holmstedt, 2013. *Beginning Biblical Hebrew: A Grammar and Illustrated Reader*. Grand Rapids: Baker Academic.

Cogan, Mordechai. 2008. *I Kings: A New Translation with Introduction and Commentary*. Anchor Yale Bible Commentary 10. New Haven, CT: Yale University Press.

Cogan, Mordechai and Hayim Tadmor. 2008. *II Kings: A New Translation with Introduction and Commentary*. Anchor Yale Bible Commentary 11. New Haven, CT: Yale University Press.

Cogan, Morton. 1974. *Imperialism and Religion*. Society of Biblical Literature Monograph Series 19. Missoula, MT: Scholars Press.

Craigie, Peter C. 1983. *Ugarit and the Old Testament*. Grand Rapids: William B. Eerdmans.

Crouch, Andy. 2017. *The Tech-Wise Family: Everyday Steps for Putting Technology in Its Proper Place*. Grand Rapids: Baker Books.

Davis, Andrew R. 2016. "Rereading 1 Kings 17:21 in Light of Ancient Medical Texts." *Journal of Biblical Literature* 135.3: 465–81.

Day, John. 1992. "Baal (Deity)." Pages 545–49 in vol. 1 of the *Anchor Bible Dictionary*. Edited by David Noel Freedman, Gary A. Herion, David F. Graf, John David Pleins, and Astrid B. Beck. 6 vols. New York: Doubleday.

DeVries, Simon J. 2003. *1 Kings*. Word Biblical Commentary 12. Second Edition. Dallas: Word.

Dubovsky, Peter. 2006. "Tiglath-pileser III's Campaigns in 734–732 BC: Historical Background of Is 7; 2 Kings 15–16 and 2 Chr 27–28." *Biblica* 87.2: 153–70.

Dungy, Tony and Nathan Whitaker. 2007. *Quiet Strength: The Principles, Practices, &*

Priorities of a Winning Life. Carol Stream, IL: Tyndale House Publishers.

Elayi, Josette. 2017. *Sargon II: King of Assyria*. Atlanta: SBL Press.

_____. 2018. *Sennacherib, King of Assyria*. Atlanta: SBL Press.

Faust, Avraham. 2012. *The Archaeology of Israelite Society in Iron Age II*. Winona Lake, IN: Eisenbrauns.

Fee, Gordon. 2014. *The First Epistle to the Corinthians*. The New International Commentary on the New Testament. Grand Rapids: William B. Eerdmans.

Fensham, F. Charles. 1960. "The Treaty between Solomon and Hiram and the Alalakh Tablets." *Journal of Biblical Literature* 79: 59–60.

Fiagenbaum-Golovin, Shira, Arie Shaus, Barak Sober, Eli Turkel, Eli Piasetzky, and Israel Finkelstein. 2020. "Algorithmic Handwriting Analysis of the Samarian Inscriptions Illuminates Bureaucratic Apparatus in Biblical Israel." *PLoS One* 15.1: e0227452.

Finkelstein, 2002. "The Campaign of Shoshenq I: A Guide to the 10th Century Polity." *Zeitschrift des Deutschen Palästina-Vereins* 118.2: 109–35.

Fox, Nili Sacher. 2000. *In the Service to the King: Officialdom in Ancient Israel and Judah*. Monographs of the Hebrew Union College 23. Cincinnati: Hebrew Union College.

Fritz, Volkmar. 2003. *1 & 2 Kings*. Continental Commentary. Translated by Anselm Hagedorn. Minneapolis: Fortress.

Gaffin, Richard B. and Wayne A Grudem. 1996. *Are Miraculous Gifts for Today?: Four Views*. Counterpoints. Grand Rapids: Zondervan.

Galil, Gershon. 2000. "A New Look at the Inscriptions of Tiglath-Pileser III." *Biblica* 81.4: 511–20.

Gesenius, Wilhelm. 1910. *Gesenius' Hebrew Grammar*. Edited by E. Kautzsch. Translated by A. E. Cowley. Oxford: Clarendon Press.

Gordon, Robert P, Ed. 1995. *The Place Is Too Small for Us: The Israelite Prophets in Recent Scholarship*. Sources for Biblical and Theological Study 5. Winona Lake, IN: Eisenbrauns.

Greenfield, J. C. 1999. "Hadad." Pages 377–82 in *Dictionary of Deities and Demons in the Bible*. Edited by Karel van der Toorn, Bob Becking, and Pieter W. van der Horst. 2nd Edition. Leiden/Grand Rapids: Brill/William B. Eerdmans.

Greenwood, Kyle R. and David B. Schreiner. 2022. *Ahab's House of Horrors: A Historiographic Study of the Military Campaigns of the Omride Dynasty*. Studies in Biblical Archaeology, Geography and History. Bellingham, WA: Lexham Press.

Groves, J. A. 2005. "Zion Traditions." Pages 1019–25 in the *Dictionary of the Old Testament Historical Books*. Edited by Bill T. Arnold and Hugh G. Williamson. Downers Grove, IL: InterVarsity Press.

Hadley, Judith M. 2018. "Hebrew Inscriptions." Pages 135–41 in *Behind the Scenes of the Old Testament: Cultural, Social, and Historical Contexts*. Edited by Jonathan S. Greer, John W. Hilber, and John H. Walton. Grand Rapids: Baker Academic.

Hallo, William W., ed. 1997–2002. *The Context of Scripture*. 3 vols. Leiden: Brill.

Halpern, Baruch. 2001. *David's Secret Demons: Messiah, Murderer, Traitor, King*. Grand Rapids: William B. Eerdmans.

_____. 1988. *The First Historians: The Hebrew Bible and History*. University Park: The Pennsylvania State Press.

Halpern, Baruch, and Andre Lemaire. 2010. "The Composition of Kings." Pages 123–53 in *The Books of Kings: Sources, Composition, Historiography, and Reception*. Edited by Baruch Halpern and Andre Lemaire. Supplements to Vetus Testamentum 129. Leiden: Brill.

Halpern, Baruch, and David Vanderhooft. 1991. "The Editions of Kings in the 7th–6th Centuries B.C.E." *Hebrew Union College Annual* 62: 179–244.

Hamilton, Victor P. 1992. "Satan." Pages 985–89 in vol. 5 of the *Anchor Bible Dictionary*. Edited by David Noel Freedman, Gary A. Herion, David F. Graf, John David Pleins, and Astrid B. Beck. 6 vols. New York: Doubleday.

_____. 1997. "נַעַר." Pages 124–27 in Vol 3 of *New International Dictionary of Old Testament Theology and Exegesis*. Edited by Willem VanGemeren. 5 Vols. Grand Rapids: Zondervan.

_____. 1997. "שָׁכַל." Pages 105–07 in Vol 4 of *New International Dictionary of Old Testament Theology and Exegesis*. Edited by Willem VanGemeren. 5 Vols. Grand Rapids: Zondervan.

Hawkins, Ralph. 2013. *How Israel Became a People*. Nashville: Abingdon Press.

Hayes, Christopher B. 2014. *Hidden Riches: A Sourcebook for the Comparative Study of the Hebrew Bible and Ancient Near East*. Louisville: Westminster John Knox.

Hays, Nathan J. 2016. "Ivory." In *The Lexham Bible Dictionary*. Edited by John D. Barry, David Bomar, Derek R. Brown, Rachel Klippenstein, Douglas Mangum, Carrie Sinclair Wolcott, Lazarus Wentz, Elliot Ritzema, and Wendy Widder. Bellingham, WA: Lexham Press.

Herrmann, Wolfgang. 1999. "Baal." Pages 131–38 in *Dictionary of Deities and Demons in the Bible*. Edited by Karl van der Toorn, Bob Becking, and Pieter W. van der Horst. Leiden/Grand Rapids: Brill/William B. Eerdmans.

Hess, Richard. 2007. *Israelite Religions: An Archeological and Biblical Survey*. Grand Rapids: Baker Academic.

_____. 2009. "David and Abishag: The Purpose of 1 Kings 1:1–4." Pages 427–38 in *Homeland and Exile: Biblical and Ancient Near Eastern Studies in Honor of Bustenay Oded*. Edited by Gershon Galil, Mark Geller, and Alan Millard. Vetus Testamentum Supplements 130. Leiden: Brill.

_____. 2012. "Katuwas and the Masoretic Text of Kings: Cultural Connections between Carchemish and Israel." Pages 171–82 in *New Inscriptions and Seals Relating to the Biblical World*. Edited by M. Lubetski and E Lubetski. Society of Biblical Literature Archaeology and Biblical Studies 19. Atlanta: SBL.

_____. 2016. *The Old Testament: A Historical, Theological, and Critical Introduction*. Grand Rapids: Baker Academic.

Higginbotham, Carolyn. 1992. "Neco." Page 247 in vol 4 of *The New Interpreters Dictionary of the Bible*. Edited by Katharine Doob Sakenfeld. 5 Vols. Nashville: Abingdon, 2006–2009.

Hobbs, T. R. "Neco (Person)." Pages 1060–61 in vol. 4 of the *Anchor Bible Dictionary*. Edited by David Noel Freedman, Gary A. Herion, David F. Graf, John David Pleins, and Astrid B. Beck. 6 vols. New York: Doubleday.

Holland, Drew. 2020. "An Alternative Approach to the Dilemma of 2 Kgs 3:27." *The Journal of Inductive Biblical Studies* 7.2: 7–31.

Honeyman, A. M. 1948. "The Evidence for Regnal Names among the Hebrews." *Journal of Biblical Literature* 67.1: 13–25.

Hostetter, Edwin C. 2005. "Beersheba." Pages 113–16 in *Dictionary of the Old Testament Historical Books*. Edited by Bill T. Arnold and Hugh G. Williamson. Downers Grove, IL: Intervarsity Press.

House, Paul. 1995. *1, 2 Kings*. New American Commentary 8. Nashville: Broadman and Holman Publishers.

Howard, Jr., David M. 2013. *An Introduction to the Old Testament Historical Books*. Chicago: Moody Publishers.

Hughes, R. Kent. 2001. *Disciplines of a Godly Man*. Wheaton, IL: Crossway Books.

Hulse, E. V. 1970. "Joshua's Curse: Radioactivity or Schistosomiasis?" *Palestine Exploration Quarterly* 102.2: 92–101.

_____. 1971. "Joshua's Curse and the Abandonment of Ancient Jericho: Schistosomiasis as a Possible Medical Explanation." *Medical History* 15.4: 376–86.

_____. 1975. "The Nature of Biblical 'Leprosy' and the Use of Alternative Medical Terms in Modern Translations of the Bible." *Palestine Exploration Quarterly* 107.2: 87–105.

Hurowitcz, Victor (Avigdor). 1992. *I Have Built You An Exalted House: Temple Building in the Bible in Light of Mesopotamian and Northwest Semitic Writings.* Journal for the Study of the Old Testament Supplement Series 115. Sheffield: Sheffield Academic Press.

_____. 1994. "Inside Solomon's Temple." *Bible Review* 10.2: 24–36.

Jivanda, Tomas. 2014. "Woman Claims Lawyers Should Have Told Her Divorce Would End Her Marriage." *Independent*, January 10. https://www.independent.co.uk/news/uk/home-news/woman-claims-lawyers-should-have-told-her-divorce-would-end-her-marriage-9051550.html.

Johnson, P. J. "Life, Disease and Death." 2003. Pages 532–36 in the *Dictionary of the Old Testament Pentateuch.* Edited by T. Desmond Alexander and David W. Baker. Downers Grove, IL: InterVarsity Press.

Katzenstein, Hanna Jacob. 1955. "Who Were the Parents of Athaliah?" *Israel Exploration Journal* 5: 194–97.

Kim, Koowon. 2016. "Hiram, King of Tyre." *The Lexham Bible Dictionary.* Edited by John D. Barry, David Bomar, Derek R. Brown, Rachel Klippenstein, Douglas Mangum, Carrie Sinclair Wolcott, Lazarus Wentz, Elliot Ritzema, and Wendy Widder. Bellingham, WA: Lexham Press. Logos Bible Software 7.0.

King, Philip J. and Lawrence E. Stager. 2001. *Life in Biblical Israel.* Library of Ancient Israel. Louisville: Westminster John Knox.

Kitchen, Kenneth A. 1995. "Sheba and Arabia." Pages 126–53 in *Age of Solomon c. 3000–30 BC.* London and New York: Routledge.

_____. 2003. *On the Reliability of the Old Testament.* Grand Rapids: William B. Eerdmans.

_____. 2005. "Chronology." Pages 181–88 in *Dictionary of the Old Testament Historical Books.* Edited by Bill T. Arnold and H. G. M. Williamson. Downers Grove, IL: IVP Academic.

Kiuchi, Nobuyoshi. 1994. "Elijah's Self-offering: 1 Kings 17,21." *Biblica* 75: 74–79.

Knoppers, Gary. 1992. "'There Was None Like Him'; Incomparability in the Books of Kings." *Catholic Biblical Quarterly.* 54: 411–31.

Koehler, Ludwig and Walter Baumgartner. 2001. *The Hebrew and Aramaic Lexicon of the Old Testament.* Study Edition. Translated by M. E. J. Richardson. 2 vols. Leiden: Brill.

Konkel, A. H. 1997. "חָפַשׂ." Pages 326–27 in vol. 4 of the New International Dictionary of Old Testament Theology and Exegesis. 5 Vols. Edited by Willem VanGemeren. Grand Rapids: Zondervan.

Kuhrt, Amélie. 1998. *The Ancient Near East.* 2 vols. London: Routledge.

Lasine, Stuart. 2004. "Matters of Life and Death: The Story of Elijah and the Widow's Son in Comparative Perspective." *Biblical Interpretation: A Journal of Contemporary Approaches* 12.2: 117–44.

LeBarbera, Robert. 1984. "The Man of War and the Man of God: Social Satire in 2 Kings 6:8–7:20." *Catholic Biblical Quarterly* 46: 637–51.

Lehmann, Gunnar and Anne E. Killebrew. 2010. "Palace 6000 at Megiddo in Context: Iron Age Central Hall Tetra-Partite Residencies and the *Bīt Ḥilāni* Building Tradition in the Levant." *Bulletin for the American Society of Oriental Research* 359: 13–33.

Leithart, Peter J. 2006. *1 & 2 Kings.* Brazos Theological Commentary on the Bible. Grand Rapids: Brazos Press.

Leuchter, Mark A., and David T. Lamb. 2016. *The Historical Writings: Introducing Israel's Historical Literature*. Minneapolis: Fortress Press.

Levenson, Jon D. 1985. *Sinai & Zion: An Entry into the Jewish Bible*. San Francisco: HarperCollins.

Levenson, Jon D. and Baruch Halpern. 1990. "The Political Import of David's Marriages." *Journal for Biblical Literature* 99.4: 507–18.

Levin, Yigal. 2012. "Did Pharaoh Sheshonq Attack Jerusalem?" *Biblical Archaeological Review* 38.4: 42–52, 66.

Low, Katherine. 2011. "Implications Surrounding Girding the Loins in Light of Gender, Body, and Power." *Journal for the Study of the Old Testament* 36.1: 3–30.

Lubetski, Meir. 1992. "Ezion-geber (Place)." Pages 723–25 in vol. 2 of the *Anchor Bible Dictionary*. Edited by David Noel Freedman, Gary A. Herion, David F. Graf, John David Pleins, and Astrid B. Beck. 6 vols. New York: Doubleday.

Maier, III, Walter A. 2018. *1 Kings 1–11*. Concordia Commentary. St. Louis: Concordia Publishing House.

Malamat, Abraham. 1989. "Prophecy at Mari." Pages 50–73 in *The Place Is Too Small for Us*. Edited by Robert P. Gordon. Sources for Biblical and Theological Study 5. Winona Lake, IN: Eisenbrauns, 1995. Reprint from "Prophets, Ancestors and Kings." Pages 79–96, 125–44 in *Mari and the Early Israelite Experience*. Schweich Lectures 1984. Oxford: Oxford University Press.

Mazar, Amihai. 1990. *Archaeology of the Land of the Bible: 10,000–586 B.C.E.* The Anchor Bible Reference Library. New York: Doubleday.

McAdams, Wes. RadicallyChristian.com (blog). https://radicallychristian.com.

McCarter, P. Kyle. 1974. " 'Yaw, Son of 'Omri': A Philological Note on Israelite Chronology." *Bulletin of the American Schools of Oriental Research* 216: 5–7.

McKay, John. 1973. *Religion in Judah under the Assyrians*. Studies in Biblical Theology 2/26. Naperville, IN: Allenson.

Meek, Russell. 2014. "The Abishag Episode: Reexamining the Role of Virility in 1 Kings 1:1–4 in Light of the Kirta Epic and the Sumerian Tale 'The Old Man and the Yong Woman.' " *Bulletin for Biblical Research* 24.1: 1–14.

Moran, William. 1963. "The Ancient Near Eastern Background of the Love of God in Deuteronomy," *Catholic Biblical Quarterly* 25: 77–87.

Moulis, David Rafael. 2019. "Hezekiah's Cultic Reforms according to the Archaeology Evidence." Pages 167–80 in *The Last Century in the History of Judah: The Seventh Century BCE in Archaeological, Historical, and Biblical Perspectives*. Edited by Filip Čapek and Oded Lipschits. Ancient Israel and Its Literature 37. Atlanta: SBL Press.

Na'aman, Nadav. 1974. "Sennacherib's 'Letter to God' on His Campaign to Judah." *Bulletin of the American School of Oriental Research*. 214: 25–39.

Negev, Avraham, ed. 1990. "Shechem." *The Archaeological Encyclopedia of the Holy Land*. 3d Edition. New York: Prentice Hall.

Nitsche, Martin. 2015. "Und das Königtum war fest in der Hands Salomos": Untersuchungen zu 1 Kön 3. Beiträge zur Wissenschaft vom Alten und Neuen Testament. Stuttgart: W. Kohlhammer.

Olley, John W. 2003. "Pharaoh's Daughter, Solomon's Palace, and the Temple: Another Look at the Structure of 1 Kings 1–11." *Journal for the Study of the Old Testament* 27.3: 355–69.

Olyan, Saul. 1984. "Hăšālôm: Some Literary Considerations of 2 Kings 9." *Catholic Biblical Quarterly* 46.4: 652–68.

Paul, Shalom. 1969. "Sargon's Administrative Diction in II Kings 17:27." *Journal of Biblical Literature* 88.1: 73–74.

Pitard, Wayne T. 1992. "Hazael." Page 83 in vol. 3 of *Anchor Bible Dictionary*. Edited by David Noel Freedman, Gary A. Herion, David F. Graf, John David Pleins, and Astrid B. Beck. 6 vols. New York: Doubleday.

Pritchard, James Bennett, ed. 1969. *The Ancient Near Eastern Texts Relating to the Old Testament*. 3rd ed. with Supplement. Princeton, NJ: Princeton University Press.

Rainey, Anson F. and R. Steven Notley. 2006. *The Sacred Bridge*. Jerusalem: Carta.

Rasmussen, Carl G. 2010. *Zondervan Atlas of the Bible*. Revised Edition. Grand Rapids: Zondervan.

Redford, Donald. 1992. "Shishak (Person)." Pages 1221—22 vol. 5 of *Anchor Bible Dictionary*. Edited by David Noel Freedman, Gary A. Herion, David F. Graf, John David Pleins, and Astrid B. Beck. 6 vols. New York: Doubleday.

Rhodes, Ron. 2011. *1001 Unforgettable Quotes about God, Faith, and the Bible*. Eugene, OR: Harvest House Publishers.

Richter, Sandra. 2002. *The Deuteronomistic History and the Name Theology:* lᵉšakkēn šᵉmô šām *in the Bible and the Ancient Near East*. Beihefte zur Zeitschrift für die alttestamentliche Wissenschaft, 318. Berlin/New York: Walter de Gruyter.

_____. 2005. "Deuteronomistic History." Pages 219–30 in *Dictionary of the Old Testament Historical Books*. Edited by Bill T. Arnold and H. G. M. Williamson. Downers Grove, IL: InterVarsity Press.

Roberts, J. J. M. 1970. "A New Parallel to 1 Kings 18:28–29." *Journal of Biblical Literature* 89: 76–77.

_____. 2006–2009. "Nebuchadnezzar, Nebuchadrezzar." Pages 245–46 in vol. 4 of *The New Interpreter's Dictionary of the Bible*. Edited by Katharine Doob Sakenfeld. 5 vols. Nashville: Abingdon Press.

Roberts, Kathryn. 2000. "God, Prophet, and King: Eating and Drinking of the Mountain in First Kings 18:41." *Catholic Biblical Quarterly* 62: 632–44.

Rollston, Christopher. 2010. *Writing and Literacy in the World of Ancient Israel: Epigraphic Evidence from the Iron Age*. Society of Biblical Literature: Archaeology and Biblical Studies 11. Atlanta: Society of Biblical Literature.

Roos, Dave. 2020. "10 Worst Business Decisions Ever Made." How Stuff Works, updated May 26. https://money.howstuffworks.com/10-worst-business-decisions3.htm.

Sabar, Ariel. 2020. "A Biblical Mystery at Oxford." *The Atlantic*, June. https://www.the-atlantic.com/magazine/archive/2020/06/museum-of-the-bible-obbink-gospel-of-mark/610576.

Sarna, Nahum. 1997. "Naboth's Vineyard Revisited (1 Kings 21)." Pages 119–26 in *Tehillah le-Moshe: Biblical and Judaic Studies in Honor of Moshe Greenberg*. Edited by Michael Cogan, Barry L. Eichler, and Jeffrey H. Tigay. Winona Lake, IN: Eisenbrauns.

Schneider, Tammi. 1996. "Rethinking Jehu." *Biblica* 77: 100–07.

Schniedewind, William M. 2004. *How the Bible Became a Book*. Cambridge: Cambridge University.

Schreiner, David B. 2012. "The Election and Divine Choice of Zion/Jerusalem." *Journal for the Evangelical Study of the Old Testament* 1.2: 147–66.

_____. 2014. "Why נִיר in Kings?" *Journal for the Study of the Old Testament* 39.1: 15–30.

_____. 2015. "Zerubbabel, Persia, and Inner-biblical Exegesis." *Journal for the Evangelical Study of the Old Testament* 4.2: 191–204.

_____. 2016. "The Ambiguity of Job's Final Words." *Bible Study Magazine*, July/Aug: 22–23.

_____. 2017. "We Really Should Stop Translating נִיר in Kings as 'Light' or 'Lamp.'" *Tyndale Bulletin* 68.1: 31–37.

_____. 2018. "'But He Could Not Warm Himself': Sexual Innuendo and the Place of 1 Kings 1:1–4." *Scandinavian Journal of the Old Testament* 32.1: 121–30.

_____. 2018. "The Annihilation of Egyptian and Neo-Assyrian Armies: A Proposal of Inner-biblical Typology and Some Literary Critical Implications." *Zeitschrift für die alttestamentliche Wissenschaft* 130.4: 529–44.

_____. 2019. *Pondering the Spade: Discussing Important Convergences between Archaeology and Old Testament Studies.* Eugene, OR: Wipf and Stock.

_____. 2020. "Wilderness, Theology of." Pages 401–03 in *Global Wesleyan Dictionary of Biblical Theology.* Edited by Robert Branson, Sarah Derck, Deirdre Brower Latz, and Wayne McCown. Kansas City, MO: Beacon Hill Press.

Shea, William H. 2005. "Historical Implications of the Archaeology of Southwestern Judah in the Late Eighth Century B.C." *The Near East Archeological Society Bulletin* 50: 1–14.

Smalley, Stephen S. 1984. *1, 2, 3 John.* Word Biblical Commentary 51. Dallas: Word.

Smith, Morton. 1975. "A Note on Burning Babies." *Journal of the American Oriental Society.* 95.3: 477–79.

Stern, Ephraim. 2001. *Archaeology of the Land of the Bible: The Assyrian, Babylonian, and Persian Periods 732–332 B.C.E.* New York: Doubleday.

Stökl, Jonathan. 2012. "Ancient Near Eastern Prophecy." Pages 16–24 in *Dictionary of the Old Testament Prophets.* Edited by Mark J. Boda and J. G. McConville. Downers Grove, IL: IVP Academic.

Stone, Lawson G. 2012. *Judges.* Cornerstone Biblical Commentary. Carol Stream, IL: Tyndale House Publishers.

Strand Winslow, Karen. 2017. *1 & 2 Kings: A Commentary in the Wesleyan Tradition.* New Beacon Bible Commentary. Kansas City, MO: Beacon Hill Press.

Swaminathan Aarthi. 2018. "Domino's Pizza Unveils U.S. Infrastructure Project Filling Potholes." *Yahoo! Finance,* June 11. https://finance.yahoo.com/news/dominos-pizza-unveils-u-s-infrastructure-project-filling-potholes-130802630.html.

Sweeney, Marvin A. 2007. *I and II Kings.* Old Testament Library. Louisville: Westminster John Knox.

Thiel, Winfried. 1992. "Athaliah (Person)." Pages 511–12 in vol. 1 of *The Anchor Yale Bible Dictionary.* Edited by David Noel Freedman. 6 vols. New York: Doubleday.

Tov, Emanuel. 2001. *Textual Criticism of the Hebrew Bible.* 2d ed. Minneapolis: Fortress, 2001.

Ullendorff, Edward. 1967. *Ethiopia and the Bible: The Schweich Lectures 1967.* London: Oxford University Press.

Ussishkin, David. 1973. "King Solomon's Palaces." *The Biblical Archaeologist* 36: 78–105.

Van Keulen, Percy. 2005. *Two Versions of the Solomon Narrative: An Inquiry in the Relationship between MT 1 Kings. 2–11 and LXX 3 Reg. 2–11.* Vetus Testamentum Supplements 104. Leiden: Brill.

Van Seters, John. 1997. *In Search of History: Historiography in the Ancient World and the Origins of Biblical History.* Winona Lake, IN: Eisenbrauns.

Versluis, Arie. 2016. "Devotion and/or Destruction? The Meaning and Function of חרם in the Old Testament." *Zeitschrift für die alttestamentliche Wissenschaft* 128.2: 233–46.

Wallace, Daniel B. 1996. *Greek Grammar Beyond the Basics: An Exegetical Syntax of the New Testament.* Grand Rapids: Zondervan.

Walsh, Jerome. 1996. *1 Kings.* Berit Olam. Collegeville, MN: Michael Glazier/The Liturgical Press.

Waltke, Bruce K. and Michael O'Connor. 1990. *An Introduction to Biblical Hebrew Syntax.* Winona Lake, IN: Eisenbrauns.

Walton, John. 2003. "Date of Exodus." Pages 258–72 in *Dictionary of the Old Testament Pentateuch*. Edited by T. Desmond Alexander and David Baker. Downers Grove, IL: InterVarsity Press.

Walton, John H. and D. Brent Sandy. 2013. *The Lost World of Scripture: Ancient Literary Culture and Biblical Authority*. Downers Grove, IL: IVP Academic.

Whitelam, Keith. 1992. "Hiram (Person)." Pages 203–4 in vol. 3 of the *Anchor Bible Dictionary*. Edited by David Noel Freedman, Gary A. Herion, David F. Graf, John David Pleins, and Astrid B. Beck. 6 vols. New York: Doubleday.

Wilson, Gerald. 1997. "חִידָה." Page 107 in vol. 2 of the *New International Dictionary of Old Testament Theology and Exegesis*. Edited by Willem VanGemeren. 5 Vols. Grand Rapids: Zondervan.

Wiseman, D. J. 1996. "Ophir." Pages 849–50 in *New Bible Dictionary*. Edited by D. R. W. Wood, I. H. Marshall, A. R. Millard, and J. I. Packer. Leicester, England; Downers Grove, IL: InterVarsity Press.

_____. 2008. *1 and 2 Kings*. Tyndale Old Testament Commentaries 9. Downers Grove, IL: IVP Academic.

Wood, Alice. 2008. *Of Wings and Wheels: A Synthetic Study of the Biblical Cherubim*. Beihefte zur Zeitschrift für die alttestamentliche Wissenschaft ZAW 385. Berlin: Walter de Gruyter.

Wray Beal, Lissa M. 2013. "Jeroboam and the Prophets in 1 Kings 11–14: Prophetic Words for Two Kingdoms." Pages 105–24 in *Prophets, Prophecy, and Ancient Near Eastern Historiography*. Edited by Mark J. Boda and Lissa M. Wray Beal. Winona Lake, IN: Eisenbrauns.

_____. 2014. *1–2 Kings*. Apollos Old Testament Commentary 9. Downers Grove, IL: InterVarsity Press.

Wright, David P. and Richard Jones. 1992. "Leprosy." Pages 277–81 in vol. 4 of the *Anchor Bible Dictionary*. Edited by David Noel Freedman, Gary A. Herion, David F. Graf, John David Pleins, and Astrid B. Beck. 6 vols. New York: Doubleday.

Wurthwein, Ernst. 1995. *The Text of the Old Testament*. 2d ed. Translated by Erroll F. Rhodes. Grand Rapids: William B. Eerdmans.

Young, Robb Andrew. 2012. *Hezekiah in History and Tradition*. Vetus Testamentum Supplements 155. Leiden: Brill.

Younger Jr., K. Lawson. 2016. "Aram and the Arameans." Pages 229–65 in *The World around the Old Testament: The People and Places in the Ancient Near East*. Edited by Bill T. Arnold and Brent A. Strawn. Grand Rapids: Baker Academic.

KERUX COMMENTARY SERIES

---

1 & 2 Kings: A Commentary for Biblical Preaching and Teaching
David B. Schreiner & Lee Compson

Psalms, Volume 1: The Wisdom Psalms: A Commentary for Biblical Preaching and Teaching
W. Creighton Marlowe & Charles H. Savelle Jr.

Jeremiah and Lamentations: A Commentary for Biblical Preaching and Teaching
Duane Garrett & Calvin F. Pearson

Zephaniah-Malachi: A Commentary for Biblical Preaching and Teaching
Gary V. Smith & Timothy D. Sprankle

Ephesians: A Commentary for Biblical Preaching and Teaching
Gregory S. MaGee & Jeffrey D. Arthurs

Philippians: A Commentary for Biblical Preaching and Teaching
Thomas S. Moore & Timothy D. Sprankle

Colossians and Philemon: A Commentary for Biblical Preaching and Teaching
Adam Copenhaver & Jeffrey D. Arthurs

Hebrews: A Commentary for Biblical Preaching and Teaching
Herbert W. Bateman IV & Steven Smith